BIRDS AND PEOPLE: resolving the conflict on estuaries

Copyright © John Goss-Custard 2017

ISBN-13: 978-1508473954

ISBN-10: 1508473951

The moral right of the author has been asserted.

No part of this publication may be reproduced, stored in a retrieval system or transmitted in any form or by any means without the prior permission in writing of the publisher, nor be otherwise circulated in any form of binding or cover other than that in which it is published and without a similar condition being imposed upon the subsequent purchaser.

Cover design & layout: www.publishonkindle.co.uk

Available to purchase as a paperback and Kindle edition on Amazon.

POTENTIAL READERS

THOSE WHO MIGHT BE INTERESTED IN THIS BOOK INCLUDE:

Students and lecturers in ecology and conservation as the book describes a new approach to evaluating the impact of human activities on shorebirds that they might not otherwise encounter. The original research papers are scattered throughout the scientific literature and it is difficult to see the whole picture, and to fully understand why the approach was adopted. The book should also give students considering a career in field research on birds an idea of what it can be like.

Government organisations, professional groups, environmental consultants, conservationists and NGOs that are concerned with managing the coast, especially estuaries. The book provides an easy access to a modelling approach that is being used by some authorities, but of which some other authorities may not be aware.

Amateur and professional biologists and ornithologists who carry out research on, or who are just interested in, the ecology and behaviour of shorebirds and in their conservation.

Members of ornithological and natural history societies who like to read about developments in science and how the research is done.

"John Goss-Custard has done the wildlife conservation profession a great service by translating huge volumes of inaccessible science on shorebird ecology and individual based models into an accessible, comprehensive and fascinating narrative. This book is a must-read for any serious student of population ecology, and for any ecological consultant modelling bird populations. If you're working to ensure that built development around estuaries used by important bird populations can go ahead without undue impacts, this book will be invaluable. John has a dig at the wildlife conservation community at regular intervals throughout this book, but, if they read and understand its content, he'll have less cause to do so! I wish I had had this book to hand two decades ago."

Mr. S C J

ABOUT THE AUTHOR

Despite growing up in land-locked Stoke-on-Trent in the English midlands, John Goss-Custard (BSc PhD DSc) became interested in the shorebirds (waders and wildfowl) of soft coasts – estuaries, embayments – primarily through Peter Scott's television programme, 'Look'. He spent many of his teenage holidays at the Wildfowl Trust in Slimbridge where he developed his enthusiasm for research on the behaviour and ecology of shorebirds. After a B.Sc. in Zoology and Psychology at Bristol University and a Ph.D. in shorebird ecology at Aberdeen University, and a spell as a research fellow at Bristol University, he joined the then Nature Conservancy at the Coastal Ecology Research Station in Norwich to work on the impact of a proposed freshwater reservoir in the intertidal zone on the shorebirds of the Wash. This is where the story told in this book began.

He has been a professional shorebird and estuary scientist for 40 years, for most of that time being employed by the UK's Natural Environment Research Council, latterly as a senior Individual Merit scientist. He has published over 185 scientific papers on the behaviour and ecology of shorebirds and has taken part in research projects and acted as consultant in many countries.

For over thirty years, he and his colleagues in the Centre for Ecology and Hydrology in Dorset developed an approach to understanding populations of shorebirds that is based on the behaviour of individual birds. This approach has made it possible for the first time to predict the impact of a whole range of human activities – ranging from shellfishing through barrage construction to recreational disturbance – on the birds' survival and body condition over the non-breeding season. Now retired, he is a Visiting Professor in the Faculty of Science and Technology at Bournemouth University where the most recent version of the approach, called 'MORPH', is continuing to be developed and applied to a much wider range of animals and issues by a research team led by its creator, Professor Richard Stillman, from whom details can be obtained at rstillman@bournemouth.ac.uk.

PREFACE

This book tells the long story of the development of a new method for predicting the impact of the many human activities that are carried out on the estuaries and embayments of the world on the shorebirds that live there. The method is based on the behaviour of individual birds and how they react to changes in their environment brought about by people, such as shellfishing, recreation, building ports, sea-level rise and so forth. It describes in very simple terms the basic ideas upon which the method is based and how the fieldwork on the birds was carried out to test these ideas. It also details the sometimes circuitous route by which the goal was finally reached. It also describes how the eventual success of the project owed a great deal to good luck and to colleagues from all over the World.

The book began when Peter Ferns of Cardiff University, a friend of many years, suggested that some ornithologists, nature managers, environmental consultants and ecology students would appreciate reading a non-technical account of the research programme that led to the development of a now widely used individual-based model (IBM) of shorebirds. Since Patrick Triplet of the Syndicat Mixte pour l'Aménagement de la Côte Picard, France – another friend of many years – had also suggested that very same thing some years before when I was still employed and thus too busy to do it, there seemed to be a potential readership of at least two professional biologists. I have also given a number of talks over the years to local ornithological societies and, in so far as one can tell, people seem to find the story of this IBM interesting, stimulating and, very occasionally, entertaining. This suggested that there might also be a potential readership among the enormous numbers of well-informed bird watchers in the UK and in other countries. So, with the final push provided by Pete's comment, I decided to write this book.

Unlike most books on birds, this one does not comprehensively summarise what is known about the breeding biology, migration, population dynamics, conservation requirements *etc.* of a particular group of birds. Nor does it summarise the current state of knowledge of a topic, such as bird migration. Rather, it describes the origin and development of a new approach to providing the advice that nature managers require to make evidence-based decisions on how estuaries might be managed to retain their value to the huge numbers of migratory shorebirds that occur there, mainly during the non-breeding season. It recounts why a modelling approach was used that had previously found little favour within the UK (and still does not, I should add), despite being developed simultaneously in a number of other countries. As I hope will become clear, it was required because it was the only means - that I could think of - by which it would be possible to forecast the impact of any change in the way in which an estuary was managed (or changed by a proposed development) on what really matters: that is, the chances of the birds surviving the non-breeding season in good enough condition to migrate successfully to their often distant breeding grounds.

When I began researching shorebirds on the beautiful Ythan estuary in Aberdeenshire, Scotland in the autumn of 1963, I could not even have formulated the questions that needed to be asked to achieve this goal, let alone think up a way of answering them! At that time, the UK's major environmental research funding authority - the Natural Environment Research Council – had designated estuaries as red zones (I think that was the colour) because of the many ecological issues that their management and use by people were raising. For shorebirds in particular, questions revolved around the impact on the birds of such things as shellfishing, disturbance from walkers, fishermen and hunters, pollution, the construction of barrages and marinas and so on.

In those early days, just finding out about the basic ecology and behaviour of shorebirds was deemed sufficient to warrant financial support. Accordingly, that is what we researched in the UK and in many other countries, perhaps especially the Netherlands. We tried to answer questions such as: how much food does one shorebird require each day to survive in good condition? (the answer is a lot!); how many individual prey does a single shorebird eat each day? (again, a lot – one redshank in winter consumes 20,000 to 40,000 small shrimp-like crustaceans in 24 hours!); where do the UK's wintering birds breed? (over a huge area of the northern hemisphere) and how far do they fly to get there? (a long way, sometimes thousands of kilometres in one hop!).

These were fascinating discoveries, made by groups of professional and amateur researchers from many countries around the world: shorebird research knows no international boundaries, just like the birds themselves. But as our knowledge expanded, we were quite rightly challenged to start using it in order to help decision-makers to decide what to do if, for example, someone proposed to build a marina on the foreshore of an estuary where shorebirds feed. Simultaneously, increasingly strong legislation was being introduced that provided powerful protection for shorebirds, perhaps especially in the European Union. Although informed by the findings of research on the basic biology of shorebirds, the legislation and the decision-makers that implemented it still had regularly to resort to the precautionary principle: if in doubt about the impact on shorebirds, say 'No!'!

With good reason, those wishing to do something on an estuary sometime wondered whether the precautionary principle was not just too precautionary, and whether a lot of mere hand-waving was going on. Surely, they would say, these birds cannot be so hard-pressed everywhere that nothing could be changed in any estuary anywhere without terminally damaging the shorebird population? Their suspicions were heightened by the sometimes extravagantly expressed concerns of some conservationists and their sometimes instant opposition to any proposal to do something on an estuary, even before the necessary research had been done.

As so often happens in science, a well-directed comment galvanised a response which, for me, proved to be highly stimulating. The idea of building a barrage across the Severn estuary to generate tidal power had been discussed for decades. This estuary is important for a number of non-breeding shorebird species, notably dunlin and shelduck. During the 1970's and 1980's, Tom Shaw, a lecturer in engineering at Bristol University, was very active in exploring the energy-generating potential of a Severn barrage, and at a number of meetings met with biologists like myself to see if the 'bird issues' could be resolved. Even after some years of research on a similar problem on the Wash in east England, I had to admit at one of these meetings that I couldn't even begin to see how we could provide the forecasts required. Looking at me, he said (more-or-less): 'We find it hard to understand why, after so much expensive research on shorebirds, you can't give us the predictions that are needed!' Ouch! This cold shower of criticism galvanised this particular research worker, and helped to set us on the track that ultimately led to the development of IBMs of shorebird populations.

The book is about the research journey that led to the development of shorebird IBMs. It explains precisely what we came to believe had to be achieved, and how the idea of using an IBM began to emerge out of misty and muddled recesses of the mind, and how we gradually homed in on the real questions that had to be answered before we could develop a workable model. The book is mainly about the science, of course, and the twisting route we took to achieve the goal. I hope it will give non-scientists an insight into the way in which advances sometimes occur in science, and just how uncertain a scientist can be as to exactly where he/she is heading and how to get there! Scientific papers are always written with the benefit of hind-sight and the Introduction to the paper can give an impression of prescience that is sometimes quite unjustified!

The book also describes how the research was carried out, sometimes in rather uncomfortable conditions, occasionally in dangerous circumstances but often in beautiful places. There are also some asides about colleagues and friends from all round the World whose own research work, generosity of ideas and comment have been vital to the development of our shorebird IBM. These asides are also intended to give the reader a flavour of how this kind of research is done. I hope they will occasionally provide some mild entertainment as well.

This is one of the tower hides that played such an essential part in the research described in this book. At any one time, there were up to six of them on different mussel beds between the mouth of the estuary and Lympstone. (photo: with thanks to Rajan Nagarajan)

A few words about references: this is not a 'heavy' academic book in which all statements have to be backed up with as many references as possible. Rather, it is the story of a group of researchers developing a new approach to making difficult ecological predictions. So instead of there being a massive list of references at the end of the book, each chapter ends with a few references that should give a reader a way into the literature on the research described in that chapter. The references are of papers produced by the team that developed the shorebird IBM. These references are themselves extensively referenced and provide anyone interested in taking a topic further a good way of opening up the wider literature on the subject.

And also a few words about the diagrams. Most of the diagrams in this book are there just to get an idea across rather than to present the data on which a statement is based: they are more schematic than precise. Anyone interested in seeing the data upon which the statements in this book are made should refer to the scientific publications, cited at the end of the chapter. This is an approach which works well in the talks I have given to clubs of various kinds, and so has been adopted here to.

I hope it works for you as well

John Goss-Custard

26th March 2014

CONTENTS

POTENTIAL READERS 2

ABOUT THE AUTHOR 3

PREFACE 4

CONTENTS 8

PREAMBLE 10

....in which the two sorts of predictions that ecologists are required to provide for answering society's questions are described and it is admitted that making one kind of prediction for shorebirds is quite beyond us at present and may remain so for many years to come.

CHAPTER 1: Origins – how the need for a model arose 17

....in which the need for some way to be found to predict the impact of all sorts of human activities on shorebirds emerged during the 1960s and 1970s and some stories are told of the birds themselves and of some of the people who study them and of others who try to conserve them.

CHAPTER 2: First steps 51

...in which is told the story of how a long-term project was set up in 1976 to research the foraging behaviour of oystercatchers that eat mussels on the Exe estuary in Devon, of the extraordinary help that was provided by so many people to ensure that it got underway successfully and the emergence of the first evidence that competition might be occurring between the birds

CHAPTER 3: Rate of food intake by oystercatchers on the mussel beds and density dependence

.... 82

...which describes the in-depth research on the foraging behaviour of mussel-eating oystercatchers and details how it came to be realised that research on individual birds could be used to test whether the mortality rate of oystercatchers depended on their density on the mussel beds.

CHAPTER 4: Competitive ability and intake rates 106

......in which the long research programme that was required to measure the considerable differences between individual oystercatchers in their ability to compete with others is described, a-model was developed that predicted intake rate from the density, size and flesh content of the mussels where a bird was feeding and the stage is set to build the first IBM for a shorebird.

CHAPTER 5: Putting it all together into an individual-based model 129

...which describes how the first version an individual-based model of mussel-eating oystercatchers was gradually developed using a game theory approach, and the important role played in its conception and construction by

friends and colleagues, and how it didn't work too well at the start but not so badly that the whole approach had to be abandoned.

CHAPTER 6: The development, structure and testing of version 3 152

...which details the extra fieldwork that had to be carried out for the third version of the IBM for mussel-eating oystercatchers to be built and then describes how the model works and concludes with the tests of its predictions that, through good fortune, resulted in a remarkable success.

CHAPTER 7: Explorations with the oystercatcher-mussel model of the Exe estuary 179

....which describes how version 3 of the individual-based model (IBM) was used to explore the effect of disturbance from people and of mussel-fishing on the mussel-feeding oystercatchers of the Exe estuary and of cockle-fishing on oystercatchers in the Burry Inlet, Wales

CHAPTER 8: Simplifying the Exe model and applying it to other shellfisheries 200

...in which the ways in which the model was further developed to enable it to be applied to oystercatchers and shellfish – cockles as well as mussels - much more quickly than had been possible on the Exe estuary are described.

CHAPTER 9: Applying the model to other shellfisheries 217

... in which the application of the oystercatcher-shellfish model to a range of management issues in shellfisheries elsewhere than the Exe is described and examples are given of the kind of management 'rules of thumb' that the model can be used to produce.

CHAPTER 10: Extending the model to species of shorebirds other than oystercatchers 245

....which describes how the need to find a much quicker way to produce models for shorebirds other than oystercatchers and prey species other than shellfish was realised and how this objective was successfully met so that, instead of taking 25 years, a model could be built in just a few months which enabled a variety of models to be produced for a wide range of shorebird species, both wading birds and wildfowl, and management issues at different spatial scales.

CHAPTER 11: Some points to end with 277

..in which the notion of 'carrying capacity' is discussed and a new definition for shorebirds is developed and the importance of testing model predictions, of knowing the animals' natural history and of density-dependence are stressed

ACKNOWLEDGEMENTS and some photographs 302

PREAMBLE

....in which the two sorts of predictions that ecologists are required to provide for answering society's questions are described and it is admitted that making one kind of prediction for shorebirds is quite beyond us at present and may remain so for many years to come.

In giving talks to natural history societies and the like, it has proved quite a good idea to begin by summarising the role of scientists in society before focussing down on the particular contributions that shorebird ecologists can make.

Scientists have three main roles: satisfying our desire to discover and understand the way in which the world around us works and our place in it; fascinating and entertaining people with stories about the extraordinary world and universe in which we live, and finally, providing advice, discoveries and technologies to help society achieve its many practical goals. For shorebirds, this last category primarily includes giving advice to government at all levels, to conservation organisations, to environmental consultants and to people making proposals that involve a change in 'land'-use (actually mud, sand, saltmarsh and water!) on coastal flats. The call for some time has been that the decisions of such organisations should be based on 'sound science'. That seems reasonable, and it should usually be better than guessing or relying on particulate experience or self-serving preconception!

This book makes no contribution to the first but may provide a little entertainment, and so contribute to the second. Its primary purpose, though, is to give an example of the third role, the tricky business of making predictions that can be applied with confidence, in this case by managers of the coast. Very many developments are proposed for the coastal zone, perhaps a lot more than are suggested for terrestrial habitats. The intertidal zone is often perceived as being wasteland and ugly where nobody lives. The proposed developments can also be on a large scale; for example, the Severn and Mersey barrages for tidal power, the Saemangeum barrage in South Korea (280 km^2 of mudflats to create land for agriculture and industry), and the proposed reclamation in the Thames estuary for a new London airport.

Unfortunately, many ecologists have seemed rather reluctant to make predictions of this kind, arguing that everything is just too complex and uncertain. Well yes, but so is the climate, and that doesn't stop meteorologists pressing on with finding better and better ways of predicting weather, with impressive success. Nor has it stopped many ecologists from doing so either: research to improve sea-fishery management is a good example. This is the spirit in which the research described in this book was carried out: if there is a way to do it, it will be found!

There are two broad categories of scientific prediction – 'future' predictions and 'scenario' predictions. In future predictions, an ecologist might, for example, attempt to predict what will happen over the next weeks, months, years or decades to the size of the population of an animal or plant species. Figure P.1(A) illustrates a hypothetical prediction for the numbers of redshank on an estuary somewhere in the UK.

But as the quote of disputed provenance says: "It is difficult to make predictions, especially about the future". Predicting the future of a shorebird population is way beyond us at the moment and will probably remain so for decades. Not only do we not know enough about their ecology to construct models that might enable us to do this, but their future by its very nature is unpredictable.

(A)

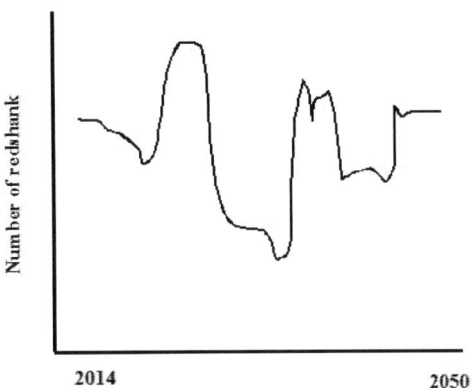

(B)

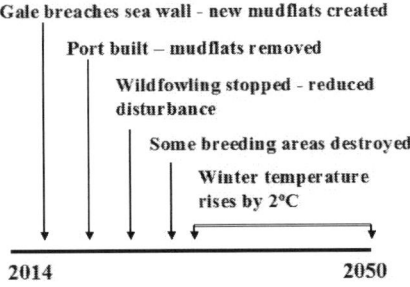

Figure P.1 *The difficulty of predicting changes in the size of a hypothetical population of redshank. (A) This illustrates a hypothetical prediction for the numbers of redshank on an estuary somewhere in the UK, and (B) shows the kind of unforeseen events that can render the predictions wildly inaccurate.*

The reason for this is that the rate at which the birds reproduce and die – the balance between which determine how many birds there will be – depend on factors and events that are themselves unpredictable. Figure P.1(B) illustrates this point using our hypothetical population of redshank. Unpredictable changes in their environment, due to weather or to local or national policy decisions, conspire to prevent reliable forecasts from being made. If asked the question: 'How many redshank will there be on the estuary in October 2031?' the answer would have to be 'Pass!'

Unlike future predictions, scenario predictions do not try to forecast something at a definite time in the future. Rather, the predictions are of the kind: 'If we change in a particular way how the estuary is managed, what will be the effect on the average numbers of redshank that spend the non-breeding season here?' Figure P.2 gives some examples of how the management of an estuary might change or be changed.

- Building a marina or heliport over mudflats
- Building a barrage to generate electricity
- Reducing disturbance from people on the sandflats
- Allowing more shellfishing of mussels and cockles
- Increasing wildfowling
- Removing *Spartina* grass from some upshore mudflats
- Breaching the seawall to create new mudflats over land
- Designating the estuary a Special Protection Area
- Controlling access by people to the intertidal zone
- Controlling dog-walking along the shoreline
- Rise in sea level and winter temperature

Figure P.2 *Some examples of how the management of an estuary might be changed.*

Such predictions are possible because they do not require forecasts for all the future values of all the factors that might affect redshank numbers, but only of those arising directly from the planned change in the management of the estuary. For example, constructing a marina on a mudflat where birds feed would reduce the extent of the intertidal zone where the birds feed and might also change the nature of the sediments in adjacent areas; by reducing the velocity of the tidal currents, the sediments might change from being predominantly sandy to predominantly muddy, for example. If sedimentologists tell the ecologists that such a change in sediment is likely to occur, the ecologist must then predict how this will affect the invertebrates that live there as these form the redshank's food supply. By investigating analogous muddy and sandy areas elsewhere in the estuary, it is usually possible to make a pretty good attempt at forecasting how the food supply adjacent to the marina would change as the sediment changed from sand to mud. In principal, and often in practise, such changes are predictable, and the effect of the changes on the birds food supply can then be forecast, with varying degrees of confidence according to how well their ecology is understood. The effect of the change in the food supply on the numbers of birds then be worked out, using a variety of methods as discussed in later chapters.

The final point about the tricky business of making predictions is that they should be quantitative. It is very easy to build up a word argument that nothing about an estuary should be changed because the system is so' fragile', 'sensitive', and so forth, and therefore that shorebird numbers are bound to decline if this or that proposal is allowed to go ahead without mitigation. But equally, one can build up a word argument that the system is more 'robust' and capable of absorbing much more change than this pessimistic viewpoint implies. With word arguments like this, you can almost pick the outcome that you want, and discussions between opponents can go on and on and on....!

The way out of such a whirly-gig of argument is for predictions to be quantitative. An example might be: 'If the estuary were to be changed in such-and-such a way, the number of shorebirds would change by 0% (zero impact) or be reduced by 5% or 10% *etc.* but, if a proposed mitigation measure were to be implemented, it would return shorebird numbers to their present levels.' If this could be done in such a way that the decision-makers had confidence in the predictions, it would save everyone a lot of time and expense, help conservation authorities to focus their limited resources on real problems, reduce the amount of hand-waving that can all too often influence decisions at present and prevent the vetoing of worthwhile projects for no good reason, and so risk losing public support for a good cause.

To be able to provide such quantitative predictions, some form of mathematical modelling is essential, of course: it goes without saying that you cannot avoid using numbers if you are required to make quantitative predictions! Ecological systems can be complex and always contain a bundle of processes that interact with each other, and the magnitude of their influence on an interaction – and not just the fact that they are interacting - can be of the utmost importance to the outcome. For example, it could be of great importance in predicting the effect of a loss of mudflat on the long-term population size of a shorebird species that, on average, the birds currently consume 25% rather than 75% of their food stocks during a single non-breeding season. It is impossible from the word statement 'the birds eat a lot' to work out the effect on bird numbers of removing some of their food supply, an action that would probably result in the birds eating a greater proportion of it than they do at present, with possibly detrimental effects on their ability to survive the non-breeding season. It is the same reason that economics models are expressed in mathematical equations: to predict that inflation might go up a little bit or by quite a lot is usually just not a good enough to guide economic policy! Apart from the difficulty of predicting the knock-on consequences for the economy of such vague forecasts for inflation, 'a little' and 'a lot' mean different things to different people, and so nothing at all to anybody!

Ecological models consist of equations – sometimes lots of them – that are chained together in a sequence that represents how the system is believed to work, with the output of one equation providing the input to the next, and so forth, until the final output – such as bird numbers - is reached. A simple and wholly imaginary example is shown in Figure P.3. Such a model is also a quantitative hypothesis about the way in which the 'system' works, not only about the way in which all the processes combine to produce the outcome but also about the magnitude of the influence that each one has on the eventual output. In shorebirds, for example, birds may feed at night at 25% or 75% or even 125% of their daytime rate. Now imagine that a proposal is made to allow shellfishing to take place at night for the first time. Using the correct value in the model for the feeding rate at night would make a big difference to the forecasts of how this change in estuary management would affect bird numbers.

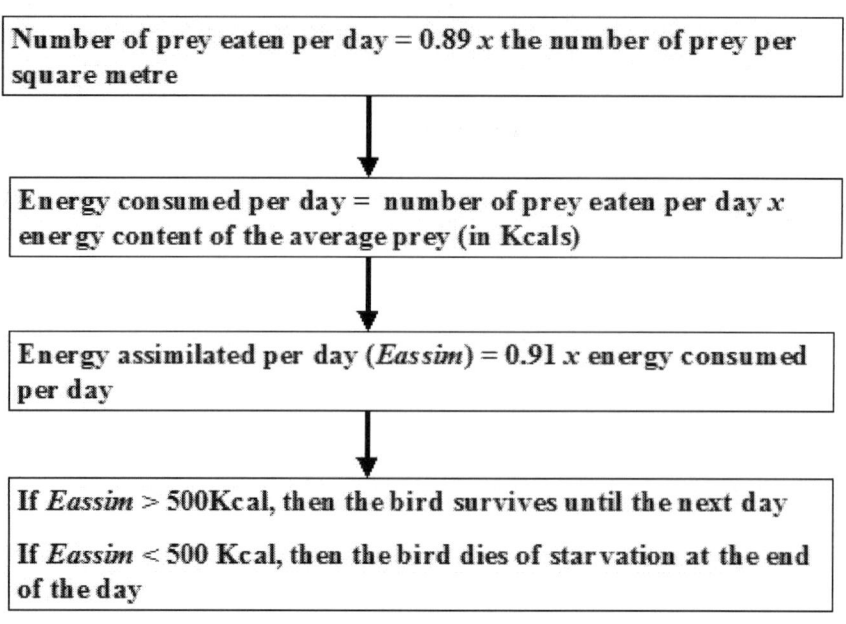

Figure P.3 *Like many other models, ecological models consist of equations that are chained together in a sequence that represents how the system is believed to work, with the output of one equation providing the input to the next, and so forth, until the final output – such as whether or not a bird starves - is reached.*

Often there is some uncertainty about the processes that should be included in a model and about the values in the mathematical expressions that are used to represent them. This can, of course, undermine confidence in using some models as a basis of decision. In these circumstances, it behoves the scientist – the expert ('hopefully'), in other words – to form a judgement of what is the most likely value to use, and therefore to be responsible for the advice. You can only do as well as the underpinning science permits, and only the scientists concerned and their peers can really evaluate how risky or otherwise the advice might be. Certainly, the responsibility of assessing the risk that a prediction might be right or wrong should not normally be left to the decision-makers themselves who usually do not have the expert knowledge with which to form a judgement (Box P.1). For the scientist to hand this responsibility over to them is just a cop-out.

There is also a powerful scientific argument for building mathematical models with which to make quantitative predictions. Such models make you think much more precisely about the processes that are going on. They allow you to explore their sensitivities to the chosen assumptions. They also encourage a continuous process of improvement and allow radical changes if necessary.

They also permit you to make much more rigorous tests of your understanding of the system being modelled. Applying a model to a real cases where a change in the management of an estuary has taken place and its effect been monitored provides a very strong way of testing our current understanding of how shorebird numbers are determined. If the model predicts that there will be 23% fewer birds after the management of an estuary has been changed, and numbers actually decrease by 23.2%, it would be difficult not to be impressed with the understanding, the hypothesis, the model upon which the prediction was based! Such a result would raise our confidence not only that the model gives reliable predictions but also that it captures the main biological processes and how they interact with each other.

It is unlikely that the prediction would get so close to the right number by chance, bearing in mind that the model predictions and the real-world values could lie anywhere between 0% and 100%! There is only a 1 in a 100 chance that you will get it right by chance - or even 1 in a 1000 if the model predicts to the first decimal place! Either way, there are many more opportunities for the model to get quantitative predictions wrong than there are to make unsuccessful predictions that are expressed in words. The prediction in words might be, for example, 'more than at present' or 'less than at present' or 'the same' where there is a 33:33:33 chance that the model will get it right by accident because are only three outcomes – increase or decrease or no change! Quantitative predictions are not only required by managers of the coast. Shorebird scientists also need them in order to be able to test rigorously their understanding of the system as it is represented in their models. Sadly, this realisation is not everywhere common in shorebird ecology and, indeed, in ecology as a whole.

P.1 Advising policy makers

The following is apparently a true story, recounted by a senior scientific administrator in regular contact with the British Government.

A minister in the Government was advised by one of his team to consult an expert scientist on a particularly thorny issue on which he had to decide between two options. The Minister was reluctant because, as he put it, 'He'll probably say: 'Well, on the one hand Minister…. but on the other hand……'" which, in effect, would mean that the Minister himself had to decide on a tricky technical matter without having the technical expertise with which to do so. Eventually he was persuaded to see the expert who, before he entered the Minister's office, was told firmly by his boss that on no account should he say: 'Well, on the one hand Minister…. but the other hand……'.

In he went, the Minister asked his question, and out came the answer: 'Well, on the one hand Minister…. but on the other hand……'. He just couldn't break the habit of an academic lifetime!

What the Minister said in response can only be imagined!

In the scientists defence, you could argue that scientists are trained to evaluate the evidence and to consider both sides of the argument, and a reasonable attitude in an academic discussion is that all options should be considered openly. But this was not an academic debate. The philosophy of not pinning your flag to a particular mast without strong evidence was not necessarily appropriate!

The Minister was no expert on these technical issues and had no basis upon which to decide whether 'the one hand' was more likely to be the case than was 'the other hand'. It was the responsibility of the scientist to take the decision as to which was the more likely to be true, and this particular person failed to do so. No doubt the Minister wondered why the country was spending so much money on scientific research if, when put to the test, the findings didn't help in situations like this.

A more helpful reply to the Minister might have been: 'Well, Minister, the evidence is rather finely balanced (so you're taking a gamble here) but, on the basis of my experience and that of other colleagues with whom I have discussed the matter at length over the last six months, I would advise that there is more evidence in favour of 'the one hand' than there is for the 'other hand'. That's the one that we ourselves would choose on present evidence. Good luck!"

CHAPTER 1:
Origins – how the need for a model arose

....in which the need for some way to be found to predict the impact of all sorts of human activities on shorebirds emerged during the 1960s and 1970s and some stories are told of the birds themselves and of some of the people who study them and of others who try to conserve them.

SHOREBIRDS

The mudflats and sandflats (the 'flats') that are exposed at low tide along the coasts of the world provide hundreds of thousands of specialist birds with the major part of their food requirements throughout much of the year. Most of these shorebirds belong to three groups; waders, wildfowl and gulls. Most species eat invertebrates, such as ragworms and cockles, but some wildfowl are herbivorous and some gulls also scavenge. Although by no means all species of shorebirds rely solely on the coast, many species do so, either throughout the entire year or during their prolonged non-breeding season, which may last up to nine even ten months. Many species migrate between their non-breeding and breeding grounds, sometimes covering enormous distances, sometimes in a single hop. The record at the moment stands at 11,000 km, the distance flown by the bar-tailed godwits that cross the Pacific Ocean between their Alaskan breeding areas and their non-breeding areas far into the southern hemisphere. Single hops of about 5,000km are quite common, this being the distance covered by several wader species migrating between North and South America.

It is not just these amazing feats of migration that have enthused huge numbers of amateur and professional ornithologists to devote much time and other resources to studying shorebirds (Box 1.1). Most shorebirds are beautiful, often in an elegantly simple and under-stated way and, in their sometimes massive flocks can provide a wonderful spectacle as they twist and turn through the big skies of the open coast. They are also relatively easy to watch on the open flats as they go about their daily lives. Unlike species living in woods, for example, the only obstacles to seeing them is usually distance, and this can easily be overcome by simple field craft and powerful telescopes (Box 1.2). Shorebirds also often live in very beautiful places. Vivid colours of dawns and sunsets reflect off the water-film covered mudflats, producing a subtle blend of colours that has been captured by photographers, artists and writers. Many coastal flats are wild and rather few people occur there so that remoteness and solitude are easy to find. They can also be dangerous to the unwary and this adds a risky - but not too risky - feel to being out on the flats and salt marshes (Box 1.3). It is perhaps not surprising, then, that shorebirds have so many enthusiasts in so many parts of the World. They and the places in which they live cater for our curiosity and senses of beauty, atmosphere and risk.

PROTECTING SHOREBIRDS

The fact that shorebirds are migratory and the fact that they attract so many committed enthusiasts has led in many countries to strong demands for their conservation and the provision of strong legal means, often involving international agreements, to enforce it. In Europe, for example, the Habitats and the Birds Directives have provided powerful means to help protect shorebird populations from the many activities that people like to carry out on the coast for both commercial and recreational reasons.

The way in which these activities might have an impact on the birds is one of the main themes of this book and will be developed throughout. But by way of introduction, here is a minimal list, in alphabetical order, of activities that either disturb the birds from their feeding or resting areas or remove some of the food resources on which they depend: **bait digging** (for fishing), usually for polychaete worms in northern Europe; **barrage construction,** for electricity generation or to create amenity freshwater lakes; **bird-watching, fishing, dog walking, hunting,** usually for wildfowl; **replacing flats** with all sorts of developments, such as marinas for leisure boats, ports for commercial shipping, building land; **shellfishing** for cockles, mussels and other molluscs; **walking, running** and **training the military.** Additionally, there is *'coastal squeeze':* as sea levels rise, the width of the shore, and therefore the area available for the birds to live, will be compressed where ever the high water line is unable to migrate inland because, for example, it is defended by sea walls.

Conservationists realised many years ago that, to be effective, measures to protect shorebirds had to be taken internationally, simply because so many of the species are migratory. Typically, the breeding grounds of migratory shorebirds lie to the north of their non-breeding grounds and the birds migrate between them along the flyways of the Pacific coasts of the Americas and Asia and the Atlantic coasts of Europe and the Americas. There would be little point in protecting shorebirds stopping to re-fuel along the coasts of the United Kingdom, for example, if their non-breeding areas further to the south had been wrecked beyond use (or *vice versa*)! Analogies involving the weakest links in the chain spring to mind! For shorebirds to survive, the integrity of the network of sites on which they depend through their annual cycle had to be maintained.

International arrangements, such as the Ramsar Convention, have committed governments around the world to protect shorebirds and their habitats so that the network of coastal areas that sustain their populations will continue to function effectively. In Europe, the Habitats Directive and Birds Directive, and its 'Natura 2000' network of coastal sites, provide powerful legislation to achieve this conservation goal through the creation of special protection areas (SPAs) and special areas of conservation (SACs). If anybody wants to introduce a new activity to an SPA or SAC that might have an impact on the 'integrity' of the site (*i.e.* its effectiveness in sustaining the shorebird populations), an 'appropriate assessment' must be carried out for the 'competent authority' (such as the local government) to evaluate whether it is likely to reduce the ability of the site to maintain the numbers of the shorebirds that were present at the time when the site was designated. If this is thought not to be the case because the 'carrying capacity' of the site is likely to be reduced, mitigation measures can be used to offset any damage to the site that is foreseen. If the competent authority is convinced that the measures will be effective, they may then grant permission for the new activity to be started. If not, they won't, and their decision could only be challenged on appeal at various judicial levels - a costly and time-consuming business, I believe.

These directives have been very effective in preventing proposed activities from going ahead, even though regularly challenged. One reason for this is that the directives, and the subsequent case law, have insisted that, if there is uncertainty whether a particular action would undermine the integrity of the site, the precautionary principle should be invoked. In simple terms, this principle states 'If there is any doubt about the effect of a proposed activity on the birds, either don't allow it or mitigate for it!'. Authorities faced with such decisions are required by the legislation to adopt the precautionary principle. They certainly have no incentive or reason to take a risk when making a decision. Just imagine if a decision to allow an activity to go ahead was to be followed by a decrease in bird numbers — even if it had been caused by something quite unrelated to the activity itself!

But it is not always easy to convince the people who are proposing a new activity, and sometimes the general public also, that this approach is always appropriate for the community as a whole. While in Britain, for example, there is very strong general support for the idea that bird populations should be protected and maintained, those people directly affected by a 'No" decision based on the precautionary principle can be deeply frustrated if they suspect that the decision has not been based on sound scientific evidence. Often people feel that the conservation authorities can be rather extreme or, at the least, rather over-precautionary (Box 1.4).

As applied to estuaries, the precautionary principle in effect assumes that the birds are in some sense so hard-pressed that any additional activity carried by people will inevitably make matters worse for them so that of them will starve or at least have a poor body condition. This is what is meant by there being a meaningful impact on the birds (Box 1.5).

One of the roles that shorebird scientists should have is to test assumptions like this on which government policy (and that of others) is based, or at least should be based. By way of illustration, assume that a developer is seeking permission to develop an area of mudflat in an estuary that is currently used by shorebirds for feeding during the non-breeding season. The area would be transformed from mudflat to ordinary land. This would, of course, reduce not only the total quantity of food that is available to the birds in the estuary but also the extent of the feeding area which can be very important, as will become apparent later.

The argument used to support the precautionary principle would then go something like this: 'Many of the birds are already finding it so difficult to get all the food that they need that even more of them will die of starvation if their food supply is reduced by even a small amount. Furthermore, while the mudflat is being reclaimed — and probably afterwards too - there will be lots of disturbance from people and machines, which will just add to the birds' difficulties. Flying away when disturbed will cost them energy that they would otherwise not have spent. It will also cost them time in which to feed, because a shorebird cannot feed while it is in flight. The reduction in the food supply and the increased frequency of disturbance is certain to make it more difficult for birds to survive during the non-breeding season. It will also make it more difficult for them to accumulate the energy reserves they need to fuel their long migration flights to the breeding grounds. They may starve *en route* and crash into the sea or arrive in such poor condition on the breeding grounds that their subsequent breeding success will be impaired. Clearly, this development should not be allowed to go ahead as it is very likely to be damaging to the birds'. I know this argument well, having used it myself in a number of precautionary environmental impact assessments in the early days of our research.

But there have always been reasons for being sceptical about this compelling line of reasoning. Generally, the survival rate of shorebirds in the UK over the non-breeding season seems to be very high for such small-sized birds in the temperate zone. Despite this, and despite their twice-yearly long and demanding migratory flights, shorebirds are viewed as 'sensitive'. Constant repetition of this mantra has fostered the belief that anything people do **must** harm these birds! Yet when the winter weather in the UK is very severe for a long period, which it has occasionally been over the last few decades, the corpses of large numbers of starved birds may be washed up along the tide line or are found at the roosts used by the birds at high water. This prompts a question: 'If we find so many corpses in extreme conditions, why do we find so few corpses – if any - in more normal and often mild winters if these birds are habitually so hard-pressed for food that more-or-less any new activity on an estuary will damage them?' Furthermore, in many species, the number of birds that spend the non-breeding season on an estuary can vary a lot from year to year. This raises another question: 'While the birds might be hard-pressed in years with large numbers, it is surely much less likely that they will be hard-pressed in years of low bird numbers when the amount of food and foraging space per bird would be a lot greater?' Similarly, studies of oystercatchers during the Burry Inlet 'oystercatchers *versus* shellfishers' debate of the 1960s showed that the birds' principal food supply - cockles – fluctuated enormously in abundance between years. Yet large numbers of corpses were not found in most winters of cockle scarcity, perhaps because the birds fed in fields instead. Another question is therefore raised: 'Although birds may have been hard-pressed in years of low cockle stocks, is it really likely that they would have been hard-pressed in years when food was extremely abundant?' These are perfectly good arguments for raising doubts about the precautionary assumption that shorebirds are generally hard-pressed and should be regarded as 'sensitive'.

Really, whether a human activity will have an impact on the birds is a question of quantities. Nobody would believe, for example, that removing just one cockle from the billions that live in a huge shellfishery area, such as the Wash in east England, would cause the oystercatchers that depend on them any further difficulty in obtaining their daily food requirements during the non-breeding season – if indeed, they do normally have any difficulty anyway! But if all the cockles but one were to be removed, nobody would doubt that the birds would be likely to suffer! So the key question is this: 'At what point as the numbers of cockles removed is increased will some threshold be reached at which the birds begin to be affected?' In terms of the numbers of cockles removed by shell fishers, at what point does 'not enough to harm the birds' become 'too much and the birds will be harmed'?

When research on shorebirds really got under way in the late 1950s and early 1960s, we hadn't even thought of this question let alone tried to answer it! Competing arguments could not be evaluated because so little was known about the ecology and behaviour of these birds. Apart from some obvious exceptions, such as oystercatchers eating cockles and mussels, we knew very little even about what they ate! This state of affairs changed dramatically over the following few decades because of the immense amount of research that has been conducted all round the world. This research effort was motivated partly by curiosity and partly by the need to advise managers of the coastal zone so that that conservation actions that limit the activities of people are based on sound science rather than on mere hand-waving protestations and the often repeated mantra that the shorebirds are 'sensitive'. Now it is possible to test the assumption underlying the precautionary principle as it has been so frequently applied to shorebirds during the non-breeding season. This book tells the story of how this came about, as seen through the experience of one team of research workers in the UK.

THE BEGINNINGS

The recognition of the need to develop methods that could make the quantitative predictions required to advise estuary managers emerged only gradually through the 1960s and 1970s as, indeed, did the research questions that had to be answered if quantitative predictions were ever to be made. It arose from the increasing frequency with which shorebird researchers were required to carry out environmental impact assessments on a number of coastal management issues: some influential examples from the UK can be used to illustrate this.

Burry Inlet: cockle-fishing

The extensive sand flats of the Burry Inlet in south Wales support very large stocks of cockles that have been fished by hand for generations. The traditional fishing method was for shellfishers to go out onto the sandy flats in a pony and cart as the tide receded to rake up bags of adult cockles in their second-winter or above which were then carted back to the shore for processing and sale.

The severely cold winter of 1962-63 brought about a huge change to what had previously been a rather stable cockle population consisting largely of relatively young cockles (2-3 years old). That severe winter killed most of the adult cockles and led to a massive settlement of young cockles in 1963 and then to a huge stock of second-winter cockles in 1964, which could be harvested by both fishermen and oystercatchers. This glut provided a temporarily more profitable basis for the fishery. But by the early 1970s, as a result of increased predation by oystercatchers (whose numbers had increased from 8 000 to 14 000) and of shellfishing, and in the absence of further substantial settlement of young cockles, the commercial cockle beds in the Inlet were returning to their pre-1963 state of persistently low stocks. It was thought that these reduced cockle stocks could not support both the high level of fishing that had become normal by 1970 and the increased numbers of oystercatchers. Accordingly, a reduction in oystercatcher numbers to previous levels was recommended and an experimental cull was carried out, yet the cockle stocks did not recover. The numbers of oystercatchers wintering in the Inlet did not change either, even though many thousands of them had been shot. Counts revealed no evidence of a reduction in the population size.

The assumption underlying the shooting experiment had been that all the oystercatchers that had 'wanted' to spend the winter in the Burry Inlet were already there. Other oystercatchers in the UK had their own preferred wintering sites and would be unaffected by any shooting of Burry Inlet birds. Had this assumption been correct, shooting would surely have led to a decrease in the numbers in the Inlet. The birds that wintered elsewhere in the UK would just have remained where they were and not moved to the Burry Inlet to replace those that had been shot.

But instead, numbers did not go down in line with the numbers that had been killed. Birds from elsewhere must have moved into the Inlet take advantage of the space vacated by the shot birds. This raised the possibility that many more oystercatchers would have wintered on the Burry Inlet if it had not supported so many already. The result seemed to imply that the capacity of the Inlet to support wintering oystercatchers had usually been used up so that any additional birds that arrived had to go somewhere else. The outcome of the cull in the Inlet seemed to suggest that the presence of 14 000 oystercatchers in the Burry Inlet had in some way prevented other oystercatchers from spending the winter there.

But the way in which this could happen was not at all clear. After 1963, the numbers of oystercatchers in the Inlet did not track the massive annual fluctuations in the abundance of their main food supply (Figure 1.1). Had oystercatchers in some sense used all the capacity of the Inlet to support them in every winter, we would not have expected oystercatcher numbers to remain high in years of low cockle stocks. Perhaps the birds coped over such winters by eating other things, such as ragworms on the flats and earthworms in the fields - which they certainly did when cockles were scarce. But if these alternative foods allowed a higher capacity in years of low cockle stocks, why weren't they used in years of cockle abundance so that even more birds would be able to spend the winter in the Inlet?

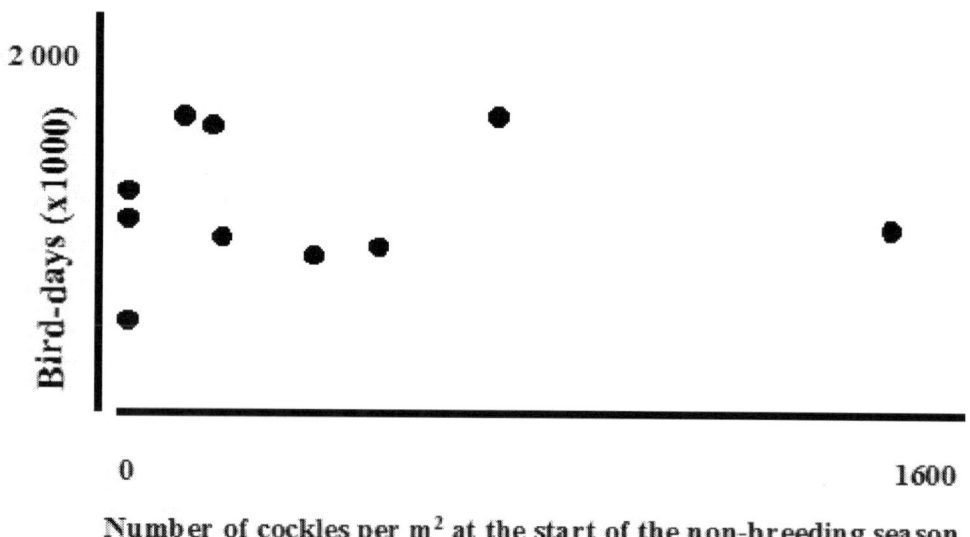

Figure 1.1 *Burry Inlet: the total oystercatcher-days between mid-November and mid-May in relation to the abundance of second-winter cockles in November.*

The results of the cull proved much more difficult to understand than those of similar experiments that had been carried out on territorial breeding birds. In these breeding studies, the removal of territory owners (originally by shooting but subsequently by humane trapping) was usually quickly followed by the arrival of other birds to take their place. In one famous experiment in the USA, territorial males were shot and were repeatedly replaced by a far greater number of other males as successive waves of 'replacement males' were themselves removed. There must have been large numbers of roaming individuals looking for a place to establish a territory. This suggested that the birds had competed for territories at the beginning of the breeding season and that all the available territorial spaces had been claimed - just as the capacity of a car park is reached when all the parking spaces are occupied (Box 1.6). The result of the oystercatcher cull could not so easily be understood then, however.

In combination with the rising influence of the conservation lobby during the 1970s, the Burry Inlet study helped to focus attention on the question of how the numbers of shorebirds wintering on an estuary is determined. It not only raised the profile of this key question for managing estuaries, it provided much information on the basic biology of shorebirds - such as just how many cockles a single oystercatcher eats in a single day, which can be as high as 500! The fact that each bird needs daily to find so many prey items provided further reason for arguing that the birds should be left in peace to find the large amounts of food they need to survive the non-breeding season in good condition.

Morecambe Bay: fresh-water reservoir

Before the controversy in the Burry Inlet had quietened down during the 1970s after the failure of the shooting experiment, it was proposed to build a barrage across part of Morecambe Bay in order to retain the freshwater that would otherwise run from its inflowing rivers into the open Irish Sea. The question was: 'What impact, if any, would this have on the shorebirds that would otherwise feed on the mud flats and sand flats that would be covered by this fresh-water reservoir?'

This was the first environmental impact assessment carried out in the UK on an issue that came to dominate much of the applied research on this shorebirds for two decades; habitat loss. The proposal was to construct an impermeable barrage on the intertidal flats where a river entered the Bay to create a large container in which fresh-water could be stored (Fig. 1.2). The area to be impounded would not have wiped out all the mudflats and sandflats of the Bay, so the first things to find out was whether any birds fed there at all. If no birds had fed in the area to be covered by freshwater, it is unlikely that the loss of feeding habitat would have mattered to them! But having quickly established that shorebirds certainly did feed there, the next thing to find out was what they ate and whether plentiful stocks of the same kind of food were also available for them to use elsewhere in the Bay.

Attention focussed on knots because Morecambe Bay was, and still is, a very important wintering and staging area for these specialised estuary birds. Many hundreds of thousands of them occur on the wide sandy flats of North-west Europe, such as the Wadden Sea, the Wash and Morecambe Bay where they provide one of the great spectacles of estuary birds as flocks of thousands wheel overhead. Generally, outside the breeding season, knots eat small and medium-sized bivalve molluscs, such as young cockles and a clam called the Baltic tellin. Individually, they are attractive and enchanting little birds, their rotund bodies and short legs giving them a portly, well-fed appearance!

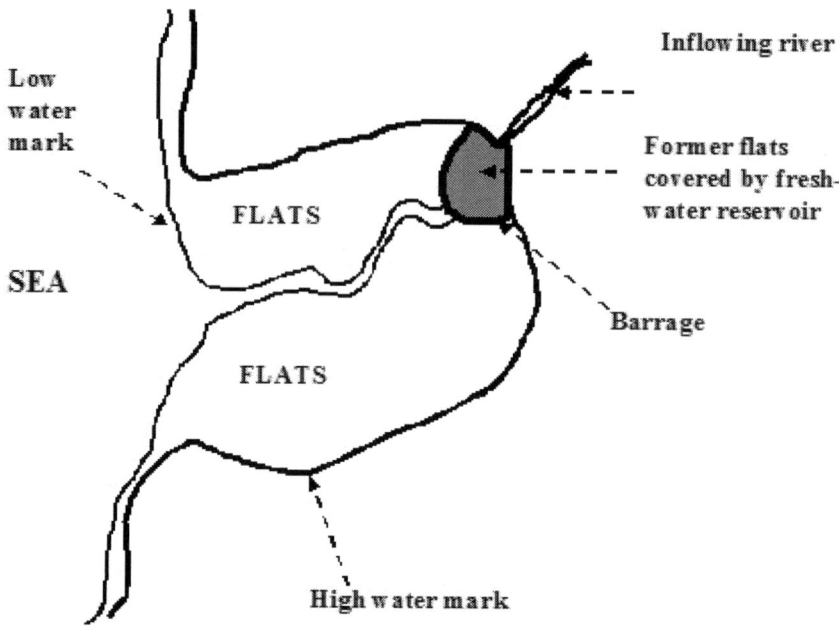

Figure 1.2 *Morecambe Bay: a sketch of the proposal to build a fresh-water reservoir at the mouth of a river where it flows into the Bay.*

This study successfully answered the questions that it had been posed: 'Do many shorebirds feed in the area that would be removed by the reservoir? Yes, they do'; 'What do they eat? In the case of knots, small bivalve molluscs'; 'Are there extensive food supplies elsewhere in the Bay? In the case of knots; yes'. The reservoir would affect the birds in that it would displace them to other feeding areas.

What a short study of this kind could not do at that particular stage in the development of the science, of course, was to predict whether this displacement would affect the birds in any really meaningful way; just moving to another feeding area may not have mattered to them at all. After all, the location of the foods of shorebirds often changes naturally within and between non-breeding seasons, so that just changing feeding grounds of itself was not necessarily damaging. Shorebirds are highly mobile animals capable of flying enormous distances in a single hop. So just forcing them to change their feeding areas within Morecambe Bay - large though it is - would not necessarily make it more difficult for them to survive the non-breeding season and to do so with enough fat reserves for them to migrate successfully to the breeding grounds. This is where the matter rested because the idea to store fresh water in Morecambe Bay was abandoned.

Teesmouth: reclamation of high-level mudflats

The proposal here was to reclaim a large area of Seal Sands (actually, no longer sand, but thick gloopy mud that was difficult and dangerous to walk on!) by covering part of it with soil, rubble and so forth in order to create dry land for building. This, of course, would have permanently removed all the shorebird food supplies in the underlying mud.

This was the first study really to attempt to define and measure 'impact' in what seemed to be at the time a biologically meaningful sense. The question asked was: 'Would the reclamation of part of the Seal Sands mudflats remove so much of the food supply that there would not be enough left to support all the birds that used the estuary?'. The idea was this: if a single bird required, say, 10kg of ragworms to survive the winter in good condition (its physiological 'daily requirement'), and there were 10 000kg present on Seal Sands when the birds arrived at the start of the non-breeding season, then not more than 1000 (10 000/10) birds could be supported by Seal Sands. If there was a proposal to reclaim half of the Sands to build a factory, there would only be enough food left for 500 birds and so 500 would either starve or go elsewhere. Either way, the numbers of birds would be expected to decrease. In this sense, the 'carrying capacity' of the Sands would be greatly reduced by the reclamation and bird numbers would decline accordingly. Although nowadays there are very severe doubts about the wisdom of defining carrying capacity in terms of daily physiological requirements, when the reclamation was carried out a considerable reduction in shorebird numbers did indeed occur.

There was, however, a particular feature of this reclamation that made it difficult to apply its finding to other estuaries where reclamation had been proposed. Before the reclamation was fully carried out, a boundary wall had been constructed out of boulders all along the top of the Sands to form the downshore edge of the forthcoming reclamation (Fig. 1.3). This boundary was porous and water could therefore flow through it. The mudflats upshore of the wall continued to be covered by water over high tide. The intertidal invertebrates remained there and continued to be a source of food that could be exploited by shorebirds. However, the porous wall delayed the advancing tide. The mudflats upshore of the wall were available to the birds after the advancing tide had covered all the rest of the Sands that lay below and outside the porous wall. By the time the tide had filtered through the wall enough to cover the flats within the reclamation area, the water had started to retreat outside. Mudflats began to emerge downshore of the wall very quickly after the last mudflats within the reclamation boundary had been covered. This first stage of the reclamation process had therefore substantially increased the length of time over a tidal cycle of *circa* 12.4hrs when the shorebirds could feed on mudflats somewhere on Seal Sands. Accordingly, when the mudflats upshore of the porous wall were finally covered with rubble, it not only caused a loss of feeding habitat but also a reduction in the amount of time that the birds could feed during each tidal cycle. For the birds, the final reclamation represented a 'double wammy'.

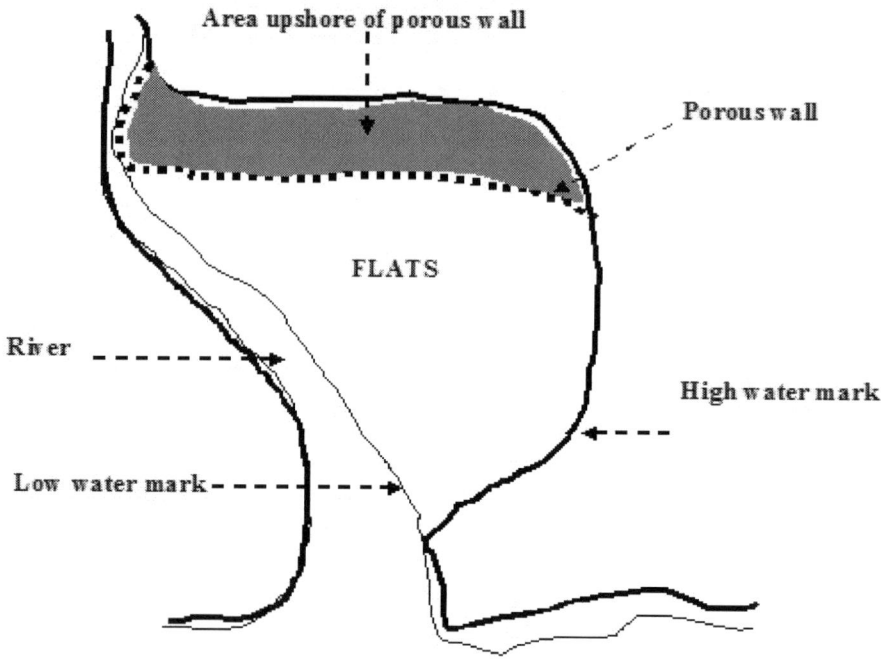

Figure 1.3 *Teesmouth: a sketch of the reclamation of the mudflats along the top of the shore.*

The study on Seal Sands began when this wall was already in place. Unfortunately, but unavoidably, little was known about the shorebirds beforehand. It was therefore not possible to disentangle the separate effects on the numbers of shorebirds of a loss of feeding habitat and of a loss of foraging time. For reasons completely out of the control of the scientists involved, the experiment of habitat loss was 'confounded' (in the jargon) by a reduction in foraging time. Two things changed with the reclamation and their separate effect on bird numbers could not be distinguished.

Since most reclamation schemes do not reduce foraging time across the entire estuary, the lessons of the reclamation at Seal Sands were difficult to apply to other estuaries. Nonetheless, this was an important study in a number of ways. It showed that shorebird numbers could indeed be reduced by only a modest change in their feeding conditions; *i.e.* by a partial reduction in foraging time and a partial loss of feeding habitat. It also made important discoveries on the biology – and particularly the energetics - of these birds. It was one of the first to measure the daily consumption of energy by a single shorebird, an issue that was to drive much shorebird research for years to come. It also showed that, even though many birds could starve during severe winter weather, shorebirds were at that time generally 'great survivors' with considerably less than <10% of adult birds dying during most non-breeding seasons. The project also provided the post-graduate research experience of many of the young scientists who went on to occupy influential positions in bird conservation organisations throughout Europe.

Wash: fresh-water reservoir

The proposal

The anticipated shortage of water in south-east England during the 1970's led to a number of proposals for water storage, one of which was for a fresh-water reservoir to be built over pat of the enormous intertidal mudflats and sandflats of the Wash in east England. The original suggestion had been to block out the sea entirely by building a barrage across the mouth of the Wash and to allow the several rivers that flow into the Wash to create a huge freshwater lake, but this plan was abandoned early on. Instead, a proposal was made to build, in effect, a huge container – a circular bund - on mudflats in the south-east corner of the Wash where fresh water from the nearby River Ouse that flows into the Wash could be stored (Fig. 1.4). As this reservoir appeared likely to remove large amounts of shorebird feeding area, a study of the impact of the scheme on shorebirds was started.

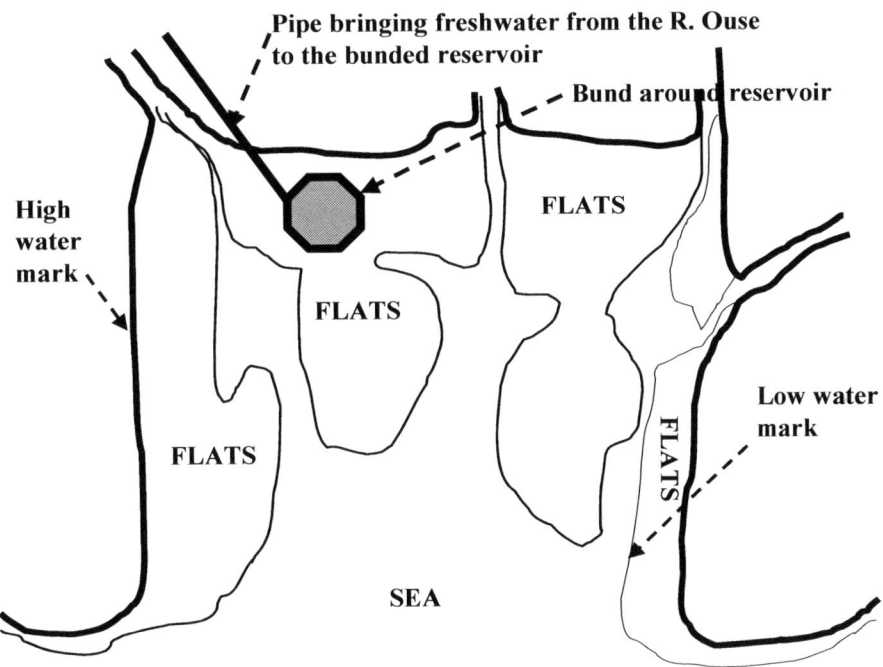

Figure 1.4 *The Wash: a sketch of the proposed freshwater reservoir*

As in the previous Morecambe Bay study, some basic questions had to be answered first: 'Do any birds feed in the area to be permanently removed by the reservoir?'; 'If so, how many birds and what do they eat?'; 'Do these food organisms occur abundantly elsewhere in the Wash and, if so, are they all already being utilised by the birds?'.

By the end of the first non-breeding season of the study, the answers were pretty clear: 'Yes, many birds did feed within the reservoir site', 'Yes, the food organisms they consumed there also occurred in many other parts of the Wash' and 'Yes, all the areas occupied by these food organisms were already being utilised by shorebirds at some point during the non-breeding season'. Although unsurprising in retrospect, it transpired that there were no unexploited stocks of food where birds displaced by a reservoir could go and feed on previously unused food stocks. The construction of the reservoir would inevitably have led to a decrease in the size of their food supply.

How to predict the impact on the birds of the loss of feeding grounds?

The next step was to try and predict whether a decrease in the food supply of the anticipated magnitude would have a significant, or meaningful, impact on the birds. A quite different approach to that adopted at Teesmouth was eventually thought out, and is best presented as a series of questions:

1. As building the reservoir would result in the same number of birds feeding in a reduced area, the density of the birds on the feeding grounds that remained – the numbers per square kilometre - would inevitably increase, at least initially. If the birds already competed for food, the competition between them would almost certainly intensify for a number of reasons, which will be detailed later. So, the first question was: 'Do the birds already compete for food, even before the extent of their feeding habitat has been reduced?'

2. If the answer to this question was 'Yes', it was very likely that any competition for food between birds would increase after a reservoir had been built. Accordingly, any difficulty they already had in satisfying their energy requirements would be made worse. So, the next question was: 'Do shorebirds already have difficulty at some stage of the non-breeding season in obtaining their energy requirements?'

3. If the answer to this question was also 'Yes', then the next question was: 'Is it likely that the difficulty is so severe that some birds actually starve during the non-breeding season or, alternatively, survive it but with too few body reserves to fly back to the breeding grounds in spring and so die *en route*?'.

4. If the answer to this question was also 'Yes', it was likely that fewer shorebirds would survive the non-breeding season in good condition after the reservoir had been built than were already doing so. It could then be concluded that building the reservoir would either increase the proportion of the birds that starved during the winter or reduce the numbers that had sufficient body reserves to reach the breeding grounds in spring, or both. The capacity of the Wash to support shorebirds during the non-breeding season would therefore be reduced by the reservoir and the numbers of shorebirds would probably decrease also.

By the time the Wash study of shorebirds was being designed, a number of research projects had shown that some birds died – apparently of starvation (because birds of prey that eat shorebirds were so scarce in those days) – even though they did not completely eat out their food supply before the end of the non-breeding season. This was known from research carried out on the Ythan estuary in Scotland and from the extensive studies in the Dutch Wadden Sea: shorebirds usually consumed well under 40% of their food stocks over the non-breeding season. This suggested that it would be very risky to base predictions on the effect of a reservoir on the welfare of shorebirds on the number of bird-days that the food supply could support after the reservoir had been built.

This is why. Imagine that shorebirds in an estuary currently eat 30% of the food supply that is present when they arrive in the non-breeding areas. That is, the combined physiological requirement of food that is needed to get all the shorebirds through to the end of the non-breeding season is equivalent to about 30% of the food supply that is there when they arrive. Somebody then proposes to remove half of the estuary for some purpose. This would leave for the birds with half of their original food stocks. If all the birds remained, they would still only consume 60% of the initial food stocks and not, by any means, all of it. That would be more than enough, one might think, for the same number of birds to continue to be supported. After all, there would still be the equivalent of 20% of the original, pre-reclamation food supply left over at the end of the non-breeding season that was in excess of their physiological requirements.

But then someone remembers that some birds already starve when they only consume 30% of the much larger, pre-reclamation food supply. Surely, a lot more of them would starve (or leave the area) if a reclamation that halved the size of the estuary caused them to consume double the proportion of their food stocks?

Now imagine another estuary where the birds habitually consume only 10% of the food supply and starvation is uncommon. At what point as the food supply is reduced by the removal of mudflats and sandflats would the shorebirds begin to starve or leave the estuary? One would not know whether, after habitat is removed, enough food would remain to support the existing numbers of birds, especially as unseen consumers, such as fish and crabs, would be taking their share as well. In other words, in terms of predicting the effect on bird survival, and therefore numbers, the finding that reclamation would cause the depletion of the food stocks to increase from X% to Y% is un-interpretable, as illustrated in Figure 1.5.

As the project on the Wash got underway, another comparable project began on Maplin Sands, Essex, which threw up a very interesting 'compare and contrast' opportunity. It was proposed that a third London airport should be built on Maplin Sands where many thousands of brent geese feed on huge beds of eelgrass as they arrive at the beginning of the non-breeding season. The loss of this food supply was seen as a serious threat to these birds. Their numbers had only just recovered from hitting very low levels in the 1930s when a disease had killed eelgrass, an important food source, in places like Maplin Sands. It seemed probable, therefore, that burying the eelgrass under an airport would have the same drastic impact on the goose population as had, apparently, the death of eelgrass years before. A study was set up to predict the effect on the geese of building a third London airport on Maplin Sands.

The scientists involved on the Wash and Maplin Sands projects worked in the same, small research station, just outside Norwich. It wasn't long before a difference between the way in which the geese on Maplin Sands and the shorebirds on the Wash exploited their food supplies was being discussed. Whereas waders and shelduck only gradually and partially deplete their food supply over the non-breeding season, the eelgrass taken by brent geese on Maplin Sands had all but disappeared within two months of their arrival due to natural die-back, gales and the geese themselves. Thereafter, the geese fed on the saltmarshes that fringe the Essex coast and, subsequently, on fields inland. It was as if the geese are faced on their arrival in autumn with a gradient of food supplies, the order of preference (as defined by the order in which they were exploited by the geese) being eelgrass → saltmarsh → grassland. They moved down this gradient, step-by-step, as the current preferred food was eaten out or removed by some other agent.

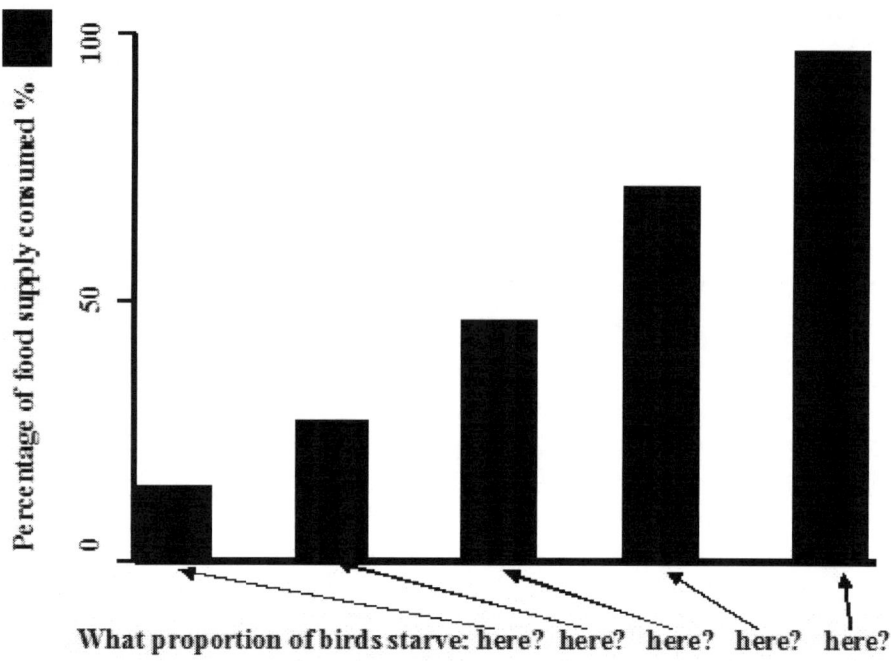

Figure 1.5 Difficulty of interpreting measurements of the impact of shorebirds on their food supply: The black columns show the proportion of the food supply consumed by shorebirds in five hypothetical estuaries. In the estuary on the extreme left, the birds consume by the end of the non-breeding season about 15% of the food stocks that were present when they had arrived on the estuary from the breeding grounds. The proportion removed by shorebirds increases from left to right, estuary by estuary, until in the estuary at the extreme right, they consume almost all the food. But at what point as the percentage consumption increases do birds begin to starve in these various estuaries? All of them could starve in all of the estuaries or none of them could! From this measure alone, there is no way of knowing how many of the birds would starve.

Most waders and shelduck - which eat invertebrates and so are carnivores - do not behave this way. Following the lead of the Maplin Sands goose ecologists, it was realised that the invertebrate food supplies of wading birds can also be thought of as a gradient because some areas (or 'patches' in the jargon) provide better feeding opportunities than do others. For example, in some parts of the Wash, cockles were large and occurred at high densities, conditions which allowed oystercatchers to ingest cockle flesh at a very high rate, and which they used first. Elsewhere, cockles were either scarce or, even more important, small so that oystercatchers could only ingest cockle flesh at a low rate. As with the geese, the food supply of waders and shelduck can be viewed as a gradient of patches that varied from the very good (*i.e.* very 'profitable' for a foraging bird) to the very poor: a schema for such as gradient is shown in Figure 1.6.

From the point of view of making the predictions that are required, it does not matter whether it is an actual gradient on the ground or a patchwork. The interesting thing to the Wash and Maplin research teams was that herbivorous wildfowl and carnivorous waders and shelduck exploited their respective gradients in very different ways. The wildfowl of Maplin Sands started feeding at one end of the gradient and moved to the next level downwards after the food supply there had been depleted to a very low level. This could happen quite shortly after their arrival and certainly well before the end of the non-breeding season. In contrast, the waders and shelduck on the Wash were generally spread out over the food gradient from the time that they arrived and subsequently depleted the food in each patch quite slowly, with much of it remaining after they had left for the breeding grounds. The question was: 'Why this difference between these two groups of birds in the way in which they exploited their food supply, and were there any implications of this difference for predicting the effect of habitat loss on shorebirds?'

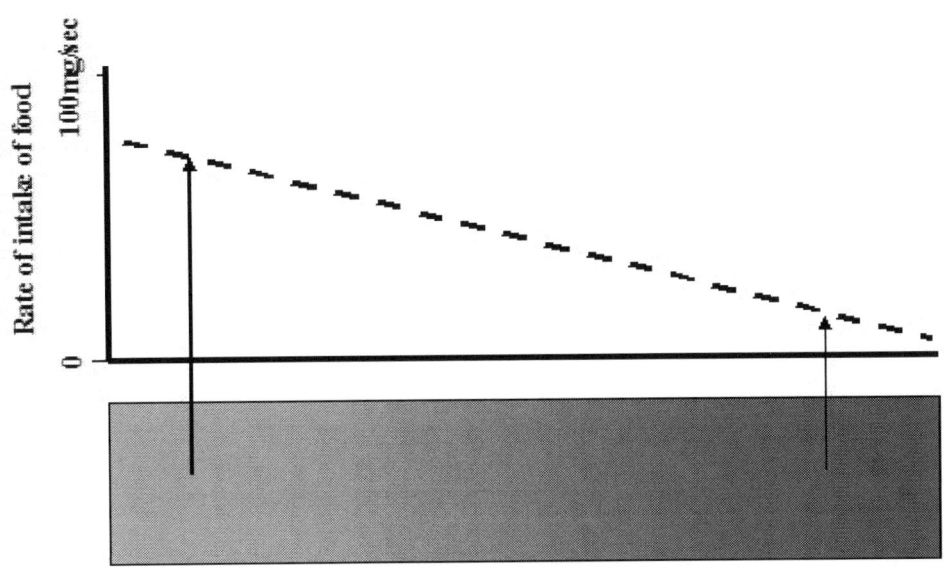

Figure 1.6 Food gradients: the shaded box represents a feeding gradient on a mudflat. The best feeding places are at the left-hand end where the birds can collect food at a fast rate and the worst are at the right-hand end where the birds can only feed at a slow rate, as indicated on the graph above by the arrows.

The answer to the first question involved the nature of their differing food supplies, and here a digression into the foraging biology of shorebirds is required. The food eaten by the herbivores for the most part sits on the surface of the mud and is almost completely accessible to the birds. Waders and shelduck, on the other hand, eat prey that protect themselves in various ways. Some are armoured by virtue of a thick shell that few, if any, waders can penetrate unless the prey is young and small enough to swallow whole. Others hide under stones and weed. A great many prey species hide in the substrate itself, either by living in a burrow or tube that provides the essential connection to the surface of the mud or sand or by being completely buried and maintaining contact with the surface through tubes, or 'siphons'. The result is that, in any one place at any one time, most of the prey animals are inaccessible to the birds. Most of them are either too thickly armoured, hidden under something on the surface or buried in the sediment too deeply to be reached by the birds, even if they can detect that they are there.

An invertebrate becomes available to a wader when it can be both detected and is within reach of the bill. The neatest illustration of how prey become available to shorebirds is the lugworm taken by some waders, mainly curlews, oystercatchers and bar-tailed godwits (Fig. 1.7). This, often plump, worm spends most of its time deep in the sediment (muddy-sand or sandy-mud), way beyond the reach of even the longest bills. It ingests sand or mud from which it digests organic matter. Eventually, its gut is full of used sediment, and the worm must expel it. Were it to do this at the bottom of its burrow, where it was eating, the worm would block the tube behind it and therefore lose its essential connection to the surface, its source of water and oxygen. It has no alternative but to back up its tube and expel its gut contents onto the sediment surface; these are the worm castes that are such a feature of many coastal flats. It is clearly visible to us – and apparently also to shorebirds - when a worm is near the surface because the muddy caste wriggles as it is pushed up from beneath. A nearby wader that sees the worm caste being formed, detects that a lugworm is close to the surface and tries to grab it with its bill. If the worm detects the threat, perhaps from the moving shadow of the attacking bird or from pressure waves made by its feet, it quickly retreats down its burrow. The wader may pursue the retreating worm if it is equipped with a sufficiently long bill and is quick enough to catch it before it descends too far. Because the worm dives down its burrow head first, the bird is most likely to get hold of the retreating rear end. The tail often breaks off, which explains why there are so many lugworms without tails!

Each lugworm comes to the sediment surface about once every 40 minutes and stays there for only a few seconds: to avoid being eaten, speed is of the essence when it is in this vulnerable state! This means that, at any one time, worms available to waders will be dotted about here at an overall density that is extremely low, even if hundreds of them are actually present in every square meter of sediment. When the sediment dries out – as many sandy areas do after the tide has left them – the worms are much less active and so even fewer of them are available to waders at any one time. Lugworms also become much less active as the temperature of the sediment declines so that, by 4°C, none come to the surface at all. Were a wader to stand in one place, it could have a very long wait indeed before another lugworm became available within reach, especially in sandy areas on cold days; it would quickly starve. So these birds have to range continuously over the flats to increase their rate of encounter with worms that are temporarily available to them, which is usually wetted perimeter at the tide edge, for example, where the worms are most active.

These aspects of wader foraging biology were first investigated at Lindisfarne on bar-tailed godwits by a Canadian PhD student of immense dedication and field skill (Box 1.7). It is a particularly clear example of what the words 'available prey' mean in waders. A prey is available when it can be both detected and captured. But the same idea applies across waders in general, and examples are legion: crab plovers rush around trying to catch the occasional crab that is too slow to get back into its protective burrow before the bird reaches it; redshank often seem to catch the occasional burrow-dwelling shrimp-like Corophium when they emerge briefly from their U-shaped burrow to grab some organic matter from the surface; many oystercatchers feed by stabbing their powerful bills into the occasional cockle or mussel that is momentarily relaxing its tightly closed shells in order to expel waste products. Waders can only feed because their invertebrate prey species have to 'break cover' from time to time to perform some essential task. The environment places contradictory demands upon them. While there is a need to have some kind of cover to avoid being eaten by predators, at the same time, they must also feed, expel waste products or obtain oxygen. This is their Achilles heel that waders exploit so effectively (Box 1.8).

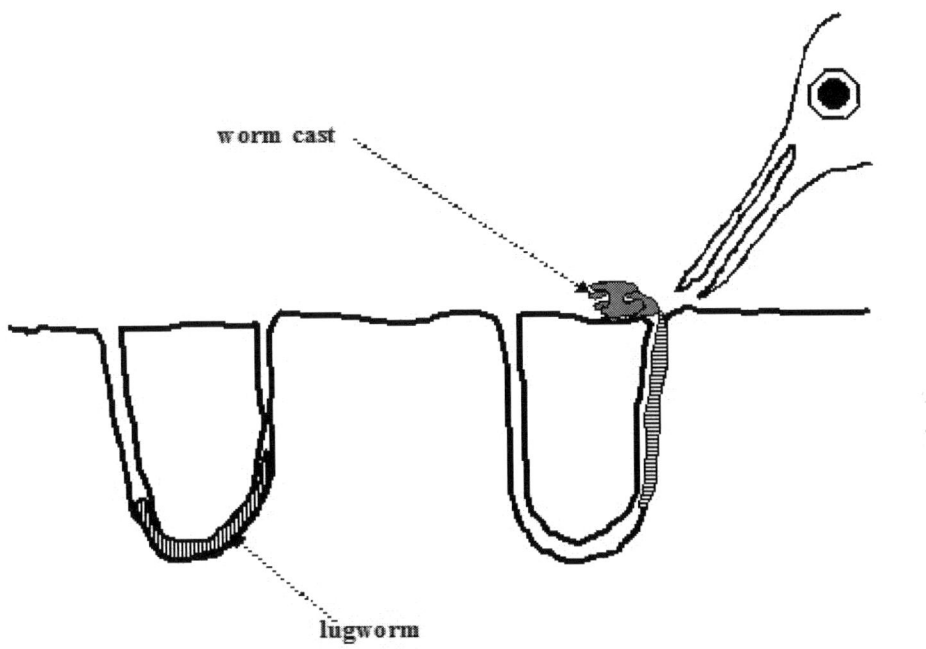

Figure 1.7 When a lugworm is forced to make itself available to shorebirds. For most of the time, the worm is deep in its burrow eating sand and digesting any organic matter that it contains. In this position, it is safely out of reach of even those birds with the longest bills. But every 40 minutes or so – in this example – the worm must back up its burrow to empty its gut onto the surface of the flats. The moving worm-cast that is being formed on the surface tells a nearby bird that a worm is near to the surface and so within reach and can be caught. The worm stays at the surface for the shortest possible time but, inevitably, it does run a risk – which it has to take in order to eat and grow.

Waders generally must keep moving onwards in order to find the next available prey item. In any small area occupied by several birds, a high proportion of the prey that make themselves available while birds are in the vicinity are taken by one or other of the birds. There is probably a high rate of depletion of the available prey in that area: not in the abundance of all the prey in the sediment but only of those that are actually available within the boundary of a bird flock as it ranges over an area. The birds must often have to spread out from each other because depletion by the flock as a whole reduces the density of prey that is available to them where the flock is foraging.

Often there is an additional factor that reduces the density of available prey encountered by foraging shorebirds. Many of the prey have anti-predator responses. For example, a ragworm foraging at the entrance of its burrow quickly retreats down its burrow when the shadow of nearby bird (or hand – try it!) passes over it, or it detects pressure waves coming from a bird's feet. Other birds nearby may depress the density of available prey items in this way too. Although having a tendency to flock – perhaps to reduce the risk of being taken by a predator – many waders have to spread out to some degree in order to avoid 'mutual interference' (in the jargon) while foraging.

In contrast, herbivorous wildfowl could in principle stand in one place and eat all the food supply within their reach without moving on. Its food doesn't dive down a burrow and all of it is pretty well available at the surface at all times. Although they often do stop for short periods to grab a beakful of vegetation, they usually don't stand still for long periods but move slowly on. As a general rule, flocks of waders move over the mudflats and sandflats very much faster than do flocks of brent geese and that other herbivorous intertidal wildfowl, the wigeon.

These differences in feeding behaviour and food organisms seem to explain why herbivorous geese and ducks can deplete almost to nothing the food supply in the best part of their food gradient while carnivorous shorebirds do not. Waders have to move on to maintain an adequate rate of encounter with the scattered prey that are available to them and consume only a tiny fraction of those present in any one 'pass'. In contrast, the herbivorous wildfowl do not have to be so active and can stand in one place and deplete their current local patch of food almost down to zero.

As a consequence, it is easy to work out the number of days that a given quantity of eelgrass could support a given number of geese because, in effect, almost all of their food is available to them at or close to the surface of the sediment. If each of a hypothetical 1000 geese arriving requires 20 kg of eelgrass per day, and there is 200,000 kg on the surface of the mud, the food supply in this most preferred part of their food gradient would last almost 10 days – 'almost' because the geese always give up feeding a little before the food is entirely removed. If half of the food supply were to be removed by habitat loss, the capacity of the locality to support geese would be reduced and the food would last the same number of geese (over which no-one has any control, of course) just five days instead of ten. It is therefore possible to predict the effect a given reclamation would have on the numbers of 'goose-days' that the area would provide.

This is an answer of sorts but, as was fully realised by the Maplin research team at the time, it begs a very important question. What happens to the geese after they have depleted the food stocks on Maplin Sands? The geese would move to the saltmarsh where the same calculation could be made, although it is technically more difficult to do so. If the geese then eat out all the saltmarsh food, or a seasonal change in its quality renders it less nutritious to the geese, they would move another step down the food gradient into fields. No doubt, they would start in the field with the most nutritious grass, and gradually work down the 'grass gradient', taking food of poorer and poorer quality as they did so.

But where does this sequence of events stop? At what point will the decreasing quality of the food supply begin to matter to the geese in a meaningful way? It will matter, of course, when the birds are feeding so far down the food gradient that the food is so poor that their body condition deteriorates and birds begin to starve. But how to predict if and when this will happen? And how to predict whether a given reduction in the food at the top end of the food gradient – the eelgrass on Maplin Sands, for example – would push the birds later in the non-breeding season so much further down the food gradient that, over the non-breeding season as a whole, more geese than at present would lose condition and starve?

This, of course, is exactly the same point that was made earlier about predicting the effect on shorebirds of building a fresh-water reservoir on the Wash. That the depletion of the food supply would increase from, say, 30% to 38%, would be an uninterpretable finding in terms of its impact on the birds' chances of surviving the non-breeding season in good condition. With grass farmland contributing so much of the food eaten by the geese later in the non-breeding season, one would first have to work out where their gradient ended; *i.e.* the point at which the food became so poor that birds began to lose body condition and starve. Not an easy task when one considers that they could use all the fields along the coasts of southern England to where so many of them move during the course of the winter anyway! Where would one draw the boundary of the food gradient? If that cannot be done, it would not be possible to calculate how the removal of some of the food on Maplin Sands at the top end of the food gradient would be translated into increased rate of starvation further down the gradient, later in the non-breeding season. Though generally on a smaller spatial scale, exactly the same argument and dilemma applies to carnivorous shorebirds, many of whom do not totally eat out their intertidal food supplies and also feed in other habitats, such as in grass fields on earthworms.

An answer could now be given to the second question asked earlier as to whether the difference between herbivorous wildfowl and carnivorous shorebirds in the way in which they occupy and exploit their food gradients would have any implications for the way in which the effect of habitat loss on them could be predicted. The answer was 'No'. In both cases, we would have to predict at what point as habitat was removed that they would begin to find it difficult to obtain all the food they required to survive the non-breeding season in good condition. Predicting the effect of a loss of foraging habitat on both groups of birds required the same questions to be answered, despite the very different way in which they exploited their food gradients.

The key question dawns - eventually

After what in retrospect seems an unnecessarily long time, a way was found to illustrate by a simple graph what really needed to be found out for both herbivorous and carnivorous shorebirds (Fig 1.8). The graph is a hypothetical relationship showing how the percentage of birds starving before the end of the non-breeding season increases as the proportion of the food gradient that is removed by habitat loss increases. Imagine that an estuary has 1000ha of mudflats and sandflats that provide all of the food that the shorebirds need. With all of these flats available to them, just 2% of the birds starve at present over the non-breeding season Now imagine that someone puts a small pontoon, measuring 2m by 2m, on the mud so that the birds can no longer feed there. It would be very difficult to argue convincingly that a loss of habitat of such a tiny magnitude - 0.00002% - would make it more difficult than at present for any of the birds to find enough food to survive. But were the estuary to be barraged across its mouth so that all 1000ha were covered by a fresh-water lake, everyone would agree that all the shorebirds would either leave or starve.

Most proposed activities that remove shorebird habitat do not lie at this highest extreme, however. A scheme might remove 5% or 10% or even 25% of the current mudflats and sandflats. The immediate effect of this habitat loss would be to increase the average density of birds across their food gradient as a whole. The key question then is: 'Would an increase in average density of this magnitude cause more birds than at present to starve (or fail to fatten up or to emigrate)?' This seemed possible because, from what was known for vertebrates in general (although not yet at that time for shorebirds), it was likely that an increase in bird density could intensify competition between them for food. As density increases, the food supply is depleted more and so becomes scarcer and harder to find, and any direct interference between birds caused by more of the prey retreating down their burrows also increases in frequency.

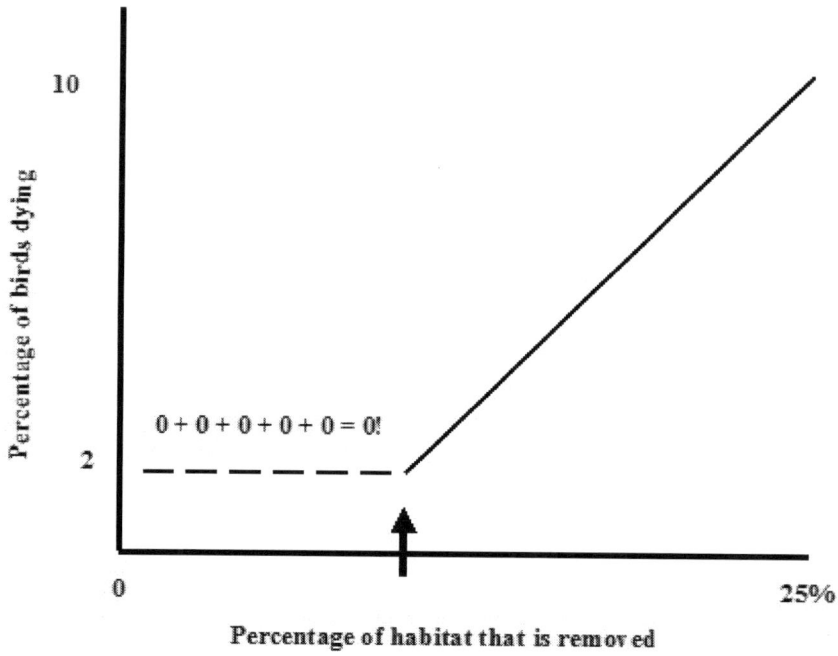

Figure 1.8 A hypothetical example of a density-dependent mortality function to illustrate how we can think about the effect of a loss of foraging habitat on shorebirds. With all the existing habitat present, only 2% of the birds die over the non-breeding season; they might be unlucky or inefficient in some way. Small parcels of habitat are then removed in succession. However, the mortality rate remains at 2% until 10% of the initial habitat has been removed. Up to this point, none of the habitat losses increased the percentage of birds dying so their aggregate impact is zero: no matter how many zero impacts are added together, the total still adds up to zero! What the successive losses of habitat does do, however, is to bring the population nearer to the threshold point of a 10% habitat loss after which subsequent losses will cause more birds to die (shown by the arrow). The proportion dying then enters the 'density-dependent' phase because, as the area of habitat diminishes and bird density therefore increases, competition between birds intensifies and an increasing proportion fail to obtain the food they need to avoid starvation. (Note that the Figure could equally well show the percentage of birds that fail to store enough energy as fat to return successfully to the breeding areas or even the percentage that move to another estuary before the end of the non-breeding season.)

By the end of the Wash and Maplin Sands projects, it had at last been realised that, for habitat loss, it was necessary to find out whether mortality (or emigration or poor body condition) was, in the jargon, 'density-dependent'. If it was not already density-dependent, it was necessary to find out at what point it would become density-dependent as more and more of the habitat was removed. That density dependence was likely to occur at some point as density increased was never much in doubt, but the location of the 'critical density' at which it would began was completely unknown. Belatedly, it was realised that this was the critical thing to know if we were to predict whether and at what stage shorebird starvation rates would start to increase as the loss of habitat increased.

Habitat loss and density dependence

Density dependence had by then emerged through modelling animal populations mathematically as a key process in determining animal numbers. Much time was spent on studies of density dependence across the animal kingdom: indeed, a leading population biologist suggested that the study of density dependence should be what ecology was all about. Many studies on many animal groups were carried out in which the mortality rate of the subject species was measured over a number – often very many – years and then each annual estimate plotted against the population density in that year. Although some theoreticians argued that density dependence was either absent or of minor importance to animal populations, the evidence for its widespread occurrence and importance became overwhelming.

In order to predict the impact – if any – of habitat loss on shorebirds, it had become clear that testing for the existence of density dependence was critical. Unfortunately for shorebird biologists, testing for the existence of density dependence during the non-breeding season in these migratory birds is extremely difficult and, at that time, no study had even attempted it. To test whether the mortality rate was density-dependent, it would have been necessary to measure the percentage of birds dying in each of a number of non-breeding seasons and then to have plotted the data against population size (or density – it amounts to the same thing, of course, if the area remains the same size). At that time, however, it was technically extremely difficult to measure the mortality rate, especially in such a huge area as the Wash. Furthermore, the size of many shorebird populations change rather slowly. With the likely errors involved in the measurement of mortality rate being so large, estimates from very many years would probably have been needed to establish a trend in mortality against density. As Figure 1.9 illustrates, we might have ended up after 40 years of hard work with just a blob of points that told us nothing about the underlying density dependence! This would not have been a profitable way to spend an entire research career!

But even if we had accumulated a number of data points across a range of bird densities, and thus establish a trend of some kind, we certainly could not have assumed that it would be safe to extrapolate the trend to the higher densities of birds that would occur after the habitat loss had happened. While it ***might*** have been safe to predict the mortality rate at a particular density within the range of bird densities that had been experienced by 'interpolation', making predictions beyond this 'empirical range' by projecting forward, or 'extrapolating', the trend to higher densities would have been very risky indeed (Box 1.9).

So whether or not many years of patient research did or did not yield a clear trend in mortality rate against density, we still could not have used it with confidence to predict what would happen to the mortality rate if part of the foraging habitat was removed. Apart from the general problem of assuming that an established trend would continue onwards and upwards as before, there is the particular and predictable danger with extrapolation when dealing with the possible effect of habitat loss in shorebirds.

This is why. Imagine that 100ha of an estuary of 1000ha is to be removed, but this 10% includes all the best feeding areas. Its loss would also reduce the amount of foraging time by 5%. It is pretty obvious that, at a given population density, mortality would be much higher than it currently is: trend lines **(c)** in Figure 1.9 represent this possibility. On the other hand, if the 100ha to be removed consisted of the poorest feeding area and the foraging time would be unchanged, the post-reclamation mortality rate might not be very different to what it had been before: trend line **(a)** in Figure 1.9 represents this possibility. Only seldom would habitat loss involve the removal of an area that would be typical of the estuary as a whole so that the present-day density-dependent relationship – represented by trend **(d)** in Figure 1.9 - would still apply after the habitat had been lost. Only then might extrapolation be appropriate.

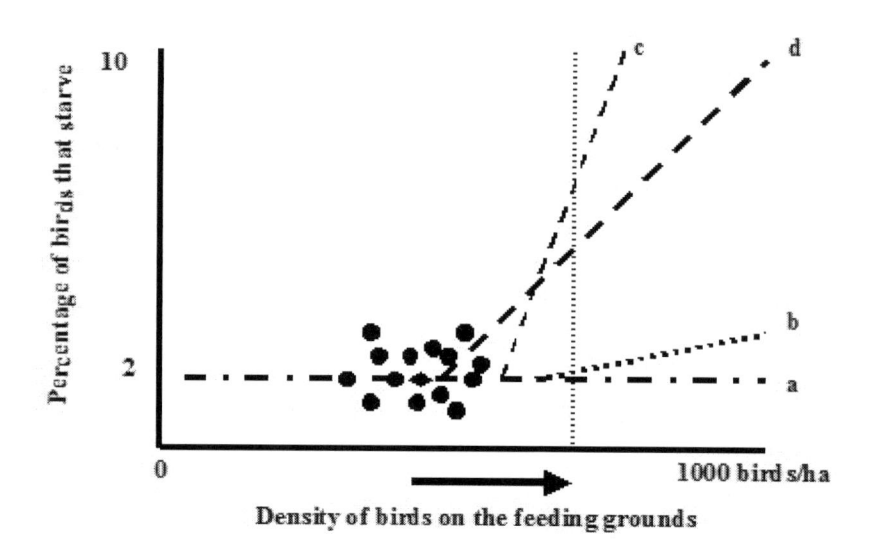

*Figure 1.9 Some hypothetical density-dependent relationships. The relationship is the same as in Figure 1.8 except that the horizontal axis shows the density of birds rather than the amount of habitat lost. Each diamond is an estimate of the percentage of birds that die during one non-breeding season: so, it took 15 non-breeding seasons to obtain these data! The population did not vary much over these years so the data points straddle a rather narrow range of bird densities. It is impossible to establish the underlying relationship between the mortality rate and bird density – if, indeed, there is one. A number of possible trends are shown as dashed lines. **(a)** In this one, mortality is independent of density across the entire range of population densities; **(b)** the population density has to be very much higher than during the 15 years studied before the mortality becomes density dependent, and thereafter mortality rises at a slow rate; **(c)** the threshold at which mortality becomes density dependent is very close to the range of densities encountered during the 15 years and the rate rises very rapidly once the threshold has been passed; **(d)** the threshold occurs at a lower bird density than in any of the other cases and thereafter increases at a medium rate. If habitat is removed and increases the bird density by the amount shown by the arrow, the increase in the percentage of birds dying over the non-breeding season will depend on which of these trend lines is the real one. The intersection between each trend line and the vertical dotted black line shows the mortality rate that would occur after the habitat had been removed.*

The predictions that were made for the impact of a fresh-water reservoir on the shorebirds of the Wash

The individual-based model of shorebirds was the eventual solution to the problem of how to predict the impact of habitat loss (and of other changes in the foraging environment) that would take into account all these possibilities. But this lay a long way in the future. A prediction was required then, in the mid-1970s, for the impact of the proposed fresh-water reservoir on the shorebirds of the Wash and a non-quantitative approach had to be adopted. Rather than predicting, for example, that the reservoir would change the mortality rate during the non-breeding season by X%, from Y% to Z%, it was only possible to predict that there was, or was not, a risk that mortality would increase, but without being able to say by how much. The predictions could only be expressed in words and not numbers, and the magnitude of any predicted impact could not therefore be gauged.

Intensive fieldwork over three years enabled these questions to be answered with varying degrees of confidence, and details can be read in the three papers that were published in 1977. Briefly, the answers were as follows:

'Yes, many shorebirds do feed where it was planned to build the reservoir'. 'They ate a variety of invertebrate species but there were no obvious areas containing these prey in the Wash that were not already being used by lots of shorebirds, so they would have to feed in the parts of the existing feeding ground that remained after the reservoir had been built'.

'As shorebirds consumed up to 40% of some important prey species over the non-breeding season and birds were often seen fighting over food items and feeding spots when bird densities were high, it seemed likely that there might already be some competition for food. Furthermore, it was likely that this competition would become stronger if their food supplies were reduced. This would be expected to make it more difficult for birds to satisfy their energy requirements at critical times of the non-breeding season'.

'Some shorebird species at some times during the non-breeding season fed for virtually the entire time that the mudflats and sand flats were exposed. This suggested that it was sometimes difficult for some species to collect all the food they required in the time available. Furthermore, emaciated corpses of birds that had apparently starved were found from time to time, especially in very cold and windy weather.'

The conclusion was that, by removing feeding areas, a reservoir would be likely to make matters worse by intensifying competition and so causing more birds to starve. This would reduce the numbers of shorebirds, and thus the capacity of the Wash to support them. The same non-quantitative logic worked successfully years later when Cardiff Bay was reclaimed: as predicted by this approach, the mortality rate of redshank did increase after the mudflats in the Bay had been permanently removed.

This is the best that could be done in 1976 when the Wash project concluded. Some progress had been made in making predictions and, as importantly, the questions that needed to be answered in shorebird environmental assessment of habitat loss of this kind had become clearly identified. But it was unsatisfactory that the predictions could not be quantitative. It really did matter whether 10,000 or just 10 more birds might starve as a consequence of building the reservoir! But it was not possible to predict the numbers affected and all that could be said was that an increase of unpredictable magnitude was likely to occur.

It was also unsatisfactory because this non-quantitative prediction was based on rather weak evidence that competition was sufficiently intense to significantly affect the ability of some birds to obtain all their food requirements. This was a precautionary assumption because this was simply not known. It would all depend on how intense the competition between birds was, and would be, after the reservoir had been built. It is the magnitude of the competition that counts, and that could not be measured with the necessary thoroughness in the Wash study.

THE FOLLOW-UP TO THE WASH PROJECT

What was needed was a study area and a study species that were amenable to the kind of long-term research that was required. Particular importance was attached to selecting a system where competition could be studied thoroughly and the mortality of the birds during the non-breeding season could be measured. It was also vital that quantitative predictions could be made which meant that some kind of mathematical modelling would be essential. The hunt was on for a suitable species, estuary and modelling approach.

REFERENCES FOR CHAPTER 1

Evans, P.R., Herdson, D.M., Knights, P.J. & Pienkowski, M.W. (1979). Short-term effects of reclamation of part of Seal Sands, Teesmouth, on wintering waders and shelduck. I. Shorebird diets, invertebrate densities, and the impact of predation on the invertebrates. *Oecologia*, **41**, 183-206.

Goss-Custard, J.D. (1977). The ecology of the Wash. III. Density-related behaviour and the possible effects of a loss of feeding grounds on wading birds (Charadrii). *Journal of Applied Ecology*, **14**, 721-739.

Goss-Custard, J.D. & Charman, K. (1976). Predicting how many wintering waterfowl an area can support. *Wildfowl*, **27**, 157-158.

Goss-Custard, J.D., Jenyon, R.A., Jones, R.E., Newbery, P.E. & Williams, R. le B. (1977). The ecology of the Wash. II. Seasonal variation in the feeding conditions of wading birds (Charadrii). *Journal of Applied Ecology*, **14**, 701-719.

Goss-Custard, J.D., Jones, R.E. & Newbery, P.E. (1977). The ecology of the Wash. I. Distribution and diet of wading birds (Charadrii). *Journal of Applied Ecology*, **14**, 681-700.

Horwood, J.W. & Goss-Custard, J.D. (1977). Predation by the oystercatcher, *Haematopus ostralegus* (L.), in relation to the cockle, *Cerastoderma edule* (L.), fishery in the Burry Inlet, South Wales. *Journal of Applied Ecology*, **14**, 139-158.

Prater, A.J. 1972. The ecology of Morecambe Bay. III. The food and feeding habits of Knot (*Calidris canutus*) in Morecambe Bay. *Journal of Applied Ecology*, **9**, 179-194.

Redpath, S.M., Young, J., Evely, A., Adams, W.M., Sutherland, W.J., Whitehouse, A., Amar, A., Lambert, R.A., Linnell, J.D.C., Watt, A. & Gutierrez, R.J. (2013). Understanding and managing conservation conflicts. *Trends in Ecology and Evolution*, **28**, 100-109.

Smith, P.C. (1975). A study of the winter feeding ecology and behaviour of the bar-tailed godwit (*Limosa lapponica*). Ph.D. thesis, University of Durham.

Box 1.1 The enthusiasm of shorebirders

There are several ways in which enthusiasm for shorebirds is expressed around the world. None more so than in the UK where, for many years, mainly amateur enthusiasts have counted every winter the numbers of birds along sections of the shore at monthly intervals throughout the non-breeding season so that virtually all the places where shorebirds occur have been censused regularly. These counts are carried out over high tide when the birds congregate at roosts or feed in fields adjacent to the coast. Every five years or so, shorebirds are also counted at low tide as they feed on the intertidal flats. The results of these two projects have provided conservation authorities with information of immense value for assessing the importance or unimportance of coastal areas for which proposals are being made that might threaten the birds.

The large-scale ringing of shorebirds also began in the UK, with the formation of the Wash Wader Ringing Group (WWRG). The objective was to find out where the birds that spend the non-breeding season on the Wash come from and where they went later if they used the area as a staging post. The WWRG pioneered techniques for catching shorebirds, such as putting out hundreds of metres of mist nest and, using cannons, firing projectiles trailing nets over roosting flocks. Large numbers of people became involved with the WWRG and other groups established themselves in many part of the UK. People would spend weekends – and whole weeks of their annual holidays - in these teams, often staying in very primitive conditions and often working in cold, wet and windy weather. The WWRG was under the inspired leadership of Clive Minton who, for his day job, had a very responsible position in industry but would, nonetheless, after work on Friday drive to the Wash and immediately set up nets to catch birds that night or the following morning.

The weather on the Wash and other coastal areas is not always challenging! In the Wash, you can stand at the edge of the water many kilometres from land surrounded by sand, mud and water for as far as you can see, accompanied only by flocks of chattering birds and the grunting and snorting of seals on a nearby sand bar, and all under the huge hemisphere of the sky that stretches from one distant low horizon to another. The light and colours range from subtle to vivid, and can provide a changing (and often distracting!), atmospheric surround for anyone working in such places. I discovered this as a teenager when I worked during many school holidays at the Wildfowl Trust (as it was then called) in Slimbridge. I would spend the evenings at the edge of the nearby saltmarsh meadow (the Dumbles) learning to identify the waders on the adjacent flats. Anyone sceptical that such beauty can really be found on muddy coastal flats that are too often regarded as ugly should immerse themselves in the paintings of Sir Peter Scott, the founder of the Wetlands and Wildfowl Trust and also the originator of so much of the interest in the birds of our coastal flats.

Box 1.2 Shorebird fieldcraft

There are many places where you can just walk slowly towards a group of shorebirds and get quite close, and certainly close enough to see them well with a telescope on a tripod. When you begin to get too close, you will see signs of agitation, and the nearest individuals will move away, while continuing to feed; then move ten paces forward and stop, then another ten and so forth. They often seem to let you approach more closely if there is a strip of water between you and them. Keep as low as you can as these birds are much more likely to fly away if you are outlined against the sky. It can be a bit uncomfortable to stand hunched over a 'scope for a long time. A wooden box, with shoulder straps attached and a flask of coffee inside an opening at the front, can go a long way to foster commitment!

Rather than chasing the birds about, however, it is much better to sit and wait for them to come to you. I realised this on the Dumbles where I used to wait for the incoming tide to drive the birds in front of it up to the edge of the marsh. This was an effective way of getting close to birds that spent most of their time many kilometres out on the huge intertidal flats there. They can come extremely close if you sit down in a place where you know that the birds will approach: just keep low and still and be patient!

Hides, of course, can be a great help and are certainly the best way to do it. I have used lots of different kinds and in different ways. An ordinary hide at the tide edge or in a flat-bottomed boat that you anchor on the receding tide over a known feeding area is very effective. Early in my career, I mounted a hide on broad skis and, with me inside, pushed it out – slowly and in short stages - to the edge of the feeding area. The redshank I was studying quite quickly came within a few metres of me. A hide supported by a collection of empty oil drums or plastic barrels can be used much as I used a hide on a boat. These days, one can buy a portable hide with an in-built seat, and these two can be used, either on foot or in a boat.

Often, a car can be used as a hide. There are many places in the UK where a road runs alongside a mudflat on which shorebirds regularly feed. Some species, such as redshank and black-tailed godwits, can become used to the people on the road and really are not at all disturbed by someone sitting in a car. There are similar opportunities to use a car where a road is alongside a field used by shorebirds over high tide.

I used a car as a hide for an entire three-year project to test the then-called optimal foraging theory in redshank eating polychaete worms. I found about thirty sites in south-west England where I could park my ancient van from which, and in moderate comfort, I could record the birds' behaviour. Although my purpose was very clear to me, it was not to others! On several occasions, while immersed in making observations through a telescope resting on the opened window, I was interrupted by a police car stopping alongside, and uniformed officers moving quickly to each door to prevent my escape. On one occasion, by chance, I was parked alongside a wide creek on which a young Prince Charles (the heir to the British throne) was learning to sail! Happily, vigorous questioning and inspection of my notebooks satisfied the police (correctly) that I was not a threat to the succession! On another occasion, again unwittingly, I parked by a narrow creek on the opposite side of which a murderer had dumped the body of his/her victim, and the police thought I may have been the murderer, returning to gloat. I wasn't! On other times, I have been suspected of having too much interest in a military airbase and in a lady's washing that was hanging out to dry on the opposite side of a narrow – and for redshank – wonderful creek in north Devon! Not so, in either case! I really only had eyes for the birds, and happily (and again correctly) this is what the police accepted!

Box 1.3: Risky flats

The common fear on sandflats is that quick-sand could swallow you completely or, more probably, hold you fast until the tide comes in and drowns you. Deep mud can do the same and even in small estuaries, people sometimes have to be pulled out.

But a much more widespread hazard is creeks. In many coastal areas, creeks can be wide and deep. On the, Wash, for example, they can be at least two metres deep, and very muddy. They can be long too, and it can take some time to circle round one to find the shallow end, especially if the surrounding sediment is muddy and deep. Going out at low water presents no real problems as you can scramble down the side of a creek and ascend the others side with nothing lost but bit of dignity and getting muddy clothes. But stay out on the flats too long, and on your return you can be faced with a real hazard and, literally, the need to make life and death decisions.

Many times on the vast flats of the Wash I have walked back up the shore with the advancing tide so far behind that I can't see it, and I'm wondering if I didn't bottle out too early and whether I could have stayed a while longer and got another few data points! But then, approaching the marsh, I arrive at a deep creek with steep, slippery sides and I notice that the current at the bottom is already moving rapidly inshore. Because the creek is so deep, the incoming tide has already got there, out of sight and way ahead of me!

So long as the water in the creek is still shallow, it's easy to cross. But imagine arriving so late that all you see ahead of you is a wide expanse of water because the tide has already over-topped the edges of the creek. While you might jettison your telescope and tripod and swim across in warm weather, this is not really an option at the coldest time of year because of the risk of exposure when you emerge, virtually without clothes, on the far side! The best thing is to get to the creek early enough to avoid the dilemma in the first place! On one occasion on the Wash, I did not do so. But I knew the creek very well and I knew that, if I walked in a particular direction, the creek would get shallower and shallower, and so I was able to cross safely by testing water depth with my extended tripod and avoiding the steep and slippery sides of the deepest parts. Nonetheless, I was soaked to my waist. Anxious moments!

Creeks filling with water as the tide advances must have been what happened to the Chinese cockle pickers who drowned in Morecambe Bay when, unwittingly, they left their return to the shore too late. The same has happened to people, even a whole family (I have been told) on a treacherous stretch of the Severn estuary. What looks like a benign creek on the way out can turn into an extensive sheet of water that hides all kinds of plunging danger on the return journey. At the very least, you should take a long stick with you to check water depth.

The consequences of getting caught by the tide are not always so dire, fortunately, but can nonetheless be very frightening. Many years ago, it is told that some people on the Wash were putting out mist nets on a warm autumn night at a site that was very low down a saltmarsh, near to the mudflats: one net too many, as it turned out! When they tried to return to the shore they were faced with a black sheet of water that could have been hiding some very deep creeks. Wisely, they decided to stand it out. But the water kept rising and rising. It is rumoured that more than one craggy veteran wept as the water rose up to their chests. Fortunately, high water passed before it reached anyone's airways, and the tide started to go down, before anyone was drowned. But they would have had to stand there, unable to move for fear of falling into deep water, for several hours. Probably, a distant storm surge had caused the high tide to rise well above the height predicted in the tide table. It must have been a long and wet night, though, and a really nasty experience.

Another real hazard is a sea mist or fog that quickly moves onshore. If this happens while you are out on the flats, you have to get ashore quickly because of the creeks that lie between you and safety. A thick mist which prevents you seeing any of your normal reference points can slow you down even if you have a compass. In some parts of the World, a flash flood following heavy rain can simply wash the unwary away.

Box 1.4 A couple of anecdotes.

Nobody should doubt the sincerity and commitment of most people now working within the very large shorebird conservation enterprise in the UK and elsewhere in the world. Especially in countries where conservation has much less public and official support than it now has in the UK, I have encountered some incredibly dedicated and seriously impressive people – pioneers in their countries - who have devoted themselves to the protection of the natural environment and its wildlife. In the UK, according to university friends, a major motivation of students applying for courses in ecology is their interest in conservation. The work is interesting and worthwhile and, for many, a self-evidently 'good cause'. It does not (intentionally) harm the environment or, apparently, unfairly exploit other people.

But as with so many single-issue movements, some conservationists can appear to be blinkered and can give the impression of having an agenda of uncertain provenance. A comment often made to me by members of the public about shorebirds is: 'Why are these shorebirds more important than people?' The answer, of course, is that the current legislation and case law leads to the precautionary approach being adopted. In democracies like the UK, however, it may be prudent to retain public support for a legislation if that legislation is to persist in the long run. The danger is that the conservation of shorebirds will become viewed as something that has to be got round rather than worked with, and society's hidden wheels might start churning against it. My experience suggests that this process may already be underway in the UK.

Here are a couple of anecdotes that illustrate why some people's approach to shorebird conservation should be a matter of concern, not only to the general public in the UK but also to other conservationists as well.

I was advising the Cardiff Bay Development Corporation on the effect that their proposal to create a freshwater lake over the mudflats of the Bay might have on shorebirds. I predicted there was a risk that an increased number of some species might starve because of the removal of their feeding habitat. This prediction was shown subsequently to have been correct. Constructively, the developers asked what could be done to offset the risk to the birds. I suggested that they punch a hole in the sea wall in a nearby part of the Severn estuary so that present-day fields could become mudflat and replace some of the area to be lost. By holding back the tide with its narrow entrance, such a lagoon would also extend the feeding time of the birds, to what we now know would have been to their great benefit. Although this suggestion has now been implemented in many places as part of managed retreat measures in response to sea level rise, at that time the idea had not been widely considered.

When I raised the suggestion at a public meeting between developers and conservationists, it was not well received by some of my conservation friends! After the meeting, three of them cornered me and, with faces distorted and empurpled with rage, demanded in very loud voices why I had suggested the idea when 'everyone' was trying to kill the development stone dead! That I was employed by the developer to find solutions to problems did not seem to occur to them, their cause being to them, it would seem, so self-evidently right and just! I said nothing but I did wonder what the assembled developers, planners and so on thought of this display! It was a bizarre end to a meeting that had been set up by the Corporation to try and find a rational solution to a conflict between two groups with different but perfectly legitimate interests.

At that time, the legislation was not as strong as it now is in the UK. This power can sometimes be used in such a way that an impression of self-serving elitism. I was at a meeting to discuss an estuary where conservationists were becoming concerned about the possible effect on shorebirds of a number of commercial and recreational activities. It happened to be an estuary that colleagues and I had researched. We had found no evidence to suggest that the shorebirds were consistently hard pressed for food. Accordingly, I remarked that at least a couple of the activities of concern were of such minor significance that they would certainly not cause the birds any harm. The gist of the reply - given in all sincerity - was: 'The trouble with your showing that the birds are not hard-pressed is that it makes it more difficult for us to stop people doing things we want to stop them doing!' In other words, it didn't matter whether the activity would actually harm the birds, that person just wanted to stop it anyway (for some reason)! To me this seems a quite inadequate justification for infringing someone else's right to carry out a perfectly legitimate activity in a public space. The only relevant and legitimate reason for their stopping it would be if it disadvantaged the birds, but that apparently was not the main issue here! I was astonished that this viewpoint appeared to be acceptable to the several other estuary managers who were also present at the meeting. Most people are properly incredulous when I recount this story!

Such happenings do make one wonder whether, in some minds, birds really are more important than people. Such fundamentalism can also be a major frustration for many conservation professionals who, to my way of thinking, have a more balanced view and regard the protection of birds as something that is done, at least in part, for the benefit of people.

In principle, good scientific research should enable independent decision-makers to distinguish between real and imagined threats. But there can be a problem here too, quite apart from the sometimes over-enthusiastic application of the precautionary principle. There seems to be widespread feeling among many shorebird ecologists that their research should demonstrate that the preconceived concerns of shorebird conservationists are justified. I have witnessed good scientists struggling with a conflict between scientific objectivity and a desire not to let down their conservation friends. It can be hard for the shorebird ecologist to resist the resulting peer-pressure and I certainly used to feel this until my experience at Cardiff Bay forced the issue. The night before the public meeting at which I raised the idea of a mitigating lagoon, a conservation friend had hinted over a beer that it would be handy if no mitigation could be found. That forced me to decide what my role as ecologist should be, and I duly presented my idea on how to mitigate the impact of the loss of the Bay. Like any other human activity, ecological science has its sociology. Ecologists and conservationists often train together in university departments entitled 'Ecology and Conservation'. Conservation is the common good cause that unites them and provides a shared *raison d'etre*.

The trouble with anecdotes, of course, is that they can distort the impression that people have of a group as a whole. I would definitely not wish to do this, for the great majority of shorebird conservationists do a great job for their cause and therefore for people. But as a holder myself of a medal awarded for a contribution to conservation research, I felt I should record how the attitudes of some conservationists can alienate members of the public on whose support, in the long run, the success of their own activities will depend. In my experience, some of them need to wise up a bit if they are to continue to retain the strong support that they currently enjoy in the UK!

Box 1.5: What is the meaning of 'meaningful'?

To an ecologist concerned with the numbers of animals, a 'meaningful effect' would be one that either increased the proportion dying (the mortality rate) or reduced the number of young birds that are produced by each adult pair (the reproductive rate), because in most circumstances, either would reduce population size. Since shorebird conservation aims to maintain bird numbers, conservationists should also aim to maintain these rates at their present levels. But this often seems to be forgotten by some of those concerned with shorebird conservation. This is because measuring and predicting both of these rates has been in the past so difficult. Their attention has therefore often focussed on surrogate measures, such as the amount of disturbance and the area and quality of the estuary habitat. The idea is that, to be on the safe side, the amount of disturbance of the birds on an estuary should not be increased above current levels by a proposed activity (and preferably it should be reduced). Similarly, the quality and the extent of the habitat should not be reduced either, even by a small amount because, bit by bit, a series of small reductions in either would gradually accumulate to a large one. In short, maintaining the integrity of the site amounts to retaining at least the *status quo*.

This precautionary thinking has led in some cases to what may seem to many people (including me) a rather over-precautionary approach. For example, I have heard it said a number of times that, if a proposed activity were merely to disturb shorebirds so that they had to move to another part of the estuary, the integrity of the site would have been reduced. On this extreme view, it simply does not matter whether the birds would be affected in any meaningful sense: just forcing the birds to change their feeding locations would be enough to condemn the proposed activity. The birds are being caused to fly to another part of the estuary and therefore the 'integrity' of the estuary has been affected. [On this argument, by the way, the holiday beach in Exmouth should be closed from August onwards because it lies within the Exe estuary SPA and shorebirds are returning from the breeding grounds at that time of year!] While the need to employ the precautionary principle can be understood, this viewpoint does seem to be excessively over-precautionary and not one likely to endear the cause of shorebird conservation to everyone!

Box 1.6 The great territory debate: does territorial behaviour limit the density of breeding pairs?

This was a really was a big issue in the 1960s and 1970s among ornithologists interested in the factors and process that determine the size of bird populations; or, more precisely, the number of pairs breeding in a location. The issue was really quite simple: 'Do all the birds that 'want' to breed in an area – say, a wood – obtain a territory and breed, or does the presence of some territorial birds prevent other would-be territory owners from establishing themselves in that wood?' Some people believed that territorial behaviour just spaced out all the birds that wanted to breed in a place whereas other people believed that territory owners actually prevented others from obtaining a place to breed.

The eventual outcome was that territorial behaviour could indeed prevent potential breeding birds from establishing themselves in the best habitat. Losers then have the choice of waiting until a space in the wood becomes available or giving up trying to get into the wood and just settle for a less good habitat instead.

The Burry Inlet cull was carried out in the belief that there were not many birds outside the Inlet looking for an opportunity to establish themselves there. In fact, by analogy with the experiments on breeding territorial birds, the results of the experiment suggested that the arrival of potentially incoming birds might have been resisted by those already present. Oystercatchers on cockle beds do not defend territories so the mechanism for this resistance to incomers would have been different, but the evidence nonetheless suggested that, somehow or other, oystercatchers already in the Inlet did prevent some others from establishing themselves there. Hence, when many were removed by shooting, others came in to replace them.

Box 1.7: The fieldwork at Lindisfarne

This work was carried out as a PhD project on bar-tailed godwits by a remarkable field biologists called Pete Smith under the supervision of Professor Peter Evans of Durham University – a pioneer in this area of science. Pete lived in a little cottage close to the beautiful flats that lie between the mainland and Lindisfarne where monks had lived many hundreds of years before. Pete's way of finding out how the birds behaved was to get in amongst them as close as he could to watch them at very close range. One method was to lay a sheet of plastic on the flats and lie on top of it and to cover himself with a sheet of tarpaulian. This meant that his profile against the sky was very low and birds would approach very closely when being pushed towards him by the advancing tide. Following the lead of wildfowlers, Pete also dug large holes in the sand and mud into which he dropped an oil drum in which he then stood, again covered by a sheet of tarpaulian. Using either method, he could get very close to the birds and see precisely what they were doing. He could see at close quarters that the godwits ran towards spots where worm castes were forming. He could see the prey being taken very clearly so when the birds switched from lugworms to a thin polychaete worm called *Scoloplos*, he could see the prey was red of this species. Godwits at Lindisfarne turned to *Scoloplos* when the temperature of the flats approached zero C^O. I still marvel at the hours of sub-zero discomfort Pete must have endured during the several winters of his PhD project in order to obtain the excellent data that he reported in his PhD thesis!

Box 1.8: Detecting prey

It is not surprising perhaps that a godwit can see a caste being formed on the sandflats by a lugworm – we can too. But often, the clues that tell a shorebird that an invertebrate is near to the surface and potentially accessible are, to our eyes, extremely subtle, not to say, invisible. Take redshank feeding on the little shrimp-like crustacean *Corophium*. These enchanting little animals live in U-shaped burrows down to a depth of 8-10cm in mud. They appear to spend most of their time down below the surface but occasionally move up to the entrance of their burrow to carry out some important task, such as feeding. I needed to test whether the frequency with which they came to surface decreased as the temperature of the mud dropped. To the amusement of locals, I put a table out on a mudflat and lay on top of it, counting how many *Corophium* came to the surface per minute. By lying on the table, I could avoid disturbing the *Corophium*. At a mud temperatures above 6°C, lots of them came to the surface. Everywhere 'popped' with the sound of the bursting air bubbles that their movement up to their burrow entrance had created. As the temperature dropped, fewer and fewer *Corophium* appeared so that by, about 3-4°C, I could see none at all, just a shining, placid, still mudflat. But at that very same temperature, redshank walked briskly over the mud surface at speed of about 10m per minute, pecking at the surface, perhaps 80 times per minute, detecting - apparently by sight - and catching 50-60 *Corophium* as they did so! I still have no idea what clues they were using to detect prey that to this human's eye were completely invisible.

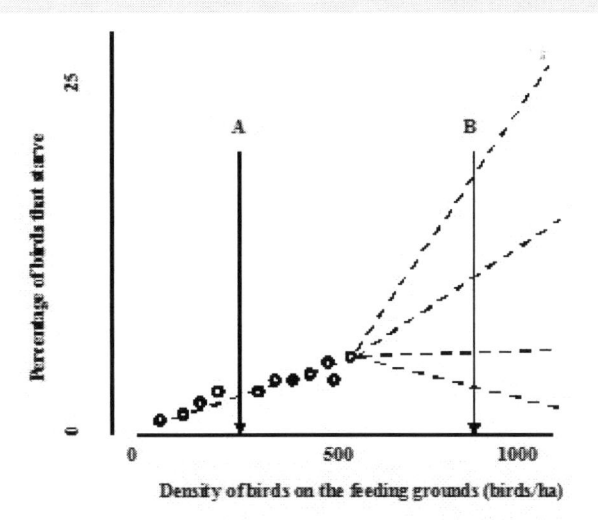

Box 1.9 The difference between 'interpolation' and 'extrapolation'.

In this hypothetical example, a study has shown that the mortality rate is density-dependent. It is a very 'tight' relationship, meaning that most of the individual data points (the circles) fall pretty close to the line that is drawn through them. There is a bit of a gap in the data around the vertical line, A, and we want to know what the mortality rate is likely to be at that density. Because the relationship is so tight, we can probably 'interpolate' with confidence the mortality rate at point A. But we also want to know what the rate would be at the density shown by the vertical line B. This might apply, for example, after a large part of the estuary had been removed to build a new harbour. As the future density would now lie well beyond the range of densities over which the real mortality rate had been measured, we would have to extrapolate 'beyond the empirical range' of the actual data points. Perhaps the real line would indeed be just an extension of the trend that had already been established. But how could we possibly know? It might go up, down or even stay level at the higher densities! Extrapolating a trend beyond the empirical range would be very risky and the chance are it would give a completely false prediction.

CHAPTER 2:
First steps

...in which is told the story of how a long-term project was set up in 1976 to research the foraging behaviour of oystercatchers that eat mussels on the Exe estuary in Devon, of the extraordinary help that was provided by so many people to ensure that it got underway successfully and the emergence of the first evidence that competition might be occurring between the birds

STARTING UP

As well as needing a place and a shorebird species from which all the necessary measurements could be obtained, it was also important to choose a species whose main prey species was amenable for a study of its population dynamics. After all, if half an estuary was to be removed, for example, and most of the shorebirds nonetheless remained, they would consume a much increased proportion of the prey. This raised the question: 'What would be the effect of this greater rate of bird predation on the prey population and what would be the long-term consequences therefore for the food supply of the shorebirds?' As the interaction between predator populations and those of their prey was at the time a 'hot' academic issue, with many theoretical models being produced, it was hoped that an empirical, long-term project on a shorebird-invertebrate interaction could make a significant contribution.

For the birds, the requirements of the species and study area were quite stringent. The estuary had to be easily accessible and not too large: that was why the Wash itself would have been unsuitable. Small size and accessibility means that the logistics of observing the birds and sampling the prey populations are much less time-consuming and costly. But not too small because small estuaries support very few birds! Additionally, the estuary had to be separated from other estuaries by a reasonable stretch of coastline that was more-or-less unsuitable for the birds. Given the chance, most shorebirds roost over high water in places near to where they feed over low tide so that they spend as little energy and time as possible commuting between the two. Were the chosen site to be, say, 10 miles from the nearest estuary, there was good chance that its bird population would restrict all of its activities during the non-breeding season to that estuary. The site needed to be not too large, but not too small, and reasonably isolated from neighbouring estuaries.

Size and isolation were important because, from the very start, it was believed to be essential to work on birds that could be identified individually. There was at that time a general belief that finding out how different individuals respond to each other and to their common environment would provide important insights into how populations would respond to environmental change and how the all-important density-dependent processes are produced. It is, after all, individual animals that respond to their changed environment, not a whole population acting as one.

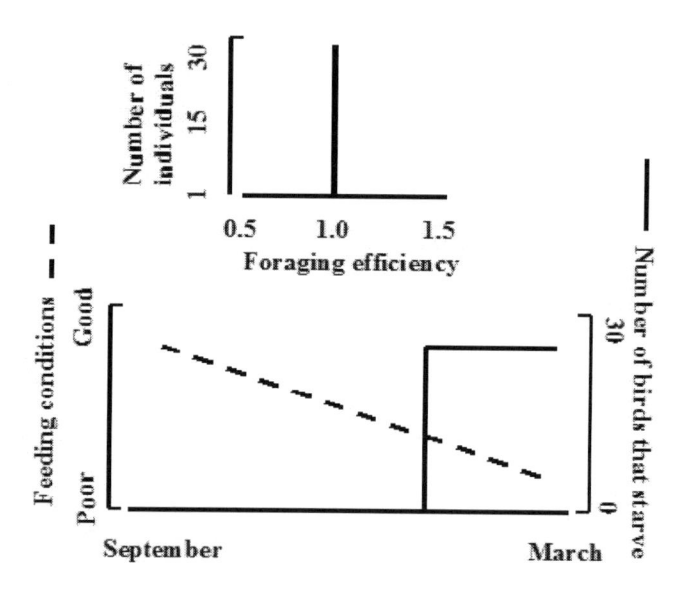

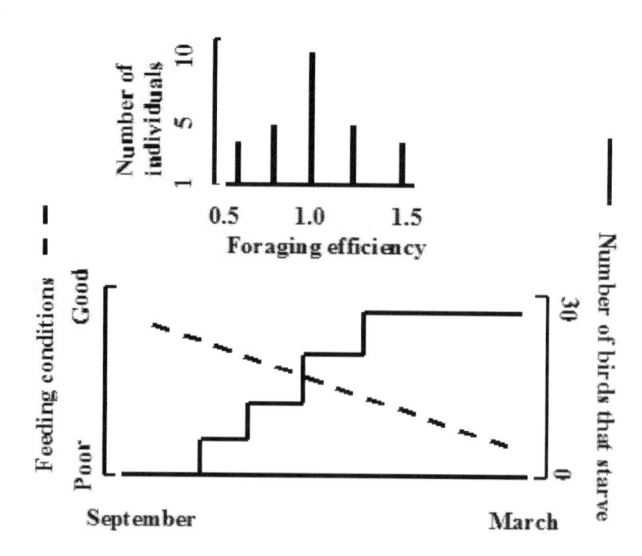

Figure 2.1 The importance of variation between individuals in foraging efficiency in determining the pattern of mortality. **(A)** In this case, all 30 birds in the population have exactly the same foraging efficiency of 1, an arbitrary unit for the purposes of illustration. So as the feeding conditions get worse as the non-breeding season proceeds, all 30 birds starve at the same time, because none is better or worse at feeding than the rest. In case **(B)**, however, some individuals are 25% or even 50% more efficient than the average birds whereas others are 25% or 50% less efficient. Accordingly, as the non-breeding season proceeds, the least efficient individuals starve first and, by the end of the season, only the most efficient ones are still alive.

Imagine a population in which all individuals are absolutely identical in the efficiency with which they exploit their food supply – it's a nonsense, of course, but sometimes these extreme comparisons can be helpful. Imagine that the food supply gradually becomes scarcer and scarcer until it is so sparse that an individual animal is not be able to find food fast enough in the time available each day to meet its energy requirements. It would use up all its fat reserves and starve to death. As all the birds are identical, they would all starve simultaneously. On one day, all of them would be alive (though emaciated), but the next day they would all be dead (Fig. 2(A)).

Now imagine a group of birds in which individuals differ in ways that affect how good they were at getting food. Some individuals might be exceptionally good at finding a prey. An example could be a bar-tailed godwit that detects a worm caste emerging onto the sand surface much sooner than any of the other godwits and at a considerably greater distance. This bird would be deemed highly efficient at detecting its prey. Another individual might be less efficient at prey detection but much more skilled at catching the worm before it retreats down its burrow. Another individual might be relatively inefficient at both of these skills: this would be the unfortunate individual that starved first as the food supply decreased. Subsequently, as the food supply continued to decline, more of the less efficient individuals would perish, and so on. Birds would gradually starve, one by one, rather than all at once. As more birds died, the rate of depletion of the prey would slow down because fewer birds remain to eat them, further extending the time that it takes for the remaining birds to starve. When there is variation between individuals in how efficiently they feed, the period over which starvation occurs (the 'starvation window') would be much extended. Only the most efficient individuals would survive to the end of the non-breeding season (Fig. 2.1(B)).

There is another way in which individual birds vary that also extends the period over which starvation occurs. In many species of shorebirds, individuals compete against each other for food items or for the best places to feed (Box 2.1). Imagine that a very efficient godwit has detected a lugworm and has dashed to where the worm caste is forming. Other godwits will see this happen, and one that is near enough might run to the same spot in an attempt to get to the worm first. If it is a good fighter, it might be able to drive the efficient bird away, and so get the worm itself, or steal worm from the other bird's bill. Either way, this socially 'dominant' individual would gain at the expense of the poorer fighter, but more efficient, individual that had found the worm in the first place.

As with individual variations in their ability to detect and catch prey – their foraging efficiency – differences between birds in their ability to fight with other birds (i.e. in their 'fighting ability') also extends the period over which birds starve as the feeding conditions decline (Fig.2.2). It is because individuals vary in both foraging efficiency and fighting ability that there is a gradual increase in the mortality rate as population size increases rather than a sudden step-up at some threshold population size. Clearly, the greater the variation between individuals, the more gentle is the slope of the relationship. The work on the Wash had identified the vital importance of researching competitive processes in shorebirds and it seemed impossible to do this without having a substantial number of birds that could be individually identified.

The other reason to have marked individuals was to measure mortality rate over the non-breeding season. [Note, it is not strictly a 'rate' which is when something is expressed against time. 'Mortality rate' has come to be accepted as a shorthand way of saying 'the proportion of birds alive at the start of the non-breeding season that die before the end': much quicker!] At that time, the mortality rates of shorebirds were estimated by putting numbered rings on the legs of a sample of birds. As these numbers were usually far too small to be read at a distance, mortality rate was estimated from the frequency with which dead ringed birds were reported by the general public. There was usually doubt about whether the sub-sample of recovered birds was representative of the whole population, and therefore whether the mortality estimates based upon them were reliable.

Since samples of birds had to be individually colour-marked anyway for the impending studies on competition, the mortality rate could be measured by recording when marked individuals disappeared permanently from the study population. The entire population was scanned at regular intervals through the non-breeding season to find out how many of the marked individuals disappeared at some point and how many were still present at the end. This would show at what stage in the non-breeding season birds disappeared – which might help identify the cause of their disappearance, as well as how many died overall.

Imagine that 10% of the birds had been individually marked. For studies of individual variation in foraging efficiency and fighting ability, it would be vital that many of them could be found and observed on the feeding grounds. For measuring the mortality rate, it would be vital also that their presence or absence in the population could be checked relatively easily. It would be no use marking 500 individuals (which would take a long time) if they dispersed over as huge an area as the Wash where they would be difficult to find. The Wash was an awe-inspiring place to work, but too big.

Nor would it be any good if the study estuary was so close to adjacent estuaries that many of the individually marked animals might regularly move next door, or even to next door but one. A huge area would still have to be searched, and time spent searching just reduced the amount of time available for obtaining data on the behaviour of the birds. For this reason, the possibility of carrying out the work on an estuary in Essex was quickly abandoned because its many estuaries are so close to each other and linked by shorebird-friendly coasts.

The choice of study species was also vital, of course. It had to be common and numerous and also of reasonable size. Dunlin are very numerous but are so small that identifying tiny colour rings as the birds splosh through mud and water or seeing tiny wing-tags would be extremely difficult. Furthermore, measuring how fast birds fed was going to be a vital part of the project and dunlin eat many small-sized prey that are difficult to see as they are being taken. This species was quickly rejected. Redshank seemed a good option in this regard and much was already known of their foraging behaviour and ecology. The relatively isolated Blythe estuary in Suffolk supported a suitably-sized redshank population during the non-breeding season and seemed to be an attractive option – it's a beautiful place too - but the main prey of redshank there was *Corophium volutator*. This enchanting little shrimp-like crustacean has two or three generations a year and this makes its population dynamics complex and difficult to study. The search was extended from the south-east coast of England to the whole of the UK.

The excellent studies of both birds and cockles on the Burry Inlet had shown that the oystercatcher-cockle system might be a very suitable. Oystercatchers are large and so are able to carry large individual markers that can be read at a distance. Their large prey can easily be identified as they are taken and it is easy to measure how many are eaten by a bird in, say, a ten-minute period.

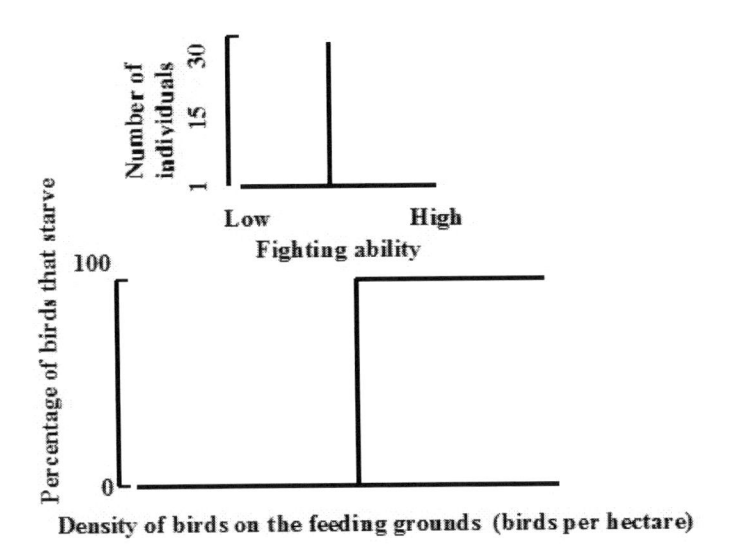

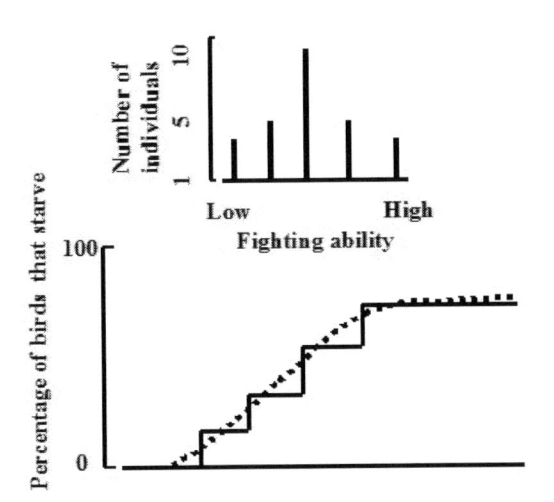

(A)

(B)

Figure 2.2 *Importance of variation between individual birds in their fighting ability in determining the pattern of mortality in relation to the density of birds on the feeding grounds.* ***(A)*** *As the density of the birds - and thus the intensity of the competition between them – increases, all 30 birds starve at the same time, because none is better or worse at fighting than the rest. In case* ***(B),*** *however, some individuals are 25% or even 50% better fighters than the average bird whereas others are 25% or 50% worse. Accordingly, as the density of birds increases, the worst fighters starve first, followed by the next worst, and so on. The dotted line averages the trend because, in the real world, birds within one competitive category will vary too.*

Furthermore, the classic study of the population dynamics of the cockles of the Inlet had shown that the population dynamics of this prey species could be studied well.

That study had also shown that the effect that oystercatchers had on the cockle shellfishery was still uncertain, and that further work on this system might be funded in the interests of developing shellfishery management policy. For a while, oystercatchers and cockles seemed to be the answer, and several areas were visited with these animals in mind, mainly along the south and west coasts of Wales and England. But sadly, the oystercatcher-cockle system has one bad feature: cockle populations of reasonable size only occur in large, sandy embayments, such as Morecambe Bay, the Wash and the Burry Inlet itself. All these sites were just too large!

As part of this search, however, the Exe estuary in south Devon was visited to see if it had a suitable population of cockles. The oystercatcher population of 2-3000 birds was just right. The estuary was very accessible, of a convenient size and quite distant to the next estuary along the coast – that of the river Teign. It was also a lovely place with some very nice villages around it where away-from-home fieldworkers would be content to stay on field trips. But the cockle beds were very small and were thought likely to be rather ephemeral and to be prone to much casual harvesting: very risky for a long-term study of their population dynamics.

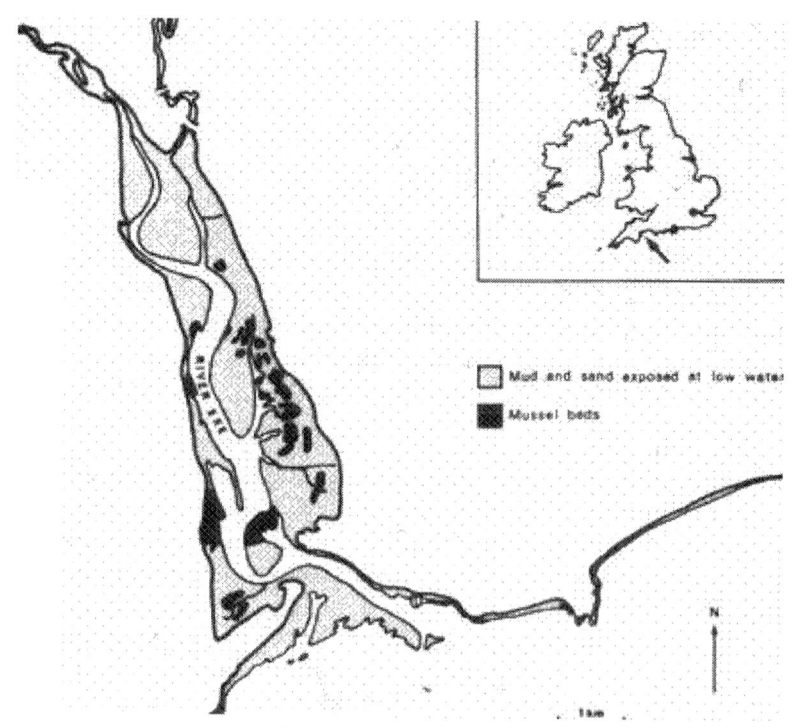

Figure 2.3 The mussel beds of the Exe estuary in south Devon in 1976.

At first this was disappointing. On the other hand, there were many mussel beds and these were individually distinct. Most of them had been laid by earlier generations of local fishing families to provide an income when the seas were too rough for inshore fishing. The mussel beds had been there for years. Because mussels sit on the surface, the different mussel beds were easy to distinguish. Furthermore, it was immediately obvious that some mussel beds had high densities of large mussels whereas others only had small mussels and, on some, even these were very sparse. The different beds provided a wide variety of food patches across which both the average size and density of the mussels varied considerably. The food gradient of oystercatchers on the Exe was very easy to identify (Fig 2.3).

If the first impression that oystercatchers on the Exe did mainly ate mussels proved to be correct, the oystercatcher-mussel system there would make an excellent system on which to investigate the mortality rate of a shorebird during the non-breeding season and for in depth studies in individual variations in foraging efficiency and fighting. Whether oystercatchers affect the abundance of their shellfish prey, and *vice versa*, was still an issue, and there seemed likely to be a market for advice on whether the abundance of either species is affected by the abundance of the other. It took only a few weeks to establish beyond doubt that most of the oystercatchers on the estuary did eat mussels – approximately 80% of them. So the decision was made and the team of three were transferred in summer 1976 from Norwich to the nearby Furzebrook research station in Wareham, Dorset, 80 miles away.

GROUNDWORK

Initial research questions - What questions needed to be answered first? There was quite a long list:

- How many oystercatchers are there on the Exe estuary in each month of the year?
- How many of them are in their first year (juvenile), second and third year (immature) or are adult?
- How many of them feed on each mussel bed, and what are their ages?
- How many feed on the mudflats and sandflats, and what are their ages?
- *How many feed along the coast between the Exe estuary and the Otter estuary to the east and the Teign estuary to the West?*
- Do oystercatchers always roost over high tide or do some feed in fields and, if so, how many and at what stage of the non-breeding season do they do it?
- What prey do they eat in each habitat?
- What is the mortality rate of each age-class over the non-breeding season?
- Do the birds that die appear to have starved or to have died from some other cause?
- Do all oystercatchers that survive the breeding season return afterwards to the Exe?
- How feasible is it to measure the number of prey consumed per unit time by an individual oystercatcher and how best to measure the size of the ones that are eaten?
- Do oystercatchers appear to compete for prey items and feeding places?
- Can individuals be marked so that they can be identified at a distance in all of the habitats that they use?

The main questions for mussels were:

- How many mussel beds are there?

- How best to measure the area of each mussel bed, in *ha*?

- How best to measure the numerical density (numbers per square metre) and sizes (maximum length in *mm*) of the mussels on the different mussel beds at the beginning and end of the oystercatcher non-breeding season?

- How to age mussels of different size?

- How to measure the energy content of mussels of different sizes on different mussel beds at each stage of the non-breeding season?

- How to calculate the proportion of mussels that are killed by oystercatchers and other agents (eg. gales, crabs) over the non-breeding season?

The methodologies required to answer the questions derived from previous knowledge and, often, trial and error. All the questions were answered over the first few years, and details of the methods employed can be found in the appropriate papers.

Finding the answers to most of the oystercatcher questions simply involved driving or walking or sitting and looking at the birds through a telescope and recording in a notebook what was seen! In all habitats, it was usually possible to approach the birds on foot to within 50-75m without disturbing them and to count the numbers in a specified area, such as on one mussel bed, an area of mud bounded by creeks or sandy areas or a field. The estuary and adjacent coast were quickly subdivided into foraging 'patches'. Some patches were mussel beds, some were mud, sand or gravel and so forth. The numbers on each patch were easy to count at low tide, either on foot or from a car in places where that was possible; alongside fields, for example. A single count of all the actual or potential patches in the entire study area at both high tide and low tide took at least five days or, more accurately, five low water periods. It was quickly established by repeated visits to a small sample of patches that, fortunately, the distribution of the birds was more-or-less stable over at least that length of time.

It was also easy to watch the birds' behaviour and to record what they were eating and how many prey items were taken over a five or ten minute period. When fights occurred between birds, these too could be noted and the outcome recorded.

All this was fine for finding out about the oystercatcher population as a whole, but it was vital to be able to identify individuals as well. Two happy coincidences enabled this to occur. One was the presence of an enthusiastic group of bird ringers, the Devon and Cornwall Wader Ringing Group, that had recently established itself in Plymouth, having previously worked with the Wash Wader Ringing Group (Box 2.2). The other was a fortuitous encounter with a colleague at the British Trust for Ornithology (BTO) who provided an idea that saved thousands of man-hours of fieldwork and mountains of frustration (Box 2.3). At the peak of the ringing effort, some 10% of the oystercatchers on the Exe were individually colour-marked. From the second year onwards, individually-marked birds were seen every time a census was made and whenever observations on their behaviour were being made, and their location and activity (foraging or resting) was always recorded.

Although at this early stage we did not know it, these individually-marked birds were to play a vital part in the development of the shorebird model that was to be the 'end-product' of the project, some 30 years later. Over the first years, however, their value was in answering questions such as: 'Do individuals feed on the same prey species in the same place day after day and from season to season?' – answer 'Yes, mainly!'; 'Do individuals return year after year to the Exe?' – 'Yes, once they have reached two years of age; 'Are Exe-marked birds ever seen or found dead elsewhere?' – 'Only very occasionally'; 'Where do the birds breed?' - 'Scotland mainly'.

Oystercatcher numbers and diet

A lot of time was spent answering the questions: 'How many oystercatchers are there? What are their ages? What do they feed on?'

Plate 2.1 *The colour-ringing scheme used on the Exe estuary oystercatchers. The tall white 'wasp' ring is actually a Darvic sandwich made up of two layers; an inner black one and an outer white one. By engraving narrow bands through the white layer, the black layer beneath is exposed. These bands can be either 'thick' (3mm width) or 'thin' (1mm width). There are three positions for a band: top, middle and bottom. Since there can also be no band in one of these positions ('blank'), there are 27 combinations for one wasp: starting from the top, a ring might be 'thin, thick, blank' or 'thick, thick, thin'. By putting a small colour ring either above or below the wasp, and by putting the rings on either the left or the right leg, the number of combinations for one colour of wasp with one colour of small ring increases fourfold to 108. A complete combination now reads as, for example: left leg, red below, thin, blank, thick (white wasp). The number of combinations for white wasps can be increased yet again by changing the colour of the small ring. And the number of combinations can be increased even more by having different colours of wasp sandwich: for example, yellow with black bands, green with black bands etc. There really is an enormous number of unique combinations, and all on one leg! The combination of the bird in this photograph is: left leg, orange above, thin-thin-thin (white wasp). The numbered BTO ring can be seen on the far leg too.*

Censuses were made at very regular intervals – fortnightly or monthly – at both high tide and low tide between 1976 and 1981 – five non-breeding seasons. At high tide (defined as the period from two hours before high water to two hours afterwards), all the known roosting sites and fields where the birds occurred were visited on foot or by car, with repeated extensive searches by car made in areas where none had yet been seen but where they might occur. At low tide (defined as the period from one-and-a-half hours before low water to one-and-a-half hours afterwards), counts were made on foot over much of the estuary.

Counts were also made from car along part of the estuary and coast and in fields where some birds occurred at low tide. The entire low tide study area had been mapped and could be sub-divided into foraging habitats, such mussel bed, sandy beach, muddy sandflat, mudflat, mudflat with eelgrass (*Zostera* spp.), rock ledge, and so forth. A full census of the estuary itself took two-three low tide periods and the coasts and fields an additional two to five low tide periods. A full census over high tide took a similar amount of time. Very frequently, a sub-sample of birds on a particular foraging habitat or roosting site was examined closely so that each individual could be aged, which can be done quite easily from a combination of beak colour, leg colour and plumage. Often while they were being aged, they took a prey item that could be identified and recorded. This whole programme lasted for five non-breeding seasons.

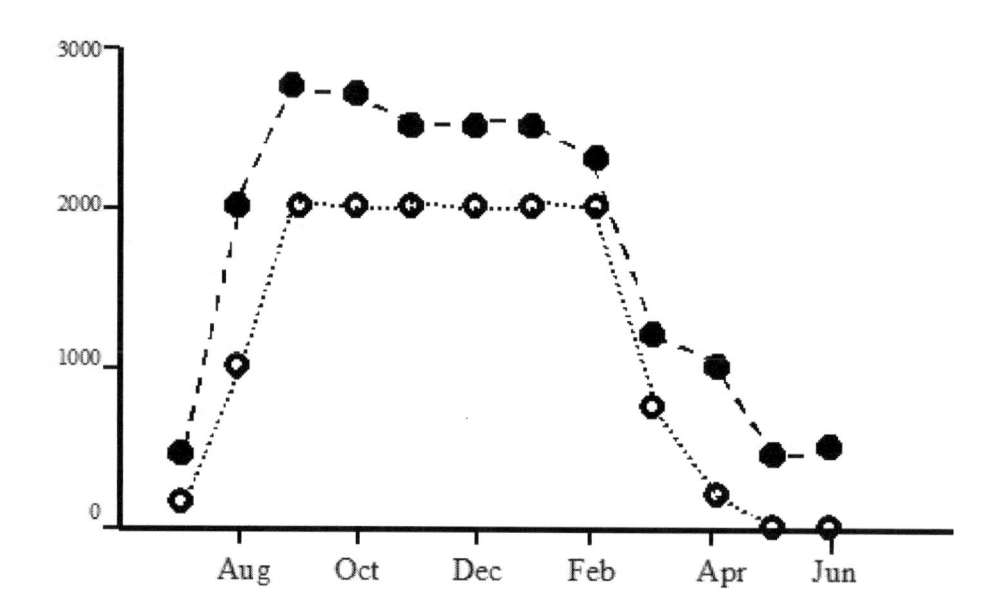

Figure 2.4 *The population of oystercatchers on the Exe estuary. The values are approximate monthly averages over the period July 1976 to November 1979 for all the birds (black dots, dashed lines) and just adults (open circles, dotted lines).*

It was a lot of work, but it yielded important basic information about the population of oystercatchers on the Exe. In brief, during the breeding season (March/April to July/August), there were just a few hundred young birds and a few adults (Fig. 2.4). They were joined by some two thousand adults during July to September as they returned from the breeding grounds. Some juveniles hatched the same year also arrived. From October until the end of the non-breeding season at the beginning of February, the population size changed rather little but may have declined somewhat, but not by much. Most of the birds were adults, most of which fed on the mussel beds. The small number of juvenile birds (4-11 months after hatching) mostly ate things other than mussels, predominantly ragworms and clams from the mudflats and earthworms from the fields. As birds matured through the two years of their immaturity, an increasing proportion began eating mussels. At the beginning of the non-breeding season, all the birds roosted over high tide but, later, a gradually increasing number went to the fields, mainly at high tide when the mussel beds were covered by the tide but also at low tide, even though the mussel beds were exposed then. Most of the birds in the fields fed on earthworms.

Mortality rate

The individually-marked birds provided the critically important information on the mortality rate over the non-breeding season, something that it had not been possible previously to estimate in any wading bird species. Over these first five years of the project, every oystercatcher that could be found within the study area was checked for rings. In these early years, the checks were carried out virtually continuously whenever the visibility permitted from August (when birds were starting to arrive from the breeding grounds) to April (by when most adults had left to breed). This huge effort was justified because of the essential need to measure the mortality rate just *within the non-breeding season* itself and because it took so long to be ensure that most of the birds that were present had actually been found and recorded.

It might be worth describing this work in some detail to convey the magnitude of the task that the single fieldworker involved had to take on. At the beginning of the non-breeding season, most of the oystercatchers at high tide congregated in one or two roosts at the tip of Dawlish Warren, the sandy peninsular at the mouth of the estuary. This would appear at first sight to provide a golden opportunity to tick off all the individuals present. But because so many were packed together in a small area, only the legs of those birds on the side closest to the researcher could be checked. The birds did move about from time to time, particularly as they walked upshore and downshore as the tide advanced and retreated from high water. Sometimes the flocks would be disturbed by a crow or something, which helped stir them up a bit. Even so, it took five visits, each of about 5 hours, on five successive days to ensure that most of the individuals that were using the roosts had been recorded. After one search that lasted several hours, only 40% of the individuals that would eventually be seen had been recorded. Over successive days, the proportion seen increased to 60% then 80% then 95%. After the fifth search, so few new individuals were located that it was considered cost-ineffective to continue for more days. Anyway, many other places also had to be searched over the same spring tide series of seven or so days.

As the non-breeding season progressed and holiday makers gradually quitted the coasts to the east and west of the mouth of the estuary, and as more and more birds began to feed in fields, particularly over high tide, the searches had to cover a lot more ground. Oystercatchers mainly use mature grass fields, where there are many earthworms. There are a great many such fields around the Exe estuary! Luckily, many of the birds were attracted to earthworm-rich sports fields and golf courses where the grass was short and the rings could be read relatively easily. But too often, this was not the case, and the grass was frustratingly deep. You could see that there was a ringed bird in the field, but getting a clear view of the ring as it wandered through the long grass was difficult. It could take up to a couple of hours to identify with certainty a single ring combination, only to discover it was the individual that had been seen somewhere else the previous day! Sometimes it was just not possible to identify an individual, and a return visit next day was required. By the end of the non-breeding season, the researcher was thoroughly exhausted: 'rung out', you might say. But quite soon it had to start all over again as the birds returned from their all too short breeding season.

But the end result was certainly worth the effort because the average rate at which birds disappeared at some stage or other of the non-breeding season had been determined. Between 19% and 27% of the birds less than four years old disappeared while only 12% of the older birds – the adults – did so. But note that the word is 'disappeared', not 'died', because those that could not be found may just have gone to another estuary! How to test this possibility?

As well as carrying plastic colour rings, each bird that was caught had been ringed with a uniquely numbered BTO metal ring. When a dead ringed bird was found by a member of the public, the number of the ring was often sent to the ringing office at the BTO. During the non-breeding season, almost all such recoveries were made within the Exe estuary study area. The only exceptions were a small number of birds that had wintered on the Exe in their first non-breeding season and were subsequently found dead, mainly in the Burry Inlet (as it happens). Few other recoveries were made elsewhere during the non-breeding season. This suggested that, after their first non-breeding season, oystercatchers on the Exe returned there for all the subsequent non-breeding seasons.

That being the case, a bird older than two years that disappeared from the Exe at some time during the non-breeding season may have died there. However, those individuals that disappeared towards the end of the non-breeding season may have indeed died on the Exe estuary but they may also have died after they had left, either *en route* to the breeding grounds or later on the breeding grounds. All that would be known of such a bird is that it never returned to the Exe again. Unfortunately, some oystercatchers left for the breeding grounds very early in February, just as the most difficult part of the non-breeding season for feeding comes to an end. Since it could take two to three weeks to establish that a bird had disappeared, it was not possible to decide whether a bird disappeared in mid-January had died then or had migrated and subsequently died elsewhere, many months after it had left the Exe.

Some such late-disappearing individuals were found dead within a few weeks elsewhere in the UK, and so it was known that they had not died on the Exe. But this was a minority of birds. Luckily, some were also found dead on the Exe during January, February or March, either by members of the public or by the researcher on his very frequent searches of the strandline that were undertaken for that very purpose.

On average over four years, between a quarter and a third of the oystercatchers that had disappeared during the non-breeding season were found dead somewhere on the Exe estuary or along the adjacent coast. If it could be shown that the chance of finding the corpse of an oystercatcher that had died there was in the region of 25-35%, it could be assumed that all the birds that disappeared during the non-breeding season – including those that disappeared in January - had actually died on the Exe.

A simple experiment was set up to measure the chance that a dead ringed birds would be found by the researcher or reported by a member of the general public. For many months before the experiment began, every road casualty of any medium-sized bird that was encountered was picked up and stored. Many pigeons that had been shot were also assembled. When it was judged that a sufficiently large sample of corpses had been acquired, each one was ringed with a metal numbered BTO ring and some kind of colour-ring. The latter was necessary as experience had shown that the finder often noticed the corpse when they caught sight of the colour ring. These marked corpses were then scattered around the intertidal zone of the estuary over a period of two days, concentrating mainly in the southern half where most oystercatchers occurred.

The happy outcome of this experiment was that 25% of these experimental corpses were indeed found by the researcher or reported by the public (Box 2.4). It was concluded that a high proportion of the birds above two years of age that disappeared during the non-breeding season had died on the Exe estuary, along the adjacent coast or in nearby fields. This allowed Figure 2.5 to be drawn and, for the first time, there was an estimate of the mortality rate of a wading bird during the non-breeding season alone, rather than throughout the whole year. Because of the larger sample size of ringed birds, the estimate for the mortality rate was most accurate for adult birds. Over these first five years of the project, a minimum of 1.5% and a maximum of 3.2% were estimated to die during the non-breeding season.

The cause of a death was sometimes obvious, sometimes obscure. One bird was hit by a train as it flew across the railway line to feed in the fields beyond. Occasionally a bird was found drowned because its legs had become tangled with nylon fishing line that was itself tangled around mussels, so the bird was unable to flee the advancing tide. On other occasions, the cause of death was unknown but the birds were very emaciated, suggesting that starvation and/or disease had played a part.

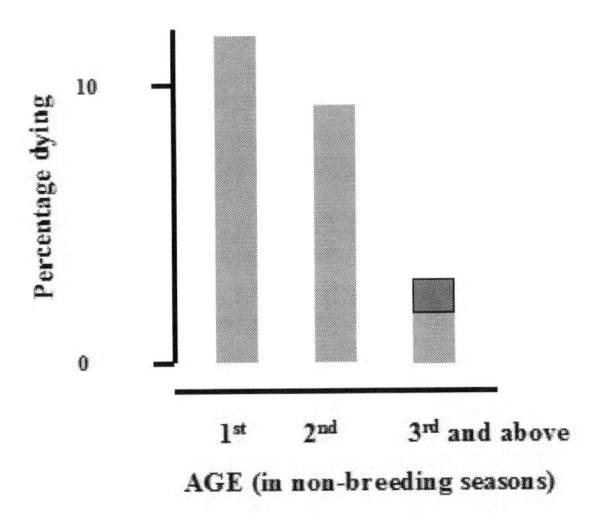

Figure 2.5 *The mortality rate of oystercatchers on the Exe estuary during their first, second etc. non-breeding seasons of their life. As birds at the end of their 3rd and subsequent non-breeding season may migrate from the Exe at the end of the non-breeding season, the chart for them shows the minimum (pale grey) and maximum (dark grey) estimate of their mortality rate.*

First evidence that competition occurs between oystercatchers
Occupation of mussel beds by oystercatchers returning from the breeding grounds

The first signs that competition between birds might play a role in the death of some of them came from the counts of the numbers of birds on the different mussel beds. The sizes of the mussels, their flesh-content and their numerical density (numbers per square metre) appeared to vary greatly between the different mussel beds in relation to environmental factors, such as the level of the shore and therefore the length of time that the mussels were covered by water when the tide was in. Since the size, flesh-content and density of the mussels on a mussel bed seemed likely to affect how well birds could feed, it seemed likely also that they might compete to feed on the most profitable mussel bed. If so, adults returning to the estuary in autumn might be expected to first occupy the most profitable mussel beds and only to occupy the less profitable ones if and when the increasing number of birds led to competition in the best feeding places. From studies in the Dutch Wadden Sea and on the Wash, increasing competition between birds returning from the breeding grounds as their numbers increased was expected to cause the mussel beds to be occupied in the sequence illustrated in Figure 2.6.

After one non-breeding season, it was clear that most of the mussels and most of the oystercatchers occurred on just 12 of the 32 mussel beds that had been identified and mapped. As these twelve varied in a number of ways likely to affect their attractiveness to oystercatchers, they were considered sufficient to investigate the way in which oystercatchers occupied different mussel beds as their numbers increased (and decreased) and to explore the various factors that might make some beds more attractive to the birds than others.

The numbers of birds using each mussel bed were counted during the population censuses and, from these data and the area of the mussel beds, the densities of oystercatchers on each bed over the low water period were calculated. Density not only varied greatly between patches but also over the non-breeding season as the size of the population of mussel-feeding birds changed. At low population sizes, the density of the birds was low on almost all of the mussel beds, with many having no birds at all. Most of the oystercatchers that were present were on just four of the 12 mussel beds. At high population sizes, densities were, of course, much higher on all of the beds but there was a difference in density between them (Figure 2.7). These field data therefore did match the expectation shown in Figure 2.6 and may imply that competition was playing a role in distributing the birds over the mussel beds.

This prompted two further questions: 'What factors caused oystercatcher density at any one population size to vary between mussel beds – the 'foraging patches'?' and 'Did the factors responsible differ between population sizes?' Answering these questions were thought likely to help understand whether competition between birds was taking place.

(A)

Number of oystercatchers on all the mussel beds combined:

Mussel bed	500	1500	2500
1			
2			
3			
4			
5			

(B)

Figure 2.6 How the numbers of oystercatchers on each of five mussel beds might change as the total numbers of birds on all the mussel beds combined increases. (A) Each white dot represents, say, 10 birds on the five black mussel beds. Bed 1 provides the best feeding conditions and bed quality decrease progressively from bed 1 to bed 5. When there are only 500 birds on the estuary, they can all feed on the best bed, mussel bed 1. But as the numbers increase, the increasing intensity of the competition on bed 1 causes an increasing number of birds to move to other beds, further down the food gradient. (B) Accordingly, as the total numbers increase from 500 through 1500 to 2500, more and more birds occur on beds 3 and 5.

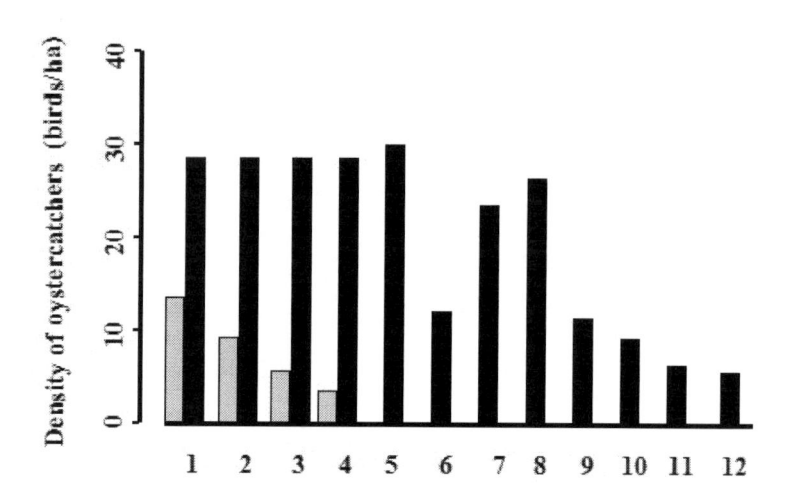

Figure 2.7 *The distribution of birds over the 12 main mussel beds was different when less than a total of 500 birds were on the estuary (pale blue) than when there were about 2000 (black). When <500 were present during the breeding season, they all occurred on four of the mussel beds but, because there were so few birds available, the density of birds was rather low on all four. When about 2000 were present in the non-breeding season, birds occupied all of the mussel beds, their densities being particularly high in the mussel beds where the oystercatchers had occurred before the start of the non-breeding season.*

The list of possible factors that might affect the density of oystercatchers at a given population size on a mussel bed was quite long: (i) based on studies in the Netherlands, mussel beds near to the roost that was used by the birds at high tide might attract higher density of birds than those further away because birds would be expected to try to minimise the time and energy spent in commuting; (ii) mussel beds with high densities of large (and therefore profitable) mussels might attract higher densities of birds than mussel beds with scanty supplies of small mussels; (iii) mussel beds with a hard substrate – such as shingle – might be more attractive than ones with sloppy mud because walking in mud might be energetically more expensive than walking on a firm surface (an hypothesis incorrectly drawn from the human condition, as it turned out) or because the birds might find it difficult to smash their way into a mussel that kept sinking into the mud; (iv) mussel beds with much surface algae might be less attractive because more of the mussels would be hidden from the birds and so be more difficult to find; (v) bumpy mussel beds might have higher densities of birds than flat ones because the birds would be seen less often by aggressive neighbours and so would not be attacked so often as they would be on a flat bed with no obstacles to vision. And so on! In all, a total of 10 possible factors were thought up, and no doubt, other researchers could have dreamed up even more!

How to identify the factors that influenced bird density on a mussel bed and eliminate those that did not? Experimental manipulations on the scale required were out of the question. Instead, an attempt was made to relate differences in the density of the birds on the mussel beds to differences in each of these factors using a statistical procedure to distinguish between factors that might influence bird density from those that were unlikely to do so. The values of some of the factors were known from the mussel population study (*i.e.* the density and sizes of the mussels on each bed). One could be read from a map (*i.e.* distance of the mussel bed from the roost at the mouth of the estuary). Others had to be measured on each bed, however, using in some cases rather bizarre procedures (Box 2.5).

(A)

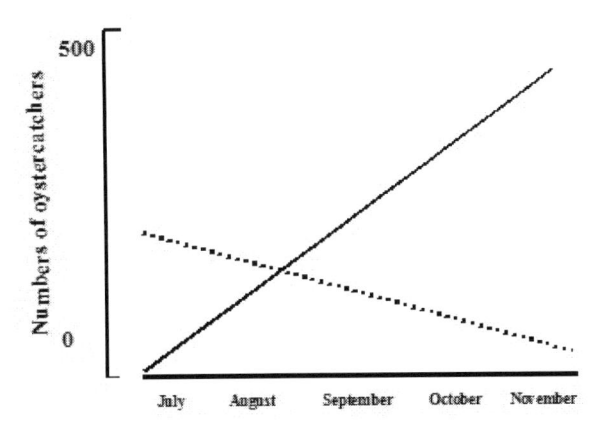

(B)

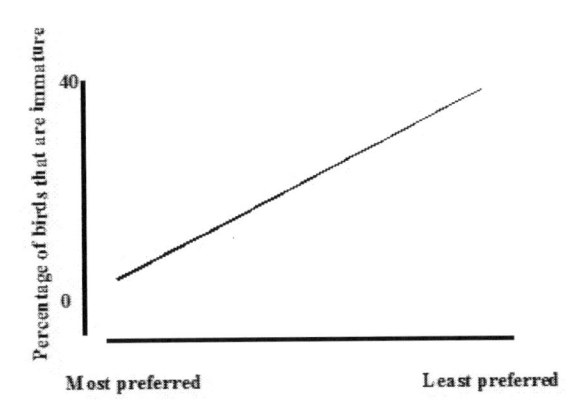

Figure 2.8 *The ages of the birds on the different mussel beds also varied as would be expected if competition for the most preferred mussel beds was occurring. **(A)** The approximate numbers of socially dominant adult (solid line) and sub-dominant immature (dashed line) oystercatchers on the two most preferred mussel beds (1 and 2) over the beginning of the non-breeding season when the adults were returning to the Exe from the breeding grounds. **(B)** The proportion of oystercatchers later in the non-breeding season that was immature in relation to the preference of oystercatchers for the mussel bed.*

Some clear patterns did emerge from this analysis. At any one population size, only from 2 to 4 factors seemed to influence the density of oystercatchers on the different mussel beds, (i) the proximity of a mussel bed to the main roost on Dawlish Warren, (ii) the hardness of the substrate, (iii) the density of the mussels in the main size class (40-50mm long) consumed by oystercatchers on most mussel beds, and (iv) the thickness of the mussel shells on the dorsal (uppermost) side.

From the point of view of exploring the idea that competition might occur between oystercatchers on the mussel beds, the most interesting finding was that, as the size of the population increased over the first part of the non-breeding season, the density of the birds became increasingly closely related to the density of the mussels. At low population sizes, the highest densities of birds occurred on four mussel beds that were close to the roost and also had relatively hard substrates: bizarrely, the mussels there also had thick shells. But as numbers built up as the adults returned from the breeding grounds, the birds spread out and occupied all the mussel beds where mussels occurred at high densities.

One interpretation of this finding is consistent with the competition hypothesis. According to this, the density of oystercatchers was highest on mussel beds with a highest average density of mussels because such beds provided the greatest amount of mussel 'feeding space within their boundary. The more feeding space there was, the more easily poor fighters could avoid better fighters and this would allow more birds as a whole to occupy the mussel bed. The amount of feeding space was low where the average density of mussels was low because such beds consisted of large bare patches of mud between scattered clumps of mussels. On the mussel beds where the overall density of mussels was high, by contrast, mussels tended to occur in solid sheets with very few bare patches to break them up. Accordingly, a high density of mussels was associated with large amounts of feeding space for oystercatchers, whereas low densities were associated with large amounts of bare ground without mussels.

Ages of birds on the different mussel beds

The age-composition of the oystercatchers on the mussel beds also changed over the non-breeding season in a manner that would be expected if competition was occurring. Most of the immature birds that had occupied the two 'best' beds during the breeding season when the socially dominant adults were absent left those beds as the adults returned (Fig. 2.8(A)). Subsequently, the proportion of immature birds was higher on the least preferred beds than on the most preferred ones, where adults were especially abundant (Fig. 2.8(B)). By the end of this initial phase of the non-breeding season, only about 10% of the oystercatchers that were on the most preferred beds were immature compared with between 35 and 40% on the least preferred beds. Therefore, not only did the numbers of birds on the various beds change as the adults returned to the estuary in a manner that would be expected if competition was taking place, but the changing age composition of the birds on the various beds was also consistent with the competition hypothesis.

Conclusions of the early research on competition

So, the early signs after five years were that competition for the most preferred mussel beds may have occurred. Both the way in which the returning adult oystercatchers re- occupied and spread out over the mussel beds over the beginning of the non-breeding season along with the simultaneous departure from the most preferred beds of the sub-dominant immature birds, and their subsequent predominance on the least preferred mussel beds, all suggested that competition was at least having an influence of the distribution of the birds. Whether competition also influenced which individuals died over the non-breeding season was a matter that would have to wait a few more years of research.

Predation by oystercatchers on mussels

Following the Burry Inlet controversy, understanding the predator-prey interaction between the oystercatcher and mussel populations of the Exe was thought likely during the late 1970s to be useful of advising managers of shellfisheries in the UK and elsewhere. The impact that predators had on the abundance of their prey, and *vice versa*, was also an important field of theoretical and empirical research at that time amongst population ecologists (Box 2.6).

What approach should be used to answer the question: 'What impact do oystercatchers have on the abundance of mussels?' It was already clear that the density of oystercatchers varied considerably between the main 12 mussel beds of the estuary. Additionally, some mussel beds were exposed over one tidal cycle for much more time than others, this depending on their location on the shore. Birds feeding on mussel beds that were located high up the shore could feed over a longer period, and therefore take more mussels, than can birds feeding on low-lying mussel beds. And furthermore, as the sizes and densities of the mussels varied between patches, the number of mussels taken by a single bird from a patch over one exposure period would also be expected vary for this reason as well. The overall predation rate on mussels by oystercatchers was therefore expected to vary a lot between mussel beds because the two factors determining that impact – the density of oystercatchers and the numbers of mussel each bird consumed over one exposure period – differed between mussel beds. Oystercatchers might have had a large impact on the mussels in some patches but not in others. Accordingly, the impact of predation by oystercatchers on mussels would also be expected to vary between mussel beds. In order to fully understand the impact of the birds on the abundance of the mussels, it was believed necessary to take into account the spatial variation on the densities of both oystercatchers and mussels.

The direct approach to finding out how many mussels were consumed by oystercatchers over the entire non-breeding season was therefore to multiply together (i) the numbers of birds eating mussels on each bed, (ii) the numbers of mussels consumed by one bird over a single exposure period, and (iii) the number of exposure periods over the whole non-breeding season. This can be expressed in this simple equation:

$$C_{total} = N.C_{ep}.E_p$$

where C_{total} is the total consumption of mussels by all of the oystercatchers on one mussel bed over the non-breeding season, N is the average number that eat mussels during each tidal exposure period, C_{ep} is the average number of mussels consumed by one oystercatcher over one exposure period and E_p is the number of exposure periods over the non-breeding season.

For example, if over the non-breeding season of 400 tidal cycles (200 days with approximately two cycles during each 24 hours) an average of 200 oystercatchers fed on a mussel bed day and night and the average bird consumed 75 mussels during every 24 hour period, the total numbers removed by oystercatchers from that bed over the non-breeding season would be: 400x200x75, or 6 million. This may sound an awful lot, but there are huge numbers of mussels on many of the beds!

Having measured the numbers of mussels on that mussel bed at the beginning of the non-breeding season, the proportion of the mussels on each patch that was removed by oystercatchers before they leave for the breeding grounds can be estimated. By combining all the calculations from all the main mussel beds on the estuary, the proportion of the entire mussel population consumed by the birds can be calculated. This tells you by how much these predators reduce the prey population over the non-breeding season

A very simple approach, but it took a lot of work and time to solve this particular equation for each of the 12 main mussel beds of the estuary. And it proved to be a bit of a blind alley too!

Rate of consumption of mussels by one oystercatcher

As it is simply not possible to observe how many mussels are eaten by one bird over the entire non-breeding season, this work was broken down into manageable components. Apart from the number of oystercatchers, the main measurements were: (i) the 'feeding rate' (in daylight and in darkness), the number of prey items picked up and swallowed within a specified period of active foraging, usually five or ten minutes, and (ii) the 'foraging intensity', the proportion of the exposure period spent foraging by the average bird during daytime and night-time exposure periods. So if the average bird consumed 10 mussels per hour of active foraging and foraged for 50% of the 6 hours for which the mussel bed was exposed and so accessible, the average bird would consume 30 mussels per exposure period.

Measuring feeding rate

The first step was to measure the 'feeding rate' of an average oystercatcher on each of the main mussel beds of the estuary. Three other small beds were also included as they were very close to the shore especially convenient and comfortable to watch, particularly in bad weather. 'Actively foraging' means the bird was searching for a prey, picking it up and swallowing it and fighting over a food item or a feeding site with another bird. To measure this, the researcher would get as close to the mussel bed as possible without disturbing the birds, and then sit on a 'Sherman Boates' box. This was an open-sided wooden box with shoulder straps and a soft seat at one end and a flask of coffee inside! The researcher would then pick an individual bird and watch it for ten minutes. Birds were chosen by a procedure that prevented all the attention being focussed on a near bird that was easy to see. For example, if there were 200 birds on the bed and the exposure period was long enough to allow 20 of them to be watched for ten minutes, every twentieth bird from the extreme left or right of the mussel bed would be selected and watched. Sometimes a chosen bird was eating prey other than mussels, such as ragworms or clams. This too was recorded because it allowed the proportion of birds on each bed that were not consuming mussels to be estimated.

For obvious reasons, most of the research effort on feeding rate was made during the daylight hours. During innumerable five minute periods, all the following actions were recorded: the number of mussels taken, the time taken to deal with a mussel from the moment it had been found to the moment the last bit of flesh was swallowed (the 'handling time'); the means by which the bird broke into the mussel (*i.e.* whether by stabbing between the two shells of the mussel or by hammering a hole in the shell, on either the dorsal (uppermost) or ventral (underneath) side); the bird's age and, if ringed, its identity; any encounters between it and any other oystercatcher (whose identity was also noted if it was ringed). If a selected bird was not eating mussels but was taking worms or clams, this was noted (as was its age) but the observation was abandoned and the next bird across the bed selected.

Aspects of the 'foraging environment' were also recorded in case anything affected the rate of feeding on mussels and would have to be taken into account when calculating the numbers consumed. These were: the number of birds on the mussel bed; a rough measure made by eye of the proportion of the mussel bed that was exposed (so that bird numbers could be converted into densities, and thus the intensity of competition); the duration of the period over which the mussel bed was exposed (in case birds took mussels faster when the available foraging time was low); the time of day (in case birds increased or decreased their rate of feeding as night-time approached); the time elapsed since the mussel bed first exposed (in case birds slackened off their feeding rate as they accumulated more and more food); number of days elapsed since August 1st (the arbitrarily-chosen start of the non-breeding season, in case birds increased their rate of feeding in response to the gradually deteriorating feeding conditions); air temperature (in case birds increased their intake rate in cold weather because they needed more energy to keep warm) and mud temperature (in case the activity of the mussels varied with temperature in ways that affected the chances of being detected by stabbing birds).

The day after the birds had been watched, a sample of mussels that had been recently opened by oystercatchers was collected to establish the sizes of those taken. In fact, these data were never used apart from establishing the maximum and minimum lengths taken. This was because shell collections were too seriously biased in favour of the larger mussels. However thorough a search was conducted, the chance of finding a large mussel that had been opened by an oystercatcher was far higher than for a small one.

Some 15-30 such 10-minute observations were obtained from all of the 15 mussels beds on a number of occasions with each bed being worked over a range of tides, seasons, years and weather conditions. The average feeding rate of mussel-eating oystercatchers on one bed on one day was the datum, giving a total of well over 10^4 pieces of data. These were then subjected to multiple regression, a nifty statistical procedure that helps to distinguish (although by no means infallibly) factors that may be correlated with feeding rate from those that are most unlikely to do so (Fig. 2.9).

The outcome of this analysis was that, out of the large number of variables that had been measured, feeding rate seemed only to be correlated with the following four: (i) average size of the mussels on the mussel bed – the feeding rate was lower where the mussels were large, presumably because large ones took so much longer to open and swallow than small ones; (ii) the numbers of days elapsed since August – the feeding rate increased towards the end of the non-breeding season because, it subsequently transpired, the birds took small mussels then; (iii) the height of the tide – this was again related to the size of the mussels that the birds took because on Spring tides the larger mussels that occur at the lower levels of the shore are accessible for longer than on Neap tides (as will be discussed in the next chapter); and (iv) feeding rate was lower where the mussels had thick shells – presumably because it just took longer for hammering birds to break into them.

All of the factors that affected the feeding rate were related to the size of the mussels that were being consumed. Small mussels can be opened and consumed much more quickly than large ones, thus leaving more time to find the next one, thus enabling feeding rate to be higher than where mussels are large. The large mussels breed at the end of the birds' non-breeding season and in doing so use up most of their energy. It is not unusual for an oystercatcher to take 5 minutes to open a large mussel and extract all the flesh from it, whereas it usually takes far less than half a minute to open a really small one! The choices oystercatchers make between large mussels that take a long time to deal with and – usually – contain a lot of flesh and small mussels that can be eaten rapidly but contain much less flesh is discussed further in Chapter 3.

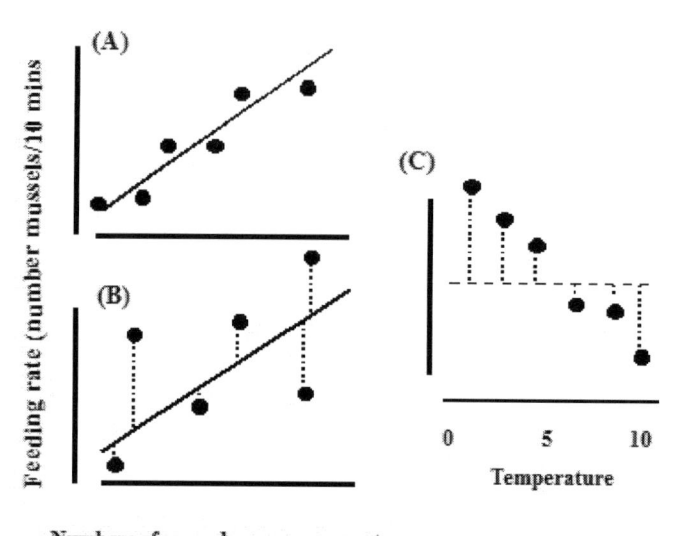

Figure 2.9 *How multivariate statistics can calculate the correlation between a 'dependent variable' – in this example, the numbers of mussels consumed over a ten minute period by an oystercatcher (the 'feeding rate') – and two 'independent' or 'determining variables'. In **(A)**, only the density of mussels affects the feeding rate, and it does so very 'tightly' – i.e. there is very little unexplained scatter in the points around the average trend line. Because the relationship is so tight, the trend line enables the feeding rate of oystercatchers to be predicted by interpolation with great confidence at a particular density of mussels without actually measuring it. In **(B)**, however, there is a great deal of scatter in the data because an additional variable – the temperature – as well as mussel density also affects the feeding rate. Consider the high point second from the extreme left: The density of mussels is very low so that, were that the only factor to affect feeding rate, the observed rate would be very low. But, in fact, it is very high, the reason being that, when that data point was obtained, it was very cold and feeding rate is increased at low temperatures. The dotted lines attached to each point show the gap – or 'deviation - between the actual data point and the trend line fitted between feeding rate and just mussel density on its own. In **(C)**, the deviations of each point away from the trend line is plotted against the temperature, with the dashed line representing the trend line with mussel density that has been held constant or 'levelled out'.*

There was no indication at all that any of the rest of the factors that had been explored had any effect on feeding rate. There was no evidence at all that the density of birds on the mussel bed affected the average feeding rate. It had been expected that, as the density of birds increased, the feeding rate would have gone down because of the intensifying competition. But the data suggested that this was not so, and it was a disappointing result. We now understand why this 'non-result' was obtained, as will be discussed in the final chapter.

Foraging intensity

The data required to measure foraging intensity during the day were obtained as the measurements of feeding rate were being made. At regular intervals (say every 30 or 60 minutes), all the birds on the mussel bed were counted by scanning the bed through a telescope. As each bird came into view within the 'scope, whether it was actively foraging or not was noted mentally, and added to the current score which could be, for example, '127 22' – 127 feeding, 22 not feeding'. At the end of the exposure period, up to a dozen or so such measurements would have been acquired, and foraging intensity calculated.

The following is an hypothetical sequence of regular counts from a patch on which birds gradually arrived and then left as the exposure period unrolled: *Count 1* - 9 birds foraging (f), 1 not foraging (nf); *Count 2* – 40f, 2nf; *Count 3* - 90f, 18nf; *Count 4* - 18f, 2nf; *Count 5* - 3f, 7nf. Over the whole exposure period, there were (9+40+90+18+3) foraging when counted and (1+2+18+2+7) not foraging; *i.e.* 160f, 30nf. Of the 190 birds counted (160+30), 84.2% ((160/190)x100) were foraging. From this it could be implied that the average bird fed for 84.2% of the time that it was on this mussel bed.

It would have been impossible to obtain as much data at night from mussel-eating oystercatchers as were obtained during the day: even researchers have to sleep sometime! Instead, a number of 'spot' comparisons were made between the foraging intensity and feeding rates of birds at night and those of birds feeding in the same place at the same stage of the exposure period on an adjacent night (Box 2.7). There were some differences but these were not generally large enough to prevent the convenient assumption being made that the birds' activities were similar night and day.

The outcome

After a few years, an attempt could be made to combine the findings on foraging and bird density into a model that could be used to predict how many mussels would be taken by oystercatchers from a mussel bed and from all the main mussel beds combined during a single non-breeding season. Basically, a model of the kind envisaged is a quantified generalisation. In response to the question: 'How many mussels would 2322 oystercatchers consume over the 200 days of the non-breeding season if the mussels on the mussel bed had an average size of X*mm*?'

But this 'systems analysis' approach turned out not to be a profitable way to proceed. The reason for this was that it proved impossible to predict the densities of birds on the mussel beds with much confidence. Although the analysis of the results themselves had produced very clear conclusions, the equations derived from them failed accurately to predict the numbers of birds recorded on each of the mussel beds in subsequent years. A model using equations based on the first three seasons of work, for example, would not predict with much accuracy the densities of birds on the different mussel beds in the fourth. If the model failed to predict the current distribution of birds, it certainly could not be relied upon to predict the distribution of birds if their feeding environment was changed, for example, by the removal of a couple of beds through over-fishing or excessive disturbance. And if the numbers of birds on each bed could not be predicted with confidence, it would be impossible to calculate accurately their impact on the abundance of mussels. Confidence in this approach waned and waned, and it was eventually abandoned!

MOVING ON

Other events were pushing in the same direction too. The study on mussel population dynamics was beginning to show that by far the most important density dependence occurred during the first year, and to a lesser extent, the second year of the mussels' life, well before they were large enough to be eaten by oystercatchers (Box 2.8). The data suggested that, beyond two years of age, mussels gradually disappeared at a rather low rate. Back-of-the-envelope calculations suggested that oystercatchers took less than 30% over non-breeding season of the mussels in their most preferred size range, even on the mussel beds where the birds were most numerous. The mortality rate they inflicted on the largest adults on other mussel beds and on the more numerous smaller adults on all the mussel beds was much lower. Overall, they consumed only about 10% of adult mussels. This was tiny compared with losses to which the younger mussels were subjected.

Furthermore, because each adult mussel produces vast numbers of young mussels, and since there always seemed to be a vastly greater number of spat available to settle than there was space for them to do so, it became obvious that oystercatchers would have no meaningful impact on the recruitment of young mussels to the population. As the mortality rate oystercatchers inflicted on adult mussels was rather low, and as their impact on mussel recruitment was trivial, pursuing a major project on their role in the population dynamics of this prey seemed futile. The scientific goal of modelling the predator-prey interaction between oystercatchers and mussels was duly abandoned.

Blind alleys occur in research, of course, as elsewhere. But fortunately for the ever-entertaining task of managing the expectations of one's line-managers, the time certainly had not been spent fruitlessly! Apart from the valuable discovery that oystercatchers did not play a dominant role in the population dynamics of the mussels, much was learned about the foraging biology of the birds that was subsequently of great value. Of particular importance was the strong suggestion from the work on the distribution of birds over the mussel beds that competition might be occurring. Where there is competition, there might be density-dependent mortality. If confirmed, this would be of great significance not only for understanding the population dynamics of the birds but also, as Chapter 1 argued, for predicting the effect on the birds of man-induced changes in their food supply.

Fortunately for the continued funding of the project, being able reliably to predict how bird numbers would be affected by habitat loss, shellfishing, disturbance and so forth were becoming by then much more of an issue with estuary managers than whether oystercatchers were a serious pest of shellfisheries. The main objective of the research was therefore reversed from predicting the impact of oystercatchers on the shellfish to predicting the impact of changes in the shellfish population on the birds. Flexibility is the key to survival in research, as in other areas of life! But admittedly, it was fortunate that the project had been set up in the first place to explore the reciprocal interactions between a population of a predator and that of its prey. It meant the project could be pointed in either direction and so follow the latest fashion in funding! It was also fortunate for the team's publication rate, and therefore support, that the estuary proved to be so amenable for answering fundamental questions about the behaviour and ecology of oystercatchers and of their prey, as the many references below indicate.

REFERENCES FOR CHAPTER 2

Boates, J.S. & Goss-Custard, J.D. (1989). Foraging behaviour of oystercatchers, *Haematopus ostralegus*, during a diet switch from worms *Nereis diversicolor* to clams *Scrobicularia plana*. *Canadian Journal of Zoology*, **67**, 2225-2231.

Boates, J.S. & Goss-Custard, J.D. (1992). Foraging behaviour of oystercatchers *Haematopus ostralegus* specialising on different species of prey. *Canadian Journal of Zoology*, 70, 2398-2404.

Durell, S.E.A. & Goss-Custard, J.D. (1996). Oystercatcher *Haematopus ostralegus* sex ratios on the wintering grounds: the case of the Exe estuary. *Ardea*, **84**, 373-382.

Durell, S.E.A., Goss-Custard, J.D. & Perez-Hurtado, A. (1996). The efficiency of juvenile oystercatchers feeding on ragworms *Nereis diversicolor*. *Ardea*, **84**, 153-158.

Goater, C.P., Goss-Custard, J.D. & Kennedy, C.R. (1995). Population biology of two species of helminth in Oystercatchers, *Haematopus ostralegus*. *Canadian Journal of Zoology*, 76, 296-300.

Goss-Custard, J.D. (1980). Competition for food and interference among waders. *Ardea*, **68**, 31-52.

Goss-Custard, J.D., Caldow, R.W.G. & Clarke, R.T. (1992). Correlates of the density of foraging oystercatchers, *Haematopus ostralegus*, at different population sizes. *Journal of Animal Ecology*, **61**, 159-173.

Goss-Custard, J.D. & Durell, S.E.A. Le V. dit (1983). Individual and age differences in the feeding ecology of oystercatchers, *Haematopus ostralegus*, wintering on the Exe. *Ibis*, **125**, 155-171.

Goss-Custard, J.D. & Durell, S.E.A. Le V. dit. (1984). Winter mortality of adult oystercatchers on the Exe estuary. *Wader Study Group Bulletin*, **40**, 37-38.

Goss-Custard, J.D., Durell, S.E.A. Le V. dit, McGrorty, S., Reading, C.J. & Clarke, R.T. (1981). Factors affecting the occupation of mussel (*Mytilus edulis*) beds by oystercatchers (*Haematopus ostralegus*) on the Exe estuary, Devon. *Feeding and Survival Strategies of Estuarine Organisms*. (Ed. by N.V.Jones & W.J. Wolff), pp. 217-229. London, Plenum Press.

Goss-Custard, J.D., Durell, S.E.A. le V. dit, McGrorty, S. & Reading, C.J. (1982). Use of mussel, *Mytilus edulis* beds by oystercatchers *Haematopus ostralegus* according to age and population size. *Journal of Animal Ecology*, **51**, 543-554.

Goss-Custard, J.D., Durell, S.E.A. Le V. dit, Sitters, H. & Swinfen, R. (1981). Mist-nets catch more juvenile oystercatchers than adults. *Wader Study Group Bulletin*, **32**, 13.

Goss-Custard, J.D., Durell, S.E.A. Le V. dit, Sitters, H.P. & Swinfen, R. (1982). Age-structure and survival of a wintering population of oystercatchers. *Bird Study*, **29**, 83-98.

Goss-Custard, J.D., McGrorty, S. & Durell, S.E.A. le V. dit. (1996). The effect of oystercatchers *Haematopus ostralegus* on shellfish populations. *Ardea*, **84**, 453-468.

McGrorty, S., Clarke, R.T., Reading, C.J. & Goss-Custard, J.D. (1990). Population dynamics of the mussel *Mytilus edulis*: density changes and regulation of the population in the Exe estuary, Devon. *Marine Ecology Progress Series*, **67**, 157-169.

McGrorty, S. & Goss-Custard, J.D. (1991). Population dynamics of the mussel *Mytilus edulis*: spatial variations in age-class densities of an intertidal estuarine population along environmental gradients. *Marine Ecology Progress Series*, **73**, 191-202.

McGrorty, S. & Goss-Custard, J.D. (1993). Population dynamics of the mussel *Mytilus edulis* along environmental gradients: spatial variations in density-dependent mortalities. *Journal of Animal Ecology*, **62**, 415-427.

McGrorty, S. & Goss-Custard, J.D. (1995). Population dynamics of *Mytilus edulis* along environmental gradients: density-dependent changes in adult mussel numbers. *Marine Ecology Progress Series*, **129**, 197-213.

McGrorty, S., Goss-Custard, J.D. & Clarke, R.T. (1993). Mussel *Mytilus edulis* dynamics in relation to environmental gradients and intraspecific interactions. *Netherlands Journal of Aquatic Ecology*, **27**, 163-171.

Nagarajan, R., Goss-Custard, J.D. & Lea, S.E.G. (2002). Oystercatchers use colour preference to achieve longer term optimality. *Proceedings Royal Society B*, **269**, 523-528.

Nagarajan, R., Lea, S.E.A. & Goss-Custard, J.D. (2002). Mussel valve discrimination and strategies used in valve discrimination by oystercatchers *Haematopus ostralegus*. *Functional Ecology*, **16**, 339-345.

Nagarajan, R., Lea, S.E.A. & Goss-Custard, J.D. (2002). Re-evaluation of mussel (*Mytilus edulis*) selection patterns by european oystercatchers (*Haematopus ostralegus*). *Canadian Journal of Zoology*, **80**, 846-853.

Nagarajan, R., Lea, S.E.G. & Goss-Custard, J.D. (2006). Seasonal variations in mussel, Mytilus edulis L. shell thickness and strength and their ecological implications. *Journal of Experimental Marine Biology and Ecology*, **339**, 241–250.

Nagarajan, R., Lea, S.E.G. & Goss-Custard, J. D. (2008). Relation between water quality and dorsal thickness of mussel (*Mytilus edulis*) and its ecological implications for wintering oystercatchers (*Haematopus ostralegus*). *Acta Zoologica Academiae Scientiarum Hungaricae*, **54** (Suppl. 1), 225–238.

Sitters, H.P. (2000). The role of night-feeding in shorebirds in an estuarine environment with specific reference to mussel-feeding oystercatchers. D.Phil. thesis, University of Oxford.

Box 2.1 Birds stealing food from other birds

You see this happening a lot amongst shorebirds on the intertidal flats of estuaries and in the fields roundabout when the prey being taken are of a reasonable size. If the prey are small and swallowed very rapidly, there is no opportunity for another bird to attack it and steal it. Shorebirds often fight over the larger worms, such as ragworms and lugworms. In fields, for example, a lapwing may find an earthworm and start pulling it out of the ground. It is seen by another lapwing nearby and this bird then runs across with the apparent intention of attacking the victim with its bill, encouraging its victim to let go of the worm which the attacker can then pick up. Often, it seems that the victim only needs to have found a promising feeding spot for it to be attacked, whereupon the attacker may take over the spot where the victim had been apparently just about to find a worm. Vigorous fights can ensue, and feathers can literally fly in the struggle. I have even seen one victorious oystercatcher standing on its hapless victim whose head was submerged in a puddle. No doubt it would have drowned had it not at last struggled free and taken flight. Sometimes the food item can be just grabbed by the attacker from the bill of its victim. On the Wash, I once saw a curlew in a gale trying to swallow a large worm which it normally does by throwing the worm up its bill. It couldn't do this in such a strong wind because the worm would have been blown away. The curlew stood there, a worm streaming from its bill tip, quite unable to find a solution. A redshank wandered by and, seeing the curlew's dilemma, grabbed hold of the free end of the wind-stretched and almost horizontal worm and gradually swallowed it! The much larger curlew was quite incapable of defending its prey without letting it go and so losing it anyway!

A lot of the bird noise you hear on estuaries is when birds fight each other, usually for a food item or a feeding spot, or to establish dominance. This continues at night too. Oystercatchers on mussel beds are particularly noisy. This is not birds chatting happily to each other to while away the hours, as a gentle ex-military friend of mine believed, until sadly I disillusioned him! The birds are fighting over a prey item or are establishing their dominance!

Box 2.2 Devon and Cornwall wader ringing group

The debt owed to this group of enthusiasts by the Exe oystercatcher project cannot be over-stated. On hearing in 1975 that this long-term project was going to happen, they at once started visiting the Exe, many of them travelling from Plymouth some 40-50 miles away, at their own expense, often immediately after a day's work. Then, the nets had to be carried out to the tip of Dawlish Warren where the birds roosted: a distance of about a mile. The heavy nets, bags to keep birds until they could be ringed and released, the canons, charges and everything had to be transported on foot, and it was exhausting. Then the nets had to be set up, and the wait began. Mist nets were used, and were particularly useful for catching juveniles (which were much in demand because their age was known precisely having been hatched the previous summer). But the numbers caught were small, and so canon nets were often used at dawn to catch large numbers of birds of all ages.

After a night in the open, often without much sleep and frequently cold, the team would take up position for the canon net firing. Often the birds did not land near the nets, and all the effort and time was to no effect. But sometimes they did and, once it was safe to fire, the nets were cannoned over the flock. Immediately the team ran out to extract the birds as quickly as possible to prevent them damaging themselves as they struggled under the net. They were put in hessian cages which kept them warm and quiet. One by one, the birds were extracted and their biometrics obtained (age, bill shape, wing length and so forth) and then ringed with a BTO numbered ring and an individual colour ring combination.

This went on for many years so that the sample of individually-marked birds was maintained at around 10% of the whole population despite 'natural wastage'. It was a prodigious and greatly appreciated effort without which the research programme that led eventually to the shorebird model would never have been possible.

Box 2.3 Colour ring scheme

Waders have the annoying habit of standing on one leg when roosting, the time when so many of the rings were read. The prospect of finding a bird with one leg visible that had a ring on it and then having to wait until it exposed the other leg was horrendous. The cumulative frustration for the observers could have been agony!

But a chance meeting with Chris Meade of the BTO led to this brilliant solution. He had devised a way in which the entire combination could be put on one leg, using a combination of small singe colour ring (either above or below the main ring), the 'sandwich' ring (Plate 2.1). This was a double layer with, for example, yellow over black. Either thick (3mm) or thin (1mm) bands could be cut through the yellow layer in three places, making rings that became known as 'wasps'. As the drawing illustrates, a sighting could be, for example: red ring over yellow wasp, with (from top to bottom) thin, thick, thick band engraved on it. As you could also have no band at all (giving a wasp that was recorded as 'blank, blank, blank' or 'thin, blank, thick', for example), there were 27 combinations of wasp with any one colour of sandwich: a sandwich could be red over black, or blue over black and so on. Since the small single colour ring could be either above or below the wasp and the whole combination could be on either the left or the right leg, there were 108 (27x4) combinations for a single colour of small ring and wasp. This provided a huge number of combinations given the range of colours available - and all on one leg! This was the biggest single innovation that allowed this project to measure the mortality rate over the non-breeding season for the first time in any shorebird species. It was of immense value also to the studies of competition on the mussel beds. I cannot recall how many times I thanked Chris for this idea, and I only stopped when he indicated that he was getting bored with my gratitude!

Box 2.4 Help of the public

When somebody returned a ring to the BTO, they were told that they had contributed to an experiment and also what the purpose of it had been. Most people seemed to accept this and to understand that they had made a useful contribution, even though the dead bird was a plant and not a genuine casualty! One or two people were offended, however, feeling that they had been 'duped'. One in particular was quite irate when he met one of the research team. 'I found seven of them, and I broke my penknife trying to get the rings of their legs!'. He was offered recompense but would not accept it.

This same person (nick-named MIF, for some reason) had had a 'history' with the research team, which no doubt influenced his attitude. During one non-breeding season, a Dutch colleague had spent many months in a hide in the middle of a mussel bed where MIF fished for bass on many, many occasions. As MIF walked across the mussel bed to his favourite location at its seawards tip, the oystercatchers flew away leaving the Dutch colleague with no birds to watch. Very frustrating and no amount of pleading would deter MIF from 'preventing an unlimited increase in the data base!', as was subsequently noted in the Acknowledgements of a scientific paper. So frustrated was the researcher, that one day he jumped out of the hide, waving his arms and expressing his frustration in loud and rapid Dutch! He was a big man too! MIF was understandably a little sensitive from then on!

Occasionally, the research raised suspicions amongst local people, which meant that some time was spent meeting locals in pubs and so forth (no hardship that!) and explaining what was going on in their estuary. A row of stakes were once put out on a mussel bed near Cockwood, and all had been removed by the next morning. The explanation of why the stakes had been put out was mentioned to someone in the pub and, from then on, all stakes were left alone. Similarly, the boat used for watching the birds in the middle of the estuary had one of its two moorings cut over the first night it was moored in the brook in Lympstone. A quite word with the friendly harbour master of the time stopped that from ever happening again. Over the years, members of the research team became very friendly with people living in the villages around the Exe, many of whom took a keen interest in the progress of the work. This was especially true of the villagers who collected winkles on the mussel beds, which provided a common interest.

Box 2.5 Measuring characteristics of mussel beds

Measuring algal cover was easy as it only required a pretty standard botanical sampling scheme. Using the same randomly assigned sample points as were used to measure mussel abundance, a 0.5x0.5m square made out of four bamboos was tossed out sideways, the researcher carefully closing his/her eyes to avoid selection bias, and the proportion of it covered by algae estimated by eye. The average of a number of such estimates gave an estimate of algal cover that proved adequate for the purpose.

The sloppiness of the substrate was also measured at a number of sites on each mussel bed. A metal rod was dropped vertically from a constant height and the depth to which it penetrated the ground measured by placing a ruler alongside the penetrating end. To avoid the observer giving the rod a biasing push downwards on occasions, the rod was just let drop through the emptied central socket of a vandalised telescope tripod.

Measuring the bumpiness of the bed required a little innovation. A bright orange ball attached to a string was pulled over the ground by one person who walked away in a randomly-chosen direction from another researcher who recorded the proportion of the time that the ball was visible at the height of an oystercatcher's eye. Rather than lie on the muddy ground to get an oystercatcher's eye view, a small mirror was attached to the end of a stick such that the middle of the mirror was at about the same height as an oystercatcher's eye. Adjusting the angle of the stick appropriately allowed the progress of the orange ball as it moved away over the mussel bed to be monitored quite easily. A weird way, some might say, to earn a living!

Box 2.6 The interest in the interactions between populations of predators and prey

An important question about the nature of predator-prey population interactions that was much researched during the 1970s was: 'Why don't predators usually exterminate their prey populations?' One approach to answering this question stressed the significance of spatial variation in the densities of both the predators and prey. While patches where prey are abundant may attract many predators and be exterminated, patches with few prey may either not attract any predators or not be found be them. In effect, these patches form 'prey refuges' which would allow the population of the prey to remain in existence, at least somewhere, because the predators are not able to seek out and find every single prey in every single patch occupied by the prey. They are just spatial equivalents of places where prey can hide, as do lugworms in their burrows. Of course, this aspect of some predator-prey interactions does not apply to mussels and oystercatchers since all the patches must be as obvious to the birds as they are to humans! Anyway, adult mussels have their own built-on refuges: their 'armoured' shells that are extremely difficult to break or to prise open!

Box 2.7 Working at night

At that time, night-viewing equipment was not well advanced and could be very expensive. In this project, a former night-sight (light intensifier) that had been used on tanks, and had been bought for the Wash project, was used. It was very bulky and very heavy and so was nick-named 'Twiggy'. It was difficult to work with and sometimes caused the tripod on which it was supported to unbalance, thus scaring all the birds away and necessitating another visit on another night. Its green illuminated image was reasonably clear but it was only possible to see an oystercatcher taking a mussel at about up to 50m or so. The birds had to be watched before they had wandered too far downshore.

The approach, therefore, was to sit at the upshore edge of a mussel bed that was right next to a good access point with solid ground, as are the mussel beds at Cockwood. Carrying such a heavy load, single-handed out onto a soft mudflat at night would have been too punishing. It was necessary to arrive before the receding tide had exposed the mussels and to sit behind a wind-break, like the ones used on beaches in summer, which acted as a hide. From then on, keeping still and quiet was vital. Oystercatchers are understandably wary at night of nearby and unfamiliar, bulky objects, especially if they move. Waiting was sometimes a bit creepy; with nothing external to focus on, it was all too easy for the imagination to work creatively and for all sorts of irrational thoughts to bubble up into the conscious mind! But oystercatchers would eventually land nearby and the serious, and distracting, business of recording their behaviour began. Perhaps up to 5-10 five minute observation periods could be obtained before the birds had moved too far down the mussel bed to see clearly. All that remained was to lumber Twiggy back to the car and go to the pub.

The next day, the same procedure in the same place was repeated but, of course, in daylight. If seven data points had been obtained the night before, the same number would be obtained in the same place and at the identical stage of the exposure period. And that was it. The observer was then free for the rest of the exposure period to get on with something else.

Box 2.8 Importance of density-dependent processes for understanding animal populations

At that time, there was a growing awareness that density dependence, and the processes that bring it about, were of great importance for understanding the properties of populations of single species and of interacting species, such as those of predators and their prey. Much space in the literature was devoted to the 'dynamical behaviour' of single and interacting populations of animals, perhaps particularly (although by no means exclusively) of insects. One prominent insect population ecologist even remarked that ecology could be viewed as the study of density-dependent processes. 'Dynamical behaviour' referred to a number of properties of animal populations, a minimal list including: average population size over a number of generations; the amplitude, frequency and regularity of the variation around the long-term average; the rapidity with which a population re-bounds back to more its usual size after a temporary knock-back caused by some environmental event, and the magnitude and persistence of any over-shoot, and the persistence of populations which could, in principle, be consumed to extinction by their predators.

CHAPTER 3:
Rate of food intake by oystercatchers on the mussel beds and density dependence

...which describes the in-depth research on the foraging behaviour of mussel-eating oystercatchers and details how it came to be realised that research on individual birds could be used to test whether the mortality rate of oystercatchers depended on their density on the mussel beds.

INTAKE RATE AND OPTIMAL FORAGING

It was fundamental to achieving the aims of the project to find a way to predict how a change in the food supply of mussel-feeding oystercatchers caused by human activities would affect the rate at which the birds could feed, and therefore their chances of obtaining their food requirements. A model was needed that could predict the intake rate of an average oystercatcher from the food supply where it was feeding, wherever and whenever that was. The model would need to predict the numbers of mussels swallowed per unit time by an oystercatcher, their sizes and thus energy content, and thereby its intake rate. This work took a long time but it was essential to achieving the overall objective.

The research interests of many researchers into animal behaviour at that time were very appropriate to this goal. During the 1960s, the new discipline of 'Behavioural Ecology' expanded enormously. The reason was that the introduction of mathematical thinking into theories on how animals behave had opened the way for a flood of theoretical models on an increasing range of issues. At the front of this trend in behavioural ecology was the then called 'optimal foraging theory'. The name was later changed to 'foraging theory' to avoid endless discussions as to whether animal behaviour could in any sense be thought of as being 'optimal'.

The starting point of this theory was that an animal would be expected to maximise the rate at which it obtains its requirements of energy and other nutrients. The idea was that, the more quickly it did this, the more time if could devote to other activities that affect its chances of surviving and of producing healthy young, such as defending a territory. Early theory therefore assumed that animals would choose where to feed, when to feed (night or day, for example) and on what to feed (food species and their size) so as to maximise their rate of food intake. In carnivorous birds, such as most wading birds, the intake rate was usually defined as the amount of energy ingested per second, per minute, per five minutes or per ten minutes (according to circumstances). Energy was therefore taken to be the 'currency' of intake rate. The assumption was that all the nutrients a bird needed would be incorporated in the flesh of the prey and that there was no need to select a prey species because it had a high concentration of a particular nutrient. Indeed, as the 'density of energy' – the amount of energy per gram of flesh - is rather similar in most of their prey species, intake rate is usually measured as the rate at which digestible flesh is consumed. The unit of measurement is 'ash-free dry mass', a measure that excludes both indigestible inorganic matter (such as sand grains and bits of skeleton) and water that have no energy value.

Having to identify a theoretical maximum rate, of course, lent itself to mathematical modelling and much of this kind of theoretical work was done. This caused some non-mathematical behaviourists at the time to feel rather excluded, but that quickly changed when the simplicity of the underlying ideas became clear.

Imagine a bird – a redshank, perhaps, or even a great tit – foraging through their respective environments where they are faced by regular choices as to whether or not they should stop and consume a prey item that they have come across. To maximise its overall rate of intake over the foraging period, a bird should stop and pick up and swallow some prey items (in the jargon, 'handle' them) but not others. Optimality theory showed that the bird should always take a prey item that had a high energy content (E) relative to the amount of time it takes to handle it (h). The ratio E/h was called the 'profitability' of the prey, a term that gave a nod in the direction of economics. Unsurprisingly, the theory showed that the birds should always prefer, and always take, prey with high profitability over a prey with a low profitability.

The theory also showed that whether the bird should take the less profitable prey depended on the abundance of the more profitable ones. When the profitable prey are abundant, the bird encounters a second one very quickly after finishing the first. Stopping to take an unprofitable prey it encounters as it moves from the first to the second profitable prey would just slow down its rate of encounter with profitable prey and reduce its overall intake rate. It is just not worth spending time on capturing the less profitable prey. A bird should eat the less profitable prey only when the more profitable prey is scarce. Otherwise, its intake rate would be very low because of the amount of time it takes to get from one profitable prey to the next. The theory also showed that a bird should then take all of the less profitable prey it encountered, and not just some of them. Once it was worth eating the less profitable prey, the bird should take all of them that it encounters.

This simple idea is illustrated with a notional example in Figure 3.1. The models predicted when an animal should stop and pick a prey of a given profitability and when they should ignore it. A large number of tests of this idea were carried out on birds in the late 1970s and 1980s, in both the laboratory and in the field, and the results generally supported the idea.

Much time and effort was spent by the Exe research team in developing and testing an optimality foraging model for oystercatchers. The model predicted the numbers of mussels swallowed per unit time by an oystercatcher, their sizes and thus energy content, and thereby its intake rate. It could therefore predict how any change in the abundance, size and flesh content of mussels brought about by some change in the environment – such as shellfishing – would affect the rate at which the birds could feed.

COMPETITION AND INTERFERENCE

The survey of feeding rates had shown that oystercatchers regularly contest for mussels and that they lived in a very competitive world. It seemed very likely that an additional factor could also have a big impact on the rate at which oystercatchers consumed mussels, and this was competition between them.

The previous chapter provided some evidence that competition may have been driving the distribution of the birds over the mussel beds as the adults returned from the breeding grounds. This implied that something must happen on the most preferred beds as bird density increased that made the bed decreasingly attractive to many birds. One possibility was that some birds occupied feeding territories and drove others away. But this explanation was quickly rejected: it was easy to see that oystercatchers did not defend territories on the mussel beds, as some wading birds do.

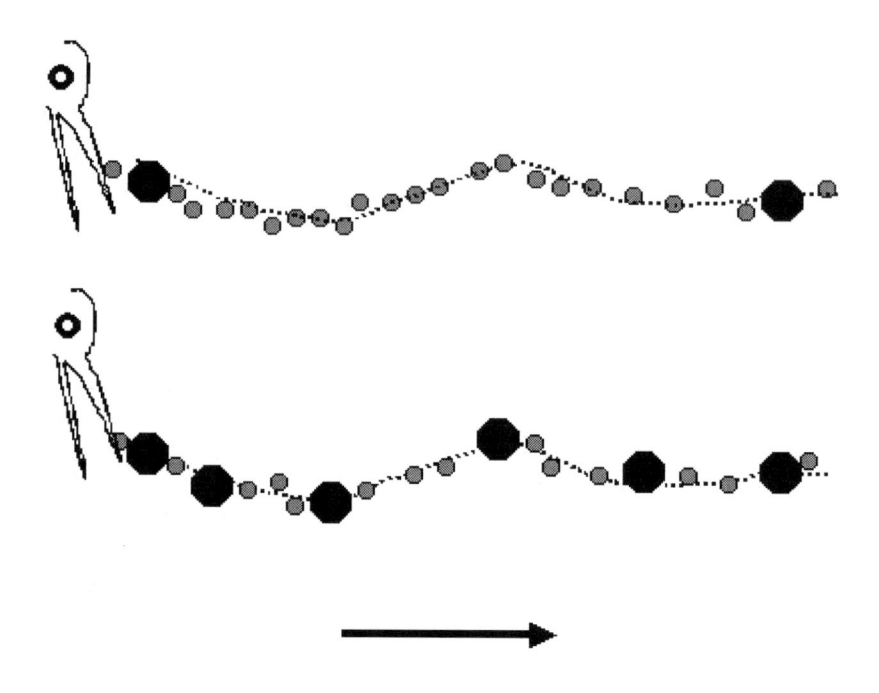

Figure 3.1 The idea underlying optimal foraging theory. The large black dots represent very large prey with a lot of flesh that can be caught and swallowed quickly and so have a very high profitability. The grey dots are very small prey, with therefore little flesh, that take quite a long time to capture and swallow, and so have a very low profitability. The top row represents a case in which large prey are very scarce and small prey are very numerous. In order to maximise its intake rate (the amount of flesh or energy consumed per minute of foraging), the bird should always take every large prey it encounters. But as these prey are so scarce, it should also take every small prey that it encounters between large prey, even though they are not very profitable. This is because it takes so long for the bird to travel from the first to the second large prey that the overall rate of food intake it would achieve by taking just large prey would be very low while taking the small prey elevates its overall intake rate. In the lower example, the large prey are very numerous. Now it pays the bird to ignore the small prey because to take them would slow its rate of progress down so much that its overall rate of food intake would be reduced because, at every stop, it would spend a lot of time in acquiring only a small reward.

On the other hand, the studies on feeding rate had demonstrated that oystercatchers fought over food items very frequently. A bird that was opening a mussel was often attacked by another bird. The 'victim' then either carried the mussel a long way off to avoid the attacker or abandoned it to the attacker. Only occasionally did the victim stand its ground and defend its mussel. Most successful attacks were launched over a distance of a few meters. Accordingly, it seemed likely that more attacks would take place when the density of oystercatchers on a mussel bed was high than when it was low. Subdominant birds on the preferred mussel beds might therefore be subjected to an increasing number of attacks as the adults returned from the breeding grounds.

Why do oystercatchers attack each other for mussels when, very often, they are walking over huge numbers of mussels lying just beneath their feet, as Plate 3.1 illustrates? The reason is the same as for the godwit eating lugworms. At any one moment as an oystercatcher walks over them, the vast majority of mussels are inaccessible. Mussels, of course, are protected from predators – such as oystercatchers – by two thick shells that remain firmly closed when the mussel is exposed to the open air when the tide is out. An oystercatcher must find the occasional mussel whose armoured defences are weakened for some reason. When it does, it forces the two shells apart if it is a 'stabbing' bird or smashes a hole through the shell if it is a 'hammerer'. Having broken through the mussel's main defence, the oystercatcher then severs the immensely strong muscle that normally holds the two shells tightly clamped together. The fleshy body of the mussel is then pulled out and swallowed.

Plate 3.1 The density of mussels can be very high, as here on the mussel bed that was most preferred by oystercatchers on the Exe estuary. Note at the bottom right the empty shell that had been opened by an oystercatcher that hammered mussels on their ventral side.

What makes a mussel vulnerable to attack by oystercatchers differs according to the technique used by the bird to get into the mussel. When mussels are under water – perhaps at the tide edge or in a pool on the otherwise dry mussel bed — the two shells may gape open slightly to allow the mussels to feed and/or "breathe". Accordingly, a quick stab into the cavity between the shells allows a bird to reach the flesh inside. But when the mussel is high and dry, its two shells are mostly closed tightly together to avoid dessication. Now the bird often has to prise its bill between the two shells at some point where it can get enough purchase to do so, vigorously twisting its head from side to side as it gradually overpowers and then severs the muscle inside.

About 40% of the mussel-eating oystercatchers on the Exe opened mussels by prising and/or stabbing. Most of them are females or young birds which generally have rather slender bills (Box 3.1). The remainder — predominantly the stout-billed males — hammer a hole through one of the shells. Some attack the uppermost, dorsal side and search for mussels whose shell on that side has, for one reason or another, become thinner than the average and so can be smashed most easily. Others tear the mussel off the mussel bed, shredding in the process the byssus threads (the 'beard' to shellfish gastronomes) with which it meshes itself to other mussels, stones *etc.* that form the structure of the mussel bed. Carrying either the whole mussel in the grip of its bill or dangling it from the byssus threads, the bird finds a nearby firm place on which it can hammer at the flattish ventral surface of the mussel until the shell cracks open and the bird can get at the flesh.

Typically, stabbing/prising oystercatchers take a minute or two to 'handle' a mussel from the time the mussel is found until the last bit of flesh is ripped out and swallowed. Hammering birds take quite a lot longer, from two to five minutes. Sometimes hammering birds give up trying to break into a mussel because the shell is too strong. It can take an oystercatcher a long time to find a mussel that is vulnerable to its particular method of opening — from just a few minutes to ten or more. Accordingly, once a vulnerable mussel has been found, it becomes a 'prize' for any other oystercatchers, herring gulls and carrion crows in the vicinity. Stealing a mussel that has been found by another bird enables the attacker to increase its intake rate because it avoids the long search to find the occasional vulnerable one. Even if the victim keeps the next mussel it finds, its intake rate is decreased because, in effect, it had to search twice for one mussel.

Interference functions

The preliminary observations on the birds' feeding rate had showed that attacks between oystercatchers for mussels were very frequent and also widespread across all the mussel beds of the estuary. It was also noticeable that attacks were particularly frequent at the beginning and end of the exposure period when only part of the mussel bed was exposed and the density of foraging oystercatchers was high. It seemed highly likely that competition between oystercatchers for mussels would cause the intake rate of some or all of the birds to decrease when the density of birds on a mussel bed was high. It was decided that the question to be answered was this: 'Does the intake rate of some or all oystercatchers decrease as the density of foraging birds on a mussel bed increases?. Or to re-phrase the question using a useful term taken from insect population theorists, 'Does interference competition occur in oystercatchers feeding on mussels?'

This idea is illustrated in Figure 3.2. This shows a hypothetical relationship between the intake rate of an oystercatcher and the density (numbers per hectare) of other oystercatchers in its vicinity. When the density of 'competitors' is low, birds have the space in which to avoid other birds that might attack them if they were closer. Aggressive interactions are uncommon and all the birds can feed at their own basic rate determined by their competence at finding and opening vulnerable mussels. But at some point as density rises, it becomes impossible for birds to avoid each other. Increasingly, birds will find that there is another oystercatcher nearby when it finds a mussel, and often that bird will be close enough to launch a successful attack. A threshold density has been passed above which stealing mussels becomes increasingly frequent. This is why the line in Figure 3.2 is a 'broken stick'. This relationship will be referred to as an 'interference function'; that is, the intake rate is a function of the density of competitors in the vicinity (within about 25m) of the subject bird.

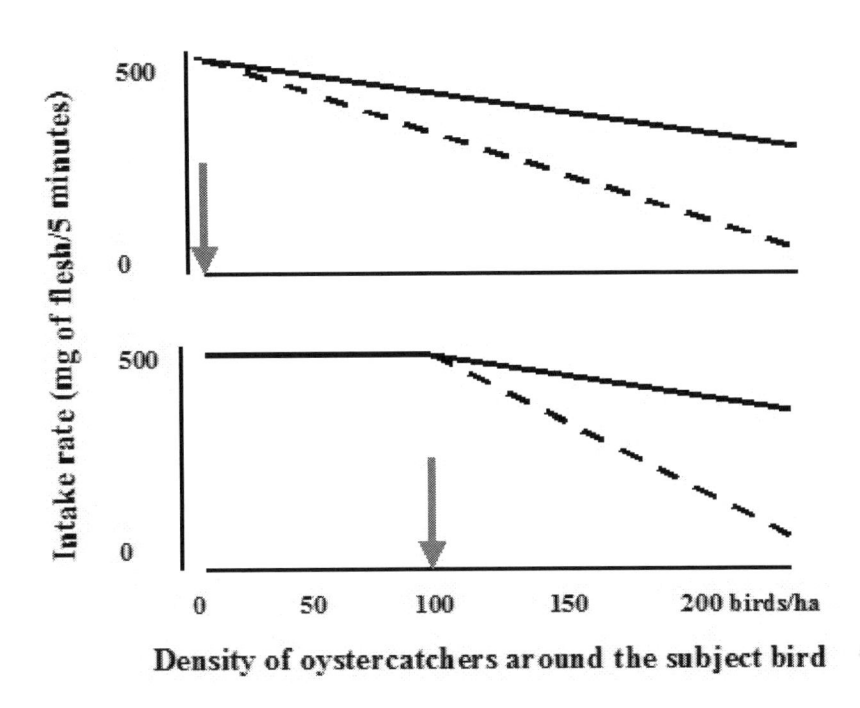

Figure 3.2 Some hypothetical interference functions. In the top one, interference begins at very low densities of competitors whereas in the lower graph, it only begins once the density of competitors exceeds the threshold of 100 birds/ha. In both cases, the bird represented by the dashed line is more susceptible to interference than the one represented by the solid line because, for a given increase in the density of competitors, its intake rate goes down by much more. The vertical grey arrow shows the critical density at which interference competition starts to reduce intake rate.

It was realised early that, if interference did occur amongst mussel-feeding oystercatchers, it would be very important to measure its strength and not just be able to show that it occurs. 'To measure' means two things in this case. First, it was necessary to find out whether the critical 'threshold' density at which intake rate starts to go down occurs at bird densities of 1/ha or 10/ha or 100/ha or 1000/ha and so on (Fig. 3.2). Establishing this was of critical importance. Imagine (improbably) that the critical density proved to be 1000 birds/ha! Interference would probably seldom have occurred on the Exe because, even if all 2000 oystercatchers fed on a single mussel bed, their density would still have been far short of 1000/ha. But if the critical threshold proved to be, say, 1 bird/ha, oystercatchers would be subjected to interference most of the time because, typically, densities ranged from 15 to 250 birds per hectare.

Second, it was necessary to determine whether, above the critical density, intake rate fell steeply or at a very gradual and gentle rate: that is, it was necessary to measure the 'slope'. By definition, a steep slope would mean that the intake rate of the birds would be depressed far more when the density of competitors was high than it would if the slope was shallow (Fig. 3.2)! The work did not only need to answer the question 'Is there interference' but also had to determine the densities at which intake started to go down and the rate at which it did so. It was not just a question of answering 'whether' something occurred but 'by how much' (Box 3.2).

The procedure for recording the foraging behaviour of a bird in a square was the same as described in Chapter 2. Over five daytime exposure periods, each of five to six hours duration, about 100 records of feeding rate and the density of other foraging competitor oystercatchers in the square in which the subject bird was feeding were obtained. They were collected over all parts of the mussel bed that were close enough to allow the feeding rate to be measured. This was roughly within 150-200m of the seawall, depending on the local topography, lighting conditions, rainfall etc. (Box 3.3). Data were collected throughout the exposure period during which time the density of birds varied considerably.

The relationship between feeding rate and bird density was then plotted on a graph. The result was deeply disappointing! Instead of feeding rate ***decreasing*** as the density of birds around the subject bird increased, feeding rate actually ***increased***! Contrary to confident expectation, these birds took more mussels per 10 minutes of foraging when bird density was high than when it was low!

Eventually, an idea occurred as to why this might be so (Fig. 3.3). It was noticed that, at the start and end of the exposure period, it took a bird much less time to open and take the flesh from a mussel than over the central part of the exposure period. Although the sizes of mussels taken could not be measured by eye at the distances at which the birds were being observed, this probably meant that the birds were eating much smaller mussels at the beginning and end of the exposure period than during the middle.

This could easily be understood. Mussels low down the shore are covered by the tide for much longer than are mussels higher up, and so can feed for longer over every high water period. This enables them to grow to much larger sizes than those higher up the shore that are covered by the tide for only a short time over high water. The mussel bed sloped down the shore and in many places there were hills and valleys, with sometimes as much as a meter between valley bottom and hill crest, as illustrated in Figure 3.3. Therefore, at the beginning and end of the exposure period, the only mussels the birds could take were small ones whereas, in the middle, they could feed on much larger ones in the valleys and at the lower levels of the shore.

At low tide, of course, the entire mussel bed was exposed whereas, at the beginning and end of the exposure period, a much smaller area was accessible. Therefore, at the beginning and end of the exposure period, the birds took small mussels because that is all that there was available to them. They had quite high feeding rates then because small mussels can be opened and consumed more quickly than large ones. And they were taking small mussels at a time when the density of birds was high because only a small area of the mussel bed was accessible. In other words, at the time when bird density was high, the birds could only take small mussels and therefore had a high feeding rate. In terms of scientific jargon, mussel size and bird density were 'confounded'.

The best way to disentangle the influence of confounding variables is to conduct an experiment, of course. Sadly, though, this was just not possible (Box 3.4). But statistics enabled the effect of these two factors to be separated. Luckily, there were occasions, contrary to the overall trend, when bird density was low at the beginning or end of the exposure period and high over low tide. Statistically, this provided enough variation to attempt to distinguish between the separate effects on feeding rate of the sizes of the mussels that were available to the birds and of bird density. This completely reversed the trend of feeding rate against bird density. With the influence of prey size taken into account ('partialled out', in the jargon), feeding rate did after all decrease as bird density increased. Unfortunately, the original data were lost during one of the series of computer upgrades so they cannot be shown here.

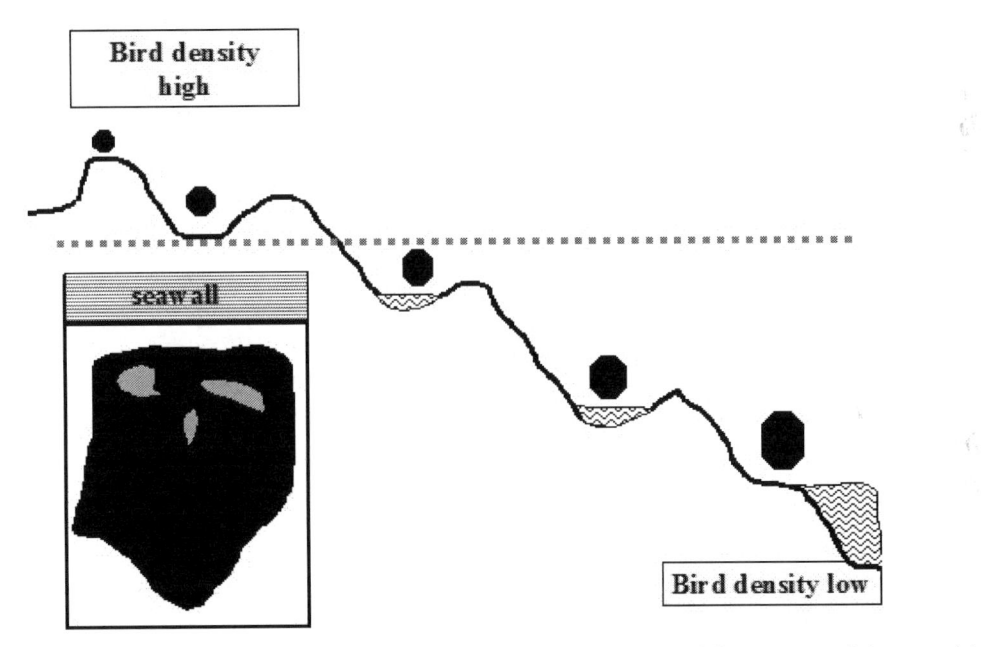

Figure 3.3 *The mussel food supply of oystercatchers down the length of a mussel bed. The top part of the mussel bed exposes first as the tide recedes and here the mussels are small and contain relatively little flesh and so can be rapidly 'handled' by oystercatchers. The number of mussels they take per 10 minutes (their 'feeding rate') is therefore relatively high because the birds are eating small prey, each of which can be opened quickly, rather than large ones that take a long time to deal with. But as only a small area is exposed at this point (shown in grey at the top of the black mussel bed in the inset), and because many hungry birds arrive quickly from the roost, the density of birds is also high. The mussels at the bottom of the shore, however, are large and contain much flesh, and it takes much longer for an oystercatcher to handle one. Their feeding rate is therefore relatively low. As a very large area of the mussel bed is now exposed, the density of birds is also low because they can spread out and avoid each other.*

No matter because, in any case, these results were by no means a conclusive test of the idea that interference occurred amongst the mussel-feeders of the Exe. Apart from the usual possibility that the correlation had arisen by chance, there may have been some unknown third factor that was correlated with bird density. It could have been this factor, rather than bird density *per se*, that was actually the real cause of the reduced feeding rate at high bird densities. Clearly, further and more convincing tests were required.

Interference competition in individual birds

Nonetheless, this preliminary finding was encouraging. The observations had been made mainly on un-marked birds so the interference function was for an average bird. A chance meeting with a Dutch colleague, Rudi Drent, stimulated the next step and was the start of a research programme on competition that lasted more than 10 years!

His insight was this: If the decrease in feeding rate was due to interference competition, the severity of the decrease might be expected to vary between individuals of different dominance. A dominant individual might be expected to attack other birds frequently because they are likely to win and steal a mussel. If so, they might even benefit as bird density increases because there would be more potential victims nearby for them to attack at high densities than at low. Dominant birds might not be affected by interference at all and, indeed, their feeding rate might even increase as bird density increased and more victims became within reach of them.

The reverse would be the case for sub-dominant individuals, however. As bird density increased, it would become increasingly difficult for them to avoid being close to a more dominant individual that could steal a mussel from them. Their feeding rate would be expected to decrease as bird density increased because they would be attacked more and lose more of the mussels they had found. Such individuals would be expected to be particularly susceptible to interference.

The idea was that focussing on how different individuals might be affected by interference could help to control for the possibility that a third, unknown factor was actually responsible for the apparent interference detected by the preliminary work. If there was such an unknown confounding factor, surely it would act on all individuals and not just on the sub-dominants? If so, all individuals would show interference. But if the decrease in feeding rate was due to interference competition, the interference would be expected to be much stronger in the sub-dominant individuals than in the dominants, where no interference might occur at all.

How to test this idea? As Box 3.5 explains, it could not be done experimentally in the field. Nor were there laboratory facilities available on the scale required. Clearly, to explore the idea in the field, a mussel bed with many marked individuals was required. Luckily, it was already known that many individuals fed on the Cockwood mussel bed day after day, and, if undisturbed by people, they occurred in approximately the same part of the mussel bed over low water. Furthermore, the individuals varied enormously in aggressiveness and social dominance. Some individuals regularly attacked other nearby oystercatchers and frequently stole mussels from their victim. Such highly aggressive birds seldom if ever lost an aggressive encounter: they had a success rate or 'dominance score' of 100% or so. Other individuals never attacked another bird and only took part in encounters when they were attacked by other birds and almost always lost: they had a dominance score of 0%, or thereabouts. Most individuals lay between these two extremes, winning some encounters but losing others. In fact, the individuals on a mussel bed could be ordered into a strict sequence according to both the frequency with which they initiated aggressive encounters – or were the victims of an attack - and in their chances of success (Fig. 3.4).

The difficulty of working from the seawall had been that its bumpy terrain made it difficult to see a colour ring and to see precisely what a bird was doing. When a bird was in a valley, for example, you might just be able to see the top of its bobbing head as it dealt with mussel but it was often impossible to measure the mussel or even to see if the flesh had been swallowed. The observer needed to be much higher up and preferably in the middle of the mussel bed. That way, he or she could look down on the oystercatchers and be able to see what they were doing most of the time.

Dutch colleagues came to the rescue! For some years, wader researchers had been building hides on towers far out on the mudflats of the Wadden Sea. In most places, the birds were far too far out from the seawall to be watched from there. Observers reached the towers by boat or on foot. Dutch colleagues came up with the great idea of building on the Exe a temporary scaffolding tower hide in the middle of a mussel bed. An undergraduate student from the University of Groningen, Bruno Ens, came over to give it a try. It was his pioneering work, under the direction of our mutual friend Rudi Drent, that provided one of the essential steps that led to the eventual development of the shorebird model (Box 3.6).

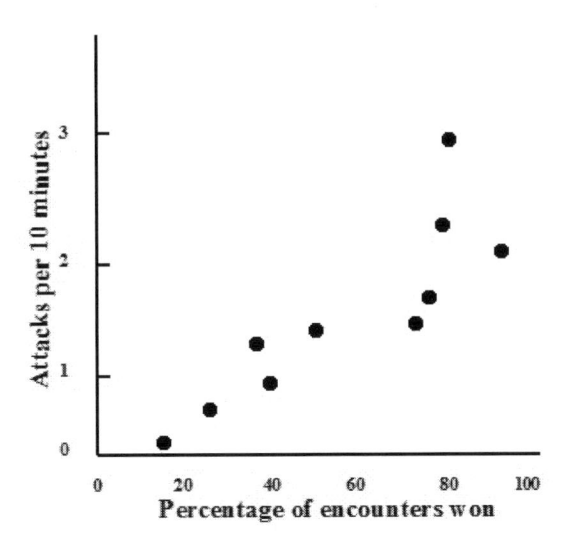

Figure 3.4 *Dominant oystercatchers feeding on mussels attack other nearby oystercatchers more than do subdominant individuals. The top dominant bird on this particular mussel bed attacked another, on average, about three times every ten minutes. It almost invariably won the encounter with the victim running or flying away, often abandoning the mussel it was opening. In contrast, the least aggressive individual almost never attacked another bird. If it did so, it almost invariably lost the encounter. It also almost invariably lost when was itself was attacked by other oystercatchers.*

Almost everything a marked individual did while it was on the mussel bed at Cockwood could be seen from the tower hide as long as the bird was within about 100m. It was even possible, with some precision, to measure the length of the mussels that a bird had taken! This was done by comparing by eye the length of each mussel to the (known) height of the colour ring on its leg! Since the amount of flesh in a mussel of a given length was already known, it was possible to measure the bird's intake rate; *i.e.* the amount of flesh consumed per 10 minutes of foraging. [Please note: the term 'intake rate' is used to distinguish this measure of flesh consumption from 'feeding rate', which is the ***number*** of mussels of any size taken over a fixed period.] As was done in the preliminary study, the numbers of other foraging oystercatchers in the 25x25m square where the subject bird was feeding were counted at the beginning and end of the ten-minute period. All the measurements of intake rate (over 10-minute periods) that were made on an individual bird were then plotted against the average density of competitors in the square where it was feeding.

The predictions were borne out. Bruno's data showed that individual birds varied greatly in their susceptibility to interference, with the dominant birds being least affected and the subdominants most affected. This result was very strongly confirmed in many other individuals on other mussel beds in subsequent projects. It was so unlikely that a third unknown factor co-varied with both bird dominance and bird density that the existence of interference amongst foraging oystercatchers seemed to be confirmed. The overall conclusion was that interference does occur in oystercatchers feeding on mussels and that its strength varies a great deal between individuals.

Competitive ability of individual birds

This year-long project demonstrated the benefits of having many oystercatchers that were individually identifiable on the mussel bed. At this time, about 10% of the oystercatchers on the estuary had been colour-ringed and, thanks to the Devon and Cornwall Wader Ringing Group, the inevitable losses were being more than replaced by the continuing ringing programme. The circumstances were in place to extend the work on interference competition in individual birds in a number of directions.

But before these empirical studies are summarised, two important ideas that arose at about this time (1981-83) need to be mentioned. One concerns 'competitive ability'. The other concerns how studies of the frequency distribution of individual variation in competitive ability might be used to derive the density-dependent mortality function, now one of the main objectives of the whole project.

Figure 3.5(A) shows in idealised form how two individuals may differ in how interference competition affects their intake rate. The intake rate of the sub-dominant bird (the grey, dashed line) decreases sharply once the interference threshold density has been exceeded. The gradient – or slope – is negative, of course, and its magnitude defines the individual's 'susceptibility to interference'. For this bird, its intake rate decreases a lot with every unit increase in bird density so it is highly susceptible to interference competition. In contrast, the intake rate of the dominant bird (black, solid line) does not decrease at all as the density of other birds around it increases. Its slope is much smaller so it is much less susceptible to interference than is its sub-dominant neighbour.

Figure 3.5(B) illustrates the other component of competitive ability. Both birds are equally susceptible to interference as they have the same slope once the critical threshold density of competitors has been surpassed. But at low competitor densities, below the critical threshold, their intake rates are very different. One (black, solid line) has a high intake rate and the other (grey, dashed line) has a low one. Since interference is absent, these differences must reflect differences in the basic competence of each bird at finding and opening vulnerable mussels. A bird's intake rate in the absence of competition is its 'interference-free intake rate' and measures its 'foraging efficiency'.

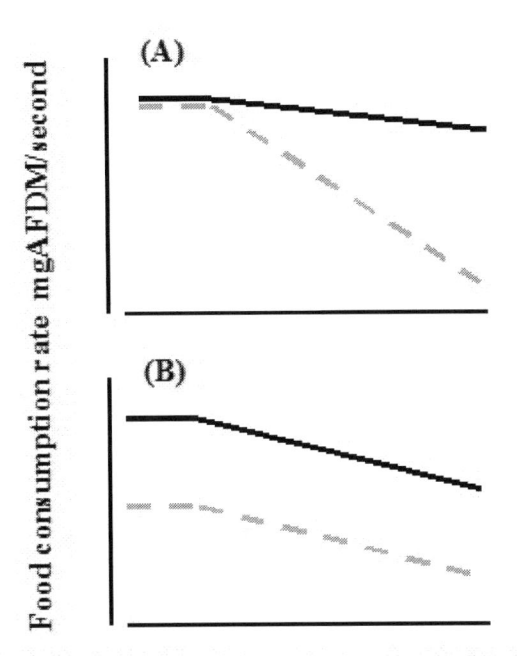

Figure 3.5 How the two components of competitive ability can vary between individual oystercatchers. In (A), individuals black and grey both feed at the same rate, shown by the horizontal black line, at densities of birds below the threshold at which interference starts. This means that they are equally efficient at foraging. But once the threshold has been passed, the intake rate of the more dominant (90% score) 'black' bird hardly decreases at all as the density of competitors around it increases. This bird is not very susceptible to interference. In contrast, the intake rate of the subdominant 'grey' bird (10% dominance score) decreases very sharply. It is very susceptibility to interference. In (B), the two birds have the same susceptibility to interference. But below the threshold, and therefore in the absence of interference, the intake rate of black is very much higher than that of grey. The black bird is much more efficient at foraging than the grey one.

How might each of these components of competitive ability influence an individual's chance of surviving the non-breeding season and contribute to any density dependence that occurs? An individual's susceptibility to interference determines how much it is directly affected when the density of its competitors is high as, for example, when most of a feeding area is covered by the advancing or receding tide. This is called 'interference competition'. An individual's foraging efficiency will determine how much its intake rate is reduced as the food supply itself is gradually depleted over the non-breeding season. This is called 'depletion competition', and is illustrated in Figure 3.6.

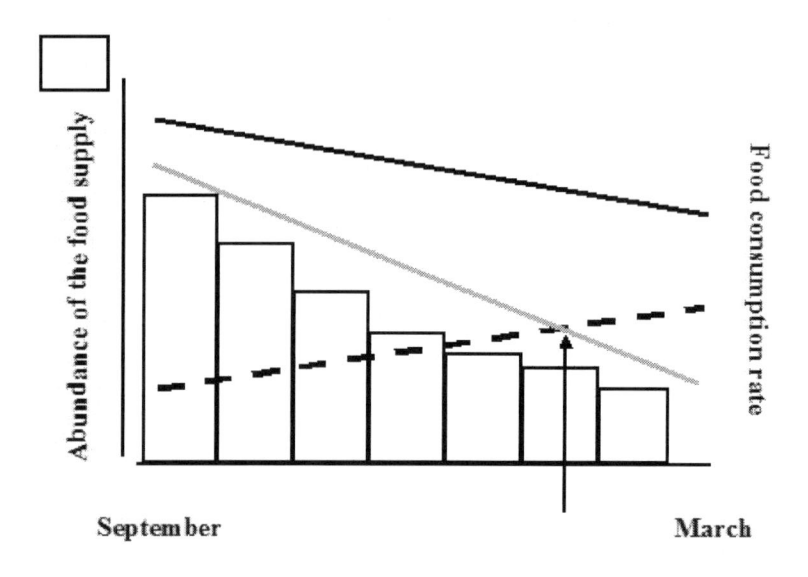

Figure 3.6 How birds with different foraging efficiency are affected by a deterioration in the food supply over the non-breeding season. The columns represent the abundance of food as it becomes gradually depleted by the birds and individual mussels lose flesh because their food is scarce. The dashed black diagonal line shows the rate of food intake that is required to keep a bird alive. The required rate increases gradually through the non-breeding season as the worsening weather raises the birds' energy requirements. The solid lines refer to the intake rates of individual birds. The black line represents a very efficient forager that can maintain its relatively high rate of intake for much of the non-breeding season. Although its consumption rate does gradually decrease as the food supply deteriorates, it is still much higher than that which it needs to avoid starvation. This is not the case with the inefficient forager, shown as the solid grey line. Its intake rate is rather low from the start and is reduced still further by the decline in the food supply. Its intake rate eventually falls below that which is required to meet its energy requirements and it therefore starves, at the time indicated by the black vertical arrow.

Both components of competitive ability can contribute to density dependence. Increasing population size increases the density of competitors on the feeding grounds. Accordingly, more and more of the individuals with a high susceptibility to interference will find it increasingly difficult to meet their energy requirements in the time available. Increasing population size also means that the food supply will become depleted at a greater rate. Accordingly, an increasing proportion of the birds with low foraging efficiency will fail to collect food at a sufficient rate to avoid starvation. An individual's susceptibility to interference determines how increasing population size affects its intake rate directly whereas its foraging efficiency determines how its intake rate will be affected indirectly by depletion.

DERIVING THE DENSITY-DEPENDENT FUNCTION FROM INDIVIDUAL DIFFERENCES IN COMPETITIVE ABILITY

It was reading a recently-published text book on ecology that provided a simple, but important, idea on how studies of individual variation in competitive ability could enable a density-dependent mortality function of oystercatchers to be obtained. The first part of the idea is expressed in Figure 3.7(A). The horizontal axis shows the amount of food that could be consumed per 24 hours by an individual bird if it fed for all of the available time; *i.e.* its 'potential maximum daily consumption'. The vertical, dashed line shows the amount that is required by a single bird in 24 hours to avoid starvation; *i.e.* its physiological food requirement. In this example, this requirement is set at 350g of flesh. In reality, of course, the energy requirement is likely to vary between individuals, but assuming a single value keeps things simple, and anyway no measurements were available. The hatched, vertical bars show the number of individuals in the population that are capable of achieving a given potential daily rate of consumption. In this histogram, two 'super competitors' **could**, in principle, obtain 700g of food per 24hrs, more than twice the amount they actually need to survive for one day. They may be top dominants or highly efficient foragers or, more probably, both. Another 20 individuals could achieve a daily consumption of 500g, 10 could achieve 600g and 10 others could achieve 400g. It is important to note that these are the 'potential' amounts of daily food consumption. A bird would actually stop feeding when it had obtained the 350g that it needs to survive the day: the two 'super-competitors' would fulfil their needs in half of the time available for foraging.

But there are also five birds that can only manage to accumulate 300g over a 24hr period, however hard they try. They are such poor competitors that they would fail to reach the target of 350g even if they spent all of the available time foraging. These individuals are doomed to die of starvation. Once their energy stores have been used up, and they are surviving only on the current consumption, they will starve to death in no time at all.

This is the very simple idea that forms the basis of the next step for deriving the density-dependent function, shown in Figure 3.7(B). The number of birds in the population increases in the series of histograms from left to right. As the population size increases, interference and depletion competition intensify and this suppresses the daily rate of food consumption of the poorest competitors. Accordingly, an increasing proportion of the individuals fail to obtain their daily requirement, and so starve. However, the daily consumption rate of the best competitors is hardly affected at all, simply because they are such good competitors. These birds are able to maintain their high rates of daily consumption even when very large numbers of competitors are present. This is why the right-hand end of the histogram stays in about the same place, whether the population size is high or low. The daily consumption of the top competitors is more-or-less immune from the general increase in interference and depletion competition that accompanies an increase in the size of the population.

By contrast, the daily consumption of the poorest competitors is much reduced when bird density is high. As a result, the daily consumption rate of an increasing number of poor competitors is reduced by competition as the population size increases. This is why the left-hand end of the histogram shifts to the left as the population size increases (Figure 3.7(B)). The poor competitors become increasingly affected by the intensifying interference and depletion competition from their increasingly numerous and superior competitors. The result is that the frequency histogram becomes more and more skewed to the left as an increasing proportion of the individuals with a low competitive ability fail to get enough food and so starve. [In the Figure, the data to the left of the starvation threshold line shows the numbers of birds that achieved a given daily consumption on the day they starve. Once they have starved, their daily consumption will be zero, of course!]. The percentage of the birds that starve is plotted against population size in the upper diagram, and a density-dependent function emerges.

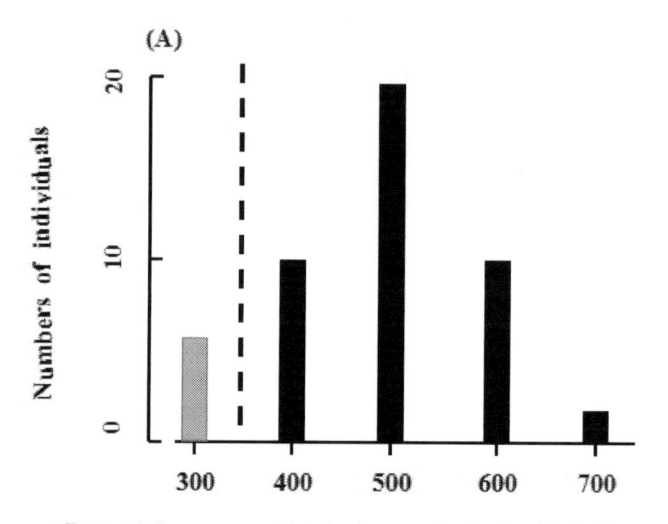

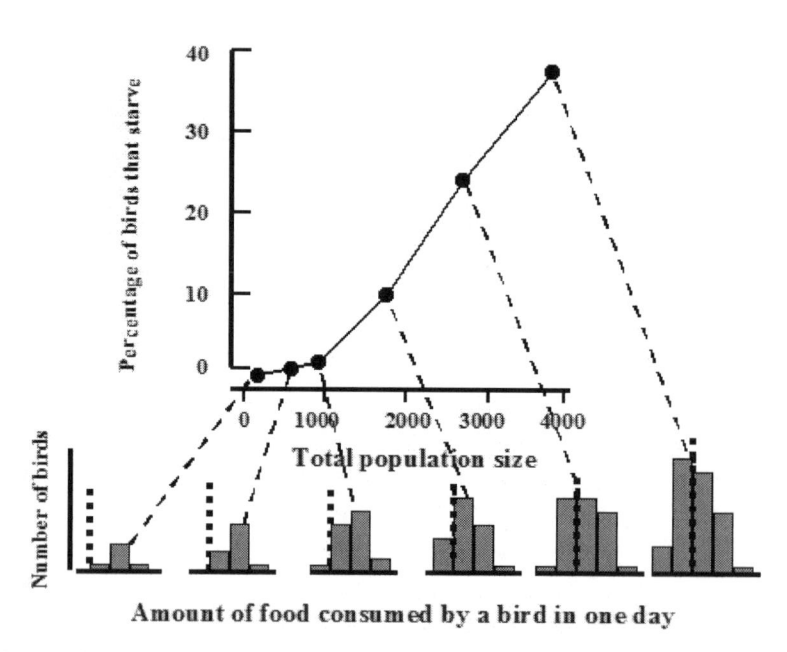

Figure 3.7 How a density-dependent mortality function can be derived from data on a population of differing individuals. In (A), the basic idea of the histograms used in (B) is presented. To avoid extensive repetition, please consult the text for the full explanation.

The idea expressed in Figure 3.7 opened the way to deriving a density-dependent function from field studies of individual oystercatchers. This is how this could be done. The foraging efficiency of a sample of 100 individuals has been measured. That is to say, the intake rate per 5 minutes of 100 individuals have been measured at low bird densities, below the 'interference threshold' of, say, 100 birds/ha. Imagine that these 100 birds are feeding on a mussel bed with an area of 25ha. The density of the birds would be so low (4 birds/ha) that even the most sub-dominant individual would not experience interference, except perhaps at the very start and end of the exposure period. By knowing the duration of the exposure period, it would be simple to calculate for each individual the maximum amount of mussel flesh it could consume during the two exposure periods in a 24-hour period; *i.e.* its maximum potential daily consumption (Box 3.7). At such a low density, all individuals could obtain more energy than they would need to survive, although the less efficient ones would take a longer time to do it than those with a high foraging efficiency. A bird would not actually consume its maximum potential daily consumption, of course, but would just stop feeding when it reached its physiological requirement and/or when its gut was temporarily full.

'Now increase the number of birds to 200, then 400, then 800 and so on. It is reasonable to assume that the distribution of foraging efficiencies across all the individuals in these larger populations would be the same as it had been in our sample of 100. [If there were reason to doubt this assumption, there would be no alternative but to measure the foraging efficiency of a larger sample of individuals in a larger populations.] On the assumption that 100 birds is enough to describe the variation in foraging efficiency at all population sizes, if there was one bird with a foraging efficiency of 0.93 in the population of 100 birds, there would be two with this foraging efficiency in the population of 200, and 3 in a population of 300, and so on.

The population size eventually reaches 2500 at which the density of birds on the 25ha mussel bed reaches the threshold of 100 birds/ha at which interference begins to occur. As the population size continues to increase, the intake rates of the least competitive individuals will begin to be reduced by interference. The next step is to calculate the amount by which the potential intake rate of an individual would be reduced by interference from its competitors.

Figure 3.8 illustrates how this can be done. Interference only begins to reduce the intake rate of subdominant birds once the density of birds exceeds 100/ha. Each bird needs 350g a day to survive. By way of an example, consider a subdominant bird whose potential daily consumption is reduced by interference by 100g when bird density increases from 100 to 200 birds/ha. It is reduced by a further 100g as bird density increases from 200 to 300 birds/ha, and so on. Currently, the density of birds is 200/ha. In the absence of interference, at bird densities below 100/ha, this bird can obtain a potential daily maximum consumption 450g – much more than the 350g it needs to survive. But bird density is now 200/ha and interference reduces the daily consumption of this bird from 450g to 350g – just enough to survive. If the density increases by a further 100 birds/ha, its potential daily consumption falls again from 350g to 250g, and it starves.

The hypothetical histograms and graph shown in Figure 3.7A and B could then be established for real birds. By doing the same for all mussel beds, the graph could be drawn for the entire mussel-feeding population. The density-dependent function would have been produced!

Although there are still many other matters to describe, this is the basic idea of the shorebird individuals-based model (IBM). The IBM tracks individuals throughout the non-breeding season and flags individuals as 'starved to death' when their daily consumption is too low to keep them alive. These starved individuals are then removed from the population, whose size goes down accordingly. Such individuals are then removed from the population that populate the virtual estuary that is the model.

We had no idea in the early 1980s exactly how the calculation above could be extended to all of the main mussel beds of the Exe. It was hoped that measuring the two components of competitive ability on a sample of beds would provide some of the most important data for doing so, however. A density-dependent mortality function could surely be derived from such data, even if it was not possible to foresee exactly how that could be done at this stage. The hope was, that as the data on individuals accumulated, ideas would emerge from somewhere or other as to how they could be incorporated into a model of the entire estuary. Luckily, this proved to be the case (Box 3.8). For the time being, though, the priority was to acquire data on the two components of competitive ability from as many individual oystercatchers as possible.

How this was done is the subject of the next chapter.

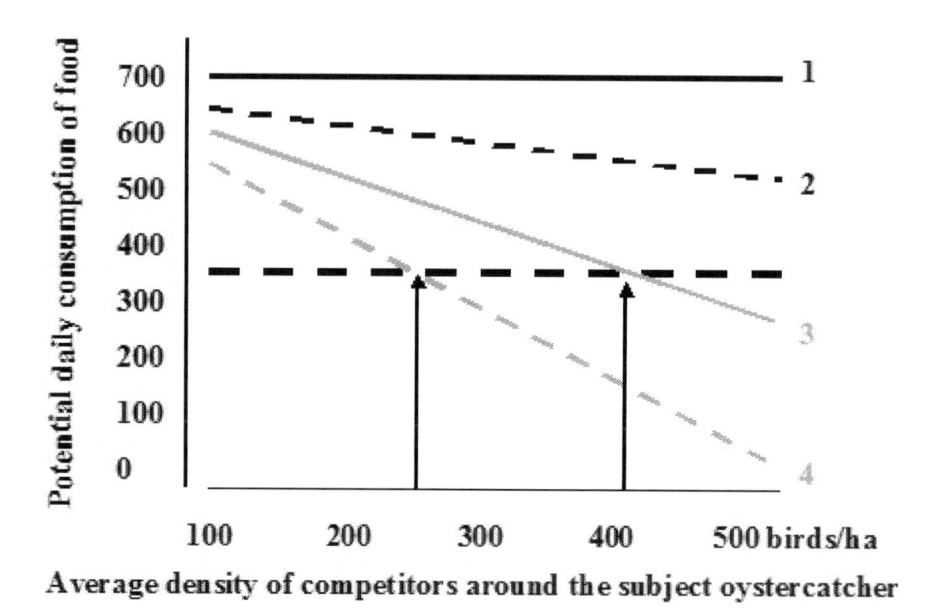

Figure 3.8 How the daily consumption of food by four hypothetical oystercatchers with differing dominance (and therefore susceptibility to interference) and foraging efficiency is affected by increasing average density of competitors on the mussel bed. Bird 1 is a highly dominant and highly efficient individual, a combination that ensures it always greatly exceeds the consumption rate 350g required for survival – indicated by the thick horizontal dashed black line – even when the highest average density of birds occurs. Bird 2 is less dominant and less efficient but can still retain an adequate consumption rate over the range of competitor densities encountered. This is not the case with bird 3, and even more so with bird 4, whose low efficiencies and low dominances mean that they starve at the low population densities – 250 birds/hectare in the case of bird 3, for example.

REFERENCES FOR CHAPTER 3

Durell, S.E.A. Le V. dit & Goss-Custard, J.D. (1984). Prey selection within a size-class of mussels, *Mytilus edulis*, by oystercatchers, *Haematopus ostralegus*. *Animal Behaviour*, **32**, 1197-1203.

Durell, S.E.A., Goss-Custard, J.D. & Caldow, R.W.G. (1993). Sex-related differences in diet and feeding method in the oystercatcher *Haematopus ostralegus*. *Journal of Animal Ecology*, **62**, 205-215.

Ens, B.J. & Goss-Custard, J.D. (1984). Interference among oystercatchers, *Haematopus ostralegus*, feeding on mussels, *Mytilus edulis*, on the Exe estuary. *Journal of Animal Ecology*, **53**, 217-231.

Ens, B.J. & Goss-Custard, J.D. (1986). Piping as a display of dominance in wintering oystercatchers, *Haematopus ostralegus*. *Ibis*, **128**, 382-391.

Goss-Custard, J.D. (1985). Foraging behaviour of wading birds and the carrying capacity of estuaries. *Behavioural Ecology: Ecological Consequences of Adaptive Behaviour*. (Ed. by R.M. Sibly & R.H. Smith), pp. 169-188. Oxford, Blackwells.

Goss-Custard, J.D., Cayford, J.T., Boates, J.S. & Durell, S.E.A. Le V. dit. (1987). Field tests of the accuracy of measuring prey size against bill length in oystercatchers, *Haematopus ostralegus*, eating mussels, *Mytilus edulis*. *Animal Behaviour*, **35**, 1078-1083.

Goss-Custard, J.D. & Durell, S.E.A. Le V. dit. (1987). Age-related effects in oystercatchers, *Haematopus ostralegus*, feeding on mussels, *Mytilus edulis*. 1. Foraging efficiency and interference. *Journal of Animal Ecology*, **56**, 521-536.

Goss-Custard, J.D. & Durell, S.E.A. Le V. dit. (1987). Age-related effects in oystercatchers, *Haematopus ostralegus*, feeding on mussels, *Mytilus edulis*. 2. Aggression. *Journal of Animal Ecology*, **56**, 537-548.

Goss-Custard, J.D. & Durell, S.E.A. Le V. dit. (1987). Age-related effects in oystercatchers, *Haematopus ostralegus*, feeding on mussels, *Mytilus edulis*. 3. The effect of interference on overall intake rate. *Journal of Animal Ecology*, **56**, 549-558.

Goss-Custard, J.D. & Durell, S.E.A. Le V. dit. (1988). The effect of dominance and feeding method on the intake rates of oystercatchers, *Haematopus ostralegus*, feeding on mussels, *Mytilus edulis*. *Journal of Animal Ecology*, **57**, 827-844.

Goss-Custard, J.D. & Durell, S.E.A. Le V. dit. (1990). Bird behaviour and environmental planning: approaches in the study of wader populations. *Ibis*, **132**, 273-289.

Goss-Custard, J.D. & Sutherland, W.J. (1984). Feeding specialisations in oystercatchers, *Haematopus ostralegus*. *Animal Behaviour*, **32**, 299-301.

Goss-Custard, J.D. & Sutherland, W.J. (1997). Individual behaviour, populations and conservation. In: (Eds. J.R. Krebs & N.B. Davies), *Behavioural ecology: an evolutionary approach. 4th edition*, pp. 373-395. Blackwell Science, Oxford.

Goss-Custard, J.D., West, A.D., Caldow, R.W.G., Durell, S.E.A. le V. dit & McGrorty, S. (1996). An empirical optimality model to predict the intake rates of oystercatchers *Haematopus ostralegus* feeding on mussels *Mytilus edulis*. *Ardea*, **84**, 199-214.

Moody, A.L., Thompson, W.A., de Bruijn, B., Houston, A.I. & Goss-Custard, J.D. (1997). The spacing of Oystercatchers during the tidal cycle. *Journal of Animal Ecology*, **66**, 615-628.

Sutherland, W.J. & Goss-Custard, J.D. (1992). Predicting the consequence of habitat loss on shorebird populations. *Acta XX Congressus Internationalis Ornithologici*, 2199-2207.

Zwarts, L., Ens, B.J., Goss-Custard, J.D., Hulscher, J.B. (1996). Why Oystercatchers *Haematopus ostralegus* cannot meet their daily energy requirements in a single low water period. *Ardea*, **84**, 269-290.

Zwarts, L., Ens, B.J., Goss-Custard, J.D., Hulscher, J.B. & Durell, S.E.A. le V. dit (1996). Causes of variation in prey profitability and its consequences for the intake rate of the Oystercatchers *Haematopus ostralegus*. *Ardea*, **84**, 229-268.

Box 3.1 The shape of the bill and of the bill-tip vary between oystercatchers.

Pointed bills are useful for catching worms that are just pulled out of their burrows. They are also used for stabbing or prising into bivalve molluscs, such as mussels. Birds with such bills – mainly females and young - cannot hammer a hole in a mussel shell because their bills would fracture. The birds that do hammer a hole in the mussel shell have very stout and strong bills that are less likely to fracture, and are generally adult males. The overall structure and strength of the bill therefore determines the feeding technique that a bird uses when opening armoured prey, such as mussels. The different shapes of the bill-tip itself are a consequence of the different amounts and types of wear that the different techniques cause. The 'chisel' tip of a stabber/priser arises because the twisting the bill tip from side-to-side abrades the bill against the mussel shells. The flat bill tip of a hammering bird arises because the otherwise sharp tip is worn down. The relatively rapid re-growth of the abraded horny beak plates at the end of the bill allow such wear and tear to occur without harm to the bird

Box 3.2 A trivial question to answer?

Conveying to non-scientists the need sometimes to quantify something precisely is often a problem! Imagine being asked the question: 'What have you discovered?' and you reply 'Well, after five years of intensive effort, we now know with some confidence that the slope of the interference function (on a log:log plot, of course) is about 0.35!' This does not sound like something worth spending five uncomfortable years doing! You then have to explain that the interference function shows that a bird's intake rate decreases as the number of competitive nearby increases, just as the average profits of restaurants in a small town decrease as more and more restaurants establish themselves there. And that sounds so obvious that your reply is likely to be received with a puzzled, even a pitying look. You must have a very small brain to devote so much of life to such a miniscule task as measuring the slope of an obvious function! Yet much science is quantifying something 'obvious'. This often means, by the way, that the questioner has no idea how many alternative possibilities do actually exist or of the significance of the precise value! As one retired gentleman said to me when he encountered me returning from yet another long and cold stint in the hide, 'Why not save yourself the bother and just make it up!' I think it was a joke.

Box 3.3 Perils on the seawall

At this location, the main line railway ran along the top of the seawall. For fear of being given the answer 'No', we never took the trouble to find out whether it was allowed to sit on the seawall, but as no train ever stopped to tell anybody off, it was assumed that it was OK!

Of course, it was uncomfortable balancing oneself on a solid stone slope that angled downwards at about 60-70°, with the telescope on its tripod. Luckily, the rough stones provided some purchase for both researcher and the tripod. A nice pad of rubber helped make it less uncomfortable underneath and provided some insulation, but without any protection from the weather, it could still be quite cold. It was mildly intimidating when a massive train thundered past at huge speed within a few feet of your head, and the wall shook so that observations had to be postponed until it had passed. Luckily, only occasionally did someone on the train flush the toilet as the train roared by!

Box 3.4 Observation and experiments - 1

We all know that testing an hypothesis with an experiment in which just one variable is changed is the most effective way to test it. But often, this just isn't possible! Rather like a scientist interested in the behaviour of planets, manipulating the objects of our ecological research in experiments is often impossible. On the Exe, it would have been very useful to have been able either to remove whole mussel beds, or to move them to another part of the estuary, to test whether our ideas predicted correctly how the birds would re-distribute themselves, but that would have taken resources way beyond our reach!

Box 3.5 Observation and experiment - 2

It would have been invaluable to be able to manipulate the dominance of individuals by appropriate hormonal implants, but even that simple experiment would have been very hard to conduct. Instead, you have to exploit natural variation and do what you can to control for the effect of other variables, usually by measurement and statistics.

To illustrate this point, consider the marked difference in bird densities between the different mussel beds. The hypothesis might be: 'Birds are more numerous on mussel beds where mussels are large than where they are small because their intake rates are higher there'. If this hypothesis is true, we would predict that bird density would be higher where mussels are larger. But as many other factors might vary together with both bird density and mussel size, finding the expected relationship between bird density and mussel size is hardly conclusive. You might be able to eliminate the possible affect of some of the confounding variables by using multivariate statistics. But that is still just a correlation that may or may not imply a causal link from one (mussel size) to the other (bird density). There may be another unknown factor that might actually be the cause; that is, the association might be spurious. For example, mussels may grow large in places where the conditions are such that the parasites that infect oystercatchers cannot survive. It is actually the absence of these parasites that causes oystercatchers to occur at higher densities where mussels are large, and not the large size of the mussels *per se*.

You can shorten the odds against achieving a spuriously successful prediction by expressing your predictions as numbers. For example, if the mussel size hypothesis predicts that bird density should be 1.37 times higher where mussels are 1.89 times larger and, lo and behold, they are 1.369 times higher, most people would regard this is pretty convincing evidence. This is because it is unlikely that another unknown factor would lead to precisely the same quantitative outcome. But such cases are rare in ecology unless hypotheses can be expressed as mathematical models. As will become clear later, the ability to test quantitative predictions became the most powerful argument that the shorebird model's predictions could be viewed with some confidence.

Box 3.6 Bruno and the tower hide

The arrival of Bruno with his tower hide was such a critical moment in the development of the research programme that led to the shorebird model that it must be described in some detail.

The tower was constructed in Groningen, and consisted of numerous poles and other bits of a light-weight metal and a heavy plank to support Bruno. Along with enough luggage to live in England for several months, Bruno himself transported this pile of ironmongery and wood on his back on the ferry to England. In London, he could not find a taxi that would take him across the city to the railway station to catch a train to Exeter. Amazingly, therefore, he had to carry all this stuff through the congested underground across London at the height of the rush hour! The next day, the tower was built in the centre of the mussel at Cockwood, about 200m out from the railway embankment. A hide was put on top and the whole structure was secured against the tide and weather with numerous guy ropes.

From then, on every day for months, Bruno was in this cat's cradle of a hide, recording on a tape recorder everything that occurred amongst the marked individuals around him. The only constraint to his data collection was the frequent presence of MIF, the local angler, who insisted that the only place to catch fish that was good enough for his cat was just a few yards from the tower hide. Eventually, Bruno did become used to this unexpected interruption to his data gathering programme, but there is no doubt that he would have obtained much more data had that cat not existed!

Nonetheless, there were enough data for Bruno to answer his research questions with sufficient confidence for the results eventually to be accepted for publication in the best British ecological and behaviour journals. The work on the Exe owes a great deal indeed to Bruno's pioneering project and dedication, even though it owed rather little to his singing!

Box 3.7 Calculating the potential daily consumption of an oystercatcher from measurements of its intake rate.

The average intake rate of the bird is 500mg of mussel flesh per 5 minutes, or 100 mg/minute.

The mussel bed is exposed and accessible to the birds for 6 hours during the day and 6 hours during the night, a total of 12 hours per 24 hours.

The bird feeds as efficiently at night as it does during the day.

As the bird can feed during each 24 hour period for 12x60 (720) minutes at a rate of 100mg/minute, its potential daily consumption is: 720x100, or 72,000 mg, or 720g.

The food requirement is only 500g, so the bird survives easily.

> In fact, it only has to forage for 500 minutes (50,000/100) during each 24 hours to obtain its energy requirements. It can rest or preen for 220 minutes per 24 hours, or for 110 minutes during each low tide exposure period.
>
> This bird will not starve!

Box 3.8 Risking a bit in research

It may seem a bit cavalier to base a large and costly research project on a belief that, eventually, an idea will turn up that will allow it to be completed! But, in fact, scientists are by no means always sure how they will reach their goal when they start a project and this may persist a long time into the project. This is, of course, the nature of research. If we already knew how to do it, it wouldn't be research but the implementation of an already-known technology. Researchers often have to base much on a belief that something will work out, on a hunch, and in so doing risk their reputation, amongst other things, although not usually their own money. You have to gamble and hope that the next step take will lead to an idea that you can't think of now but will occur to you – or to someone else - later. Research by its nature is speculative and risky, and having the opportunity to build up one's confidence in one's own hunches is an important part of the development of young scientists.

Yet, at the same time, scientists are required to produce outputs that demonstrate – quite correctly – that the money that is being used is actually yielding results. Perhaps the most highly-valued of these outputs are scientific papers in well-respected, peer-reviewed journals. No such journal would accept some hand-waving article full of not-yet realised promised outcomes of staggering significance – although it has felt at times that some 'theoretical' articles in ecology and behaviour journals came pretty close to this!

In the Exe project, the strategy was to work towards the overall goal of building a model that would predict the density-dependent mortality function under any probable scenario of environmental change. The important thing was to do so in bite-sized chunks of research that asked an interesting question in their own right, the findings on which could be published on their own in a good journal. The several projects on competition in oystercatchers and on their foraging behaviour and survival are good illustrations of how well this strategy worked.

Funding is, of course, vital. Although there was substantial core funding from the British Government's Natural Environment Research Council that played a pivotal role in allowing this risky research programme to be continued, the requirement to earn research funds (quite rightly, in my opinion) increased over the decades. Contracts could be obtained from Government agencies, companies and the European Union, the latter being a particularly good source of support towards the latter stages of the development of the IBM. But most of these sources were not interested – for very good reasons – in supporting research where the achievement of the final goal was so uncertain and so far in the future – perhaps a couple of decades away! So all kinds of contracts were undertaken, most of which did not contribute directly to the development of the IBM. But this contract money helped to keep the research team together. It also kept our researchers in close touch with the organisations that would one day benefit from the development of an IBM. To 'survive' in this research environment, the trick was both to earn money and to publish lots of scientific papers in good journals. As one very well-respected ornithologist colleague said to me; 'Whichever way the wind of current fashion blows between earning contact money and publishing scientific papers, if you do both, they would be too embarrassed to get rid of you!' It proved to be good advice!

CHAPTER 4:
Competitive ability and intake rates

......in which the long research programme that was required to measure the considerable differences between individual oystercatchers in their ability to compete with others is described, a model was developed that predicted intake rate from the density, size and flesh content of the mussels where a bird was feeding and the stage is set to build the first IBM for a shorebird.

OBSERVING FROM THE HIDES

So began a very long programme of fieldwork. Sadly, the Dutch tower hide disintegrated after a short while, and an alternative had to be found. Scaffolding towers (just over a square meter) of the kind used to decorate ceilings and so forth provided the answer. A purpose-made canvas hide was 'dropped' over the top. Planks supported the observer inside, and several guy ropes anchored the whole structure in place and kept if more-or-less steady in strong winds (Plate 4.1). The towers consisted of sections about 40cms high that were slotted together to form a structure 4-5m high.

These sections had to be tied together otherwise, over a high tide with a strong wind, the whole top section, consisting of scaffolding poles, planks and canvas hide, would be lifted off the lower sections of the tower and carried, perhaps a couple of km, up-river. On one occasion, the top must have been dropped in deep water because it was never found. The whole structure was therefore bound together with rope and anchored firmly to the mussel bed with large stakes. It looked like a cats-cradle but the hide on top was generally a great place in which to spend the working day (and/or night) (Box 4.1)!

Hides like this were used every non-breeding season for at least 10 years and were erected on all the main mussel beds, with up to six being present at any one time. With their spindly legs, imposing height and solid upper structure emerging through the morning mists, the estuary looked like it had been invaded by 'War of the World' aliens! In most cases, the hides were inaccessible by foot and had to be entered by boat on the receding tide, before the birds arrived, and could only be vacated when the tide returned. On low-lying mussel beds, a single watch might last just 4 or 5 hours but on mussel beds further up the shore, watches could last for 9 or 10 hours. A succession of PhD students, research fellows and colleagues used these hides and, between them, acquired a large and very valuable data set that formed the heart of the IBM. They were used at night (Box 4.2), most notably by Humphrey Sitters who, with the help of modern night-viewing technology and video, advanced understanding of how shorebirds spend the night more than anyone else had ever had the fortitude and ingenuity to do previously.

This part of the programme took so long for several reasons. First of all, the data were highly variable, and so large sample sizes were required to measure the foraging efficiency of individual birds and their susceptibility to interference. The data were variable because it was usually only possible to watch an individual for 5 minutes. If a bird swallowed the flesh from two or three mussels in one five-minute period, its intake rate could be as much as 2000mg whereas, if it swallowed none, its intake rate was 0mg: a huge range!

Plate 4.1 *One of the many tower hides that were used on the Exe mussel beds.*

Five minutes was the limit because so much had to be recorded and held in the memory: the colour-ring combination of the subject bird; the number of oystercatchers in the 25x25m square at the start; the length of any mussel found and whether it was opened or rejected; the feeding method of the subject; the duration of the handling time; whether a fight with another oystercatcher took place and the outcome (eg: mussel stolen by an attacker); the ring-combination of the other bird, if it was ringed or its age, if it was not; the numbers of oystercatchers in the square at the end. As typically only one mussel could be taken in five minutes, all this information could just about be held in the head until it could be written down in a notebook immediately afterwards. During the five minutes, both hands were occupied – one with a stop-watch to measure handling time, the other turning the telescope to track the bird. All of this could have been dictated into a voice recorder, of course, but this approach was rejected. It would have taken so long afterwards to transcribe the information. Better to spend the time relaxing and warming up in Cockwood's two great pubs – The Anchor and The Ship. Further, it would not have allowed data to be collected very much faster because noting, in code, at the end of the 5 minutes what had happened took very little time. On most mussel beds, the target for an exposure period would be 30-50 5-minute observation periods.

The second reason was that obtaining data at high bird densities was difficult, yet such data were vital for measuring accurately the strength of the interference experienced by individual birds (Fig 4.1). For most of the exposure period on Spring tides, when the largest areas are exposed at low water, there was enough space for the birds to spread out. This allowed them to keep their density low enough to minimise, and usually prevent, any interference that would otherwise have occurred: an example is shown in Figure 4.2. On Spring tides, high densities of birds usually only occurred at the beginning and end of the exposure period when only a small part of the mussel bed was exposed and accessible to the birds. But because it was a Spring tide, and the height of the water at high tide was so high, the water flowed in and out very quickly and there was only a short period when only a small part of the mussel bed was exposed. Additionally, some individuals tended not to occur on the bed at these states of tide. Sometimes high densities occurred at low tide on Spring tides when a winkle fisher was somewhere on the mussel bed and the birds could only feed in a limited area. Unfortunately, the birds often did not feed for some time after they had been disturbed, further restricting opportunities to record their behaviour. Densities were, however, generally much higher on Neap tides when the tide receded and advanced much more slowly and only a restricted area was exposed all through the tidal cycle, but then there was another limitation. On the Exe, low water on Neap tides occurred at the beginning and end of the day so that mussels were exposed for only a short period in daylight at dawn and dusk. On such tides, you could spend six hours in a hide and collect a tiny number of observations! Nonetheless, data were collected on Neap tides whenever the opportunity arose.

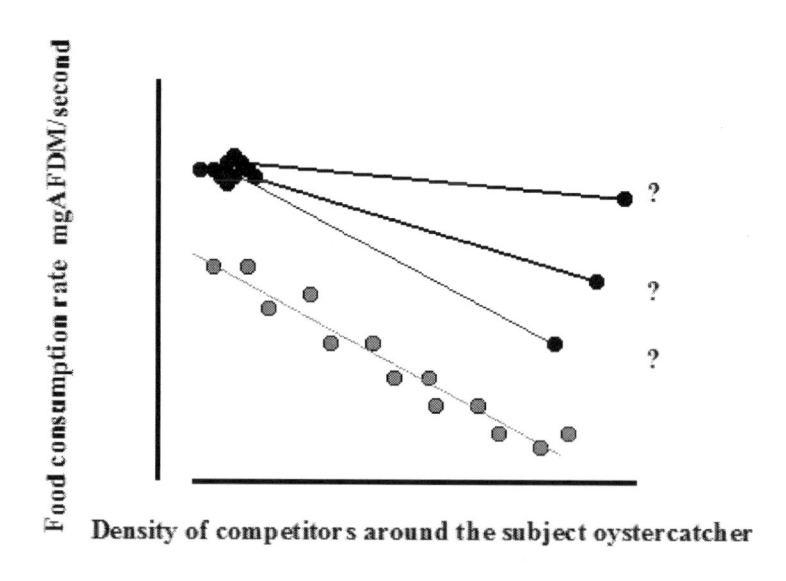

Figure 4.1 *The difficulties of estimating the slope of the interference function. The grey dots show the ideal distribution of data for estimating the slope. That is, a large number of data points with a good spread across the range of competitor densities. The black dots show what usually occurred! For most of the exposure period, the birds are spread out over the mussel beds so that the density of birds is low. Data on intake rate at low competitor densities can therefore be acquired very easily. The density of birds is high for only a small proportion of the exposure period so that only very few data points can be obtained from a given*

individual. The danger is that, without adequate data, the estimate of the slope can be hugely influenced by the chance location of one or two data points obtained at high bird densities.

Often, of course, bad weather prevented observations from being made from the towers. Sometimes people on the mussel bed also disrupted the data collection (Box 4.3). And, of course, the researchers has many other tasks, just like everyone else: managing teams; supervising students; competing for contracts and carrying them out; analysing data; writing scientific papers and contract report and, of course, servicing the bureaucracy.

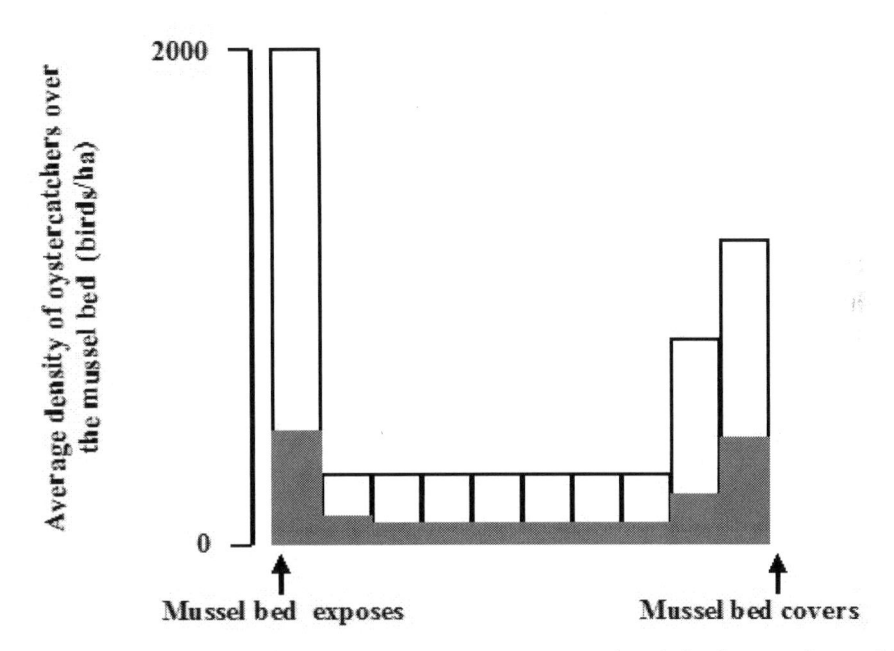

Figure 4.2 The average density of oystercatchers in 25mx25m squares across the whole of a typical mussel bed on spring tides (open columns) and neap tides (grey columns). The exposure period is divided into ten periods of equal length. The first interval refers to the first tenth of the exposure period, and so forth. This way of dividing up the exposure period allows the data from spring tides – when the exposure period is long - and from neap tides – when the exposure period is much shorter - to be superimposed.

INDIVIDUAL VARIATIONS IN COMPETITIVE ABILITY
Foraging efficiency and dominance

As will become obvious, it is first important to establish the shape of the relationship between intake rate and the density of competitors if the interference function is to be compared across a number of classes of birds and across individuals. A number of attempts were made to do this, but the definitive analysis of all the available data was published in 1996. This analysis reached some firm conclusions because there was by then available a very large data set from unmarked and marked individuals of different feeding methods and ages. There were 2749 5-minute observation periods on stabbing birds and 2176 on hammerers, divided roughly equally between dorsal and ventral hammerers. Many of these data were obtained from individual birds. With these individuals, every attempt was made to collect data at various stages of both the exposure period and of the non-breeding season to ensure that as wide a range of conditions as possible were represented in the sample. Preliminary work had suggested that a large amount of data was required to obtain a reasonably precise estimate of an individual's foraging efficiency and susceptibility to interference. Accordingly, a target was set of least eight hours of data (*i.e.* more than 100 5-minute long periods of observation) from each marked individual. This goal was achieved with many of the birds that were watched on the two or three mussel beds where this work was carried out. For reasons given in Box 4.4, the measure of intake rate used in this analysis was the 'standardised' intake rate.

This analysis showed that, contrary to the predictions of a number of theoretical models of interference that were published about that time, the intake rate of oystercatchers did not begin to decrease immediately as the density of competitors began to increase. Rather, a certain density of competitors had to be reached before the intake rates of the birds began to go down. This made sense: when the density of birds is low, individuals have every opportunity to avoid birds to which they are sub-dominant. This 'threshold density' occurring at about 50 competitors/ha in oystercatchers that hammered into the mussels on either the dorsal or ventral side and at about 150 competitors/ha in those that stabbed into a mussel (Fig. 4.3). Once the threshold had been passed, however, the intake rate decreased more sharply in stabbing birds than in the hammerers; *i.e.* the slope was steeper in stabbers than hammerers (Fig. 4.3). That is, once the density of competitors had reached the threshold level at which interference began to occur, stabbing birds were more susceptible to interference than were hammerers. A given increase in the density of competitors would reduce the intake rate of stabbers by much more than it would reduce that of hammering birds.

The analysis further showed that, for birds of a given age with a given feeding method, the value of the threshold density at which interference began to take effect did not differ between birds of different dominance. That is, there was no relationship between the interference threshold of an individual – its foraging efficiency - and its dominance. A dominant bird could be highly efficient or very inefficient and a sub-dominant likewise. In contrast, the susceptibility of a bird to interference above the threshold density varied enormously between individual birds and was related to their dominance. Birds of lower dominance were much more susceptible to interference than were those of higher dominance. Indeed, there was some evidence that the intake rate of some of the most dominant stabbing birds actually increased as the density of the birds where they were feeding increased. Presumably, for them, a higher density of birds nearby just represented a higher abundance of potential victims from whom mussels could be stolen, and therefore more opportunity to steal. For hammering birds of a given dominance, and for an unknown reason, interference was most intense at the start of the exposure period as the mussel beds began to expose.

The reason why the intensity of interference increased towards the end of the winter could easily be understood. This is the part of the non-breeding season when the feeding conditions are most difficult for oystercatchers. The reasons for this can be sought in changes in both the mussels and in the birds. The flesh-content of mussels decreases over the non-breeding season by as much as 40% (Fig. 4.4). Vulnerable mussels still take a long time to find but, when they are found and opened, they contain much less flesh than a mussel of the same size would have contained six months previously. At the same time, the energy requirements of the birds increases because of the decreasing air temperature. It is therefore likely that dominant birds had an increasing incentive to steal mussels found by sub-dominant birds in order to maintain their consumption rate. Accordingly, the slope of the individuals that were vulnerable to interference would have become steeper: *i.e.* they would have become more susceptible to interference. At a given bird density, their intake rate would have been suppressed more towards the end of the non-breeding season than it had been at the beginning.

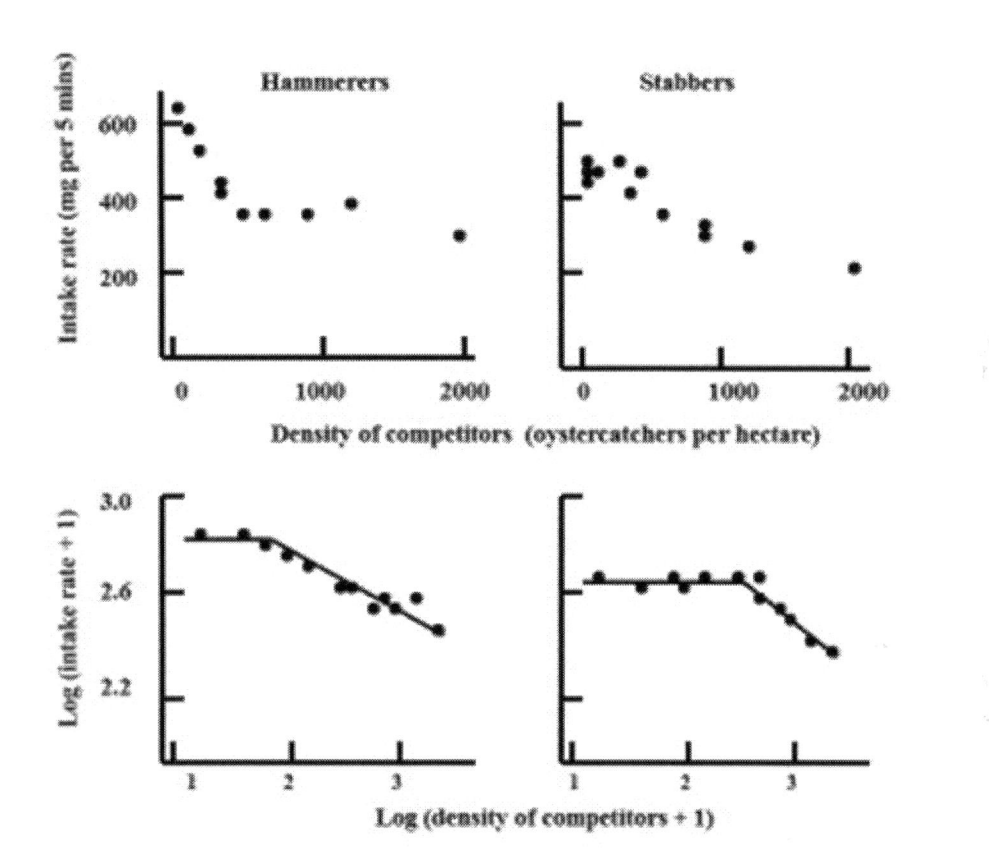

Figure 4.3 *Interference functions for the average hammering and average stabbing oystercatcher on the two main mussel beds where interference studies were concentrated. In the lower graphs, bird density is transformed to logarithms to stretch out the axis so that the location of the interference threshold can clearly be seen.*

Perhaps partly as a consequence of this intensified interference, an increasing number of mussel-feeding birds fed upshore of the mussel beds on the receding and advancing tide when the mussel beds were covered by taking cockles, ragworms and clams. Many oystercatchers also went to fields to feed on earthworms when all the flats were covered over high water. As it became increasingly difficult for the birds to obtain the food they required each day, many oystercatchers extended their feeding time and expanded their diet to include a much wider variety of prey other than mussels.

This increasing intensity of interference that occurred as the non-breeding season progressed is best illustrated with data from juvenile (first-winter) birds that almost always opened mussels by stabbing. Some arrived on the mussel beds at the very beginning of the non-breeding season (August), apparently without their parents. Many of them gave the impression of being desperate for food. They rushed around at high speed, pecking at and picking up all sorts of things that could not be eaten, such as empty shells and small sticks. Their rate of pacing was therefore quite a lot higher than that of adults feeding in the same place. When they did find a mussel, it often contained much less flesh than mussels of equivalent length that had been opened by an experienced adult bird feeding in the same place. It looked as though the juveniles often just fed on the scraps of flesh that other birds had left behind in a mussel that they had opened. A surprise was that juveniles in August frequently attacked adults that had found a mussel and, what's more, the adult victims often ran away and often abandoned the opened mussel to the juvenile. The juveniles were very aggressive at this time of year, presumably because they were so short of food that they were prepared to risk injury by stealing mussels from the more powerful adults. For their part, the adults presumably did not risk injury by defending a mussel at a time of year when it is very easy for them to collect their daily food requirements in the time available.

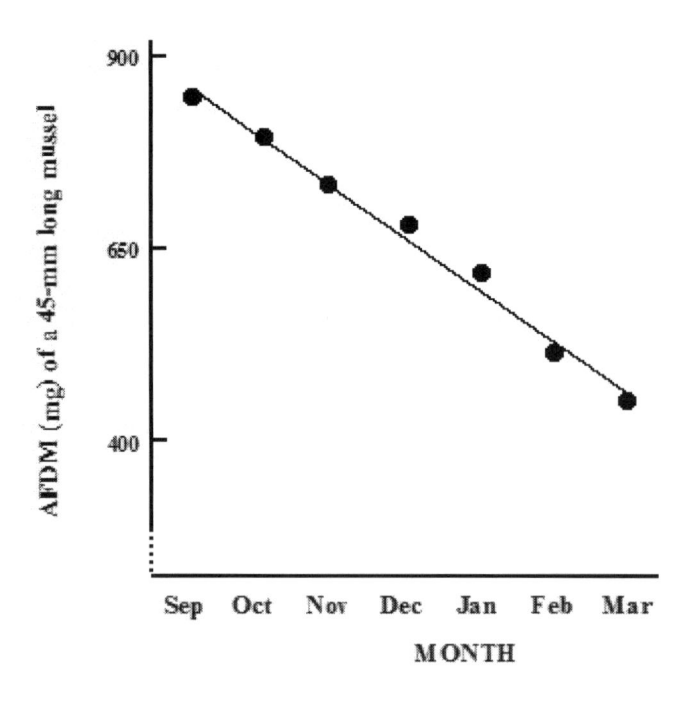

Figure 4.4 The average decrease in the flesh content of mussels 45mm long from a sample of mussel beds across three non-breeding seasons. Note that the vertical axis is truncated and does not go down to zero.

As the non-breeding season progressed, however, and feeding became more difficult for all oystercatchers, things changed quickly. Although the rate at which juveniles found mussels for themselves did gradually increase through September and October- presumably as they gained experience - the adults increasingly resisted any juvenile that attacked them, and often with extreme vigour. It was not unusual for an enraged adult to grab hold of the attacking juvenile with its beak and not let go for a long time, occasionally twisting the juvenile down onto the ground and holding it there, sometimes under water. For the juveniles, this meant that attacking other oystercatchers became increasingly risky as well as unprofitable. The combination of low foraging efficiency and lowly dominance must have caused the juveniles to have low rates of consumption. Most of them abandoned the mussel beds after just two to three months of their arrival.

Let us return now to the main point. The analysis revealed differences in susceptibility to interference between individual oystercatchers, between oystercatchers of different ages and between birds using different techniques to open mussels. The general intensity of the interference also varied in any one individual according to the stage of the tidal cycle and of non-breeding season.

The analysis also showed that there were highly significant differences between individuals in their interference-free intake rates. In the absence of interference, the intake rates of birds of the same age and using the same feeding method and feeding in the same place could be very different indeed. Some were very much more efficient than others. Taking the average bird to have a score of 100, the least efficient individuals had a score of about 70 while the most efficient bird had a score of about 130, almost twice as high. This massive difference between individuals revealed by the analysis did not really come as a surprise. It was very obvious to experienced observers in the hides that some individuals were very effective at foraging when on their own whereas others, in virtually the same place, were just hopeless (Box 4.5).

These individual differences in foraging efficiency were unrelated to an individual's dominance. An individual could be of very high dominance and capable of stealing many mussels from other birds but it could have either a high foraging efficiency or a very low one. Conversely, an individual could be at the lowest level of the dominance hierarchy but have a very high foraging efficiency or a very low one. This was contrary to expectation. It had confidently been expected that individuals would excel either at being very efficient foragers or very dominant, whereas in fact, these two aspects of competitive ability were quite unrelated to each other across individuals. Some individuals were good at both, some at just one and some at neither!

From the point of view of the eventual development of the shorebird IBM, these findings were of great importance. First, they demonstrated that individuals of any one age and feeding method varied a great deal in both foraging efficiency and dominance which, between them, determined an individual's 'competitive ability'. But just as importantly, they also provided the measurements that could be used to define an individual's competitive ability in the model.

First of all, the fighting ability of an individual in a future model could be defined in terms of its dominance on a scale of 0 to 100%. This in turn could be used to determine an individual's susceptibility to interference because this was closely linked to a bird's dominance. The data provided an equation which, in effect, said this: 'If a bird has a dominance of 100%, then its susceptibility to interference is 0 and it will not be affected by interference. But if the dominance of a bird is, say, 20%, then its intake rate will decrease, say, by 30% as the density of birds where it is feeding increases from 100 to 200 per hectare'. The data provided an equation that would enable a future IBM to calculate for any bird of any dominance, age and feeding method and at any stage of the exposure period or of the non-breeding season by how much its intake would be decreased by interference from other oystercatchers, whether the density was 100 birds/ha or 1000.

Second, the data also allowed any individual in any future model to be ascribed a value for its foraging efficiency. This was measured as its interference-free intake rate relative to the interference-free intake rate of the average bird of the same feeding method and age feeding in the same place. If a bird of average foraging ability fed in a place at 500mg/5min, then a bird with a foraging efficiency of 0.8 would feed at 400mg/5min (0.8x500).

These two quantities would be used to define, or to measure, the competitive ability of each individual in the future model. For example, a good competitor might be given a dominance score of 90% and a foraging efficiency of 1.2. By contrast, a poor competitor could have the corresponding scores of 10% and 0.8. It was timely that these results became available because the first versions of the IBM were being developed, as will be described shortly.

Mussel theft: the cause of interference?

As well as just demonstrating that interference occurred in mussel-eating oystercatchers, there was a great deal of interest in what caused it. The questions were: 'What causes the intake rate of sub-dominants to decrease as the density of competitors increases?'; 'Does intake rate go down solely because more mussels are stolen from them or are other processes involved?'; 'How does the density of competitors affect the behaviour of both the dominants and the sub-dominants?'; 'Can the sub-dominants take steps (quite literally!) to minimise the interference they experience by avoiding more dominant birds?'. In-depth studies of robbing behaviour ('kleptoparasitism' in the technical jargon) were required, and a number of such studies were carried out.

The main findings were these: As the density of competitors increases, the number of birds that are close enough to attack the subject bird also increases (Fig. 4.5). As a consequence, the sub-dominant birds become increasingly diverted from searching for mussels as they try to avoid being attacked by others. Although an increasing proportion of the mussels that sub-dominants find are stolen from them as bird density increases, these losses are entirely insufficient to account for all of the decrease in their intake rate at high densities of competitors.

What happens instead is that, as competitor density increases, the sub-dominants find fewer and fewer mussels in the first place and take longer and longer to open any that they find. This occurs because the look up more and more frequently, presumably to see if another bird is about to attack them. If they detect an attacking bird soon enough, they can often run or fly away with the mussel. But if competitors are close by, this option is less successful and they often lose the mussel to the attacker. It appears that interference mainly arises because the sub-dominants are 'hastled' into feeding more slowly by the ever-increasing threat of being attacked as the number of competitors within 'attacking distance' increases. If things get so bad that their intake rate is substantially reduced, they either stop feeding and wait until circumstances become less competitive or they leave the mussel bed altogether and try their luck elsewhere.

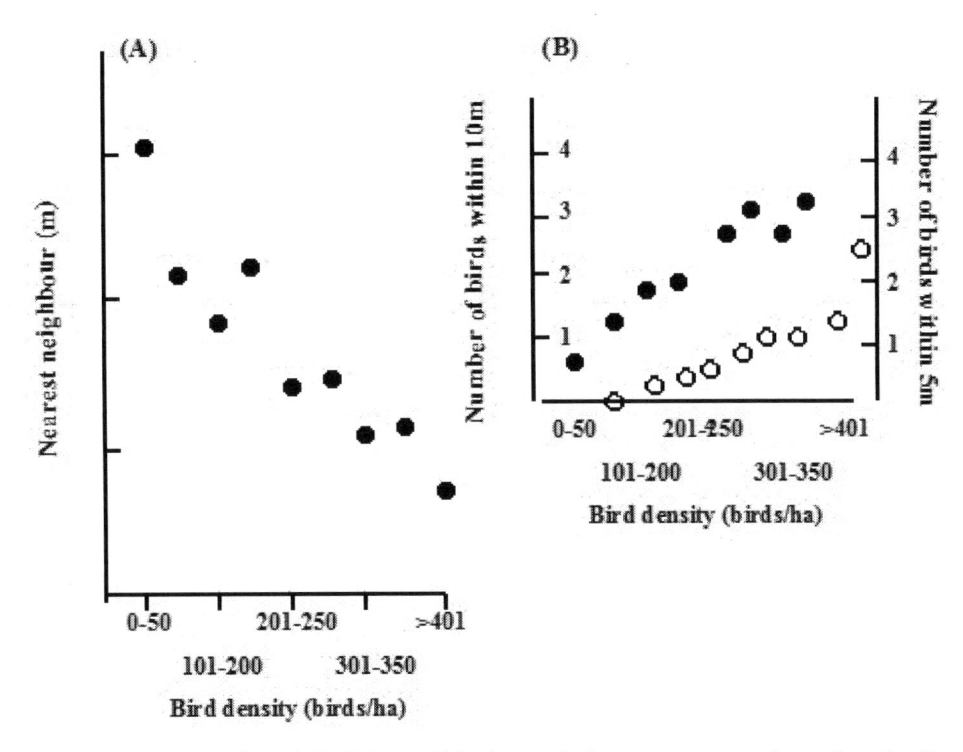

Figure 4.5 *Two ways of showing just how difficult it would be for a sub-dominant oystercatcher to keep its distance from other birds when there are a lot of other oystercatchers on the mussel bed.* **(A)** *The distance from a randomly chosen individual on a mussel bed to the bird that is nearest to it (its 'nearest neighbour'). It decreases from 12m to 3m – a fourfold decrease – when the density of oystercatchers is high.* **(B)** *How the numbers of birds within 5 m (open circles) or 10m (solid circles) of a subject individual – and thus at a distance which they could attack - rises very sharply as bird density increases.*

Implications for understanding the role competition in determining oystercatcher distribution over the mussel beds at different population sizes

Before moving on from the work on interference, it is timely to discuss how its findings provided a retrospective explanation of the change in the distribution of oystercatchers over the mussel beds as the population size increased with the return of the adults from the breeding grounds.

During the breeding season, the number of oystercatchers on the Exe estuary (where no oystercatchers bred) was very low and most were immature birds from one to three years old. Almost all of these birds foraged on the four large mussel beds that were close to the roosts on Dawlish Warren or Cockle Sand and where mussels were abundant. Because in many places the mussel bed extended down to low water mark of Spring tides, the birds could feed on mussels that contained very favourable amounts of flesh.

The enormous amount of time spent 'loafing' around by these young birds showed that they obtained their daily food requirements very easily at this time of year. Nonetheless, they competed vigorously with each other for mussels, and aggressive encounters were common. The result was that the least aggressive (and therefore least dominant) individuals had relatively low rates of food intake (Fig. 4.6). It was not clear whether these fights occurred because individuals were 'laying down a marker' for their future status amongst their peers or whether it was just less expensive of energy and/or quicker for the dominants to steal mussels than to find them for themselves.

With the return of the more dominant adults over the first part of the non-breeding season, competition on these mussel beds intensified even more. The result was that most of the immature birds left the highly preferred beds and fed on other mussel beds. As described in the previous chapter, bird densities very quickly became correlated with the numerical density of mussels. As argued in Chapter 2, his probably happened because the proportion of the ground covered by mussels increased directly in parallel with the average numerical density of mussels across the whole bed. Therefore, there was more space for mussel-feeders to forage on mussel beds with high average mussel densities than on ones with low average densities, and thus more room, or foraging space, for sub-dominant birds to avoid the dominants.

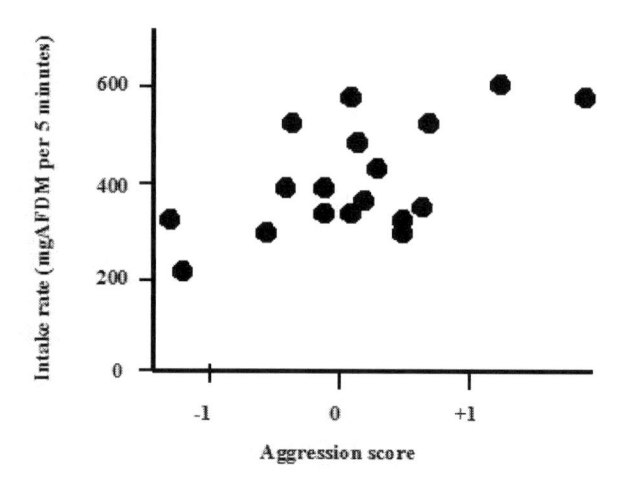

Figure 4.6 The most aggressive individuals achieve the highest average intake rate of mussels. Each point shows the average intake rate of one marked individual bird. The 'aggression score' measures the aggressiveness of the individual. If a bird attacked other birds once every 5 minutes but was itself never attacked during those 5 minutes, its aggression score, or net rate of aggression, would be 1-0, or +1. If, on the other hand, it was attacked by other birds once every five minutes, and never attacked other birds itself, its aggression score would be 0-1, or -1. If it attacked other birds once but was itself also attacked once per 5 minutes, its aggression score would be 1-1, or 0. 'AFDM' is the mass of the mussel, excluding water and indigestible inorganic matter.

Implications for modelling the mussel-feeding population of oystercatchers

Important implications for modelling the system arose from the main findings of the research on interference functions that began in earnest with Bruno's arrival in the early 1980s and finished some 10-15 years later with Richard Stillman's analysis of all of the data. The results showed that interference did not begin to suppress a bird's intake rate until the density of competitors where it was feeding had exceeded a particular threshold level. The value of the threshold differed between birds that used different feeding methods to open mussels.

Among the birds using a particular method for opening mussels, individuals varied greatly in aggressiveness and dominance and these two aspects of their behaviour were closely correlated. The most aggressive birds were also the most dominant and stole many mussels from sub-dominant individuals. Overall, but not exclusively, young birds less than four years old tended to be less aggressive and less dominant than the adults – particularly the oldest ones. Overall, an individual's dominance had a big influence on its susceptibility to interference, especially if it opened mussels by stabbing. The intake rate of sub-dominant individuals was suppressed at high competitor densities by far more than were those of the dominants. However, an individual's foraging efficiency – its interference-free intake rate - was quite unrelated to its dominance.

All this work showed that, in order to model this population of mussel-eating oystercatchers, the competitive ability of individuals in the model would have to consist of two quantities – their foraging efficiency and their dominance, and thus susceptibility to interference. Both quantities would need to be assigned to one individual bird independently of each other and at random, and both would have to differ between birds of different feeding method and ages. In effect, about six categories of oystercatchers would need to be included in the model if realism was to be achieved and, within each category, individuals would vary in both aspects of competitive ability.

MUSSEL SIZE SELECTION AND INTAKE RATE

The intake rate of an individual would depend not only on its competitive ability, of course, but also on the food supply where it feeds. The study of unmarked birds across a large sample of mussel beds (Chapter 2) had thrown up some surprises, most notably that the feeding rate (the number of mussels consumed per five minutes of foraging) appeared to be unrelated to the numerical density of the mussels where the bird was feeding. It had also shown that feeding rate increased rapidly towards the end of the non-breeding season, whereas it had been expected that it would go down as the birds gradually depleted the mussels.

Subsequent studies had shown that the increased feeding rate at the end of the non-breeding season persisted into the breeding season in the immature and the few adult birds that remained on the Exe at that time of year. This was associated with a marked switch from large mussels to small ones by birds using all three feeding methods, although only one method illustrates this point in Figure 4.7(A). Instead of consuming one large mussel about every five minutes, most birds took up to several very small ones instead. It was necessary to understand the processes that determined the sizes of mussels the birds ate and their feeding rate and thus their intake rate. Unless this could be done, it would not be possible to predict how the interference-free intake rate of oystercatchers would be affected by changes in the numerical density and size of the mussels brought about by a human activity, such as shellfishing.

Why do they select the large mussels for most of the year but not in spring? Large mussels certainly have a great deal more flesh inside them than do the small ones. On the other hand, it also takes a lot more time for an oystercatcher to break into a large mussel and to extract the flesh than it does a small one. It can take well over 5 minutes sometimes, and even then, success is not guaranteed and the bird often gives up. In addition, there is the risk when consuming a large mussel slowly that it might be stolen, the victim having by then done all the hard work! A more dominant oystercatcher or a carrion crow or herring gull could be biding its time before attacking to steal the opened mussel. If it takes too long to open a mussel, and despite its large potential reward, it can be better to reject it and spend the time instead looking for another one that will take less time to penetrate and be less at risk of being stolen.

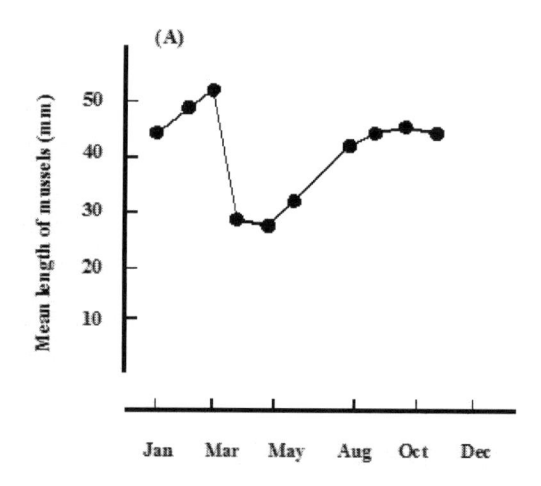

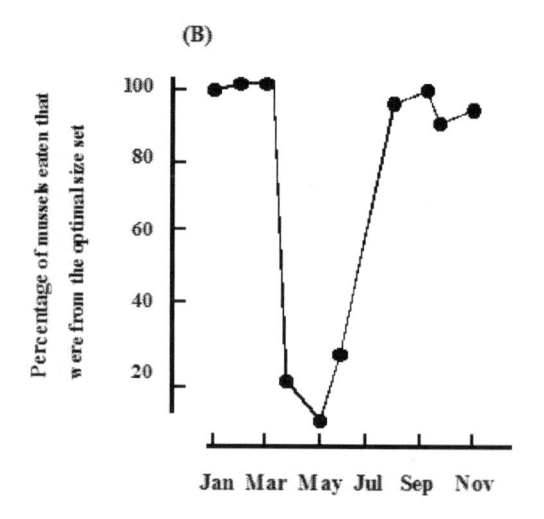

Figure 4.7 *Seasonal changes in the sizes of mussels eaten by oystercatchers that use the dorsal hammering technique.* ***(A)*** *The monthly mean length of the mussels taken.* ***(B)*** *The percentage of mussels that the birds took each month that belonged to the most profitable size classes; that is, the mussels they should have always taken if their objective was always to maximise their intake rate. For all the non-breeding season, the great majority of the selected mussels belonged to the most profitable size classes that they 'should' have taken, but this was not the case in spring.*

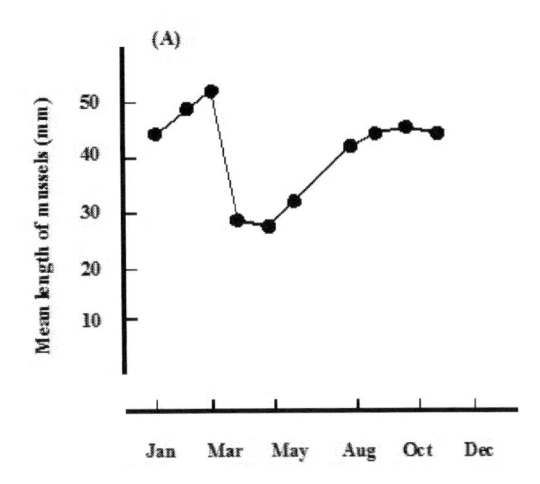

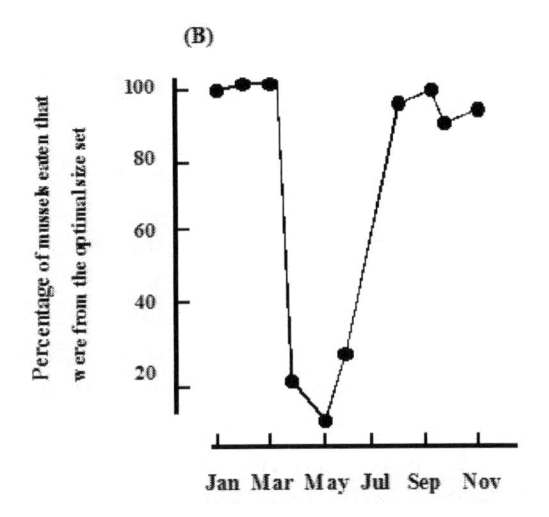

Figure 4.7 Seasonal changes in the sizes of mussels eaten by oystercatchers that use the dorsal hammering technique. **(A)** The monthly mean length of the mussels taken. **(B)** The percentage of mussels that the birds took each month that belonged to the most profitable size classes; that is, the mussels they should have always taken if their objective was always to maximise their intake rate. For all the non-breeding season, the great majority of the selected mussels belonged to the most profitable size classes that they 'should' have taken, but this was not the case in spring.

Nonetheless, evidence from the Exe and elsewhere in Europe strongly suggested that the extra time cost of dealing with large mussels is usually more than compensated by the greater amount of flesh that they contain. The profitability (E/h ratio) of the large mussels is high compared with that of the smaller ones, even though small ones can be 'handled' much more rapidly. A foraging model that described the 'economics' of foraging on mussels showed that, in order to maximise their intake rate, oystercatchers should eat only the large mussels (Fig 4.8). Surprisingly, this remained the case even in spring – even though it was less clear-cut - after the adult mussels had liberated their gametes into the water and so lost a great deal of their flesh content. It would still have been more marginally more profitable even then for oystercatchers to eat the large mussels, yet they switched to the smaller ones instead. As a result, only a small proportion of the mussels taken by the birds in spring actually came from the most profitable size classes. In contrast, well over 90% of the mussels they ate belonged to the most profitable (large) size classes during the remainder of the year.

It is still not clear why oystercatchers switch to small mussels in spring. It might be associated with changes in the composition of the flesh in adult mussels after they have liberated their gametes - but that is just a guess. From the point of view of modelling the oystercatcher-mussel relationship during the non-breeding season, however, what happened in spring, during the oystercatcher's breeding season, could be ignored, though it was of great interest.

The most important finding was that, throughout the entire 6-8 months of the non-breeding season, oystercatchers using all three feeding methods selected the large mussels of high profitability that maximised their intake rate most sharply. Importantly, however, the optimality foraging model that had been built to test this idea provided a means with which to predict the effect of a change in the sizes and flesh content of the mussels available to the birds on both the sizes of mussels they eat and on their intake rate. It enabled the interference-free intake rate of an average oystercatcher to be predicted from the numerical density, size composition and ash-free dry mass of the mussels on any mussel bed on which it was feeding.

If an environmental change resulted in a change in the sizes of the mussels available to oystercatchers on an estuary, or to the amount of flesh they contained, it would now be possible to predict how this would affect the intake rate of the birds. The development of the optimality foraging model allowed the following question to be answered,: 'How would the intake rate of the average oystercatcher be affected by a change in the density, average length and flesh content of the mussels within the size range 30-65mm?' So, for example, if shellfishing were to reduce the numerical density of these mussels by 30% and, by removing many of the largest ones, reduce their mean length from 50mm to 43mm but, through reduced competition for food, enable the average mussel of 43mm to increase its flesh content by 10%, it would now be possible to predict the effect that such a change would have on the intake rate of the average oystercatcher.

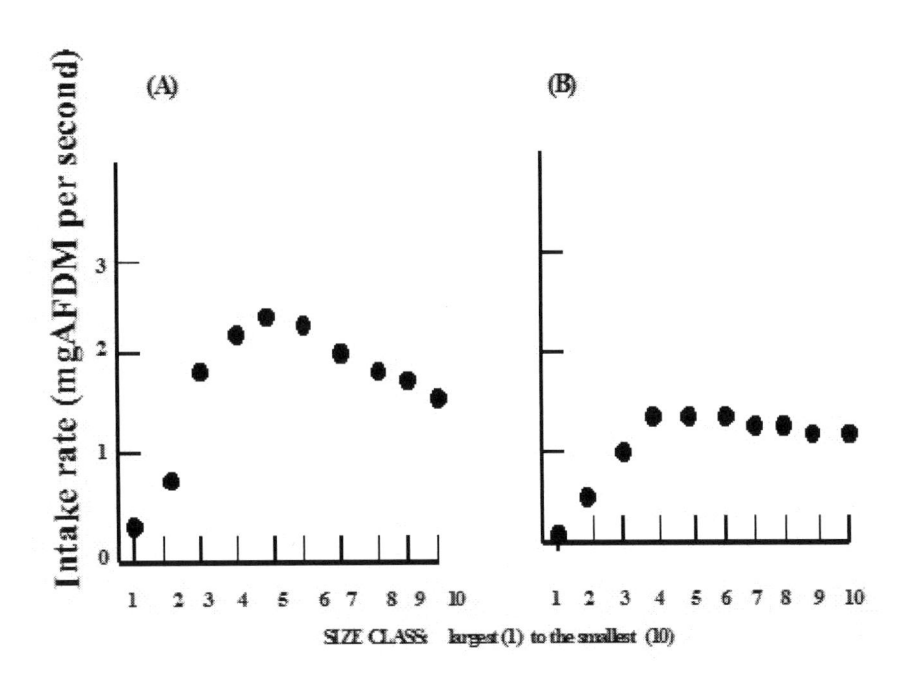

Figure 4.8 Intake rate and the selection of mussels of different profitability during a typical month during most of the non-breeding season – August **(A)** and at the end of the non-breeding season – April **(B)**. The intake rates are the outputs of an optimality foraging model that takes into account the rate at which birds 'encounter' vulnerable mussels as they search over the mussel bed, the 'time costs' of handling a mussel that is consumed and the amount of flesh obtained by eating it. The first point on the left of each graph shows the intake rate that a bird would achieve by taking only the largest and most profitable size class – size class 1. The next point to its right shows the intake rate that would be attained by taking both the largest size class and also the second largest size class – size class 2. The third point shows the intake rate when the three largest and most profitable size classes are all taken, and so on. The results show that the highest intake rates are obtained when only mussels that are in the top five **(A)** or four **(B)** largest size class are consumed. This is pretty much what oystercatchers do throughout the year by mostly consuming mussels 35-65mm long. The exception occurs in at the very end of the non-breeding season when the oystercatchers take mainly the small, unprofitable size classes. The optimality foraging model shows that this is not what they should select if the objective is to maximise intake rate.

REPRESENTING THE INTERFERENCE FUNCTIONS OF INDIVIDUAL OYSTERCATCHERS IN THE MODEL

The interference function of an individual bird could now be represented in a model in two simple steps. At low bird densities, intake rate is unaffected by interference. The intake rate achieved by an individual in these circumstances would depend on (i) the numerical density, average size and average flesh content of the mussels in the size range 30-65mm long where the bird was feeding which could be calculated by the optimality foraging model, and (ii) its own individual foraging efficiency.

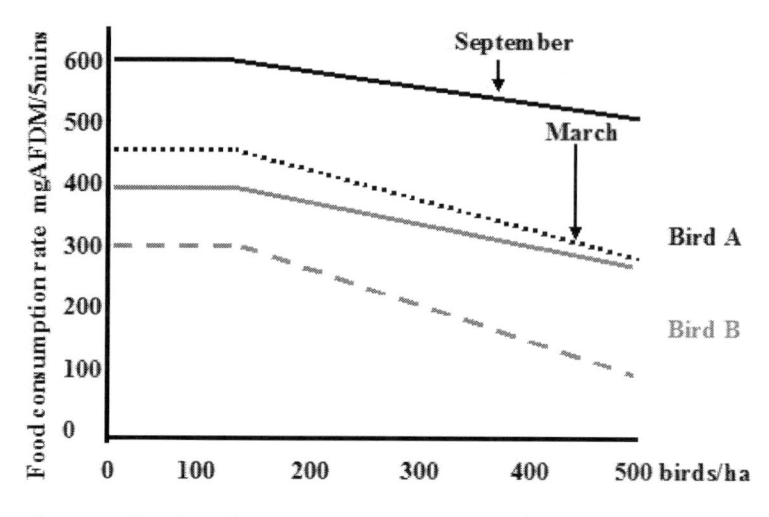

Figure 4.9 How competitive ability affects the intake rates of two contrasting birds at different densities of oystercatchers foraging on a mussel bed and at the start and end of the non-breeding season. In September, the density, size classes and flesh content of the mussels where the birds are feeding would enable a bird of average foraging efficiency to have an interference-free intake rate of 500mg/5minutes. Bird A (solid black line) has a foraging efficiency of 120% while that of bird B (solid grey line) is 80%. Accordingly, and respectively, they have interference-free intake rates of 600 (500x1.2) and 400 (500x0.8) mg/5 minutes at the start of the non-breeding season. When bird density increases, the intake rate of these two individuals declines at a rate determined by their respective susceptibility to interference. At the end of the non-breeding season in March (bird A, dotted black line; bird B, dashed grey line), the interference-free intake rates of individuals A and B decrease to 450 and 300 mg/5 minutes respectively because the flesh content of the mussels has decreased. Furthermore, the intensity of interference competition has intensified so their intake rates are decreased by a larger amount at high densities compared with the preceding September.

Consider a mussel bed where the density, average size and average flesh content of the mussels in the 'oystercatcher size range' enabled a bird of average foraging efficiency to attain an intake rate of 500mg/5min in September when the mussels contain a lot of flesh. There are two individuals feeding there: bird A has a foraging efficiency of 80% while that of bird B is 120%. Therefore they have, respectively, interference-free intake rates of 400 (500x0.8) and 600 (500x1.2) mg/5 minutes. But at certain stages of the tidal cycle, when only a small area of mussel bed is exposed, the density of birds on the mussel bed exceeds the threshold density at which interference begins to take effect (say 150 birds/ha). If bird density continues to rise, the intake rate of these two individuals would decline at a rate determined by their respective susceptibility to interference, as illustrated in Figure 4.9. Later on during the non-breeding season, in March, the interference-free intake rates of individuals A and B decrease to 450 and 300 mg/5 min respectively because the flesh content of the mussels has decreased. When the density of birds where they are feeding is high at that time of year, their intake rates can be reduced to very low levels because interference is more severe at the end of the non-breeding season that at the beginning, in September (Fig. 4.9).

These two characteristics of foraging efficiency and susceptibility to interference of the birds in combination with aspects of the food supply – in this example, the flesh content of the mussels – would enable us to calculate the intake rate of the individual according to the food supply where it is feeding and according to the density of the competitors present at the time. The time had come to start putting all this into a model.

But how?

REFERENCES FOR CHAPTER 4

Caldow, R.W.G. & Goss-Custard, J.D. (1996). Temporal variation in the social rank of adult oystercatchers *Haematopus ostralegus*. *Ardea*, **84,** 389-400.

Caldow, R.W.G., Goss-Custard, J.D., Stillman, R.A., Durell, S.E.A. le V. dit, Swinfen, R. & Bregnballe, T. (1999). Individual variation in the competitive ability of interference-prone foragers: the relative importance of foraging efficiency and susceptibility to interference. *Journal of Animal Ecology,* **68,** 869-878.

Cayford, J.T. & Goss-Custard, J.D. (1990). Seasonal changes in the size selection of mussels, *Mytilus edulis*, by oystercatchers, *Haematopus ostralegus*: an optimality approach. *Animal Behaviour*, **40,** 609-624.

Goss-Custard, J.D., Cayford, J.T. & Lea, S.E.G. (1998). The changing trade-off between stealing and independent foraging in juvenile oystercatchers, *Haematopus ostralegus*. *Animal Behaviour*, **55,** 745-760.

Goss-Custard, J.D., Cayford, J.T. & Lea, S.E.G. (1999). Vigilance during food handling by oystercatchers, *Haematopus ostralegus*, reduces the chances of losing prey to kleptoparasites. *Ibis*, **141,** 368-376.

Goss-Custard, J.D., Clarke, R.T. & Durell, S.E.A. Le V. dit. (1984). Rates of food intake and aggression of oystercatchers, *Haematopus ostralegus*, on the most and least preferred mussel, *Mytilus edulis*, beds on the Exe estuary. *Journal of Animal Ecology*, **53,** 233-245.

Goss-Custard, J.D., West, A.D. & Durell, S.E.A. le V. dit (1993). The availablity and quality of the mussel prey (*Mytilus edulis*) of oystercatchers (*Haematopus ostralegus*). *Netherlands Journal of Sea Research*, **31,** 419-439.

Stillman, R.A., Goss-Custard, J.D., Clarke, R.T. & Durell, S.E.A. le V. dit. (1996). Shape of the interference function in a foraging vertebrate. *Journal of Animal Ecology*, **65,** 813-824.

Box 4.1 Working in a tower hide

It is a strange way in which to earn a living, sitting alone for up to nine or ten hours in a cubic meter of space surrounded by a sometimes-flapping canvas wall and roof! Over the years, various improvements were added as flaws in the comfort of the design emerged. Number one flaw was the fish-eating birds, mainly cormorants, that used the roof as a perch. Here they deposited their foul-smelling droppings in copious quantities which, when mixed with abundant rain, turned into a malodorous and deep puddle, smelling like rotten fish-soup. Worse still, as its volume and weight accumulated through the autumn rains, it dripped through the canvas. While it could be kept out of the hair with a waterproof hat, it was impossible to stop it clinging to clothes, which therefore stank. It was often horrible.

The first solution to the fish-soup problem was, on entering the hide, to use the feet of the telescope tripod to push the roof of the hide upwards so that the soup cascaded over the side down to the mussel bed, where it belonged! But this was tricky and it was all too easy for much of it to flood in through the gaps in canvas, splattering the occupant and his/her notebook, sandwiches and coffee flask, and covering the floor with its slimy maloderousness! Eventually, curved steel rods were put inside the top of the hide that arched the roof upwards so that much of the stuff washed away in rain. This worked quite well but by no means perfectly. This research worker can still conjure up the clinging odour of the cormorant fish-soup in which he worked for so many years!

The numbing assault of one's rear end from the hard wooden seat was easily solved by taking out a nice rubber cushion on every trip. It couldn't be left in the hide because it would either be blown away or, more probably, get sodden with fish-soup. The cold was a more enduring problem, especially when it was windy, despite flasks of coffee. In the first flush of the project when nothing mattered but getting the data, you just got used to the idea that, after an hour or two, you would not be able to feel your legs from the knee downwards. You also got used to clambering 4m down a rope-infested tower with no feeling in the lower half of your legs and then stumbling back to base while going through the agony of returning circulation! Eventually, with Terry, a villager and store-holder in an outdoor market who was himself used to working in the cold, a number of solutions were tried. Sticking stocking feet inside a bag containing the freshly-shaved hair from Terry's poodle, Bella, was one failed solution! Terry found the answer: moon boots, as worn by one of his colleagues in the market. They worked pretty well, but only delayed the numbness for a few hours. On long watches on cold days, the returning circulation just had to be endured! Surely, these days it would be possible to find something warmer……

Box 4.2 Nights in the hides

However many bearings were taken during the day, finding a camouflaged hide in the middle of the estuary at night, even with a moon, in those pre-GPS days was not easy! It could take ages to locate the hide, which had to be done before the tide had receded enough to start exposing the mussel bed so that the hide could be entered before birds arrived.

Many night visits to the hide were carried out on Neap tides when low water occurred around dawn. These occasions provided good opportunities for watching the birds feeding at high densities of competitors. High tide would be around midnight, or not long afterwards. That is when the boat was launched and the fumbling around began: luckily, because it was a Neap tide, the current speeds were generally low. Often, it was necessary to wait a few hours in the hide for the dawn – some of which were spectacularly beautiful, of course. Once inside, it was all too easy to fall asleep, calmed by the sound of water lapping against the boat moored alongside the tower and half-drugged by the ever-present aroma of cormorant soup. [The only acceptable antidote against these otherwise charming birds was to stick a hand out of the side of the hide when one landed on top, thus giving it the fright of its life and hopefully discouraging its early return!] On one occasion, the researcher had been at a dinner party the night before and, after driving 100 miles and boating for sometime before settling down inside the hide, he fell asleep, exhausted. He only woke when the returning tide caused the boat moored alongside to started to bang against tower, by which time all the birds had left for the roost. No target achieved that night!

Box 4.3 Unusual happenings around the hide

Fired up by the vision of the results that would one day emerge from all this work, working in the hide was usually enjoyable despite the sometimes maloderous discomfort, cold, and cramp. To use the telescope, you had to lean forward in a hunched posture that was exactly contrary to how we are now instructed to sit in front of a laptop! A target for the number of data to be obtained during a watch was set every time: today, for example, 40 five-minute observations on the five birds for which we had rather few data.

Achieving the target focussed the mind and mostly diverted from the cold discomfort that even Bella's hair could not dispel! Also, occasionally, distracting things happened to break up the day. On one occasion, a gentleman wandered along the shore just 200m from the tower hide. He looked towards the green-ish hide that was smeared with cormorant soup. He then walked towards it, scaring all the birds away and preventing any more data from being obtained for some time. As he got near the hide, he stopped, looked up and asked what it was: 'It's a bird hide', came the answer through gritted teeth! 'I thought it was' came the answer, and he turned to get back to the shore. Huh! What about scaring the birds away just to satisfy his curiosity! But it's a free country!

A few days later, another guy appeared in the same place, apparently with the same question in mind. The researcher in the hide was already below target that day and, fearful that the birds were going to be scared away again, decided that preventive action had to be taken. As the guy stood looking towards the hide that was some 100m from the shore, the researcher yelled in a huge voice: 'IT'S A BIRD HIDE!'. He stood absolutely rooted to spot, turning his head rapidly from side to side, even upwards, to find the source of this voice! He hadn't seen the hide at all because it was so well camouflaged in the feeble light against the hills beyond, on the other side of the estuary! He had been looking for his boat which had broken its mooring. And a voice addressed him from nowhere, but apparently from somewhere on high! Were he an atheist, he might have thought momentarily of reconsidering his position!

Sometimes unaware that someone was in the hide, people did sometimes perform some quite eye-catching antics, including one vigorous and impressively prolonged attempt on the seawall to self-replicate! On another occasion, an old lady managed to empty her bladder, drawers around her boots, all the while crab-crawling forward and picking up winkles (ahead of her, it should be pointed out) for sale. She must have been on piece rates and short of money!

The many people living around the estuary and working or playing on it got used to the tower hides, and many interesting conversations took place in the pubs around the area. It was always entertaining to hear a person's pet (and always unsubstantiated) explanation of why this or that aspect of the ecology of the estuary had changed over the last 20 years or so: usually, it was because there were now more brent geese! But nobody seemed to mind the towers, and some even used them for navigation or for resting against if tired from wind-surfing. One gentleman even asked if he could shoot ducks from one of them! A fishermen told the story that, on returning in his boat on a foggy night from a fishing trip, he navigated home as usual by using as a way mark a tower that had formerly been 200m from the seawall. Unknown to him, it had been moved 100m inshore, and so he collided with the seawall! He bore the researchers no grudge, and found it rather amusing!

Box 4.4 A technical point – the use of length-standardised measure of intake

Now is a good time to point out that, in this analysis, the same values for the flesh content of an individual mussel of a given length had been used to calculate a bird's intake rate irrespective of where the bird was feeding and the stage of the non-breeding season. This was done because the flesh content of an individual mussel of a given length varied according to the location of the mussel on the shore. The mussels containing the most flesh occurred low down the shore where they could feed for longer over high tide. The flesh content of mussels also changed over the non-breeding season. By March, after the winter, a mussel of a given length had lost some 40% of the flesh, and therefore energy, it would have had at the start of the non-breeding season in September.

You can think of the length-standardised intake rate as a measure that was unaffected by the flesh content of the mussels where the birds happened to be feeding. Consider two birds, A and B that are eating mussels in the same place at the same time of year. Bird A eats two large mussels in five minutes whereas bird B eats only one small one. Bird A would therefore have a very much larger absolute rate of intake than bird B; the difference could easily be as large as 1500mg/5min to 500mg/5 min. In the absence of interference, bird A would be judged the more efficient forager of the two.

But now consider what happens to the comparison if bird A is watched feeding high up the shore in March whereas bird B is watched in September at the very bottom, at the water's edge. As before, bird A eats two large-sized mussels in five minutes while bird B eats just one small one. But in those different places and at that these different times of year, bird B might now have a much higher absolute rate of intake than bird A even though it is taking smaller mussels at a lower rate. This is because the mussels taken by bird B contain much more flesh than do those being eaten by bird A, despite their smaller shell size. Bird B's mussels come from the bottom of the shore in September whereas bird A's mussels from the top of the shore in March. Making the comparison between the two birds on the basis of their absolute rate of intake would give the misleading conclusion that bird B was more efficient than bird A. Therefore a single value of the flesh content of mussels of a given length were used in calculating the intake rate of individual birds, irrespective of where and when they were feeding. These 'length-standardised' measures of intake rate allow the foraging efficiency of individuals to be compared without the comparison being distorted by the different amounts of flesh in the mussels when and where they happened to be foraging.

It had been expected that the foraging behaviour of the oystercatchers would have changed in either of two directions over the non-breeding season. On the one hand, the decline in the flesh-content of the mussels might have caused the birds to increase their 'feeding rate' – the **number** of mussels eaten per 5 minutes. They might have done this in order to compensate for the 40% reduction in the flesh content of individual mussels that occurred between September and March. If they had done this, their length-standardised measures of intake rate would have increased by about 40% between the start and end of the non-breeding season. This would have enabled them to compensate for the decrease of the same magnitude in the actual flesh content of each mussel they consumed. On the other hand, the abundance of mussels might have decreased over the non-breeding season as the food supply was gradually depleted by the birds themselves and by other factors, such as gales. But, in fact - and to our surprise – there was no evidence to suggest that either of these two things happened.

Box 4.5 Impressions of differences between individuals

It really did not take long in the hide to see that some individually-marked oystercatchers were very aggressive and very dominant while others were exactly the opposite. Distinguishing the aggressive from the less aggressive was helped by the fact that many individuals tended to restrict their foraging to limited regions of the mussel bed. This meant that some birds that fed near to the hide were seen very regularly.

After a while, it would become equally obvious that some individuals were extraordinarily effective at finding and opening large mussels whereas others were not. You could see the really efficient forager 'calmly' moving only a short distance from one opened mussel to the next and extracting lumps of flesh so large that it struggled to swallow them. Such birds were also noticeable because they spent so much time just standing around, presumably while they digested the large amount of food they had ingested. In complete contrast, the least efficient birds rushed around the mussel bed, pecking frequently but only occasionally finding a mussel. And when they did, the mussel often contained rather a meagre amount of flesh. Such birds seemed always to be 'on the go'. It was easy to distinguish individuals at the extremes of the range in dominance and foraging efficiency but most individuals, of course, lay in between! Only large amounts of data and statistical comparisons enabled the dominance and foraging efficiency of this majority of individuals to be measured.

CHAPTER 5:
Putting it all together into an individual-based model

...which describes how the first version an individual-based model of mussel-eating oystercatchers was gradually developed using a game theory approach, and the important role played in its conception and construction by friends and colleagues, and how it didn't work too well at the start but not so badly that the whole approach had to be abandoned.

SELECTING THE MUSSEL BED ON WHICH TO FEED

Spatial variation in the food supply

It would have been a simple matter to model the oystercatcher population if there had been only one large mussel bed and the density of mussels, their size and energy content had been the same in every part of it. But such a uniform distribution of a food resource is extremely rare in nature, and was certainly not the case with the mussel food supply of oystercatchers on the Exe. All three of the most important aspects of the food supply varied between the 12 main mussel beds: the numerical density of the mussels, their size and their flesh-content. They also varied within each mussel bed, usually in relation to the level of the shore. In the jargon, the food supply was spatially variable at two spatial scales – between the various beds and within one bed.

Had the food supply not been so spatially variable, modelling the density-dependent mortality function for oystercatchers would have been simple. A sample of birds watched on that bed would have provided estimates of the variation between individuals in their foraging efficiency and susceptibility to interference. The results from this sample could then have been extrapolated to all the birds on the bed, as described in Chapter 4. The interference-free intake rate achieved by the average bird on that mussel bed could have been predicted from the optimality foraging model, also described in Chapter 4. It would then have been simple to calculate for each individual (i) its interference-free intake rate and then, from its dominance score, (ii) by how much, if at all, its intake rate would have been reduced as the numbers of birds on the bed increased. The numbers of birds at each population size that would have failed to achieve the average intake rate needed to survive could then have been calculated, as described in Chapter 3. The density-dependent mortality function would have been obtained.

Although this simple approach is essentially what the eventual IBM did, it leaves out the important reality that the food supply is spatially variable. It was very important that the model could work out how many birds, and indeed which particular individuals, would feed on each mussel bed at any population size considered. This is because, in combination with its foraging efficiency, a bird's interference-free intake rate depends on whether the mussels are large or small, scarce or abundant, full of flesh or skinny, which all depend on where the bird is feeding. Getting the interference-free intake rate right is important because it is the bird's 'starter' intake rate before it is eroded by interference competition as bird numbers increase. But how to predict which individuals would feed on which bed at whatever population size considered?

The arrival of game theory

Around this time, several behavioural ecologists had introduced game theory into their thinking. Whereas the earliest theoretical foraging models had only considered how individual animals make choices on their own, people began to think about how their choices might be affected by the presence of other animals of the same or different species. Real animals that are choosing between this or that prey species or this or that feeding location must often take into account what the other animals are doing. Given what had already been found out on the Exe, interference competition seemed highly likely to have a large influence on the decisions that individual oystercatchers made. Game theory provided a suitable conceptual framework for thinking about how the presence of competitors might affect what would be the best choice for a particular individual as to where it should feed.

Perhaps the best way to illustrate the game theoretic approach is to go straight to oystercatchers foraging for mussels on the Exe as so much of the basic biology has already been described. Figure 5.1 aims to get the basic ideas across.

Imagine an estuary at the beginning of the non-breeding season that contains three mussel beds. The first oystercatcher, bird 1, arrives. It quickly tries each of the mussel beds and finds that bed A, at the top of Figure 5.1, provides it with its highest interference-free intake rate because the mussels there are large and each one contains much more mussel flesh than do the mussels on the other two beds. Choosing to feed where it maximises its intake rate, bird 1 decides on bed A.

Shortly afterwards, bird 2 arrives. It quickly makes the same choice as bird 1 and settles down on bed A. Although being a less efficient forager than bird 1, bird 2 is a very aggressive bird and a good fighter and steals the mussels found by its neighbours whenever the opportunity arises. It quickly establishes its dominance over bird 1 and steals mussels from it whenever it is close enough to be pretty sure of success. But there are only two birds on the mussel bed, which has a surface area of 1ha. It is therefore very easy for bird 1 to avoid bird 2. As it looks for mussels, bird 1 keeps a close watch on bird 2 and stays as far away from it as it can, especially when it has just found a mussel. Only seldom does the sub-dominant bird 1 lose a mussel to its aggressive neighbour and the loss is certainly not large enough to wipe out the advantage of remaining on bed A. Both birds, then, feed at the interference-free intake rate determined by their foraging efficiency and the density, size and flesh content of the mussels on bed A.

Then another bird arrives on the estuary, and then another, and then another and quite rapidly there are many birds that have discovered that the potential feeding conditions are better on bed A than they are on the other two beds, beds B and C. These newly-arriving birds show a range of foraging efficiency and of aggressiveness. Some individuals are even more aggressive than bird 2 and others are even less aggressive than bird 1. A dominance hierarchy emerges in which every individual can rank itself relative to the other birds that it encounters as it forages around mussel bed A. But the density of birds on bed A still does not exceed the interference threshold density. The intake rates of all individuals present are still unaffected by interference from competitors.

Figure 5.1 The idea underlying the game theory approach to modelling how oystercatchers distribute themselves across the different mussel beds of the estuary. See text for full explanation.

With the continuing arrival of more birds to the estuary, the density of oystercatchers on bed A increases and eventually surpasses the interference threshold density of, say, 150 birds/ha. The density of oystercatchers is now so high that the least dominant individuals can no longer avoid the more dominant ones, and so their intake rate starts to decline by an amount determined by their susceptibility to interference. As yet more birds arrive, the intake rate of the sub-dominants decreases still more. The most sub-dominant individuals then start to look for alternative places to feed where their intake rate may be higher than their current, and still declining, intake rate on bed A.

From their visits to the other beds when they first arrived on the estuary, these most sub-dominant individuals remember that bed B also had large numbers of large and fleshy mussels, although they were not as profitable as those on bed A. A very sub-dominant bird, bird 3, whose intake rate had been much reduced by the intensifying interference competition on bed A, decides to try bed B. As it is the first individual to make the move, it can feed at the full interference-free intake rate allowed by the size and flesh-content of the mussels that are there and by its own foraging efficiency. It discovers that, because it is free from interference, its intake rate is higher on bed B than it was on bed A, even though the mussels on bed B are not so profitable as the mussels had been on bed A. Bird 3 decides to remain on bed B.

As numbers continue to build up on the estuary, more and more of the sub-dominant birds that initially settled on mussel bed A find that their intake rate is being ever more suppressed by the increasing number of superior competitors around them. More and more of them decide to try bed B. Like bird 3 before them, they discover that, because there is not yet any interference competition on bed B, and notwithstanding the less profitable mussels there, their intake rate on bed B is actually higher than it had been on bed A. They too decide to remain on bed B. They also try bed C but find that the less profitable mussels there provide such a low interference-free intake rate that, at the moment, it is better to remain on bed B.

The numbers arriving on the estuary continue to increase. The best competitors amongst the new arrivals find that, for them, bed A is the best option, despite the ever-increasing density of competitors. But the addition of these birds results in some of the currently poorest competitors on bed A now deciding that the time has come for them also to move to bed B. And so on.

As the build-up in numbers continues, the density of birds on bed B also approaches, and then surpasses, the threshold density of competitors at which the intake rates of the least dominant birds begin to decrease. Just as bird 1 eventually decided to try the next mussel bed down the food gradient, the least dominant birds on bed B now decide to try bed C. Here the mussels are even less profitable than those on bed B but there is no interference competition because there are so few birds there. For inferior competitors, bed C now becomes the best mussel bed in the estuary to maximise their intake rate.

And so it goes on, with birds moving between the three beds according to where they can currently obtain the highest intake rate. Which bed this is, of course, depends on the level of competition on each bed and that, of course, changes as the total numbers of birds increases. The key point to appreciate in this story is that the decisions made by each individual bird depend on the decisions that have been, and are still being made, by all the others. If, for example, and for some unknown reason, all the most aggressive birds on the estuary chose to feed on bed C from the moment they arrived, many of the sub-dominant individuals would remain on bed A instead of going to beds B and C. The decisions taken by the sub-dominant birds still enable them to maximise their intake rate but **which** option (*i.e.* on which mussel bed to feed) actually allows them to achieve that goal is influenced by the choices made by all of the other birds. Every bird is making its decision on the basis of the same principle; *i.e.* where to feed in order to maximise its own intake rate. But the best choice for maximising intake rate differs between individuals because they vary in competitive ability.

This description of how oystercatchers occupy mussel beds is a very simple example of the kind of problem that is addressed by game theory. In a very influential piece of work, the conceptual framework provided by this 'game theoretic' approach had been first applied to the distribution of animals over a spatially varying habitat by two American scientists, Fretwell and Lucas, who were considering territorial breeding birds. The game theoretic approach was first applied to foraging animals by two British scientists, Geoff Parker and Bill Sutherland, in whose highly influential theoretical model individuals varied in both foraging efficiency and susceptibility to interference, highly appropriate for oystercatchers feeding on mussels. For the purposes of individual-based modelling of oystercatchers eating mussels, such an approach could not have arrived at a more appropriate time (Box 5.1)!

MODELLING WHERE EACH INDIVIDUAL OYSTERCATCHER FEEDS

Before a game theoretic model could be built of the way in which individual oystercatchers choose the mussel bed on which to feed, a problem of scale had to be resolved, however. Almost all of the data that had been obtained to measure the dominance and susceptibility to interference of an individual birds had been obtained on a single mussel bed. An individual that was watched on one mussel bed was seldom, if ever seen, on another.

Why did this matter? Consider the three mussel beds A, B and C in Figure 5.1. Imagine that all the birds that are going to spend the non-breeding season on the estuary have now arrived and made their individual decisions on where to feed. Given the importance of a bird's aggressiveness in determining where it chooses to feed, it is highly unlikely that the birds on the highly competed bed A will have the same absolute levels of aggressiveness and fighting ability as the birds on bed C. It is much more likely that bed A will be populated by birds whose aggressiveness and fighting ability is well above the average for the whole population while bed C is populated by birds whose aggressiveness is well below the average. In short, birds that are very belligerent and very good at fighting wherever they feed would be expected to settle on bed A while the timid ones with poor fighting ability would seek refuge on bed C.

There was, of course, some evidence for this belief from the studies done during a previous summer and autumn on the two most preferred ones of the estuary. As the more aggressive adults returned from the breeding areas, the less aggressive immature birds that had been able to occupy those two prime mussel beds during the summer gradually moved elsewhere, as described in Chapter 2.

In an important insight, Sherman Boates had suggested some years before that a distinction could be drawn between a bird's 'local dominance' and its 'global dominance' or 'global aggressiveness' or 'global fighting ability'. The assumption (which to this day remains untested) is that individuals have a basic level of aggressiveness and fighting ability – a rank relative to all the other oystercatchers on the estuary - that stays with them wherever they are feeding. This would be a 'global' attribute, not in the sense that it applies everywhere in the World, but in the sense that it remains the same wherever a bird is on the Exe estuary. But while it was relatively easy to measure a bird's local dominance on a particular mussel bed, there was no method available for measuring its global aggressiveness or fighting ability.

The difficulty this caused for modelling how model birds would choose between mussel beds was this. All of the estimates of the susceptibility of an individual bird to interference had been obtained on just one mussel bed. Most of individuals had only been watched on the mussel bed at Cockwood. Some others had only been watched on a mussel bed off Sowden End, just to the south of Lympstone. A few more had been watched on a mussel bed mid-way between Exmouth and Lympstone. Again using Figure 5.1 to illustrate the point, a bird that was dominant on bed C would

133

almost certainly find itself at the bottom of the dominance hierarchy were it to move to bed A. Its high dominance on bed C would ensure that it was little affected there by interference; *i.e.* the slope of its interference function would be about 0. On bed A, on the other hand, its low dominance would make it very susceptible to interference, and the slope of its interference function could be as high as –0.5, or even steeper. A bird's dominance, and therefore its susceptibility to interference, would depend on its aggressiveness relative to that of the other birds amongst which it was feeding. Its dominance would therefore depend on which mussel bed it was foraging.

A way had to be found by which the model could calculate a bird's dominance on whichever mussel bed it was foraging, taking into account the different levels of aggressiveness of the birds on the different mussel beds. Thanks to Sherman's insight, the solution popped into the mind one day during a period when daily observations were being made from a tower hide in the middle of the estuary (Box 5.2).

On the assumption that the birds have a global aggressiveness or fighting ability, the most aggressive bird 1 in the population would have the highest rank on whichever mussel bed it was feeding. Likewise, the next most aggressive bird 2 would rank above all other birds on every bed, except bird 1. And so on, right down the ranks of global aggressiveness until the least aggressive, and therefore least dominant, bird in the whole population is reached. Were it possible to arrange, it should be possible on this hypothesis to rank each bird in terms of its global rank when all birds were in one, 'neutral' place, such as a roost. In fact, attempts were made to record the dominance scores of a sample of individuals at the communal roost on Dawlish Warren. This attempt was quickly abandoned because birds seldom fought there as there was not much to fight over!

How does the hypothetical construct of a global rank help with building an IBM? Imagine a notional population of 30 birds inhabiting mussel beds A, B and C in Figure 5.1. To keep things simple, let us assume that we are now well into the non-breeding season and that the birds have chosen the mussel bed where they are going to feed. Bird 1 – the most highly ranked individual on the estuary – is on bed A, as, in order of declining global aggressiveness and rank, will also be birds 2,3,4,5,6,7,8,9 and 10. The remaining individuals in the population – birds of global rank 11 down to 30 (the least aggressive bird of all) are on beds B and C.

On bed A, the fortunate bird with the rank 1 will be dominant to bird 2 and so forth, so the hierarchy on that bed is in the sequence 1>2>3>4>5>6>7>8>9>10. No matter that bird 10 is only one third of the way down the global scale of rank, it is the lowest ranking bird on bed A. In other words, its 'local dominance' is very low even though its 'global rank' is pretty high. An observer, of course, won't see this because all the less aggressive birds over which bird 10 would be able to assert its dominance are feeding elsewhere in the estuary, so bird 10 never encounters them. [This is analogous to the 10th best player in a local tennis club finding himself/herself ranked 100,000th in the World!] Bird 1 will win all its encounters with other oystercatchers, and thus have a local dominance of 100% on bed A. By contrast, bird 10 would lose most, and probably all, of its encounters and thus have a local dominance on bed A of 0. A bird's local dominance depends on its own global rank relative to the global ranks of all the other birds where it is feeding.

Remember now that an individual's susceptibility to interference is calculated from its local dominance score, which is the percentage of encounters it wins against all opponents on the particular mussel beds where it is watched as it feeds. Somehow, it was necessary to find a way that would enable the model to convert the global rank of a bird into its local dominance score on whichever mussel bed it was feeding. Another way of saying this is that a way had to be found to estimate the percentage of aggressive interactions it would win wherever it was feeding at the time.

The solution was to assume that the percentage of encounters a bird wins on a particular mussel bed - its local dominance score - would be equivalent to the percentage of the birds on the same mussel bed that had a lower global rank than it does itself. Consider bird Z with the global rank of 151 on a mussel bed where 100 birds are feeding that have global ranks of 101, 102, 103, 104 and so on down to 200. 50% of the birds on that mussel bed would have a global rank below that of bird Z. It would therefore be assumed that bird Z would win 50% of its encounters, and so have a local dominance of 50%. Its susceptibility to interference could then be calculated from its local dominance score of 50%, as described in Chapter 3.

This was a simple idea whose validity rested on two assumptions. The first assumption is that bird Z would win all the encounters it had with birds below itself in the global hierarchy (*i.e.* with global ranks of 150 to 200) but lose any encounters it had with birds with a higher global ranks than itself (*i.e.* 152 to 101). That is, it would be assumed that bird Z would win or lose irrespective of the magnitude of the difference between its global rank and that of its opponent. Bird Z would be as likely to win an encounter against an opponent that was ranked 155 as it is against an opponent ranked very much lower, say at 195. In reality, it was realised that bird Z might sometimes win some encounters with birds that are ranked above it in the global hierarchy and, equally, might lose to some birds that have a lower global rank. However, the assumption is that such 'reversed outcomes' would be infrequent and not related to the magnitude of the gap between the global ranks of the two birds involved.

The second assumption is that the sub-dominant birds do not restrict their feeding to parts of the mussel bed where they can mostly avoid birds of higher rank. By avoiding the places where birds of a higher rank feed, bird Z might raise its local dominance to 60%, or even 70%, with a consequent large reduction in its susceptibility to interference. However, even though avoiding areas with many dominants would be a profitable thing for sub-dominants to do, it may not happen if they are 'pursued' by higher ranked birds that regard a nearby sub-dominant as an easy source of mussels. In other words, the more dominant birds may 'keep an eye open' for birds that are less dominant than themselves and stay nearby so that they can launch a rapid surprise attack. If the dominants do behave this way, it would tend to lower the local dominance score of the subdominant, with a consequent increase in its predicted susceptibility to interference. If true, any tendency of sub-dominants to avoid the dominants might be partially or completely negated by the tendency of the dominants to pursue the sub-dominants!

To summarise, in order to convert a bird's global dominance score to its local dominance score on any of the 12 mussel beds of the Exe, two assumptions would have to be made: (i) that birds won or lost encounters with opponents irrespective of the magnitude of the difference between then in their global ranks, and (ii) the birds encountered those that were above or below them in rank in proportion to their numbers.

How to test these two assumptions? Once again, it could only be done by using observations made on a single mussel bed, and therefore on local, rather than global, dominance scores. Data collected from many marked individuals on six mussel beds over 13 years were extracted from notebooks to construct the graphs shown in Figure 5.2. The data showed that the magnitude of the difference in local dominance between birds involved in an aggressive encounter made little difference to the outcome. If one bird had a score just 5 percentage points above that of its opponent, it was almost as likely to win its encounter as if its dominance was 95 points higher (Figure 5.2A). The second assumption was supported by the data shown in Figure 5.2.B. The percentage of birds below an individual in the local dominance hierarchy predicted reasonably well the percentage of encounters it won. If there were 40% of the birds below a bird, its success in encounters, its dominance score, would also be about 40%.

These results were fortunate. They meant that it was not too unreasonable to assume that a model could calculate a bird's local dominance from its global rank relative to the global ranks of all of the other birds that were present on the bed at the same time.

Figure 5.1 can be used to illustrate how the model could calculate a bird's local dominance from its global dominance. Let us return to the beginning of the non-breeding season when the birds are arriving on the estuary and occupying mussel beds A, B and C. At some point, when all three mussel beds have been occupied by 999 birds 300 on bed A, 400 on bed B and 299 on bed C), bird Z with a global rank of 500 finally arrives. To which mussel bed should it go?

Bird Z first considers the bed with the best mussels, mussel bed A, where the birds range in global rank from 1 to 300. Bird Z's global rank of 500 is below the global ranks of all of the birds already on bed A. Bird Z's local dominance on this mussel bed, the best of the estuary, would be 0% and so it would be very susceptible to interference. Even though it might find many highly profitable mussels on bed A, it loses so many of them to its competitors that the actual intake rate it achieves is very low indeed.

But perhaps it would feed at a much better rate on bed B or bed C, so it tries each of them in turn. On bed B, it is about halfway down the dominance hierarchy because the global ranks of the birds on that bed range from 301 to 700. Its susceptibility to interference is appropriate for a bird of its feeding method with a local dominance of 50%. On the other hand, bird Z would be the top dominant on bed C where the birds with global ranks of 701 to 1000 occur. On this bed, bird Z is not affected at all by interference competition. Even though the mussels on bed C are of rather poor quality, bird Z's intake rate there is higher than the intake rates it would achieve on either of the other two beds where interference would greatly suppress its potentially much higher intake rate. Across all three beds, bird Z's intake rate would be 200, 350 and 400 mg/5min on beds A, B and C respectively. So bird Z decides to feed on bed C.

This is exactly how the IBM works. It ascribes to every individual a global rank that is unique to itself. If there were 100 birds in the population being modelled, the scores of the individuals would be 100, 99, 98, 97 and so on, down to 1. If there were 1000 birds, the scores would be 1000, 999, 998 and so on. The model now 'knows' the global rank of all the birds in the population being modelled. Indeed, the global rank of an individual in the model gives it its unique identity, or 'name: for example, individual 778.

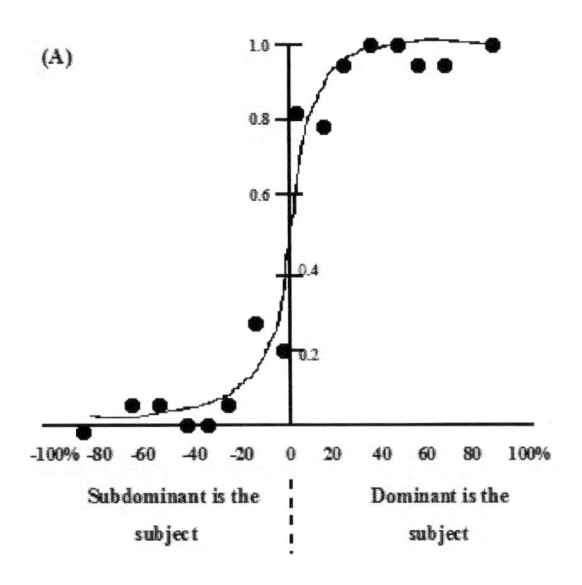

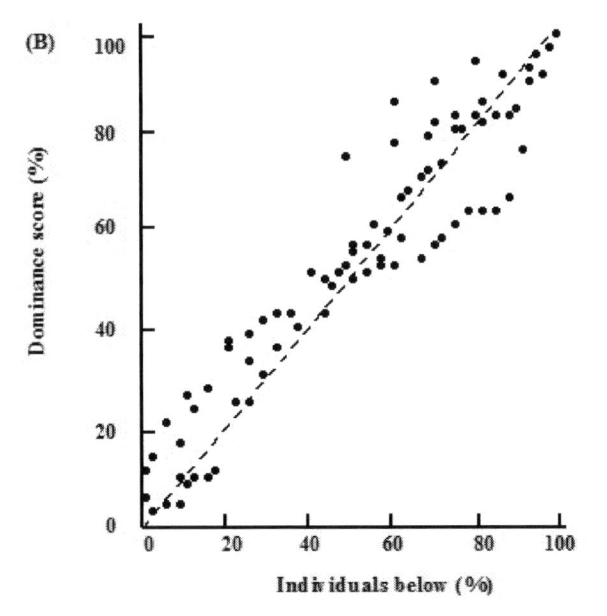

Figure 5.2 *Tests of the two assumptions made when calculating an individual's local dominance on one mussel bed from its global rank across all mussel beds.* ***(A)*** *The magnitude of the difference in local dominance between birds involved in an aggressive encounter made little difference to the outcome: the dominant won whether it was ranked 5 or 95 percentage points above the sub-dominant.* ***(B)*** *The percentage of birds below an individual in the local dominance hierarchy predicted pretty well the percentage of encounters it won: if about 40% of the birds were below a bird, its success in encounters, its dominance score, would also be about 40%.*

Each bird in the model is then given, at random, a value for its foraging efficiency that is independent of its global dominance. The range of values from which the model selects a value for a particular individual is drawn from a distribution of values obtained from the field data, as illustrated in Figure 5.3. It is assumed that a bird's foraging efficiency remains the same on whichever mussel bed it is feeding. From the supply present on each bed and from the individual's foraging efficiency, the model then calculates the interference-free intake rates of each bird on each of the mussel beds, as described in Chapter 4.

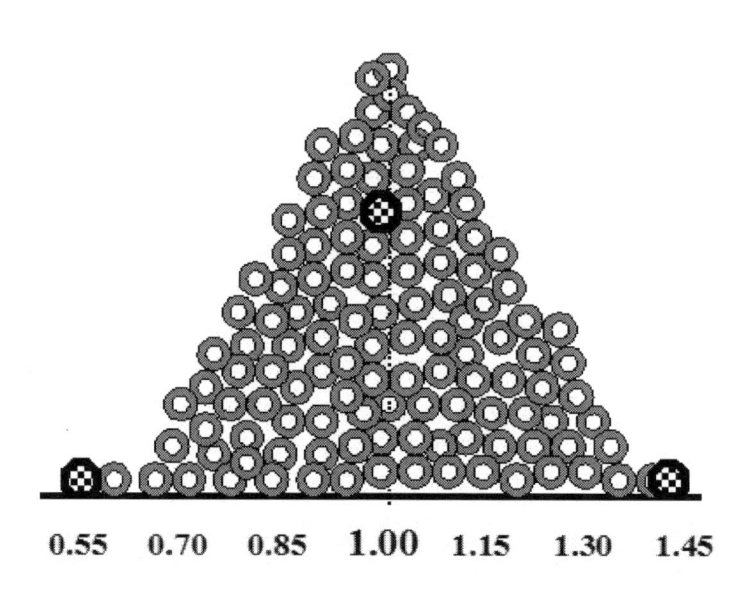

Figure 5.3 How the model calculates the foraging efficiency of each bird in the model population. Each grey circle represents the foraging efficiency of a single oystercatcher. An oystercatcher with an average foraging efficiency has a score of 1: the middle black, chequered bird is one such individual. The black bird on the extreme right is exceptionally efficient and its interference-free intake rate will be 45% higher than that of the average bird feeding in the same place at the same time. The black bird on the extreme left is extremely inefficient and its interference-free intake rate will be only 55% of that of a bird of average efficiency. In ascribing a value for the foraging efficiency to a model individual, the model picks a value at random from this frequency distribution of individual foraging efficiencies. Based on the field data described in Chapter 4, it does this from a normal distribution with a standard deviation of 15% of the mean.

The next step is for the model to work out the mussel bed where each individual should be placed. This of course depends not only on its own interference-free intake rate on each bed but also on the density of birds currently on a bed and on its local dominance, which determines by how much its actual intake rate is reduced by interference.

Imagine that all the birds in the model start by being 'stored' at a roost from which they will be taken and placed on a mussel bed as the tide goes out. The model picks an individual at random from the roost. Then from the food supply present on each bed and from the individual's foraging efficiency, the model calculates the bird's interference-free intake rate on each bed. The model then places that individual on the bed where its intake rate is highest. It then does the same with the next bird, also chosen at random, and so on, bird by bird.

Initially, of course, there are so few birds on the mussel beds that the density is nowhere high enough anywhere for interference to suppress the intake rate of even the most sub-dominant individual. All the birds will be placed on the mussel bed which provides all of the birds with their highest interference-free intake rate: that is, bed A in Figure 5.1.

Nonetheless, as every new bird arrives on the mussel beds, the local dominance of all individuals already present is re-calculated - even though there is no need yet to reduce their intake rate by interference. But eventually, the density on bed A reaches the threshold density at which interference does begin to occur. The model then calculates the susceptibility to interference of all the individuals that are then present from their local dominance. It does this using an equation that relates the slope of a bird's interference function to its age, feeding method and dominance and from the stage of the non-breeding season, as described in Chapter 3. Then, from the density of competitors present at the time, the model calculates by how much the potential intake rate of each bird on bed A is suppressed by interference.

Next, the model compares the intake rates that each bird would achieve on bed A with the interference-free intakes they would achieve on each of the other beds. Initially, of course, the density of birds on these other beds will still be well below the interference threshold (Fig. 5.4). The model places the bird on the mussel bed where at the time it would obtain the highest intake rate. The birds have now begun to spread out from bed A and are occupying other beds in the estuary.

As yet more birds arrive from the roost, the densities of birds on more and more of the beds exceed the interference threshold density. As every additional bird arrives from the roost, the model recalculates for all individuals on all beds the intake rates each one of them would achieve on each bed, given that the competitive environment everywhere has changed with the arrival of even one more bird. In random order, the model recalculates for each individual in the entire population on which mussel bed it would currently obtain the highest intake rate, and moves it there.

Eventually, all the birds have been removed from the roost and are on one or other of the mussel beds. Sometimes, the difference in intake rate that the model predicted a bird would obtain on two different mussel beds was very small indeed. This had the effect of preventing the model from finalising where birds would feed. A slight change in the intake rate of some birds when one other bird moved could have considerable knock-on consequences. In the jargon, 'instability' was the problem. Field studies suggested that an oystercatcher could detect a difference between the intake rates it would achieve on two mussel beds only if the difference was greater than 3%; *i.e.* it could detect the difference between 100 and 104mg/min but not between 100 and 102. Therefore, in the model, the birds regarded a difference of less that 3% as indistinguishable and its bed choice was made at random between the two beds.

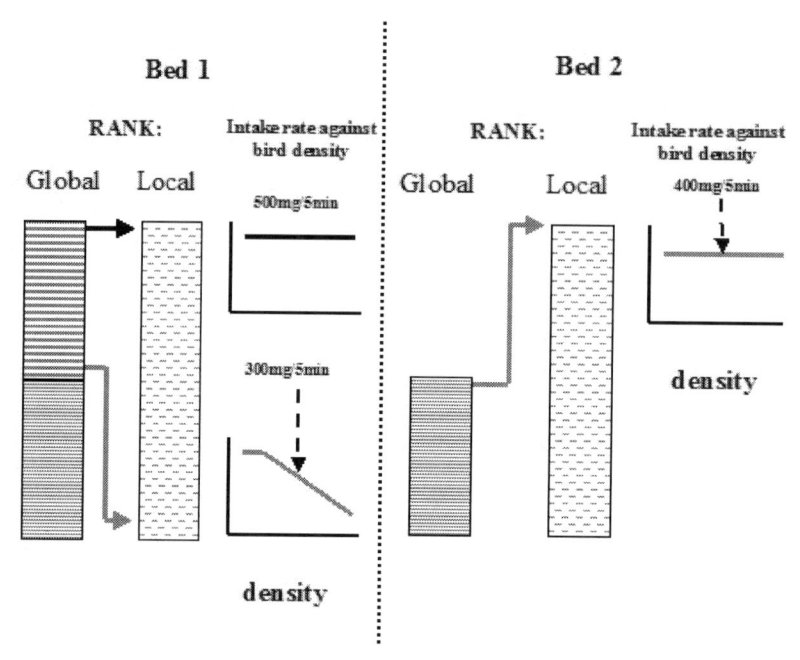

Figure 5.4 How the model calculates the potential intake rate of two model oystercatchers on two mussel beds. On bed A, the food supply enables birds of average foraging efficiency to achieve an interference-free intake rate of 500mg/5mins whereas, on bed B, the equivalent value is 400mg/5mins because the mussels there are smaller than on bed A. On bed A, black bird has a local dominance of 100% because, as the left-hand column shows, it has a very high global dominance. Although grey bird is only about half way down the global dominance hierarchy, it is very near the bottom of the local hierarchy because most of the birds below it in the global hierarchy – shown by thin horizontal lines – have previously decided to leave bed A. Black bird has such a high local dominance score on bed A that it is unaffected by the density of its competitors there and so its interference function is flat. In other words, it feeds at the rate of 500mg/5mins across the whole range of bird densities that occur there, this rate being determined by its average foraging efficiency and the quality of the mussels. As this intake rate greatly exceeds the intake rate it could achieve on bed B, it remains on bed A. In contrast, were grey bird to remain on bed A, its intake rate would be reduced below its potential of 500mg/5mins to 300mg/5mins because – as its interference function on bed A shows – at the average density of birds occurring on that bed (indicated by the dashed vertical black line), interference greatly reduces its intake rate. On bed B, however, grey bird is the top dominant and so has a local dominance score of 100%. This allows it to feed across the whole range of competitor densities at its interference-free intake rate of 400mg/5mins. As this rate is higher than its potential (interference-reduced) rate on bed A, grey bird decides to stay on bed B.

FIRST STAB AT AN INDIVIDUAL-BASED MODEL OF OYSTERCATCHERS: VERSION 1 OF THE IBM

The first version of the model was now built by our outstanding colleague, Ralph Clarke. A number of tests of the model predictions were carried out and these suggested that it replicated some of the main features of the way in which oystercatchers exploited the mussel beds of the Exe. But the agreement between what the model predicted and what had actually been observed on the estuary was by no means perfect, as can be illustrated with the following examples.

The densities the birds on all the beds were higher, of course, when the total population of mussel-eating oystercatchers was 2000 than when it was only 500 (Figure 5.5). As can be seen from this Figure, there was marked tendency for the mussel beds that supported high densities of birds when the population was high to also support high densities when it was low. This trend was replicated by the model (Fig. 5.5). However, there were two mussel beds for which the model predicted densities of about 80/ha and this was about double the densities that had actually been recorded there. Although the model replicated the overall observed trend, there were some large quantitative discrepancies between the predicted and observed values.

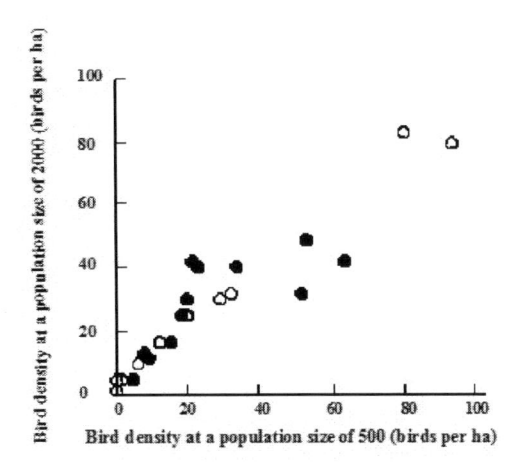

Figure 5.5 *A test of the model's predictions for the distribution of birds over the 12 mussel beds of the Exe estuary at low and high population sizes. The density of the birds on all the beds was higher, of course, when the total population of mussel-eating oystercatchers was 2000 (non-breeding season) than when it was only 500 (the breeding season). There was an overall tendency for the densities actually observed (closed circles) to follow those that were predicted by the model (open circles).*

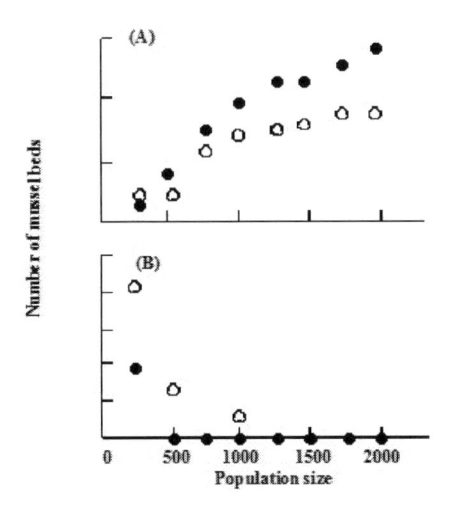

Figure 5.6 *A second test of the model's predictions for the distribution of birds over the 12 mussel beds of the estuary. As the population size increased at the start of the non-breeding season, the numbers of mussel beds where **(A)** the density of birds exceeded 10/ha, and **(B)** there were no birds present at all increased and decreased respectively. The predictions of the model (open circles) fell below the observed values (solid circles) in (A) but exceeded them in (B)*

A second test was made of the model's predictions for the distribution of birds over the 12 mussel beds of the estuary. As the population size increased at the beginning of the non-breeding season, the numbers of mussel beds where the density of birds exceeded 10/ha – an arbitrarily chosen value – increased. Simultaneously, the numbers of beds where there were no birds at all decreased. Once again, the predictions of the model matched the overall trend that had been observed. However, the match between predicted and observed values was again by no means perfect. The predicted numbers of beds fell below the observed values in the first case and exceeded the observed values in the second (Figure 5.6). In other words, the birds in the model spread out over the mussel beds more slowly as the population size increased than they actually did on the real estuary itself.

Other tests of the model's success at predicting the changing distribution of oystercatchers over the mussel beds as the population increased gave essentially the same result. The model predicted the observed trends quite well but there was not always an exact quantitative concordance between the predicted and observed values.

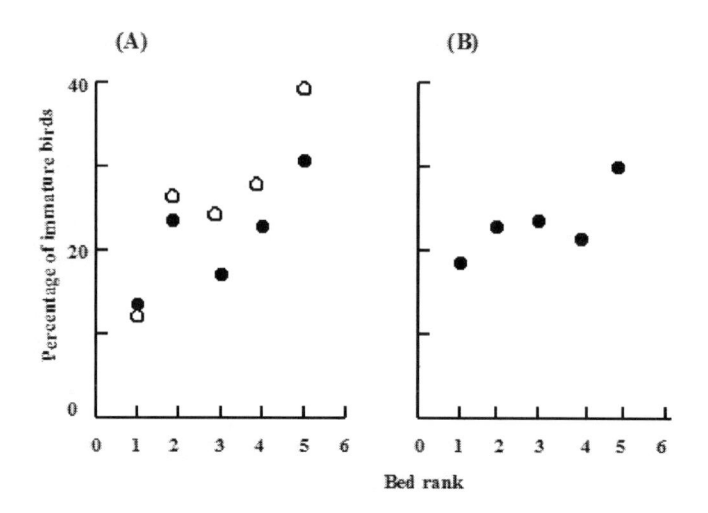

Figure 5.7 A test of the model predictions for the ages of the birds that fed on the different mussel beds. For this comparison, ten of the 12 mussel beds were combined into five pairs of beds with similar characteristics. The pair ranked 1 comprised the two most preferred mussel beds whereas the pair ranked 5 comprised the two least preferred. The proportions of the oystercatchers on each of these pairs of mussel beds that were immature are plotted against the rank of the mussel bed. (A) This shows the observed proportions of immature oystercatchers on each pair of beds were measured in two ways: from the ages of all the ringed birds that were seen (closed circles) and from direct counts of samples of un-ringed birds (open circles). The model predictions for the same pairs of beds are shown in (B).

Tests were also made of whether the model predicted accurately the age of the birds that fed on the different mussel beds. To do this, ten of the 12 mussel beds were combined in pairs with similar densities and sizes of mussels and distances from the main roosts. The proportion of the oystercatchers on each of these five pairs of mussel beds that were immature had been counted, as described in Chapter 3. In addition, the ages of all the ringed birds seen on each bed were known and the proportion that were immature could be calculated from this sample of ringed birds as well.

In Figure 5.7, the pair ranked 1 were the two most preferred mussel beds. The proportion of immature birds increased from the beds ranked 1 to the lowest-ranked beds, ranked 5, and this trend was replicated by the model. However, once again, the quantitative agreement between the predicted and observed values was not as close as it might have been. The model over-predicted the proportion of immature birds on the highest ranked beds and under-predicted the proportion on the lowest ranked beds.

A second test was made of whether the model predicted accurately the age of the birds that fed on the different mussel beds. As the population size increased at the start of the non-breeding season, the numbers of adult birds on the two most preferred beds of the estuary increased while the numbers of immature birds decreased (Fig. 5.8(A)). The model predicted the same trends (Fig. 5.8(B)). However, in comparison with the observed values, the model predicted that more adults and more immature birds would occur on these two most preferred beds than had actually been observed. Once again, the model predicted the observed trend but failed precisely to match the observed values.

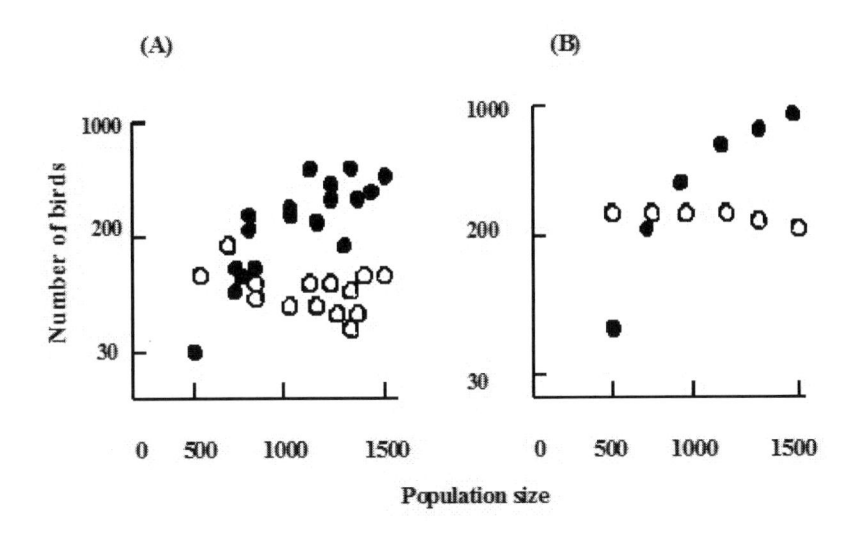

Figure 5.8 A second test of whether the model predicted accurately the age of the birds that fed on the different mussel beds. (A) As the population size increased at the start of the non-breeding season, the numbers of adult birds (closed circles) on the two most preferred beds of the estuary increased while the numbers of immature birds (open circles) decreased. (B) The model predicted the same trends but, in comparison with the observed values, over-predicted the numbers of both the adult and immature birds over the whole of the period of population increase. Note the non-linear scale on the vertical axis.

Taken together, these comparisons between the predictions of the model and what had actually been observed provided some encouragement. The important thing was that they suggested that the model did represent reasonably well the competitive processes that had been shown to occur in the oystercatcher population. Had this not been the case, the model would not have predicted - even approximately - how the birds spread out over the mussel beds as the population size increased at the start of the non-breeding season. Nor would it have predicted the movement of immature birds from the most preferred to the least preferred mussel beds as the more dominant adults returned from the breeding grounds. On the other hand, the comparisons suggested that the model under-estimated the intensity of the competition that occurred on the most preferred mussel beds. This was shown by its tendency to over-predict the numbers of birds of all ages that occurred on these beds and the numbers if sub-dominant birds that fed there.

This probably happened because the model was insufficiently 'fine-grained'. In this model, it was assumed that the density, size and flesh-content of the mussels were everywhere the same within one mussel bed. That is, it was assumed that the food supply was uniform over one mussel bed. But as was described in Chapter 3, all three of the characteristics of the mussels vary within a mussel bed in relation to shore level. Furthermore, there is a very pronounced down-shore gradient in some mussel beds – including the two most preferred ones – and a much less marked gradient in others. In other words, oystercatchers would tend to aggregate much more in some mussel beds than in others as they sought the most profitable places within each mussel bed.

In the model, however, the simplifying assumption had been made that the food supply within each mussel bed was uniform. Accordingly, within the model, the birds would have spread out much more on each mussel bed than they would have actually spread out in nature. This means that the model under-estimated the densities at which oystercatchers actually have fed on the mussel beds of the estuary. What's more, the magnitude of the under-estimation in the density of birds would have varied between mussel beds.

It was way beyond the means of the project to measure the extent of the spatial variation in the density, size distribution and flesh-content of the mussels within each of the mussel beds. So nothing could be done at this stage to compensate for the resulting under-estimates of bird density that this model necessarily introduced. It was a useful lesson, however, and one that was remembered as future versions of the model were developed.

FIRST ATTEMPT AT DERIVING A DENSITY-DEPENDENT MORTALITY FUNCTION

Despite some quantitative discrepancies between model predictions and the observed distribution and behaviour of the birds, the overall agreement was sufficiently encouraging to use this first version to illustrate how such a model could be used to generate a density-dependent mortality function. Only one new parameter had to be introduced for this to be done, and that was a threshold intake rate required by a bird to achieve its daily energy requirements.

This threshold was required so that the model could 'decide' whether or not an individual bird was feeding at a rate sufficient to keep it alive: this idea was introduced in Chapter 3. If at any point during the non-breeding season that was being simulated an individual did not achieve that rate, it would be immediately 'deleted' from the model population. That is to say, it would be assumed to have starved to death. All the model had to do was to track each individual and remove it if from the population its intake rate fell below the chosen value of the 'survival threshold'.

When one individual had been removed, the remaining birds, of course, re-distributed themselves around the mussel beds. When no more birds died, the proportion of the initial numbers that had 'starved' by the end of the simulation was calculated.

The actual value of the threshold intake rate below which birds starved was not known. Accordingly, two values were chosen that were thought likely to encompass the real value in oystercatchers. The threshold was set in one series of simulations at 150 mg/5min and in another at 200 mg/5min. These values were approximately equivalent to the rate required to consume over two exposure periods of 6hr two times the basal metabolic rate of an oystercatcher. A series of simulations were run in which the only value that was varied was the size of the oystercatcher population. Population sizes of 1000 and 2000 birds approximated the actual population size but much higher values were also used in case density-dependence only occurred at very high population sizes.

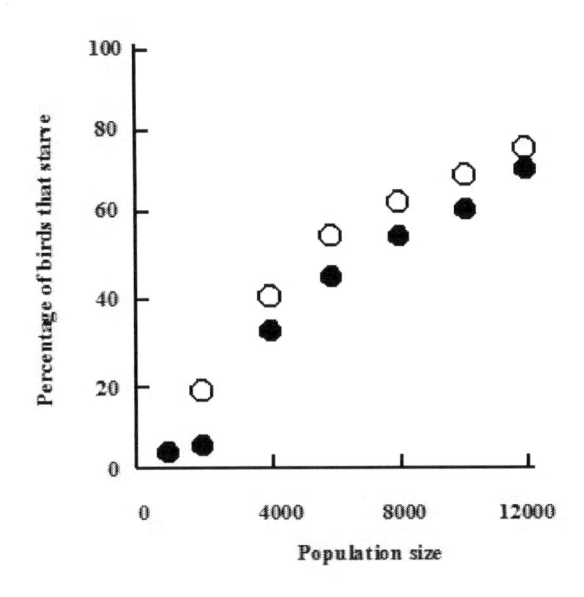

Figure 5.9 The density-dependent function obtained from version 1 of the IBM. As the intake rates required for an individual oystercatcher to meets its daily energy requirements was unknown, two values were used that were believed to straddle the actual values in nature, these being 150mgAFDM per 5 minutes (solid circles) and 200mgAFDM 5 minutes (open circles).

The simulations suggested that mortality was density-dependent over most of this range of population sizes (Fig. 5.9). This was an important finding. It suggested that at the population sizes actually recorded on the Exe, the mortality rate was density-dependent. Furthermore, at the then current population size of about 2000 birds, the predicted mortality rate depended a great deal on the value chosen for the survival threshold intake rate. Mortality rate increased from under 5% to about 20% when the threshold was increased from 150 to 200 mg/5minutes.

When you consider the outcomes that there might have this was an important finding. As Figure 5.10 illustrates, density dependence may not started until the population size had been very much greater – say 10,000 or even 20,000 birds, and so 5-10 times its actual size. In these circumstances, it may not have seemed sensible to invest much more time and effort in taking the model of oystercatchers on the Exe any further forward. But this was not so. This preliminary evidence suggested that the mortality might be density-dependent at the population sizes that had been recorded on the estuary. It suggested that the model should be developed further to be as realistic and accurate as possible. After all, it might well be needed to provide predictions that could be used by estuary managers, and particularly the managers of shellfisheries.

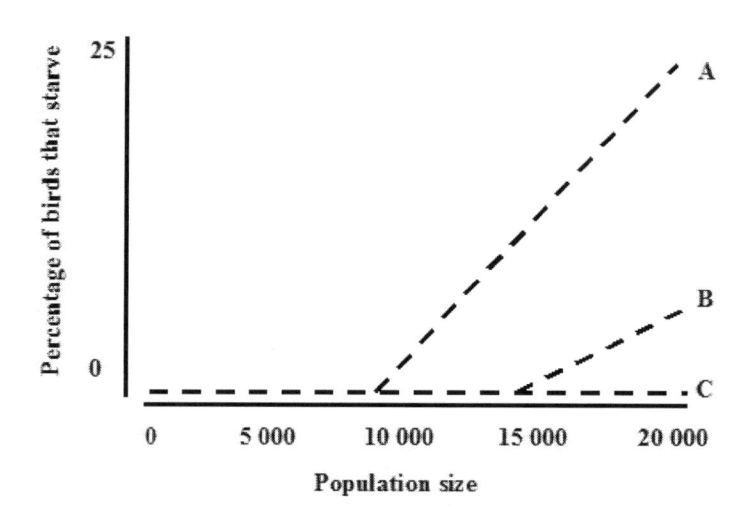

Figure 5.10 Three mortality functions that might have been predicted by version 1 of the IBM. In one (C), there is no density-dependence and the mortality rate remains near to 0 across the entire range of population sizes up to 20,000 birds. The other two are density-dependent but in (A), the density dependence begins at a much lower threshold population size, and reaches much higher mortality values, than in (B).

ADDING MORE REALISM: VERSION 2 OF THE IBM

Version 2 extended the very much simpler version 1 in a number of ways that enabled the model to represent the real oystercatcher-mussel system much more realistically. This was again done very skilfully by Ralph Clarke by adding features of the birds' natural history and of their environment.

The following changes were made: (i) a time-base was added: one simulation now ran from September 1st to March 15th in 24hr periods, each day having the actual day length on the Exe; (ii) the daily consumption of mussel flesh by each individual oystercatcher was tracked and, if it obtained in a 24hr period more than its current daily requirement (which is well known for oystercatchers), the surplus consumption was stored as fat up to a limit, and with an efficiency, that had been determined by studies elsewhere; (iii) the feeding location and current level of fat reserves of each individuals were tracked on a daily basis; (iv) the numerical density, mussel size distribution and flesh-content of the mussels on each mussel bed were also tracked on a daily basis; *i.e.* depletion of the mussels by the birds themselves and by other mortality agents – such as gales – was therefore included, and (v) the proportion of each mussel bed that was exposed at different stages of the tidal cycle on Neap and Spring tides was also included. With these additions, it was hoped that the model would much more realistically represent the feeding conditions of mussel-feeding oystercatchers than had version 1.

Only the addition of the new component (v) required the collection of yet more field data. With the exception of extremely low Neap tides, no mussels are exposed over high water. As the tide recedes, mussel beds begin to emerge, with those at the highest levels of the shore appearing first, of course. Thereafter, more and more area is exposed until all the mussel beds are accessible to oystercatchers. When the tide starts to return, the whole process is repeated in reverse.

The surface area of each mussel bed at each stage of the exposure period determines, of course, the density of the birds and therefore the intensity of interference competition. The duration of the exposure period determines how much time the birds have available to feed on mussel beds during any one tidal cycle. Both of these quantities seemed very likely to influence whether birds would be able to obtain their daily energy requirements during the two exposure periods in each 24 hours.

The time at which the first part of each mussel bed was exposed on a typical receding Spring tide and the time at which most or all of the bed was exposed was therefore recorded. This was repeated on an advancing tide, but in reverse of course. It was also repeated for a typical Neap tide. These data described for how many minutes each mussel bed was fully exposed over low tide on a typical Neap tide and on a typical Spring tide. They also gave the amount of each mussel bed that was exposed as the tide receded and advanced.

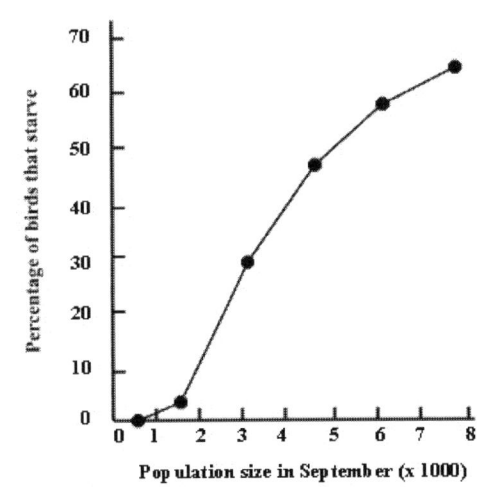

Figure 5.11 The density-dependent function obtained from version 2 of the IBM.

Simulations with version 2 of the model using the actual number of birds on the estuary predicted a winter mortality rate that was quite accurate for young birds but much too large for the adults. The probable reason for this was that the model assumed that the birds only fed on mussels whereas, in reality, they also fed on 'supplementary' foods in two habitats. One is mudflats and sandflats that lie upshore of the mussel beds that are used by oystercatchers at the beginning and end of the tidal exposure period. Here, they take ragworms, cockles and clams. The other is grass fields where oystercatchers feed on earthworms. As the intake rates of birds on these food sources was not known at the time, a 're-scaling coefficient' of 1.2 to 1.7 was employed to bring the predicted mortality rates into line with the observed rates (Box 5.3). This enabled a preliminary prediction to be made of the form and parameter values of the density-dependent mortality function (Figure 5.11).

This again suggested that mortality was density-dependent within the actual population range of 1500-2000 birds that occurred on the Exe at that time. This provided further encouragement to continue refining the values of parameters already in the model and adding new processes – such as supplementary feeding. Thus encouraged, we started to plan version 3 of the IBM as is described in the next chapter.

REFERENCES FOR CHAPTER 5

Clarke, R.T. & Goss-Custard, J.D. (1996). The Exe estuary Oystercatcher-mussel model. *The Oystercatcher: from individuals to populations,* (Ed. J.D. Goss-Custard), pp. 389-392. Oxford University Press, Oxford.

Goss-Custard, J.D., Caldow, R.W.G., Clarke, R.T., Durell, S.E.A. le V. dit & Sutherland, W.J. (1995). Deriving population parameters from individual variations in foraging behaviour: I. Empirical game theory distribution model of oystercatchers *Haematopus ostralegus* feeding on mussels *Mytilus edulis*. *Journal of Animal Ecology,* **64**, 265-276.

Goss-Custard, J.D., Caldow, R.W.G., Clarke, R.T. & West, A.D. (1995). Deriving population parameters from individual variations in foraging behaviour: II. Model tests and population parameters. *Journal of Animal Ecology,* **64**, 277-289.

Goss-Custard, J.D., Clarke, R.T., Briggs, K.B., Ens, B.J., Exo, K-M., Smit, C., Beintema, A.J., Caldow, R.W.G., Catt, D.C., Clark, N., Durell, S.E.A. le V. dit, Harris, M.P., Hulscher, J.B., Meininger, P.L., Picozzi, N., Prys-Jones, R., Safriel, U. & West, A.D. (1995). Population consequences of winter habitat loss in a migratory shorebird: I. Estimating model parameters. *Journal of Applied Ecology,* **32**, 317-333.

Goss-Custard, J.D., Caldow, R.W.G., Clarke, R.T., Durell S.E.A. le V. dit, Urfi, A.J. & West, A.D. (1995). Consequences of habitat loss and change to populations of wintering migratory birds: predicting the local and global effects from studies of individuals. *Conservation: the Science and the Action* (eds. J. Coulson & N.J. Crockford). *Ibis,* **137**, S56-66.

Goss-Custard, J.D., Clarke, R.T., Durell, S.E.A. le V. dit, Caldow, R.W.G. & Ens, B.J. (1995). Population consequences of winter habitat loss in a migratory shorebird: II. Model predictions. *Journal of Applied Ecology,* **32**, 334-348.

Box 5.1. Bill Sutherland

It was no accident that the model devised by Geoff Parker and Bill Sutherland at Liverpool University was so readily applicable to oystercatchers on the mussel beds of the Exe. Not only did Bill Sutherland have a long-standing interest in the behaviour of foraging animals, but he had started his career by doing a PhD on oystercatchers eating cockles in a lovely estuary on Anglesey, north Wales! Accordingly, it was natural to suggest to him that his theoretical game theoretic model of foraging animals could be applied to Exe oystercatchers. He duly came to the Exe to discuss the matter (and to photograph an extremely rare plant found on the local Dawlish Warren Nature Reserve) and very generously agreed to give it a try.

Just inserting empirical values from the Exe study into that theoretical model proved to be far more difficult than had been imagined because of some technical problems in calculating a bird's susceptibility to interference from the Exe data in a way that was compatible with Bill's model. It was also very difficult to find a way of applying field estimates of susceptibility to interference that had been made on a single mussel bed to all the mussel beds of the estuary. This prompted a re-think. A resolution to the problem popped into the mind of one of the Exe team sitting in a hide off Lympstone, and it was an exciting moment. This idea opened the way for the Exe research team to build its own game theoretic model, which they began to do immediately. This meant that we did not - with very guilty conscience - have to keep pestering an extremely busy university lecturer and scientist. It also meant that the model could be built from scratch and so designed exactly to fit the requirements of the oystercatcher-mussel system of the Exe estuary. Contact with Bill was of course continued thereafter and, some years later, one of Bill's own PhD students – Richard Stillman – was head-hunted to join the Exe team to develop the IBM. This he succeeded in doing and to a degree that had previously not even been thought possible! More of this later.

Box 5.2: Another hide story – not a good place to be when the baby arrives!

About this time, my wife's first child was expected but, of course, the baby's arrival was unpredictable. So, hide work carried on as usual. Then, one day, sitting in the hide, I received on the shore-to-ship radio the message that the baby was on its way. But I had reached that hide by boat! The boat was stranded high-and-dry outside the tower, waiting for the tide to re-float it, and that would be sometime later. I said: 'Hang on!', which didn't go down too well. But, luckily, my wife was able to hang on and I rushed back as quickly as possible, the moment the water was deep enough to float the boat. Expecting to see an ambulance outside the house, or to be met by an infuriated neighbour saying that my wife had gone to hospital ages ago, along with comments such as 'Where the heck were you?!', I was relieved to find everything quite normal: as so often happens, the early signs had not been followed by immediate action! That night, though, there was a drive to hospital, and no hide work over the next few days either!

> ## Box 5.3 Re-scaling coefficients
>
> Imagine that the model over-predicted the observed mortality rate two-fold. That is, the real rate is 5% but the model predicts it would be 10%. This might happen if one or more of the parameters in the model had been incorrectly estimated. For example, the energy content of the prey taken by oystercatchers might be greater than is assumed in the model if the birds are very good at selecting mussels with an above-average amount of flesh.
>
> The model might also over-predict mortality because an important aspect of the birds' natural history – its 'survival strategy' - might not yet be included. For example, oystercatchers on the Exe that are failing to obtain all the food they require from the estuary feed in fields over high tide when the estuary is unavailable to them. Failure to include this bit of their natural history would increase the chances that model birds would starve.
>
> It might take another ten years or more to do the research to find out where the model needs to be changed to close the gap between observed and predicted mortality rates. Meanwhile, predictions may be needed to solve a particular management problem or just to be able to produce scientific papers to advertise progress and to meet the publication targets required by managers.
>
> The answer is often to introduce a 're-scaling coefficient'. In the case of the shorebird IBM, the usual practice is to adjust the foraging efficiency of the birds at night until the model predicts the observed mortality rates. So, in the example here, the foraging efficiency of the birds at night would be reduced step-by-step until the model 'homed in' on the actual mortality rate of oystercatchers. The model having been 're-calibrated', it can now be used to make the predictions required to answer the management issue that is being investigated; for example, whether to double the shellfishing quotas
>
> Although some people may regard this practice as cheating, it is more constructively viewed as a procedure that allows the model to be used before all of the I's have been dotted and all the T's have been crossed. The magnitude of the re-scaling coefficient also gives a measure of how far you still have to go before the model is as good as you would want it to be.

CHAPTER 6:
The development, structure and testing of version 3

...which details the extra fieldwork that had to be carried out for the third version of the IBM for mussel-eating oystercatchers to be built and then describes how the model works and concludes with the tests of its predictions that, through good fortune, resulted in a remarkable success.

WHAT NEEDED TO BE DONE

The mortality rates predicted by version 2 were too high. What might have caused this? The most likely possibility seemed to be that version 2 did not include the supplementary feeding done by oystercatchers when the mussel beds are covered by the tide over high water. After the mussel beds had been covered, many oystercatchers flew to sandflats and mudflats further up the shore where they fed on several species of invertebrates. Some then continued feeding on earthworms in fields after the upshore flats had also been covered by the advancing tide. This behaviour had since the 1960s been interpreted in shorebirds as something the birds did when they were unable to satisfy all their energy requirements from their main food sources in the intertidal zone. It seemed highly likely that omitting this behaviour would largely explain why version 2 of the model over-predicted the actual mortality rate of oystercatchers on the Exe.

Measuring the intake rate of oystercatchers on the upshore flats at the beginning and end of the tidal exposure period and in the fields too another couple of seasons of fieldwork. The intake rates of birds at the top of the shore on clams, ragworms and cockles were measured in much the same way as those on mussels had been measured. The Boates box was used for upshore areas but, in the fields, the tower hides again had to be built because it was necessary to be very close to a bird to be able to see when a small worm had been taken. The possible effect of the ambient temperature had to be taken into account and this did indeed prove to be important in the fields (Fig 6.1), although not in the upshore intertidal areas.

At about this time, a new and extremely important member of the team – Richard Stillman - arrived and took over all the modelling. As well as adding the feeding done in supplementary places, he completely re-structured the model to enable a number of other important components to be added. One of these was the rate at which the gut assimilates food that research in The Netherlands had shown might sometimes impose important constraints of the birds' ability to obtain all their energy requirements in the time available. His description in his first paper on version 3 of the model is reproduced in a slightly modified version here, without the formulae (and parameter values) that can be found in his original papers.

VERSION 3 OF THE MODEL

General approach

As has already been described, the development of the model was guided by its accuracy at predicting the mortality rates of different oystercatcher age classes. These had been first measured over four non-breeding seasons between September 1976 and March 1980 and the model was 'calibrated' for these years. That is, these were the years chosen to guide the development of the model, as described in Box 6.1. In order to obtain accurate predictions while keeping the model as simple as possible, version 3 was developed by adding new components to reduce the discrepancy between the mortality rates predicted by the model and those that had been measured over the four 'calibration' winters. Based on the then current understanding of the system, components were added in order of their known, or probable importance, in closing the remaining gap between predicted and observed mortality rates over those calibration years.

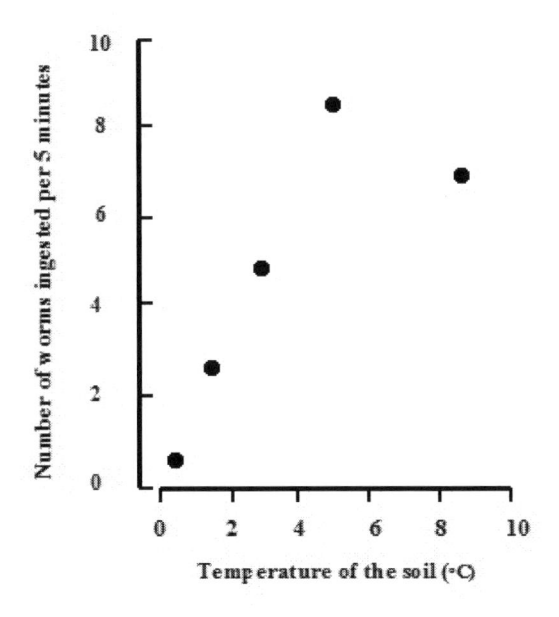

Figure 6.1 How the intake rate of oystercatchers feeding on earthworms decreases as the temperature of the top layer of the soil falls from 9°C to 0°C.

Overall structure

Version 3 of the model follows the location, behaviour and body condition of each individual oystercatcher in the population. At the start of a simulation for a single non-breeding season, each bird is ascribed a unique combination of age, feeding method, foraging efficiency and global dominance. As already described in Chapter 5, the model uses a game theoretic approach to determine where each individual feeds at each stage of the tidal cycle. All individuals base their decisions on the same principle, which is to make the choices that maximizes their intake rate. The options chosen by the model birds differ, of course, because what is best for a given individual depends on its own particular characteristics, notably its competitive ability and feeding method.

The overall structure of version 3 is shown in Figure 6.2. The model includes two behavioural sub-models that predict the response of the birds to their food supply. The rate-maximizing 'optimality' prey choice sub-model predicts how the consumption rate of each individual bird on a given mussel bed over the low tide period would be affected by changes in the flesh-content, density and sizes of the mussels where it is feeding. The game theoretic distribution sub-model predicts where each bird will feed during each stage of the 12.4hr long tidal cycle.

By combining the two outputs of these two sub-models, the model calculates at the end of each 24hr period the consequences for the energy reserves of each bird of the change in its consumption rate arising from the responses it has made to its food supply during that day. When daily energy consumption exceeds daily expenditure, individuals add to their energy reserves or maintain them if a permitted maximum level has already been reached. But when daily requirements exceed daily consumption, individuals draw on their energy reserves. If an individual's energy reserves fall to zero, it dies of starvation, the only source of mortality in this version of the model, and the main source of mortality in the wild.

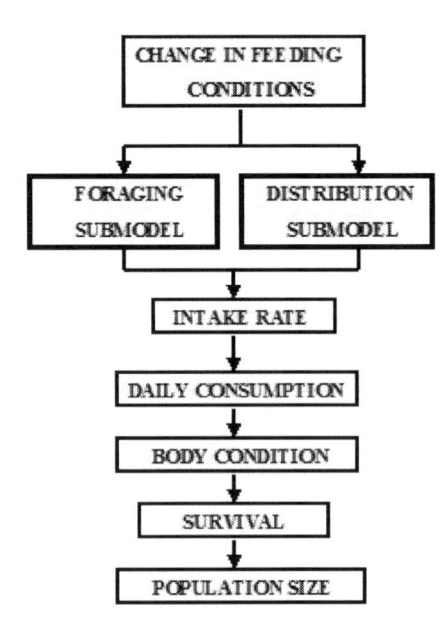

Figure 6.2 *The overall structure of version 3. The two behavioural sub-models are outlined with heavy lines. The boxes below them show the sequence in which the major calculations of the IBM are made to predict the survival rate, the converse of the mortality rate. The final step is also shown, that of predicting the effect of a change in the survival rate on the size of the population. This requires an additional model that is quite separate and different in structure from the IBM itself, as will be described later.*

Components of the model

Patch types

Most of mussel-feeding oystercatchers on the Exe estuary feed on the 10 mussel beds that lie from mid-shore down to the low water mark (LWM). All of them are included in the model. As supplementary feeding occurs on other intertidal areas at a higher shore level, and also in fields adjacent to the estuary, two other patches are included: one upshore area of mudflat and sandflat and one field. In the model, there are therefore 12 feeding patches of three types. The single upshore area and single field are considered adequate to represent the several such areas in the real system. The different patches vary in their tidal exposure patterns and in the populations of the prey that occur there.

Seasonal and tidal cycles

The model starts on 1st September and proceeds by 24-hour days until it finishes on 15th March. Daylength is described by a sine curve ranging between 18 h on 21 June and 9 h on 21 December. The model assumes that the hours of light are equally divided either side of midday, and finds the proportion of each tidal stage that falls within the hours of daylight and of darkness. This is needed because darkness can affect the foraging efficiency of the birds. Daily temperature declines by equal steps each day from 17°C in September to 5°C in February, the typical temperature range on the Exe. The seasonal change in the ambient temperature affects the energy requirements of the birds and the rate at which they can collect earthworms in the fields.

The major factor influencing the availability of feeding patches to oystercatchers is their successive covering and exposure through the tidal cycle. A 'tidal cycle' here refers to the period from one high water to the next. In the model, there are only four tidal stages, or time-steps, in every tidal cycle, as is detailed below. There are two tidal cycles on each of the 196 days from September 1st to March 15th. So, in total, in a simulation of one non-breeding season, the model runs through 1568 (4x2x196) time-steps. At the beginning of each and every time-step, the model places each individual oystercatcher on the foraging patch that is most profitable for it at that time. Birds do not change their location during the remainder of that time-step, but may do so at the start of subsequent time-steps.

A simplification in the model is that the duration of a tidal cycle remains constant at 12.44hrs throughout the non-breeding season whereas, in reality, neap cycles are rather longer than spring cycles. However, the tidal range – the difference in height between high water and low water – does vary in the model over the fortnightly sequence of spring and neap tides. In this sequence, there are approximately seven days of spring tides followed by seven days of neap tides.

Patch exposure

Each patch has a maximum area when fully exposed at low water on spring tides. On most mussel beds, the area exposed on neap tides is much smaller than it is on spring tides. Indeed a few mussel beds are not exposed at all over low water on neap tides. Accordingly, the area of a mussel bed that is exposed at low water changes through the 14 days of a spring-neap cycle. For all the tidal cycles between the extreme spring and extreme neap ones, the model calculates the area of the patch that is exposed at low water by linear interpolation between these spring and neap extremes, as illustrated in Figure 6.3.

In the model, each 12.44hr tidal cycle is divided into the four stages (or 'time-steps') of high water, receding tide, low water and advancing tide. The height of the water remains constant throughout each of these stages. This is unrealistic, of course, because in the real world the tide gradually exposes and then covers a feeding patch. If would be possible to mimic the gradual exposure and recovering of a patch by making the tidal stages very short; for example, just 5 minutes long. But this would add greatly to the complexity of the model and lengthen the time it takes to run a single simulation. As always, a trade-off has to be made between the complexities of the real world and the need to represent it in a more simplified fashion within the model (Box. 6.2). In this case, four tidal stages seemed to be a reasonable degree of simplification with which to begin.

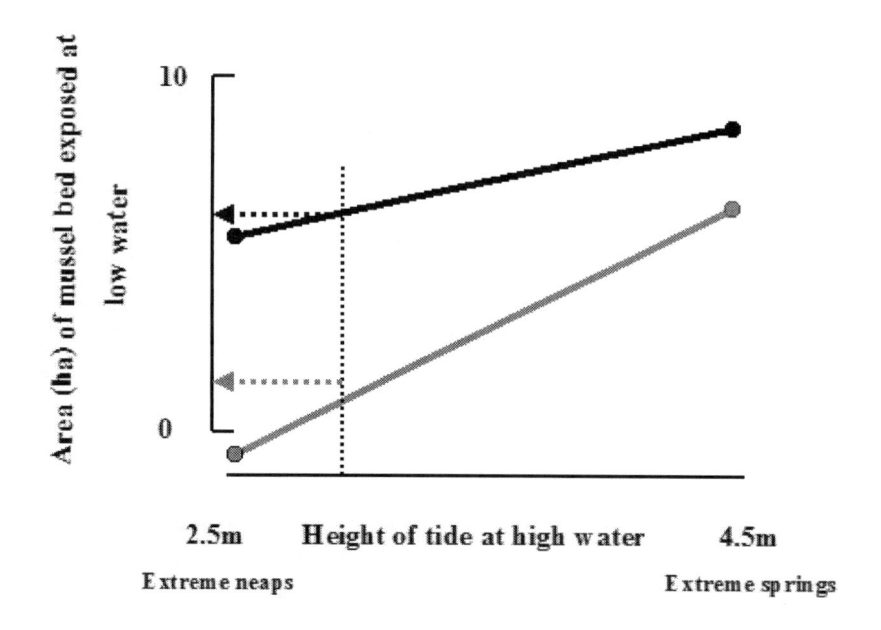

Figure 6.3 How the model calculates the area of a mussel bed exposed at low water on each low tide of a 14-day sequence of spring and neap tides. Two mussel beds are shown – black (top) and grey. The circles show their areas as measured in the field at low tide on an extreme neap tide and on an extreme spring tide. The 'black' mussel bed is situated high upshore and most of it is exposed at low tide on all neap tides as well as on spring tides. The 'grey' mussel bed lies much lower down the shore and is not exposed at all at low water on an extreme neap tide. The model calculates the area of a mussel bed that is exposed at low tide on all the intermediate tides from the straight lines drawn between the two extremes. In this example, the area of each bed on a tide with a high water of 3m is shown, the arrows pointing to the interpolated areas of about 1.5ha and 6.5ha on the grey and black beds respectively. The model used the same procedure to calculate the duration of the low tide stage by interpolation between the exposure times that had been measured in the field on an extreme spring and an extreme spring tide.

For even more simplicity, the low water stage is defined only as the period over which some or all of the mussel beds are exposed. That is to say, the mussel beds in the model are not exposed at all on receding and advancing tides, as they may sometimes be in reality: indeed one mussel bed is even exposed over high water on an extreme neap tide. Only the upshore flats are exposed and accessible at these two stages of the tidal cycle. In the model, as in reality, mussel beds are exposed and accessible to oystercatchers at low water at night as well as during the day. The upshore patch in the model is exposed on the receding tide, at low water and on the advancing tide, in darkness and in daylight, but not over high tide. In contrast, the field patch is exposed over all four tidal stages but only during the day as oystercatchers seldom feed in fields at night.

The duration of the four tidal stages within one tidal cycle are also affected by the 14 day springs-neaps cycle. On a spring tide, the tide recedes and advances very rapidly. The water then has much further to fall and rise than on a neap tide but only the same amount of time in which to do so. On neaps, the tide ebbs and flows much more slowly. Accordingly, the duration of the low tide stage when the mussel beds are exposed is longer during a spring tidal cycle than during a neap cycle.

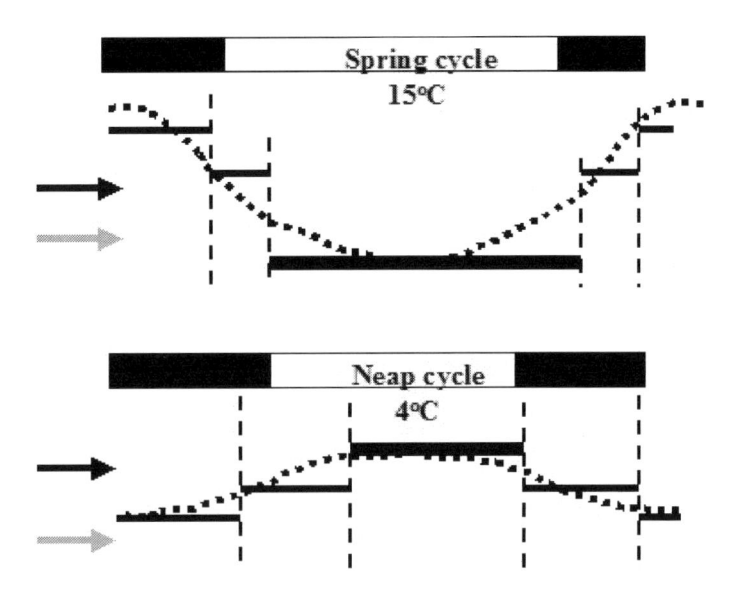

Figure 6.4 *How the tidal cycle and springs-neaps cycle is represented in the model at different stages of the non-breeding season. Shown are two representative tidal cycles of 12.44hrs, the upper one being a spring cycle in October and the lower one a neap cycle in January. The black portions of each horizontal box indicates night time and the white portions show the day time. The daylength and ambient temperature are both greater on the October spring tide than on the January neap tide, of course. The dotted line shows height of the water level as the tide recedes and advances. The four vertical dashed lines separate the four tidal stages, or time-steps, into which each 12.44hr tidal cycle is divided: high tide, receding tide, low tide and advancing tide. The start of the next high tide is indicated too. The arrows show the level on the shore at which two mussel beds are located. The one represented by the black arrow is high up the shore, the one represented by the grey arrow is low down the shore. On a spring cycle, both mussel beds are exposed over the low tide period, as indicated by the thick black horizontal line. They are not exposed as the tide ebbs and flows and over high tide. In contrast, on a neap cycle, the low-level mussel bed (grey) is not exposed at all, even at low water. The horizontal solid lines illustrate the simplifying assumption in the model that the water level remains constant throughout each tidal stage; a patch is either fully exposed or totally covered throughout a stage. On the Exe, high tides generally occur in the morning and evening on spring tides but during the middle of the day on neap tides.*

The model calculates the duration of the low tide tidal exposure period at a given point in the spring-neap cycle by linear interpolation between measurements of the exposure time made in the field on an extreme spring tide and an extreme neap tide; that is, by using the same approach as it uses when calculating the area that is exposed at low tide (Fig. 6.3). Figure 6.4 illustrates how the time for which each mussel bed is exposed and so accessible to oystercatchers is represented in the model according to the spring-neaps cycle and the season.

Prey populations

The populations on each bed of mussels between 20mm and 70mm long are divided into ten 5-mm size classes (*i.e.* 20-25mm; 25-30mm up to 65-70mm). The densities (number/m^2) of each size class on each mussel bed at the start of the non-breeding season were the average values of those obtained in eight surveys made every September from 1976 to 1983 (Box 6.3). The 5mm size classes were chosen to be compatible with the oystercatcher optimal foraging model, as described in Chapter 5.

At the end of each tidal cycle, the model deducts the numbers of mussels in each size class that had been removed over the preceding period by the oystercatchers. The proportion that have been removed by other causes of mortality, such as gales, are also deducted at a constant daily rate. Thus the model tracks, day-by-day, the decrease in the densities of each of the ten size classes of mussels on each mussel bed.

The model not only includes the numerical density of each size class of mussels on each bed but also incorporates the strong tendency mussels located high on the shore to contain less flesh than equivalent sized mussels further down the shore. This was considered likely to be important because, on neap tides on most beds, the birds could only feed on the topmost parts of the mussel bed where flesh content was relatively low. In the model, the average flesh content of a given size class of mussel is related to the proportion of the mussel bed that is exposed so that, when only the higher shore levels of a mussel bed are exposed on ncap tides, the average flesh content of the mussels is decreased.

The model also tracks the day-by-day decrease in the flesh content of the mussels that occurs over the non-breeding season. The size of the daily decrease is specific to both the size class in question and to the mussel bed in question. The flesh content declines at a constant linear rate over the winter, decreasing to an average of about 60% of its initial value by the end of the non-breeding season.

By tracking the daily reduction in the numerical density and flesh-content of each size class of mussel on each mussel bed, the model replicates the decrease in the abundance and quality of the main food supply of oystercatchers that is known to occur in nature.

The foraging of oystercatchers on upshore areas and fields is represented quite simply as the average of the intake rates that had been obtained from the fieldwork. The model therefore does not store details of the kinds of prey eaten by oystercatchers in these two kinds of patch. Although the data obtained to measure the intake rates of oystercatchers in the upshore areas and in fields were acquired over a range of sites and winters, only the average of all the available estimates from each kind of habitat was used in the model as the variation between sites was not large. Oystercatchers feed in the upshore feed in the model both night and day, as they do in reality. As oystercatchers do not usually feed in fields at night, birds in the model were not allowed to do so either.

Population size and structure of the oystercatchers

The model is run with a population of 1550 oystercatchers, the average winter population on the main mussel beds during 1976-80, in three age classes: juveniles (first winter) – 2% of birds, immatures (second winter) - 7% and adults - 91%, as recorded on Exe mussel beds. Juvenile and immature birds tend to be of lower dominance than adults and hence are more susceptible to interference. Each bird either stabs open gaping mussels (stabbers) or breaks the shell by hammering (hammerers). All juveniles, 80% of immatures and 43% of adults are stabbers, as was recorded on Exe mussel beds. On average, hammerers have both a higher interference-free intake rate and susceptibility to interference than stabbers, as was discussed in Chapter 4.

Within an age class and a feeding method class, individuals differ in their foraging efficiency on all three patch types and in their global dominance, and hence susceptibility to interference. The foraging efficiency of each individual is drawn from a normal distribution with the amount of variation that had been measured in the field in mussel-feeding oystercatchers, as described in Chapter 5. An individual's global dominance was drawn at random from the series 1,2,3,4,5 up to 1411, in the case of the 1411 adult birds. No two birds could have exactly the same global dominance, again as detailed in Chapter 5. As there were no data to test the possibility, it is assumed that the foraging efficiency of an individual can be different when it is feeding on mussels compared with when it is feeding on upshore invertebrates or in fields. Similarly, it is also assumed that a bird's local dominance is unrelated to its foraging efficiency in all three feeding habitats, although this had only been shown by fieldwork in birds that were eating mussels. The age, feeding method, foraging efficiencies and global dominance of each individual oystercatcher in the model are fixed throughout the entire non-breeding season.

Feeding times and locations

The model allocates each individual to one of the patches at the beginning each stage of the tidal cycle using the game theoretic procedure that was described in Chapter 5. Throughout the non-breeding season, individuals are chosen by the model in random order when they are being allocated to a patch at the beginning of each successive tidal stage, or time-step. A bird might be the first to be allocated in one tidal stage and then be the 100th to be allocated in the next and the last one in the next tidal stage.

In reality, oystercatchers do not feed constantly when their food supplies are accessible and also roost during periods when their food is unavailable. This is because oystercatchers are thought to balance their energy budgets over a relatively long period, estimated as just over one 24hr period. Therefore, for each pair of tidal cycles (equivalent to little over 24 hours), the model calculates each bird's energy requirements and then finds the feeding locations and tidal stages that allow it to meet its requirements in the shortest possible time, even if this meant feeding in the field over the low water period when the mussel beds are exposed and accessible. During tidal stages in which a bird does not need to feed because it has already obtained all the energy it requires during the current 24hr period, it moves to the roost.

Intake rate on mussel beds

The model calculates the intake rate of a given individual using a rather complex calculation, the details of which can be found in the original papers. Only an outline is given here. The intake rate of a given individual is calculated for a whole low water stage on a given mussel bed in three steps. The model first calculates the interference-free intake rate (IFIR) of a bird of average efficiency on the mussel bed using the foraging sub-model. As described in Chapter 5, it does this by first finding, separately for stabbing and hammering birds, the range of size classes that maximizes - within a discrimination ability of 3% - the interference-free intake rate of the average bird feeding in daylight on mussels of average flesh content.

In the second step, the model calculates the IFIR of an individual bird from its daytime foraging efficiency and the IFIR of the average bird on the patch where it is feeding – as described in Chapter 5. It then deducts the proportion of mussels stolen from it by carrion crows – as had been recorded in the field on a sample of mussel beds - and the proportion of flesh that is not removed from the mussel shell (scraps are often left behind). The same calculation is made for an individual that is feeding at night except that no mussels are lost to carrion crows (there are no crows on the beds at night) and the night-time foraging efficiency, if different from the daytime efficiency, is used.

The third step is to calculate the actual intake rate an individual achieves taking into account the amount of interference it experiences. Based on field data described in Chapter 4, the model assumes that interference is absent if the density of birds where it is feeding is below the threshold competitor density at which interference begins to occur. If the density of competitors is above this threshold density, the IFIR of the individuals is reduced by the appropriate amount, as determined by the bird's local dominance and as described in Chapter 5. As the field data showed that interference intensifies as the winter progresses, the model also makes the intensity of the interference experienced by an individual increase with the number of days that have elapsed since 1 September. That is, as the non-breeding season progresses, the amount by which the intake rate of a bird is suppressed by interference gradually increases.

In the model, the density of competitors is calculated in two stages. First, the overall density of birds is calculated by dividing the number of birds that the model has allocated to a mussel bed by the exposed area of that bed at the time. This approach assumes that birds are uniformly distributed over a mussel bed. However, in reality, birds concentrate in areas of high food availability, or away from disturbed areas, or feed at the start or end of the exposure period when densities are particularly high. The density of competitors actually experienced by birds is therefore calculated by multiplying the overall density by a fixed value. This 'aggregation factor' was determined empirically on the Exe as being 8 for stabbers, which feed throughout the exposure period. It was estimated to be 4 for hammerers, which avoid the beginning and end of the exposure period when bird densities are at their highest.

Intake rate on upshore areas and fields

Intake rate on supplementary feeding areas is modelled in a much simpler way than it is on mussel beds. This is because fieldwork had shown that (i) prey in supplementary areas are not depleted significantly during the course of winter; (ii) intake rate in supplementary areas does not change throughout the course of winter and (iii) oystercatcher densities in supplementary areas are generally low, indicating that interference will be absent or negligible. The model therefore assumes that the average bird has a fixed intake rate on the upshore areas and in fields, irrespective of both the food supply and the density of competitors (*i.e.* no prey depletion or interference competition occur).

However, even though it has not yet been measured, the model does assume that individuals vary in their foraging efficiency on these supplementary feeding patches. There were no data to explore whether the foraging efficiency of individual birds on either of the supplementary food sources was positively or negatively related to, or varied independently of, their efficiency when eating mussels. But as the shape of the bill tip that is mainly acquired on mussel beds may have unknown implications for the birds' foraging efficiency on the other prey species, it has to be assumed that the efficiency of individuals on the supplementary prey varied independently of their efficiency on mussels. Again based on fieldwork, intake rate on the field in the model is related to temperature, falling to zero at 0°C. On the Exe, oystercatchers mostly consume cockles on the upshore patches, and so the foraging efficiency on the upshore patch is lower than during the day, as determined by field studies in the Netherlands.

Energy assimilation

Digestion is incorporated because it is a significant bottleneck that can limit the amount of flesh that can be consumed by oystercatchers within a tidal cycle. It is modelled from the food storage capacity of the gut and the rates at which food is passed into and out of the gut. Gut storage capacity and processing rate are assumed to be fixed whereas the rate of food entry depends solely on intake rate. If a bird's intake rate exceeds the gut processing rate, the gut may fill to capacity. When this happens, it limits the amount of time the bird can spend feeding and thus the total amount it is able to consume during a tidal stage.

The amount of energy that is actually assimilated therefore is calculated from the length of the tidal stage, the intake rate while feeding, the proportion of the tidal stage spent feeding, and the prey energy density and assimilation efficiency.

Energy expenditure

Energy expenditure is taken from the results of Dutch experiments on oystercatchers in outdoor aviaries with an extrapolation to field conditions. Daily energy expenditure is divided into (i) general expenditure on activity, digestion and other body functions, and (ii) thermoregulatory expenditure. The latter increases at a constant rate per degree reduction in temperature below a critical temperature, as measured in captive oystercatchers, again in The Netherlands. All individuals in the model are assumed to have the same daily energy expenditure. Although this is certainly an over-simplification, the data were not available to incorporate individual variation in energy demands.

Energy storage

Whenever the amount of energy consumed during a 24hr period exceeds expenditure over that period, the excess is converted into storage tissues and the mass of the bird increases. When the reverse occurs, and birds do not meet their requirements from current consumption, the storage tissues are converted back to energy and the bird loses mass. The mass gain and loss during energy storage and release are calculated using efficiencies measured in waders in The Netherlands.

In the model, birds of each type have a maximum, empirically determined, body mass at each stage of winter, which they attempt to achieve. When a bird is at its maximum mass it regulates its intake by reducing the amount of time it spends feeding in order to prevent any further mass increase. If expenditure exceeds intake, birds lose mass. They die of starvation if their weight falls to the 'starvation' value, as measured from emaciated corpses in the wild.

Calibration

The calibration of version 3 had been a process of 'homing in' on the least complicated model that would best close the gap between the mortality rate predicted by the model and the rate that had been measured in the field over the first four years of the project. Figure 6.5 shows how well this version reproduces the observed mortality rate by the end of this calibration procedure. As the characteristics of each individual were randomly generated at the start of each simulation, model outputs for the mortality rate varied slightly between replicate simulations. Therefore, the average outputs from 10 replicated simulations, and the error bars of the averages are shown in the Figure.

Overall, the model's mortality rates for immature birds and adults are only 7% below the average that had been measured in real oystercatchers over the four calibration years. The rate predicted by the model for the juveniles corresponds much less well with the rate that had been measured in the field, being 31% lower. However, the error range around the model's outputs for this mortality rate is very wide. The wide error range arises in this case because very few juveniles were included in each simulation and this produced a very large variation in the outputs across the ten simulations. On the other hand, there is a very reasonable correspondence between model's outputs and the observed mortality rates for the much more numerous immature and, especially, adult birds. Accordingly, it was provisionally judged that the model reproduces the observed rates in the years for which the model was parameterized sufficiently well for no further development to be necessary - unless, and until, further tests suggested otherwise.

Validation

It would, of course, be absurd to call the model outputs for mortality rate over the years 1976-80 'predictions' because the observed rates were used to calibrate the model in order to achieve those observed rates! It is inevitable that the observed and predicted rates will be similar because the one is used to guide the attainment of the other!

Real predictions are model outputs that refer either to what will happen in the future or to what would happen in circumstances that are not encompassed within the structure of the model itself. In other words, a 'real' prediction refers to situations that lie outside the empirical range, as discussed in Chapter 1. Predicting the mortality rate with half the mussels removed would have provided a really good test of the model because the 'predictions' refer to novel circumstances that lie outside the narrow range of conditions over which the model was developed. Accurate predictions in these circumstances would be regarded by most people as a good test of a model's validity, and therefore reliability. But such experiments are not only impractical but also unthinkable in an area that is strongly protected for birds!

But at this point there was a very lucky break. Over the prolonged period over which the model had been evolving from version 1 to version 3, a further seven estimates of the mortality rates over the non-breeding season had been obtained for adult birds. Furthermore, between the winters 1980/81 and 1990/91, the population size of the oystercatchers on the Exe had increased. There was therefore not only an opportunity to find out whether the mortality rate had also increased as the population density had increased but also to test whether the model would predict that it had done so. In other words, good fortune provided a natural opportunity to test how well the model predicted mortality rates in novel circumstances that lay outside the empirical range over which the model had been calibrated.

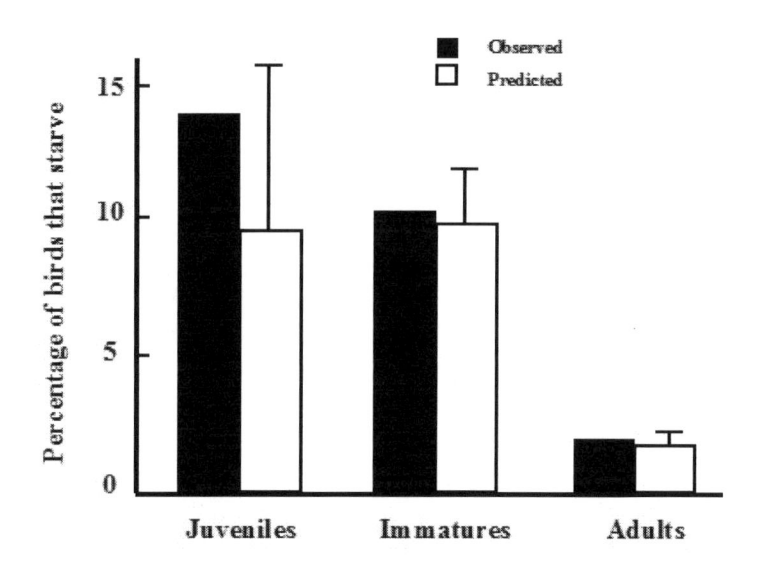

Figure 6.5 Calibrating the model's outputs for the mortality rate of oystercatchers over the non-breeding season. Birds that had died of accidents, such as by drowning after having become entangled in fishing line caught up on a mussel bed, are excluded from the observed mortality rates. The vertical thin lines show the error range within which the true value of the mortality rate produced by the model lies.

Model simulations were therefore run for each of these winters using the oystercatcher population sizes recorded in the year in question. As the size of the mussel population size varied rather little between years, the average value recorded over the period 1976-1983 could be used with confidence. No other parameter values were changed between years. The model outputs showed that, as in the case of versions 1 and 2, the predicted mortality rates were again density-dependent (Fig. 6.6).

At this point, the raw data for calculating the mortality rate of birds in the wild over these seven years were still sitting in the computer, un-examined! After a flurry of analysis and, with some trepidation, the seven observed rates were eventually calculated and plotted against population size (Figs. 6.6).

As the scientifically terse published report stated: 'Plotting the model-predicted and observed winter starvation rates against the density of oystercatchers on the mussel beds in September revealed unexpected density-dependent overwinter mortality rates in both'. Scientifically, this was a conventional, and quite appropriate, under-stated remark. There was absolutely no certainty that this would be the happy outcome, and that it happened was enormously encouraging. The early indications from versions 1 and 2 of density dependence across the range of population size seen on the Exe provided no real guide as these models over-predicted the mortality rate so much. There was no guarantee that this more realistic version 3 of the model would give the same prediction.

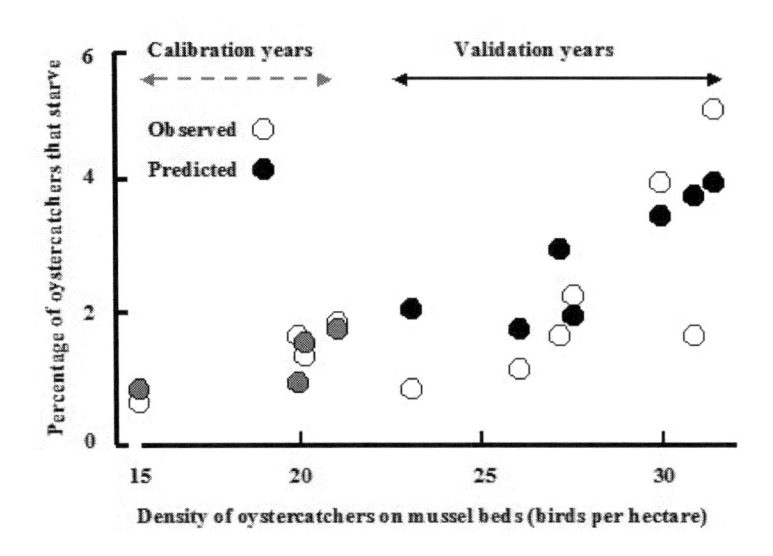

Figure 6.6 Test of the model's main prediction: the mortality rates of adults over the non-breeding season for individual years. The observed rates (open circles) and predicted rates (closed circles) are shown individually for each of the 11 years. The values below 23 birds/ha refer to the calibration years so cannot be regarded as part of the validity test but are included to show mortality rates across the whole range of population density.

As there were no estimates of the values of critical parameters that might vary from year to year – such as the flesh-content of the mussels and the weather – the results are also presented as the means of groups of years in Figure 6.7. This shows very clearly both the density dependence and the success of the model in predicting it.

That the mortality could be density-dependent was confidently expected because of the high incidence of competition between foraging birds. However, it was by no means certain that it would occur at population sizes at which the model predicted it would occur. Mortality may not have started to become density-dependent, for example, until there were 5000 birds on the mussel beds, and the density had reached over twice the highest densities recorded. What is more, the predicted rates at high population sizes could have been much higher or lower than those that were actually recorded in the adult oystercatchers of the Exe. The model could have got its predictions very wrong indeed in several ways, as illustrated in Figure 6.8. It was not only important that the model predicted that the mortality would be density-dependent, the predictions had to be of the correct magnitude and thus in the correct place in Figure 6.6. The fact that it did this quite well was very encouraging. It provided some confidence that the model adequately represents the real population quite well.

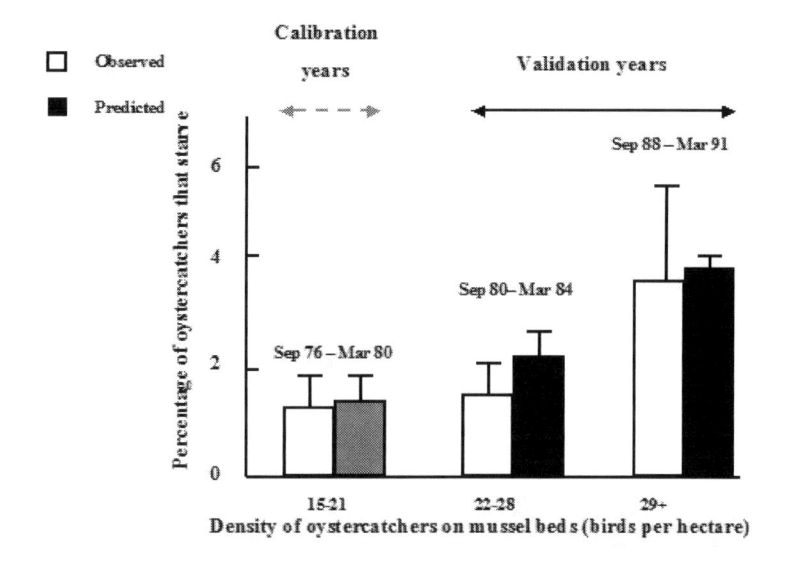

Figure 6.7 Test of the model's main prediction: the mortality rates of adults over the non-breeding season. This compares the observed and predicted values averaged for years of similar population density. The values birds/below 22 birds/ha refer to the calibration years so cannot be regarded as part of the validity test but are included to show mortality rates across the whole range of the population density.

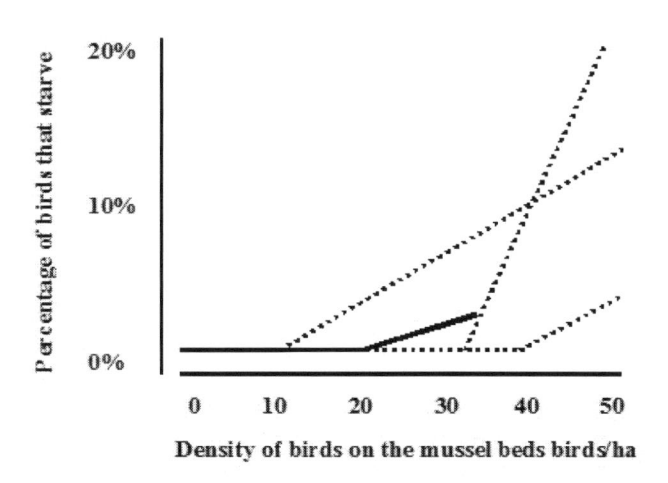

Figure 6.8 How the predictions could have been very wrong. The thick solid line shows approximately the relationship in real adult oystercatchers between their density on the mussel beds and their mortality rate over the non-breeding season. The dashed black lines show three predictions that the model might have made, but did not.

165

The 'lucky-break' was not that the model predicted density dependence, but that density dependence occurred over the range of bird population sizes that occurred over years following model calibration (Box 6.4). Prior to this, density dependence had not been demonstrated in the non-breeding season mortality rate of any wading birds. The food supply on the Exe was so consistent over those years that the feeding conditions themselves could not be used provide the novel conditions 'outside the empirical range' required to validate model predictions. As large-scale experiments were out of the question, the only thing that could provide the novel conditions, therefore, was a change in the size of the bird population. Luckily, that is what happened - and at the right time too. Had bird numbers not varied much over those years, the model would undoubtedly have predicted the observed average mortality rate because, in effect, with no change in circumstances, this would have represented little more than a confirmation of the calibration procedure. But in fact, bird numbers varied and, over that range, mortality was density dependent in reality and in the model.

Tests of subsidiary predictions of the model

While it was encouraging that version 3 predicted well the values of the birds' starvation rate over a series of non-breeding seasons during which the population size had unexpectedly increased, it may have done so for the wrong reasons. One way to explore this possibility was to test whether the model accurately predicted various aspects of the biology of the birds. If it did so, it would suggest that it represented their biology well, and that it might be appropriate to believe its predictions for the mortality rate. If it did not do so, however, it would strongly suggest that its predictions had been correct for the wrong reasons.

Many of these 'subsidiary' tests were concerned with the seasonal patterns in the occurrence of mortality, in body condition and in the behaviour of the oystercatchers. These changes reflect the increasing difficulty the birds have in achieving their energy requirements as the non-breeding season progresses. This happens because of the flesh content of the mussels decreases while, simultaneously, the ambient temperature also decreases and this raises the energy requirements of the birds.

Seasonal timing of mortality

The model successfully predicted that the birds would have increasing difficulty in meeting their energy requirements as the non-breeding progressed and that starvation would be restricted to the second-half of the non-breeding season (Fig 6.9). However, compared with real oystercatchers, the mortality in the model population occurred closer to the end of the non-breeding season. This suggests that, compared with real birds, those in the model had rather less difficulty than real oystercatchers in obtaining their energy requirements during the early part of the non-breeding season but more difficulty at the end. Nonetheless, the concentration of both the actual and predicted deaths towards the end of the non-breeding season raises some confidence in the model.

Body masses of different classes of oystercatchers

Oystercatchers gradually increase their fat reserves from the beginning of the non-breeding season and may draw on them when the feeding conditions deteriorate towards the end. In the model, the birds were given for their target mass the average body mass of surviving oystercatchers, as measured on the Exe. As the non-breeding season progressed, some birds in the model could not meet their daily requirements from their current daily consumption and so drew on their energy reserves and lost mass. But as most birds in the model were able to achieve their target mass throughout the non-breeding season, and as the target mass was set to be same as the actual mass in real Exe birds, the predicted masses of immature birds and adults were inevitably close on average to the observed masses!

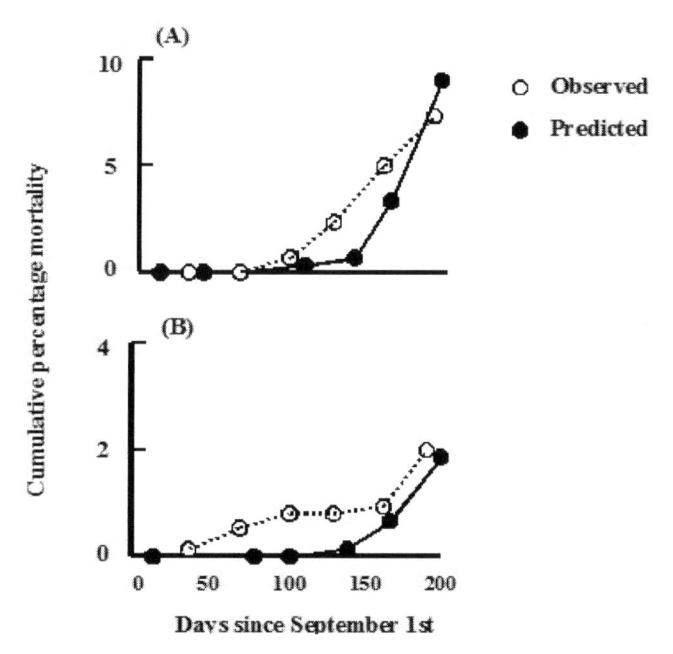

Figure 6.9 Test of the model's ability to predict the stage of the non-breeding season when **(A)** young birds (juveniles and immatures) and **(B)** adults starve to death. The graphs plot the cumulative frequency of starvation so, by the end of the non-breeding season, 10% of the young birds had starved while only 2% of adults starve.

This would hardly be a convincing test of the model, and it was never thought of as such. The only legitimate test of the predictions made by the model for body mass is the extent to which different classes of birds fell short of their common target. For example, if the model predicted that more immature stabbers than adult stabbers would fail to reach their body mass target, and this is indeed what happened in nature, it would suggest the model was doing well.

This test was carried out by comparing the model's predictions for the body mass of hammering birds with those of stabbing birds. Over the first half of the non-breeding season, the model correctly predicted that immature and adult hammering birds and adult stabbing birds would achieve the target mass. However, it failed to predict that immature stabbing birds would be less successful, as was actually the case in nature. This of course reflects the point made earlier that the model makes life too easy for some oystercatchers during the first half of the non-breeding season.

But in the second half of the non-breeding season, when most of the mortality occurs on the Exe, the model predictions were broadly correct. Even though they were given the same target mass in the model, both immature and adult hammerers achieved a higher mass than stabbers, as occurred in real oystercatchers. The average mass of the hammerers in the model was virtually the same as the target mass so nearly all of them were able to meet their daily energy requirements from current consumption. In contrast, the average mass of the stabbing birds in model was well below the target. Clearly, many stabbing birds in the model were unable to meet their daily energy requirements from current consumption. Overall, then, the model predicted reasonably well the relative body masses of oystercatchers of different age and feeding method.

Use of supplementary feeding areas

Many oystercatchers on the Exe cannot meet their energy requirements by feeding only on the mussel beds and so use supplementary sources of food on the upper flats and in fields, especially late in the non-breeding season. It was not possible to test how well the model predicted the numbers of birds that used these two supplementary habitats because the numbers feeding on the upshore flats and in fields around the estuary could not be counted. However, the model predicted that oystercatchers would start feeding in the fields during the last 10 days of October, which coincides well with the observed dates of the middle to end of October.

Individual oystercatchers on the Exe vary considerably in the frequency with which they use the upshore flats and fields. The fieldwork suggested that it was the birds with a low foraging efficiency on mussel beds, rather than those with low dominance, that were most likely to use the supplementary food supplies.

The model successfully predicted that inefficient individuals would use the fields more than the efficient ones. It predicted, in fact, that the least efficient would use the fields about one and a half times more often than birds of average foraging efficiency, while the most efficient ones would use then half as frequently. This prediction accords well with the observations made on the Exe (Fig. 6.10(A)).

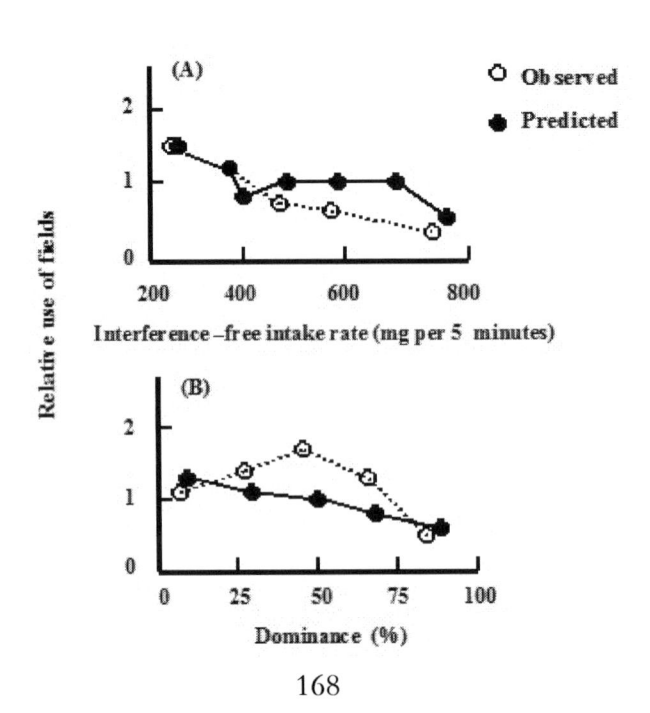

168

Figure 6.10 *Test of the model's ability to predict the (A) foraging efficiency and (B) dominance on the mussel beds of birds that use the fields for supplementary feeding during the second half of the non-breeding season.*

The field data suggested that an individual's dominance had little effect on its use of fields. In contrast, the model predicted that the least dominant would use the fields more than the dominants (Fig. 6.10(B)). This suggests that the model over-estimated the importance - or strength - of the interference that occurred on the mussel beds. This is probably because real birds in the wild are able to avoid interference from other birds rather than the model recognises.

Interference-free intake rate

In version 3 of the IBM, the interference-free intake rate of a bird of average foraging efficiency is calculated by the optimality foraging sub-model. This sub-model does this for each mussel bed at the beginning of each low water period, as described in Chapter 4.

The predictions of this sub-model were tested by a 'jack-knife' procedure, as further described in Figure 6.10. The predictions matched the observed rates quite well (Fig. 6.10). However, there was a slight tendency for the sub-model to under-predict at high values and to over-predict at low values. [This is probably a result of the sometimes large errors involved in measuring the density of the highly clumped mussels, as is discussed in the original paper]. On the other hand, the error range of the observed values overlapped the predicted rates in 34 of the 38 comparisons made. Although the match between observed and predicted interference-free intake rates was by no means perfect, it was thought to be sufficiently close over a wide range of values to be able to conclude that the sub-model predicted the intake rates reasonably well.

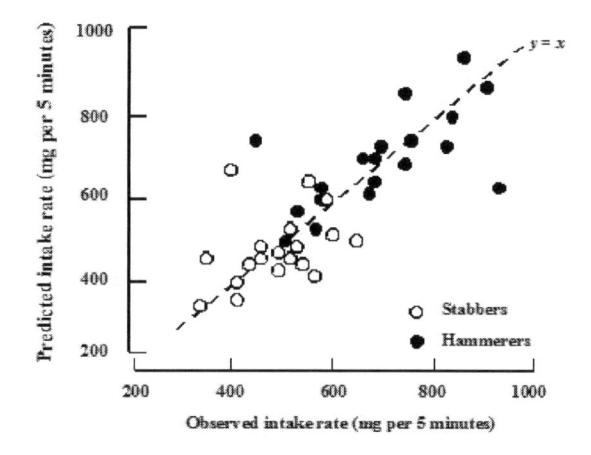

Figure 6.10 *Test of the model's ability to predict the interference-free intake rates of oystercatchers on the mussel beds. The results of a jack-knife test are shown. The optimality foraging sub-model was re-parameterised using the date that had been collected from all of the mussel beds except one. The intake rate on that excluded mussel bed was then predicted and compared with the intake rate that had been measured there during fieldwork. It is assumed that, on that mussel bed, the sample whose intake rates had been measured represented a bird of average foraging efficiency. The procedure was repeated, mussel bed by mussel bed, dropping out a different bed on each occasion and predicting its intake rate from the now re-parameterised optimality foraging sub-model. The line y=x represents the line of perfect fit between the predicted and the observed values.*

Distribution over the mussel beds

Over the low water period, most oystercatchers fed on the mussel beds and only small numbers fed on the supplementary upshore flats and fields. The model predicted that 99.5% of the oystercatchers would be on the mussel beds and this accords well with what was actually observed. This occurred, of course, because virtually all the birds obtained their highest intakes on the mussel beds.

The interference-free intake rates of oystercatchers feeding on mussels differed between mussel beds. Accordingly, the different mussel beds supported different numbers and densities of oystercatchers. The densities and numbers of oystercatchers predicted by the model to be on each of the ten beds accorded quite well with the densities and numbers that were actually recorded there (Fig. 6.11). However, there was again a tendency for the model to under-predict at high values and to over-predict at low values, especially in the case of the density of the birds.

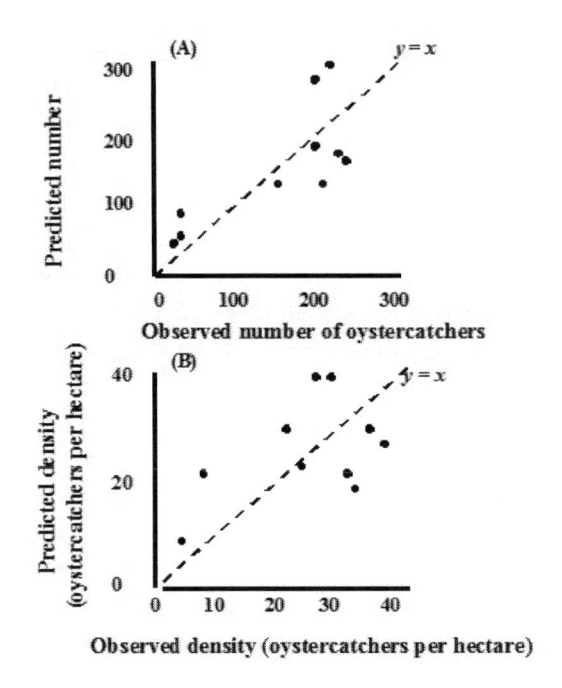

Figure 6.11 Test of the model's ability to predict the number (A) and density (B) of oystercatchers on each of the ten mussel beds. The line of perfect fit is $x=y$.

Tests of the overall performance of the model

Two tests could be carried out with model outputs that incorporated all aspects of the birds' behaviour and ecology. These were regarded as being particularly good tests of the model's overall, or integrated, performance.

Time spent foraging

The time that the birds spend feeding was viewed as one such output as it would depend on many components of the model. The amount of time spent feeding by the average oystercatcher on the mussel beds of the Exe is difficult to measure because so many of the birds move around the estuary so much as the tide ebbs and flows. However, by attaching radio-tracking transmitters to a sample of oystercatchers, Humphrey Sitters was able to time the arrival of birds on the mussel beds as the tide receded and to time their departure on the advancing tide. Direct observations had shown that, when on mussel beds, the average bird spent 90% of the exposure period foraging. This value was combined with the results of radio-tracking to calculate the number of minutes spent foraging by an average oystercatcher on mussel beds through a typical daytime and night time tidal cycle. There was a good agreement between these observed values and those predicted by the model (Fig. 6.12).

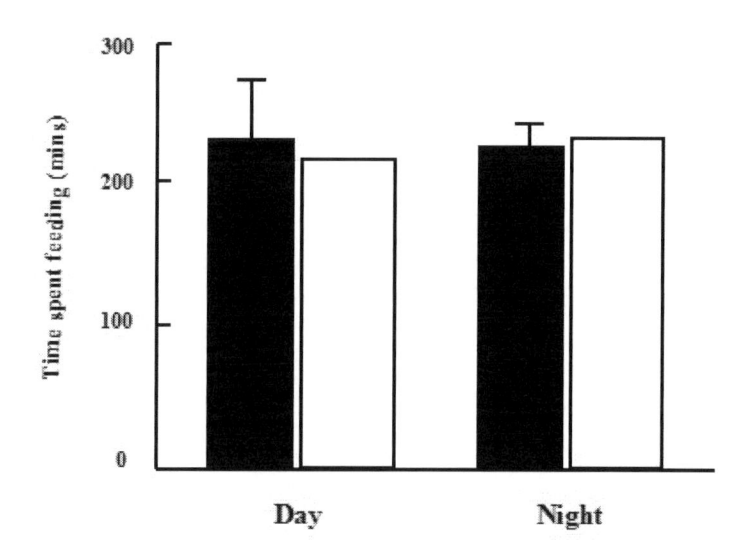

Figure 6.12 Test of the model's ability to predict the number of minutes spent foraging on mussels by an average oystercatcher on a daytime tidal cycle and a night time tidal cycle.

Depletion of mussels

Another test of the overall performance of the model was how accurately it predicted the quantity of mussels that were consumed by oystercatchers over the non-breeding season. As with the time spent feeding, this will depend on many components of the model.

The proportion of the mussels taken was estimated in two ways. In the first, oystercatchers were excluded from a number of small areas of mussels by a 'cat's cradle' of string supported by bamboo posts pushed into the ground. The string soon became festooned with weed and other floatables, such as bits of paper and, in those days when some raw sewage was discharged into the river, other items that are, perhaps, best not detailed. Anyway, all this flapping stuff kept the oystercatchers out of the excluded areas. The densities of the mussels inside the exclosures and in the control areas were measured at the beginning and end of the non-breeding season, and the decrease in both compared.

These experiments showed that the great majority of the mussels that disappeared from the mussel beds over the non-breeding season had been removed by oystercatchers. Very few disappeared from inside the exclosures, where the birds could not feed, but over 10% disappeared from outside where they could. This opened the way to obtaining a second estimate of the impact of oystercatchers on the mussels. The densities of mussels had been measured at the beginning and end of the non-breeding season on the main beds of the estuary from September 1976 to March 1983.

Since most of the mussels that had disappeared at that time would have been removed by oystercatchers – nowadays, many are also removed by herring gulls and carrion crows - the decrease in density from a September to the following March would provide another, estuary-wide measure of the depletion inflicted by these birds. The number of mussels pulled from the mussel bed by birds, but then not opened, was quite large but many of them would have re-established themselves by attaching themselves to other mussels with their byssus threads.

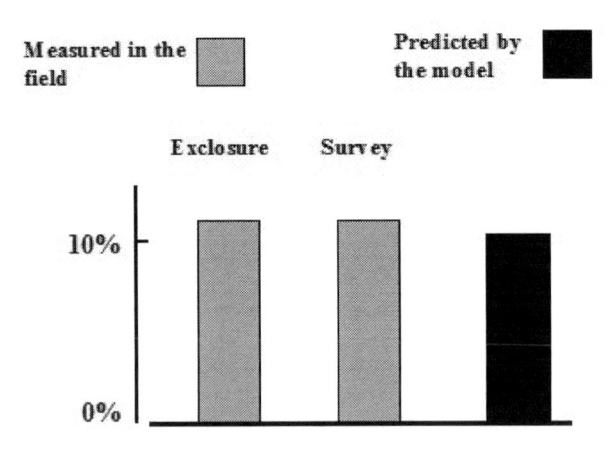

Figure 6.13 Test of the model's ability to predict the proportion of mussels taken by oystercatchers over the non-breeding season. The actual loss was measured in two ways: (i) by exclosure experiments and (ii) by comparing mussel density on the main mussel beds over eight winters in September and March.

The model predicted very well the proportion of their mussel food supply that oystercatchers removed during the course of the non-breeding season (Fig. 6.13). The total amount of mussels removed reflects everything that the birds in the model did over the non-breeding season. In particular, it would reflect the daily consumption of energy and the proportion of it that was obtained from mussels rather than other prey species at different stages of the non-breeding season. The model could very easily have made very inaccurate predictions for the depletion of mussels by the oystercatchers. The fact that it did not do so again raised confidence in the model.

CONCLUSION

Taken together, all the tests of the model's predictions described in this chapter suggest that version 3 gave a reasonably accurate representation of the oystercatcher population and of their dependence on the mussel and supplementary food supplies. It was particularly encouraging that the model had predicted that mortality would be density-dependent over the range of population sizes recorded on the Exe, even before

it had been discovered that this was the case. This was a genuine prediction of something that had already happened but had not at the time been discovered! As important, the magnitude of the predicted rates of starvation also matched the observed rates quite well. Since this is what the model was being developed to produce, this early success was critical and very welcome. It signaled that further development of the IBM approach might well be worthwhile.

REFERENCES FOR CHAPTER 6

Durell, S.E.A. Le V. dit, Goss-Custard, J.D., Caldow, R.W.G. Malcolm, H.M. & Osborn, D. (2001). Sex, diet and feeding-method related differences in body condition in the Oystercatcher *Haematopus ostralegus*. *Ibis*, **143**, 107-119.

Durell, S.E.A. le V. dit, Goss-Custard, J.D., Clarke, R.T. & McGrorty, S. (2000). Density-dependent mortality in oystercatchers *Haematopus ostralegus*. *Ibis*, **142**, 132-138.

Durell, S.E.A. Le V. dit, Goss-Custard, J.D., Clarke, R.T. & McGrorty. S. (2003). Density-dependent mortality in wintering Eurasian Oystercatchers *Haematopus ostralegus*. *Ibis*, **145**, 496-498.

Durell, S.E.A. le V. dit., Goss-Custard, J.D., Stillman, R.A., & West, R.A. (2001). The effect of weather and density-dependence on oystercatcher *Haematopus ostralegus* winter mortality. *Ibis*, **143**, 498-499.

McGrorty, S., Clarke, R.T., Reading, C.J. & Goss-Custard, J.D. (1990). Population dynamics of the mussel *Mytilus edulis*: density changes and regulation of the population in the Exe estuary, Devon. *Marine Ecology Progress Series*, **67**, 157-169.

McGrorty, S. & Goss-Custard, J.D. (1993). Population dynamics of the mussel *Mytilus edulis* along environmental gradients: spatial variations in density-dependent mortalities. *Journal of Animal Ecology*, **62**, 415-427.

McGrorty, S. & Goss-Custard, J.D. (1995). Population dynamics of *Mytilus edulis* along environmental gradients: density-dependent changes in adult mussel numbers. *Marine Ecology Progress Series*, **129**, 197-213.

McGrorty, S., Goss-Custard, J.D. & Clarke, R.T. (1993). Mussel *Mytilus edulis* dynamics in relation to environmental gradients and intraspecific interactions. *Netherlands Journal of Aquatic Ecology*, **27**, 163-171.

Stillman, R.A., Caldow, R.W.G., Goss-Custard, J.D. & Alexander, M.J. (2000). Individual variation in intake rate: the relative importance of foraging efficiency and dominance. *Journal of Animal Ecology*, **69**, 484-493.

Stillman, R.A., Goss-Custard, J.D., West, A.D., Durell, S.E.A. le V., Caldow, R.W.G., McGrorty, S. & Clarke, R.T. (2000). Predicting to novel environments: tests and sensitivity of a behaviour-based population model. *Journal of applied Ecology*, **37**, 564-588.

Stillman, R.A., McGrorty, S., Goss-Custard, J.D. & West, A.D. (2000). Predicting mussel population density and age structure: the relationship between model complexity and predictive power. *Progress in Marine Ecology Series*, **208**, 131-145.

Box 6.1 Choosing what things to add to the model

As in multivariate analysis, there are two broad approaches to building a model. One is the 'step-up' procedure. With this, you include in the first version of the model the minimum number of processes and factors that you are certain are vital if the model is to represent the system being modelled with any realism. On the Exe, there had to be, for example, the mussel food supply and how it determined the intake rate of an average bird, the daily energy requirements an average oystercatcher and the competitive abilities of the different individuals in the population. If there remains a gap between what the model predicts and what happens in the real world, you then 'step-up' by adding processes and factors until the discrepancy between observed and predicted has been removed.

The other approach is the 'step-down' procedure. Here, you include at the start everything that you have reason to believe, or suspect, might have an influence on the model's predictions. In the case of the Exe model, the list could have been immensely long and would have included, not only the obvious processes given above, but also possibilities such as differences between individuals in the efficiency with which they assimilate the energy in their food, the efficiency with which they store and subsequently mobilise fat reserves and the hour-to-hour change in the ambient temperature. Then, one step at a time, you delete processes that prove to have little or no effect on the outputs of the model, until all that remain are those that actually do seem to matter.

For the Exe IBM, a step-up procedure was employed. Processes were added, step-by-step, until the model accurately predicted the mortality rates over the non-breeding season that had been measured in the field from 1976 to 1980. The sequence in which processes were added in this approach was based on our understanding of the system. So, when version 2 predicted mortality rates that were much higher than those which actually occurred in nature, a choice had to be made as to what needed to be added to the model to improve its predictions.

Having first checked that the values given to all its parameters were still the best that were available at the time, attention turned to things that had been left out of the model. It was simply experience-based intuition that – rightly or wrongly - led to the selection of supplementary feeding on intertidal foods upshore of the mussel beds and in fields. Our understanding of the system made this seem likely to be the best bet.

There is a danger, of course, in building up a model this way. There may be another process whose importance has been under-estimated that is the real reason for the current model's poor performance. Its inclusion may even have removed the need for many of the other processes in which case the model may have ended up being more complex than it needed to be! You have to remember that, after the step-up model process has eventually produced a version that accurately predicts mortality, it may give the right answers but for the wrong reasons, and do so in an over-complicated way! The danger then would be that the model would give false predictions when it is used to explore a real issue concerning the management of estuaries.

The only way to approach the whole business is always to keep in mind the possibility that new understandings, new ideas and new findings may need to be included in the model and that ones that are already in the model may need to be removed. Some flexibility and a little scientific humility – even about your own wonderful model – is always desirable!

Box 6.2 Physics envy?

Even in something as complex as ecological systems, there has been much success in producing relatively simple mathematical models that represent well the essence of the process that is being described. Good examples of how successful this can be appear, for example, is the work on the interactions between the populations of predators and their prey and between parasitoids and their insect hosts. Some of these elegant and intellectually satisfying models have been applied successfully to real-world cases, such as the spread of some diseases.

There has been some enthusiasm for devising similar 'analytical' models amongst shorebird ecologists concerned with predicting the effect of a whole range of human activities on these birds. The ideal outcome of this approach would be a simple equation, as comprehensive and elegant as $E = mc^2$. How handy it would be if a simple equation could be devised of the form $M = cD^2$, where M = mortality, D = population density and c is a constant!

But no such luck yet with real-world populations of shorebirds! Instead, simulation or 'mechanistic' models have been produced in which the processes that are believed to be important are represented by equations and the output of one forms the input of the next equation. The IBM of Exe oystercatchers is an example of such a model. It attempts to capture the many processes which current evidence suggests are important in determining shorebird survival and body condition over the non-breeding season.

The danger with this approach is that the resulting model can be immensely complicated and include all kinds of things that were not actually relevant to making the desired predictions but which take time and resources to include. We tried to avoid this danger by adopting a step-up procedure, as described in Box 6.1. The aim was to make the IBM as simple as possible without leaving out so much of the natural history that the model's predictive ability would be diminished.

This emphasis on simplicity may seem rather strange to some when one considers the well-established areas of research where models are pretty complex: climate models, economic models, hydrological models, sediment models, fishery management models, to name but a few. Perhaps the difference is that these are all areas of modelling that have been used to guide policy for many years. The models are presumably rather complex because this was needed to produce reliable predictions. Just like the Exe IBM!

Box 6.3 Sampling the mussel beds

The mussel beds were sampled every September and every March for eight years in succession, and then on several occasions subsequently as and when the need arose. A single survey was a monumental task, often carried out in heinous weather and involving plodding or floundering through deep mud. This is how a single survey was carried out.

The first task was to map the boundaries of the mussel beds as these changed year by year as gales eroded the edges to windward. To do this, a baseline was marked out alongside each mussel bed using bamboo sticks. A series of regularly-spaced transects, at right angles to the baseline, were then walked across the mussel bed. A triangular pacing stick was used to measure the distance between the two edges of the bed on each transect.

Mussels did not occur in a continuous sheet. The proportion of the surface of a mussel bed where mussels occurred varied a great deal between beds, from as low as 10-20% up to 90%. This percentage cover was measured by recording at every meter whether or not mussels occurred within an imaginary quadrat, with the same dimensions as was used later to sample the mussels, placed at the leading point of the pacing stick. As this was done along every transect, a very precise and representative value for the percentage of the mussel bed that had mussels was obtained.

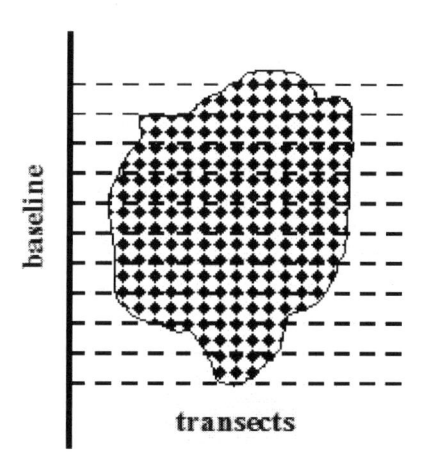

The next step was to take a series of quadrats at random from all over the bed. Random locations were pre-selected and located on the mussel bed. At each sampling spot, a quadrat was thrown with closed eyes to avoid bias. Only quadrats that contained mussels were used, the mussels in them being put in plastic bags to transport back to the laboratory.

Bags of mussels are heavy, and required much effort and muscle to be taken ashore. Whatever transport device was tried, such as a sledge, to get the samples ashore still involved very heavy labour. It is to the immense credit of the three principal scientists involved – Selwyn McGrorty, Chris Reading and Andy West – that this enormous task that took so many years was so outstandingly successfully completed, and all in a spirit of chuckling good humour.

Box 6.4 What if there had been no lucky break?

Without the lucky break, it would not have been possible on the Exe itself to test the model's ability to predict accurately to new circumstances until something in the environment had changed radically. The 'something' could have been a loss of some mussel beds in a storm, for example, or the complete removal of some feeding areas through continuous disturbance of some sort. In fact, as both circumstances were very unlikely to arise, it would probably have been necessary to test the model on a different estuary. In fact, this did happen when the model was applied to other shellfisheries, using funds obtained in contracts. But, without the successful testing on the Exe itself, the opportunity obtain a contract elsewhere may never have presented itself!

CHAPTER 7:
Explorations with the oystercatcher-mussel model of the Exe estuary

....which describes how version 3 of the individual-based model (IBM) was used to explore the effect of disturbance from people and of mussel-fishing on the mussel-feeding oystercatchers of the Exe estuary and of cockle-fishing on oystercatchers in the Burry Inlet, Wales

OYSTERCATCHERS AND PEOPLE

It had taken the best part of 25 years to develop and test the Exe estuary oystercatcher-mussel IBM but, for the first time, there was evidence from both the model and the empirical studies that the mortality rate over the non-breeding season – or, more precisely, the starvation rate – of a shorebird was density-dependent over some of its range of population size. As should be evident by now, this was an important finding. It implied that any deterioration in the feeding conditions due to an action by people or for other reasons was likely to reduce oystercatcher survival and thereby decrease the size of their population. This assumption had always been made in environmental impact assessments of how a proposed – or existing – activity might affect shorebirds, even though there had been no convincing evidence previously that either habitat loss or habitat deterioration in shorebirds would lead to decreased survival. The findings from the Exe empirical work suggested that, at least for this species eating mussels on this estuary, caution had been appropriate.

But this is a far cry from saying that every human action on the Exe would necessarily have a negative impact on the oystercatchers! The results prior to 2000 suggested that, at low population sizes, there was some 'slack in the system' because oystercatcher mortality depended very little, if at all, on their density. This implied that the birds were not always so hard-pressed that any intervention by people would necessarily reduce survival by intensifying competition amongst the birds. Perhaps some mussels could be removed and the birds could be somewhat disturbed without inevitably causing a reduction in their survival rate and body condition.

Even at higher population sizes, a reduction in survival and body condition would not necessarily arise from interventions by people. As was discussed at length previously, whether this is likely to occur is all a question of quantities. Removing one mussel or disturbing one bird once in the winter would change nothing. Removing all of the mussels, either by physically doing so or by disturbing all the mussel beds all the time, would almost certainly reduce the birds' survival rate and body condition enormously, even though they could switch to alternative prey, such as ragworms, cockles, clams and earthworms. As discussed in Chapter 1, at some threshold point as the number of mussels removed increased, the survival rate of the birds, and their body condition, would begin to be reduced, this happening sooner when the oystercatcher population size was high than when it was low.

In the early 2000s when version 3 had been built and tested, there was no immediate demand to explore the possible effect of any human activities on the oystercatchers of the Exe estuary itself. However, it was believed likely to be of benefit elsewhere if the model was first used to explore with Exe oystercatchers the effect of three common scenarios; disturbance from people, shellfishing and habitat loss. Apart from any lessons that might be learned about the potential impact of such activities on oystercatcher survival, it was thought useful to demonstrate to a largely sceptical audience how the IBM could be used to help resolve any management issues that might arise from such activities on other estuaries.

DISTURBANCE OF SHOREBIRDS

For years, conservationists had been concerned that people doing all kinds of things on the feeding grounds of shorebirds might be having a damaging effect on their survival and body condition, and therefore numbers. Most studies of disturbance and wading birds have focussed on measuring the effect of disturbance on the observable behaviour of the birds and sometimes the underlying physiology. The means by which the effect of disturbance on survival and body condition could be measured were simply not available.

A few examples will suffice to illustrate the many studies of this kind that had been carried out. Measurements had been (and still are) made on (i) differences between species in the responses of birds to an approaching person and, in particular, the distances at which they take flight; (ii) the effect that the detection of an approaching person has on how intensely the birds feed; (iii) the potentially harmful physiological responses, such as elevated corticosterone levels, of having people nearby; (iv) the amount of parental care given to oystercatcher chicks when parents are disturbed by humans; (v) the distance to which birds that have been disturbed by people move and the amount of time it takes for them to return to their previous location; (vi) the effect of frequent disturbance from people on the numbers of birds in a locality; (vii) the effect of the frequent presence of people on the distribution of birds between different feeding sites over a range of spatial scales, sometimes with food abundance also being taken into account; (viii) the under-exploitation of resources in areas that are frequently disturbed; (ix) whether wading birds can compensate for the losses of time and energy resulting from disturbance by increasing their subsequent intake rate or by feeding for longer, and (x) whether the birds get used ('habituate') to repeated disturbances.

None of these studies, however, made it possible to predict the effect that disturbance was having – if any - on the survival and body condition of the birds and therefore on their numbers. That a bird changes its behaviour and foraging location, or does not exploit all of its potential food supply, for example, does not necessarily mean that its chances of surviving the winter have been reduced. Nor does it mean that its body reserves have been so eroded that it is unable to migrate back to the breeding grounds and breed successfully. What really was required was a means to assess whether the frequency, intensity and duration with which birds were being disturbed was high enough to reduce their survival chances over the non-breeding season or their body condition prior to migration. The development of the IBM allowed this to be done for the first time.

In short, many studies had shown effects but had been unable to measure meaningful impacts. Because of this gap, some people have made, and still make, the very precautionary assumption that, if the birds' behaviour is affected, there is a risk that their chances of surviving and their body condition might also be affected. It would then be concluded that the source of the disturbance should be seen as potentially damaging, and so stopped. But this risks constraining people's activities without good cause, and perhaps losing in the long run popular support for the measures taken.

DISTURBANCE OF OYSTERCATCHERS ON THE MUSSEL BEDS OF THE EXE ESTUARY

People regularly occur on some of the mussel beds of the Exe estuary for a variety of reasons: to collect mussels and cockles for private consumption; to pick winkles for sale, usually to mainland Europe; to fish with rod and line for flatfish and bass from the seaward edge of the mussel bed; to dig up polychaete worms for fishing bait; to land a boat to have a rest or carry out some repairs or simply to amble about, sometimes with a dog, because it is a nice place to be, and interesting things can be found in the pools. In addition, there has been a commercial mussel fishery on the Exe for some decades in which small mussels that are dredged up from below the Low Water Mark are laid alongside an existing mussel bed where they remain until large enough to be harvested for sale. On top of these disturbances due to people, oystercatchers can be disturbed by birds of prey. They may also be frequently attacked by crows and herring gulls which attack oystercatchers to 'steal' mussels that they have opened. It is very easy to understand why, from looking at a couple of the most-disturbed mussel beds of the Exe, conservationists can be concerned about the possible effect of disturbance on the oystercatchers, and of other species that also occupy mussel beds.

How do oystercatchers respond to an approaching person? Typically, as a disturber approaches, they raise their heads and start to walk away, sometimes while feeding. Eventually, they stop feeding and take flight. Sometimes they fly to a sand bank and rest and preen before returning to a mussel bed. Other times they fly to another part of the same mussel bed or to another mussel bed. They often do not resume feeding immediately after they land on a mussel bed but rest and preen for a while. Every time a bird is disturbed, therefore, it may lose some time it would otherwise have spent feeding and it may expend energy in flight that it would not otherwise have used. The concern of conservationists is that disturbance can increase the energy costs of living while reducing the time available to recupe the lost energy: potentially, then, a double whammy.

There may be less obvious consequences too. Experimental studies show that disturbance can cause physiological effects, usually referred to as 'stress', even before birds take flight. This could suggest that birds may be being affected by disturbance before they actually show a clear-cut response. However, the limited data available suggest that disturbance may not normally be frequent enough in the wild for stress to have a significant effect on the birds in nature, so this possibility is ignored here.

A much more likely outcome of disturbance is that competition between oystercatchers might be made more intense. If, for example, people occur on half the mussel beds for the entire period for which the beds are exposed, the birds would be forced to feed for the whole exposure period in only half the space that they would otherwise have occupied. They would not be able to spread out as much as they would normally do in order to avoid interference competition. This is akin to the increase in bird density that occurs at the beginning and end of the exposure period. One effect of disturbance, therefore, is that interference competition may be significantly intensified. And if the disturbance occurs frequently enough, the birds may deplete their food supplies in the undisturbed areas enough to intensify competition there through depletion.

It is very easy to build up a non-quantitative 'word argument' that disturbance must do harm to the birds by making it more difficult for them to balance their energy budget, and this claim is made frequently. But on mussel beds of the Exe, there are several mitigating circumstances which mean that we should not immediately rush to that conclusion.

Most importantly, disturbance over the exposure period was, and still is, only frequent on two of the main mussel beds. Elsewhere, it is uncommon. As the data from one of the two most disturbed mussel beds illustrate, fewer people go out into the intertidal zone at low water on neap tides than on spring tides (Fig. 7.1(A)) and occur there on a lower proportion of low water periods (Fig. 7(B)). [This may partially explain why more oystercatchers occurred on the mussel bed on neap tides than on spring tides (Fig. 7.1(C)), although the numbers of people on the adjacent mussel bed also seemed to have an influence (Fig. 7.1(D))]. Figure 7.1 also illustrates that people are not present on the mussel beds for the entire exposure period and on every tide.

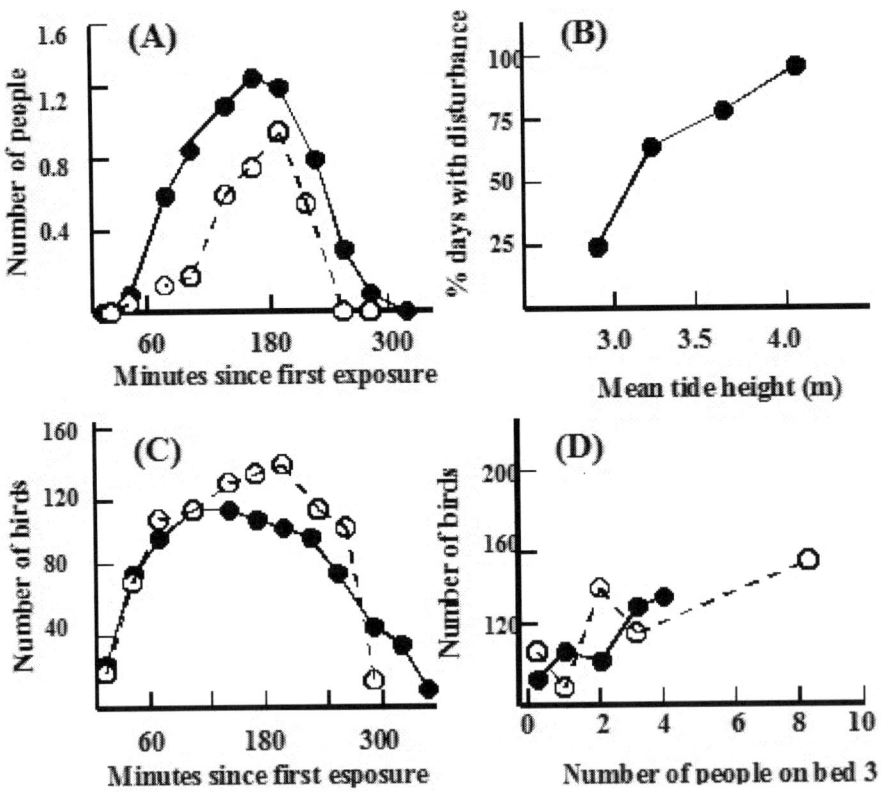

Figure 7.1 *Disturbance on one of the most frequently disturbed mussel beds of the Exe estuary during the autumn and winter of 1989. With the exception of **(B)**, data for neap tides are open circles and spring tides are closed circles. **(A)** The average number of people on the mussel bed through the exposure period. **(B)** The average number of oystercatchers present in relation to the height of tide at high water. **(C)** The average number of oystercatchers on the mussel bed through the exposure period. **(D)** The numbers of oystercatchers on the mussel bed in relation to the numbers of people present on the immediately adjacent mussel bed of similar size.*

A number of other factors that are not shown in Figure 7.1 also affect the amount of disturbance that occurs on the mussel beds. Very few people occur on mussel beds during heavy rain and in strong wind, as many of their activities are carried out for enjoyment. Many of the disturbers are more-or-less stationary once they have arrived and so mostly disturb birds for a very brief period as they arrive and depart the mussel bed. Some mussel beds are so large that a single person in one corner of it disturbs very few of the birds that are present. On many mussel beds, it therefore takes several people wandering about independently of each other to disturb all the birds that are on the bed. Finally, only an occasional person goes onto any mussel bed at night and, on the great majority of nights, nobody is there at all. What takes place on two or three mussel beds over low water on spring tides during the day gives a very one-sided, and dire, impression of the amount of disturbance to which oystercatchers are subjected. It is extremely unrepresentative of the whole estuary population. There is much less disturbance – and frequently none – at other times and in other places where birds can feed undisturbed throughout the exposure period.

Furthermore, the oystercatchers have a number of options available to them to compensate for disturbance. During many stages of the non-breeding season they do not have to feed for all of the time that the mussel beds are exposed. If disturbed, they can then 'make up for lost time' when the disturber has left, either during the day or at night when no disturbers are present. If this is insufficient, they can continue feeding on prey other than mussels on mudflats and sand flats upshore of the mussel beds and feed on terrestrial prey in fields over high tide.

It is therefore by no means self-evident that disturbance will necessarily reduce the survival chances and body condition of the birds. They may be able to minimise the impact of disturbance by moving to an undisturbed area. If the time for which they can feed there is insufficient so that they are still short of the food that they require, they have a number of options open to them to compensate. The net effect between the disturbance and the compensatory responses of the birds to it has to be worked out, and this can only done using quantitative methods. That is, a model is required to test the hypothesis that disturbance of the frequency, duration and intensity that it occurs actually might affect the birds in a meaningful way.

Modelling disturbance

Disturbance was confined to the mussel beds in these simulations with the IBM. The upshore area and field were left undisturbed. Disturbers were distributed over the mussel beds at random and avoided each other where possible so that the areas they disturb - their 'disturbance areas' - did not overlap. Simulations were run with either 10% or 50% of the total area of mussels across all beds disturbed. The model was run for each of these conditions with two types of disturbance: 'major' and 'minor' disturbers, as illustrated in Figure 7.2. A person walking across a mussel bed would be a major disturber. Minor disturbers represented people moving near to a mussel bed, around the edge. To reflect this difference, the area affected by a minor disturber was 10% of that affected by a major disturber. So, for example, 10% of the total area of mussels in the estuary could be disturbed by two major disturbers or by 20 minor disturbers.

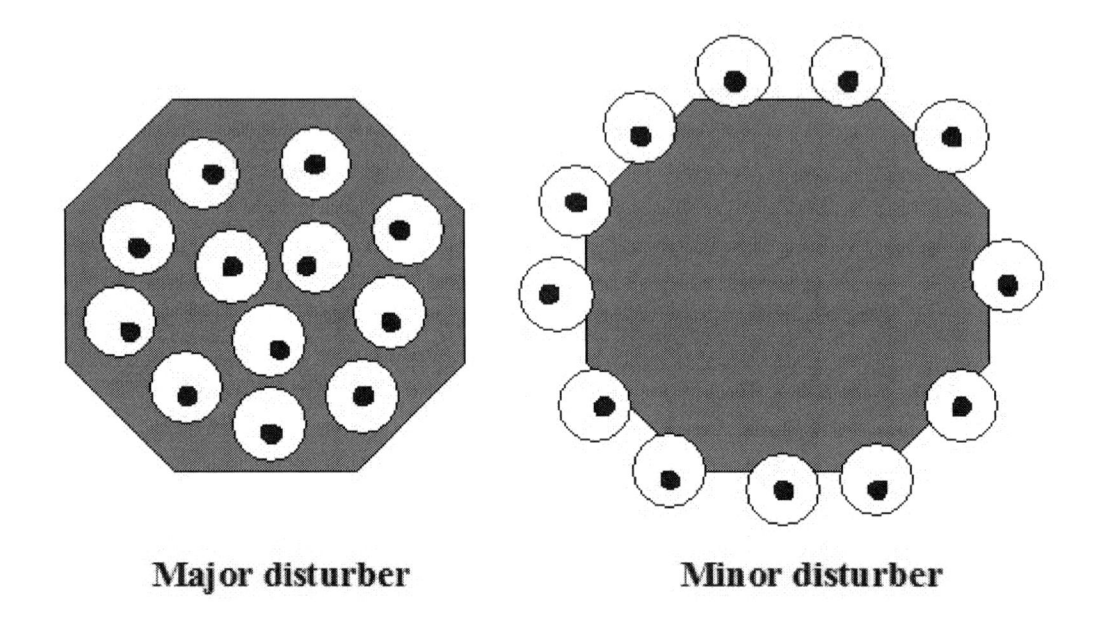

Figure 7.2 *How 'major' and 'minor' disturbers were represented in the model.* **(A)** *There are 12 disturbers (black dots) on this mussel bed, each one of which denies to the birds a circular area of 200m diameter. In aggregate, they prevent the birds from foraging in 50% of this mussel bed.* **(B)** *There are again 12 disturbers but they are at the edge of the mussel bed. As a consequence, each one only prevents the birds from feeding in an area that is just 10% of that caused by a major disturber.*

How disturbance was represented in the model is illustrated in Figure 7.3. A major disturber was placed on a mussel bed at the beginning of the low water stage and was there for the whole of that low tide stage. A minor disturber was placed alongside the mussel bed and also remained there for the whole low water stage. In both cases, all the model birds on a disturbed mussel bed flew up once when a disturber was present, as if it had just arrived. The assumption that all the birds on a mussel bed with a disturber were actually disturbed had to be made because this early model was set up to represent whole mussel beds, and not parts of them. In the real world, of course, this assumption would seldom be appropriate because some birds would be too far away to be affected by an arriving disturber. Similarly, in the model, a disturber remained on the mussel bed throughout the entire low water stage whereas, in reality, most disturbers remained for only part of it. Assuming that all the birds on the mussel bed would be disturbed and that the disturber would remain throughout low water were thus 'precautionary assumptions'. That is to say, assumptions that made it more likely, rather than less likely, that the survival chances and body condition of the model birds would be reduced by disturbance. On the other hand, in reality, some individuals may be disturbed two or three times as the disturber moves around the mussel bed. That a bird is disturbed only once per disturber was thus a 'contra-precautionary' assumption.

(A) Disturbance-free

(B) Low tide 2 – re-distributed

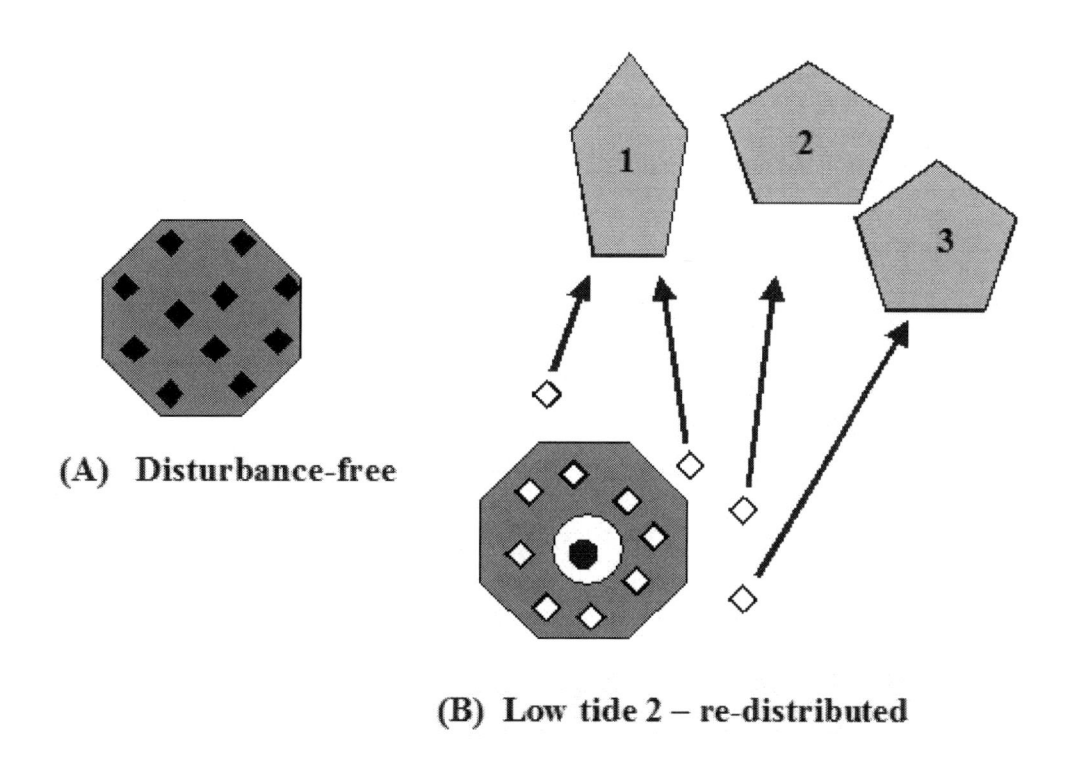

Figure 7.3 Disturbance from a person on a mussel bed during the low tide stage was represented in the model in two stages, or runs of the model. The first stage was the 'disturbance-free' run **(A)**. Having considered all the individuals in the population, the model has placed eleven of them on the 'subject' mussel bed (the grey area) at the start of the low tide stage. (There are many other oystercatchers on the other nine mussel beds that are represented in the model, but these are not shown here.) The second stage is the 'disturbance-present' run **(B)**. In this, the model is 'instructed' to place one person (shown as a black blob) on the subject mussel bed. All of the eleven individual birds that were on the mussel bed at the start of the low tide stage had been identified and marked ('flagged') by the model at the end of the 'disturbance-free' simulation. Each of these individuals incurs a time cost of 30mins and an energy cost of 1kJ because the model assumes that all the birds on a mussel bed are disturbed by a person on it. The white circle of 200m diameter shows the area from which all birds are excluded when the model considers all the birds in the population again and re-allocates them to the mussel bed where their intake rate is now the highest. This results in this instance in two birds moving to mussel bed 1 and one each moving to mussel beds 2 and 3. Thus seven of the original eleven individuals remain on the subject mussel bed in the reduced space that is now available. The birds now remain on the beds to which they have been allocated for the remainder of the low tide stage.

Having been disturbed, all the oystercatchers then rested before resuming feeding. The time and energy costs resulting from a 'disturbance event' were applied to all the individual birds that had been on the disturbed bed. The time cost (the time spent in flight and resting before resuming feeding) had been measured in oystercatchers on an Exe mussel bed. Typically, birds spent one minute in flight after being disturbed and did not resume feeding until 30 minutes after they landed again; accordingly, both these values were used in the model. While flying, a disturbed bird in the model occurred the additional energy cost of 1kJ, roughly equivalent to the energy expended in flying for one minute.

Again as in the real world, a disturber in the model prevented oystercatchers from feeding within his or her disturbance area, measured in oystercatchers on the Exe. A disturber therefore denies a circle of mussel bed to the birds, thus temporarily reducing the surface area on that mussel bed where the birds can feed and so increasing bird density in the remaining part of the mussel bed. This, of course, increases the chances that interference competition will intensify on the disturbed mussel bed and on other mussel beds too, if some of the disturbed birds fly there instead of remaining where they were.

In order to find out how many of the disturbed oystercatchers left the disturbed bed to feed elsewhere, the modelling of disturbance was carried out in two steps. First of all, it was necessary to establish which individuals were feeding on the mussel bed that was going to be disturbed. This was necessary so that the time and energy costs of being disturbed could be applied to the particular individuals that were actually going to be disturbed. An initial 'disturbance-free' simulation was therefore carried out to identify the mussel bed on which each bird in the population was feeding at the beginning of the tidal stage when the disturber was present. This 'disturbance-free' run of the model was made at the start of the tidal stage to allocate each of the birds to their 'first-choice' or 'preferred' or 'disturbance-free choice' of mussel bed (Fig. 7.3(A)). At the end of this, the model 'flagged' the individuals that fed on a mussel bed that was going to be disturbed. Those would be the individuals that would be affected by the disturbance that was to come and could now be identified as such by the model.

The second step was to introduce the disturber(s) onto the mussel bed (Fig. 7.3(B)). In this next run in which the disturber was present, the model re-distributed the birds over all of the mussel beds and not just the one where the disturber was situated. In this 'disturbance-present' run, some of the birds would be able to remain on their first-choice mussel bed but others would find it more profitable to move to another one. Accordingly, some of the birds on the undisturbed mussel beds could have been penalised indirectly through an increase in bird density on the mussel beds that were feeding. Once allocated to a mussel bed in this run, each bird then stayed on its allocated mussel bed for the remainder of that tidal stage.

Predicted impact of disturbance on oystercatchers

The first simulations showed that, at the then population size of 1500 oystercatchers, continuous disturbance throughout the non-breeding season and throughout every low water period - day and night, on neaps as well as spring tides and irrespective of the weather - could reduce the birds' chances of surviving the non-breeding season to levels far below its disturbance-free value of 2.5%. Indeed, with the worst case scenario of 50% of the mussel bed area being disturbed by minor disturbers, the mortality rate could be almost ten times higher at 22% (Fig 7.4).

A consistent result, however, was that minor disturbers had a noticeably greater impact on the oystercatchers than did the major disturbers, even though both disturbed the same total area. This seemed to happen because the minor disturbers were spread out over a greater number of patches.

More birds therefore incurred the direct time and energy costs of disturbance. Additionally, more birds incurred the indirect costs of disturbance arising from the increased competitor density on undisturbed feeding areas, especially if the major disturbers happened to be on the less preferred mussel beds.

If confirmed, this finding could have important implications for the management of disturbance. A large and noisy disturbance, such as water skiing, in one part of an estuary might appear to be very damaging as it disturbs birds over a large area, yet people walking quietly across the feeding areas in several places may actually have a much greater impact on the birds. Similarly, a group of bait-diggers or bird watchers, for example, could cause less significant disturbance than the same number of people spread throughout the estuary.

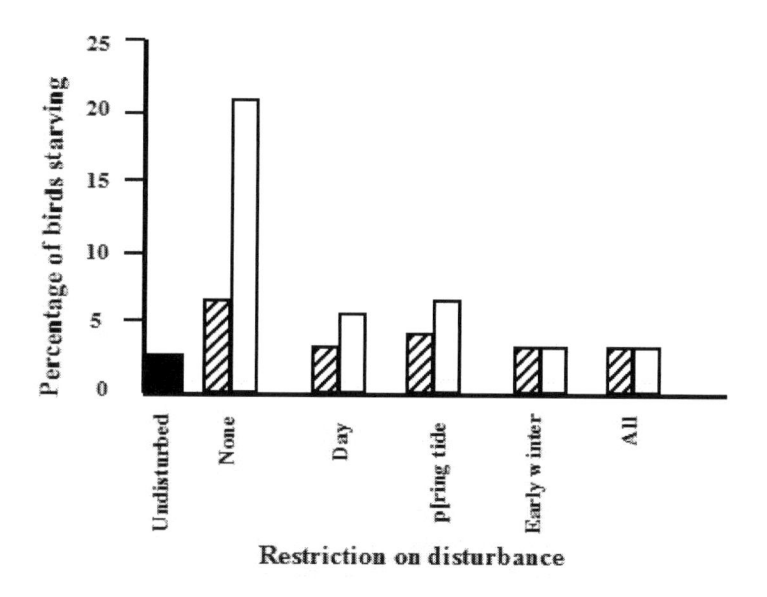

Figure 7.4 *The effect on the mortality rate of a population of 1500 oystercatchers of various amounts of disturbance caused by people. The results refer only to minor disturbers. The solid bar shows the mortality rate when there is no disturbance at all during the non-breeding season. Hatched columns refer to 10% of the mussel beds being disturbed and the white columns to 50%. 'None' means that there were no restrictions on people, and that disturbance occurred day and night on all tides throughout the non-breeding season, irrespective of the weather. 'Day' means that disturbance only occurred during the day and not at night. 'Spring tide' means that disturbance only occurred on spring tides, but occurred night and day. 'Early winter' means that disturbance only occurred before December 1st, but again at night as well as during the day. 'All' means that all these restrictions were applied at the same time.*

A further series of simulations was carried to illustrate how the predicted impacts of disturbance were affected by more realistic assumptions about the frequency and circumstances in which disturbance actually occurred. Others were carried out to illustrate how the model might be used to explore the effectiveness of introducing a number of hypothetical regulations. To be sure to obtain clear-cut comparisons, the simulations were carried out with minor disturbers rather than major disturbers because they had the larger impact on the birds. The changed assumptions were: (i) disturbers were only present in daylight; (ii) disturbers were absent on neap tides, and (iii) disturbers were banned, day and night on all tides, during the second half of the non-breeding season.

These changes were first applied individually, and then all three were applied together, and the results are also shown in Figure 7.4. All three changes in assumption caused a noticeable drop in the rate of starvation caused by disturbance. Just preventing disturbance during neap tides was the least effective, but nonetheless reduced mortality substantially. The most effective single change was to ban all disturbance during the second half of the non-breeding season – which is when most mortality occurs anyway, so this is perhaps unsurprising.

These simulations were run primarily to illustrate how the IBM could be used to measure the impact of disturbance on oystercatchers. The frequency and intensity of the disturbances used in this investigation were far in excess of those that actually occurred then (and now), however. For example, disturbers seldom occurred on more than two of the ten main beds at the same time and rarely remained throughout the low water period. Nonetheless, these simulations had illustrated how the IBM could be used to explore not only the impact of disturbance on the mortality rate but also the likely effectiveness of introducing regulations that limit the amount to which the birds are subjected. Although the particular scenarios considered at this time were very unrealistic, the impact on shorebirds of much more realistic scenarios have been explored subsequently in other estuaries, as will be described in a later chapter. At the time, the important thing about these early simulations on Exe estuary mussel-eating oystercatchers was that they had shown how the consequences for bird survival of mobile, unpredictable disturbances could be predicted by an IBM. This is something that had not been possible previously.

Population consequences of significant amounts of disturbance

At the then population size of oystercatchers, the impact of disturbance, and therefore of the measures that could alleviate it, could appear to be rather small in some scenarios. However, it is important to remember that, in long-lived animals with low rates of annual mortality, even a small increase in mortality rate can, over successive generations, lead to a much more obvious impact. While a decrease in survival rate from 98% to 96% may seem to be rather trivial, it actually represents a doubling in the mortality rate from 2% to 4%.

To illustrate this point, a separate and very different kind of model of the Exe population of oystercatchers – a 'demographic population model' - was used to calculate the long-term cumulative effect on the size of the oystercatcher population of small increases in the mortality rate over the non-breeding season that had been caused by disturbance. These simulations showed that major disturbers on 10% of the mussel bed area would cause only a 2% reduction in the long-term equilibrium population size (EPS) whereas minor disturbers would reduce it by 8%. With 50% of the estuary being disturbed, both types of disturber would, of course, lead to substantially larger reductions in the EPS.

HABITAT LOSS – PERMANENTLY REMOVING SOME MUSSEL BEDS

The basic simulations of disturbance had assumed that either 10% or 50% of the total mussel bed area was denied the birds at all times by disturbance. In effect, 10% or 50% of the habitat was removed. The only difference between permanent habitat loss and this disturbance scenario is that, when disturbed, the birds incurred additional time and energy costs whereas, with habitat loss, this would not be so.

In order to work out the impact of habitat loss, simulations were therefore run under both these conditions but without the birds incurring these costs. Excluding costs only made a difference to the predictions at unrealistically high population sizes. The most important outcome from these simulations was to illustrate, again for the first time, that a way had been developed to predict the impact of the loss of a shorebird's feeding habitat on their chances of surviving the non-breeding season.

MUSSEL FISHING ON THE EXE ESTUARY

Despite intensive research over many years, the effects on oystercatchers of current and potential shellfishery management policies were usually unpredictable prior to the development of the IBM, not just on the Exe estuary but also elsewhere in the World. It was often an issue that provoked intense debate. The advantage of the IBM is that it is able to evaluate the impact on the birds of not only the current shellfishing regime but also that of alternative regimes that might be considered by the authorities. This is because it incorporates the main responses of oystercatchers to shellfishing, which are behavioural.

How might fishing mussels on the Exe have affected the oystercatchers in the 1980s and 1990s? Shellfishing would have removed some of the large-sized mussels that are most profitable to oystercatchers, leaving them with the smaller and less profitable ones on which they would have had a reduced intake rate. The mussel fishers themselves may also have disturbed the birds if they carried out harvesting over low tide rather than by dredging, for example, from a boat over high water. The removal of mussels from the most productive beds, along with any disturbance it caused over low water, would have driven the birds from their preferred feeding areas to poorer quality areas where they would feed at a reduced rate. Additionally, increased bird densities would have intensified interference amongst the oystercatchers and, perhaps, intensified exploitation competition as well. This might have reduced the intake rate of the birds and so increased the chances that some oystercatchers would have died of starvation towards the end of the non-breeding season, when they may already have had difficulty in obtaining their energy requirements anyway.

Modelling shellfishing

Shellfishing is incorporated into the model by following the location and activities of a number of 'fishing units' which comprise a single person or group of people or boats, depending on the method used to harvest the mussels. Fishing effort can be varied by changing the number of fishing units and/or by changing the size of the quota that each fishing unit is allowed to collect during a single tidal cycle. A specified number of fishing units occupy the mussel bed or beds with the highest densities of the large mussels that they harvest. These are the mussel beds on which the shellfishers can collect mussels at the highest rate: like oystercatchers, the shellfishers choose to go to the most profitable mussel beds. As the mussel fishers deplete the shellfish stocks in the initially most preferred beds, fishing units – again like the birds - spread out to occupy a wider range of beds with lower densities of large mussels. It was necessary to prevent all fishing units unrealistically occupying the same mussel bed. Accordingly, shellfishers were assumed in the Exe estuary simulations to occupy any beds with densities of mussels of fishable size greater than 75% of that on the bed with the highest density. In effect, the mussel fishers spread out over the top 25% of the area of the estuary covered by mussels.

For fishing that is carried out over low tide, disturbance is again incorporated by assuming that birds are displaced from a circular zone around each fishing unit. If more than one unit is present on a mussel bed, the total exclusion area is the sum of individual zones. This procedure makes the precautionary assumption that units disperse widely across the patch and also implies that their disturbance zones do not overlap as long as there is enough space for this to be possible. When there are enough of them are present to disturb the entire bed, no birds can feed on it over the low tide period because the combined disturbance zones of the shellfishers blot out the whole mussel bed. Disturbance is assumed to persist throughout low tide even if the time spent actively collecting mussels to reach the quota is shorter than the duration of the low water period. This would usually be a precautionary assumption and can be thought of as realistically including time spent by mussel fishers in arriving, departing, lunching, chatting and resting on the mussel bed!

Oystercatchers displaced from one mussel bed by mussel fishers move to another one where, under the conditions prevailing at the time, they can maximize their intake rate. The energy and time costs of moving between beds can also be included in the model although this was not done in these Exe estuary simulations because the distances involved are so small.

Although the model can simulate any method of shellfishing, only those that were then being used on the Exe estuary, or might have been employed there, were the shellfishery regime to be changed, are discussed here. In hand-picking, individual mussels were selected by hand over low tide. In hand-raking, areas were raked by hand, again at low tide. In dredging, mussels were dredged from a boat at high tide. Hand-picking and raking were at that time the main ways of fishing for intertidal mussels on the Exe.

These fishing methods may affect the populations of both the mussels and the oystercatcher in different ways. Hand-picking mussels only removes shellfish within a target size range and does not reduce the density of smaller ones or reduce the surface area of the mussel bed as a whole. In contrast, both hand-raking and dredging mussels remove all size-classes of mussels and so also reduce the surface area of the mussel bed. Although usually happening at a slower rate, hand-raking mussels can potentially reduce bed area more than dredging. This is because repeated dredging fragments a mussel bed and this makes the submerged mussels increasingly difficult to locate through murky water from a boat overhead at high water. In contrast, hand-raking can remove complete beds because the mussels are clearly visible to the mussel fisher at low tide. Based on the evidence available at the time, it was assumed that hand-picking mussels had no adverse effects on the survival of shellfish outside the target size range that was harvested.

Simulations for the current and possible alternative shellfishery management regimes were examined together to allow a comparison between them to be made. At the time when the simulations of the Exe mussel fishery were done, the daily fishing effort that occurred amounted to no more than two fishing units: hand-pickers or hand-rakers only, as no dredging was carried out in the intertidal zone. On most days, the shellfishing effort was considerably less than this. Although the model can include intermittent and variable fishing like this, for simplicity these first simulations for the then current shellfishery regime were run with two fishing units on all suitable tides that fell in daylight.

Predicted impact of shellfishing on oystercatchers

Despite using a rate of fishing that considerably exceeded that which actually occurred on the Exe estuary at the time, the model predicted that the fishing methods and effort used then had no significant effect on either the average body mass of the oystercatchers or the proportion of them that starved over the non-breeding season (Fig. 7.5). But as the amount of mussel fishing was gradually increased above the then current levels, and when dredges were introduced, the average mass of the birds at the end of the non-breeding season fell increasingly short of the target mass and an increasing percentage of the oystercatchers starved (Fig. 7.5).

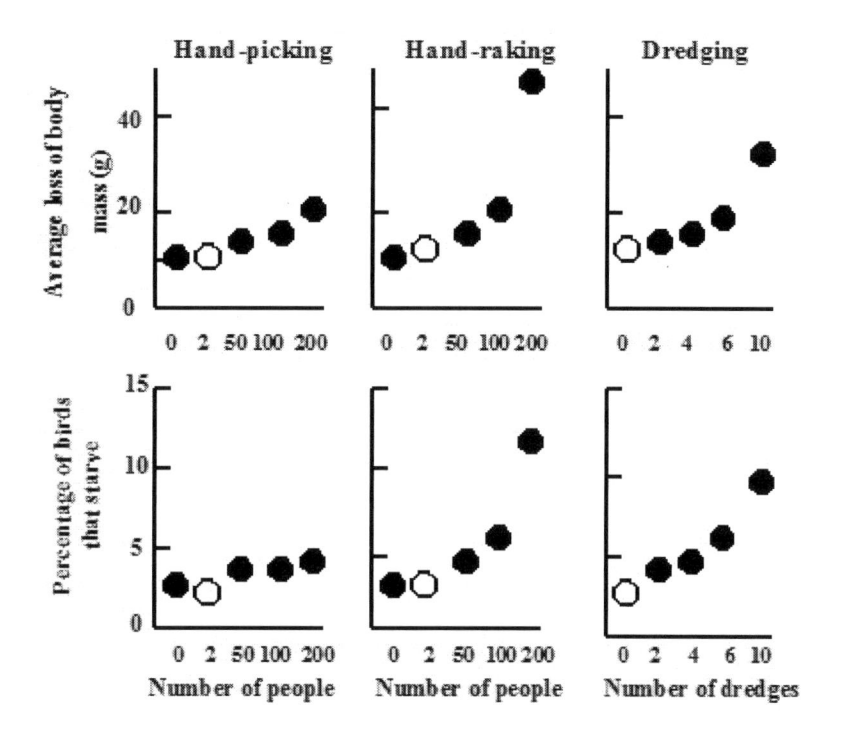

Figure 7.5 *The predicted effect of three kinds of mussel-fishing on the average body mass (top) and mortality rate of oystercatchers on the mussel beds of the Exe. The white circles show the predicted effects for the level of fishing that was carried out at the time the model represented. The upper row of graphs shows the difference between the actual body mass of oystercatchers at the end of the non-breeding season and their target weight at that time. The lower row shows the percentage of birds predicted to starve by the end of the non-breeding season. The horizontal axis shows the numbers of people hand-picking or hand-raking mussels over low water or the number of dredges employed over high water.*

The version of the model used in these simulations used an optimal foraging sub-model to calculate the intake rates of oystercatchers on mussels. Accordingly, the birds in the model took more and more small mussels as the intensive fishing reduced the abundance of the larger and more profitable ones. Expanding their mussel size selection to include the smaller-sized mussels is something that real birds on real mussel beds would be expected to do if the abundance of large mussels were to be reduced by high levels of fishing (Fig. 7.6).

Nonetheless, there came a point as the fishing effort increased when many oystercatchers could not compensate for their reduced consumption rate on their preferred larger mussels by eating more of the smaller ones. Although not shown here, there came a point also when they could not compensate either by feeding in the fields over high tide or by feeding for longer in the intertidal zone. It was at this point, of course, that the least successful birds in the model then drew on their energy reserves, lost mass and eventually starved.

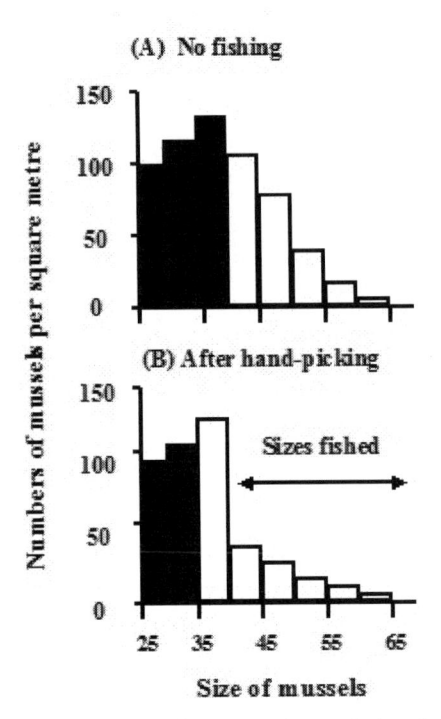

Figure 7.6 *Predicted effect of shellfishing on the range of mussel size classes taken by oystercatchers on the Exe estuary. The predictions are for 200 hand-pickers. The histograms show the range of mussel sizes that are remaining on the mussel beds at the end of the non-breeding season when oystercatchers have left the estuary. The black columns show the size classes that were not consumed by the birds while the white bars show the sizes that were consumed by the birds. By reducing the abundance of the larger mussels, fishing caused the oystercatchers to reduce the lower size limit of the mussels they consumed.*

The increasing fishing effort above the levels actually in operation at the time increased oystercatcher mortality rate by different amounts according to the method used to harvest the mussels. The differences were due to the different ways by which the mussels were depleted and to the different amounts of disturbance caused by each fishing method.

Fishing mussels by hand-raking increased mortality by the greatest amount per unit area fished, followed by dredging and lastly by hand-picking. Hand-raking over low water had the greatest effect partly because it reduced the surface area of the mussel beds by creating bare patches of substrate with no mussels on them. This reduced the surface area of the mussel beds and therefore permanently increased interference between the foraging oystercatchers. Because it was carried out at low tide when the birds were on the mussel beds, hand-raking also disturbed birds, which temporarily increased interference as well. In contrast, dredging over high tide did not disturb the birds. This method only decreased the surface area of the mussel bed by removing whole swathes of the mussels and exposing the bare substrate beneath. Hand-picking was the least damaging to the birds because, although it caused disturbance, it did not reduce the surface area of the mussel beds: it merely thinned-out the larger mussels. It increased the density of birds, and thus interference, only temporarily.

Although the impact of fishing may often be small within a single year, subsequent fishing may have a greater effect if the abundance of oystercatchers or shellfish, or both, do not recover by the following year. In other words, the cumulative effects over several years can be a lot more serious for both the mussels and the birds than their immediate effect over one non-breeding season might suggest. For example, hand-raking reduces the surface area of a mussel bed that is occupied by mussels. This means that fewer spat mussels can be recruited to the mussel bed the following breeding season because the spat require the presence of adults to give them protection against crabs. Therefore, unless replaced by natural increase or by re-stocking – which used to be a common practice on the Exe - , the impact of fishing will increase year by year, and threaten the long-term future of both the mussels and the oystercatchers that depend on them.

This was illustrated by a series of simulations with the IBM that were run over a series of ten successive non-breeding seasons. At the start of each successive non-breeding season except the first, the surface area of each mussel bed was reduced to the size to which it had been reduced by shellfishing at the end of the previous non-breeding season. Similarly, the size of the oystercatcher population was reduced to the numbers that had survived the previous non-breeding season, with the addition of juvenile birds (at a typical rate of reproduction per pair) that had been produced during the intervening breeding season. Because the actual fishing effort that was current at the time the model was built had no long-term effect on either the mussel stocks or birds, multiple-year simulations were run with 50 times the then current fishing effort.

The fishing methods used in these simulations were hand-picking and hand-raking (Fig.7.7). Although hand-picking did deplete the mussel stocks each winter, the recruitment of young mussels maintained the stocks at 90% of those without fishing. Consequently, hand-picking over 10 years cumulatively reduced the oystercatcher population by only about 15%. In contrast, hand-raking substantially reduced the surface area of mussel beds. This reduced the space available for recruiting spat mussels so the mussel beds were all but wiped out after a few years so that mussel-feeding oystercatchers also became extinct. Fishing mussels using that method at that intensity was therefore not sustainable because after a few years it wiped out the mussels and the birds that depended on them.

These simulations illustrated just how quickly populations of mussels and oystercatchers can be reduced by a fishing method that, in effect, removes the habitat where the birds feed. Some rather more subtle potential impacts of shellfishing on oystercatchers were explored using demographic models of both the mussels and birds. As pointed out earlier in this chapter, in bird species with a low annual mortality rate, a small absolute increase in the rate of adult mortality can cause large reductions in the long-term size of their population, unless there is a compensatory increase in recruitment during the breeding season. In oystercatchers, an increase in annual mortality rate from, say, 3% to 6% can substantially reduce their population size. Although the increase in mortality rate is only three percentage points, it actually represents a doubling in the annual rate.

The simulations with the oystercatcher demographic population model showed that relatively small increases in mortality due to intensive shellfishing could indeed greatly reduce population size (Fig. 7.8). For example, the mortality rate of oystercatchers over the non-breeding season was increased from 2·9% to 4·6% by 200 hand-pickers. This superficially modest increase in the mortality rate of oystercatchers resulted in a reduction in population size of 35%. A small increase in mortality caused by fishing should not necessarily be assumed to be of little importance.

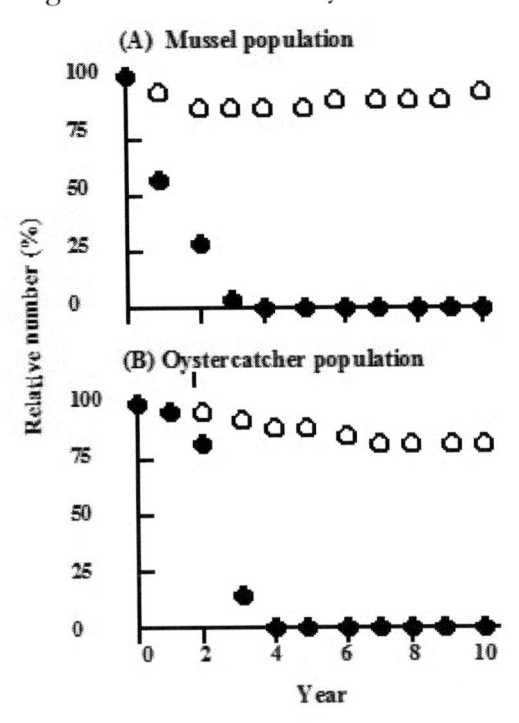

Figure 7.7 The predicted effect of hand-picking (open circles) and hand-raking mussels (closed circles) over a ten-year period on the numbers of mussels (top) and oystercatchers (bottom), measured at the start of each non-breeding season. 'Relative number' expresses the abundance of each species as a percentage of what their abundance would have been without mussel-fishing. In these simulations, there were 100 hand-pickers or hand-rakers that collected mussels throughout each non-breeding season. This is equivalent to 50 times the amount of mussel-fishing that was actually occurring on the Exe estuary at the time.

These results also illustrate the perhaps self-evident point that, because the levels of mussel fishing at the time this research was carried out did not affect the oystercatcher population size, it certainly did not mean that increasing the fishing effort would not do so either. To repeat, in these matters, it is all a question of quantities and hence the need for quantitative thinking and therefore the application of a mathematical model!

Cold weather increases the birds' energy demands and freezes over the fields and this prevents birds feeding there over high tide. Shellfishing would therefore be expected to have its largest effect on oystercatcher survival during cold winters. To simulate cold weather on the Exe, the ambient temperature was reduced in the model from approximately 5^0 C to 0^0C for two weeks in late January, this being the stage of the non-breeding season when the birds were most pressed. Supplementary feeding in field around the Exe was removed from the model for that period because earthworms would not be accessible at such low temperatures.

The impact of fishing on survival was accentuated by both the lowered ambient temperature and by the removal of supplementary feeding in fields over high water (Fig. 7.9). With cold weather and without any fields, the survival of oystercatchers decreased more rapidly with increasing fishing effort than it had done so when fields had been present and the climate was more clement. These simulations illustrate by how much more oystercatchers could be affected by fishing for mussels in hard winters and on estuaries without suitable fields nearby. They underline the need for the effects of each fishery on oystercatchers to be considered on a case-by-case basis.

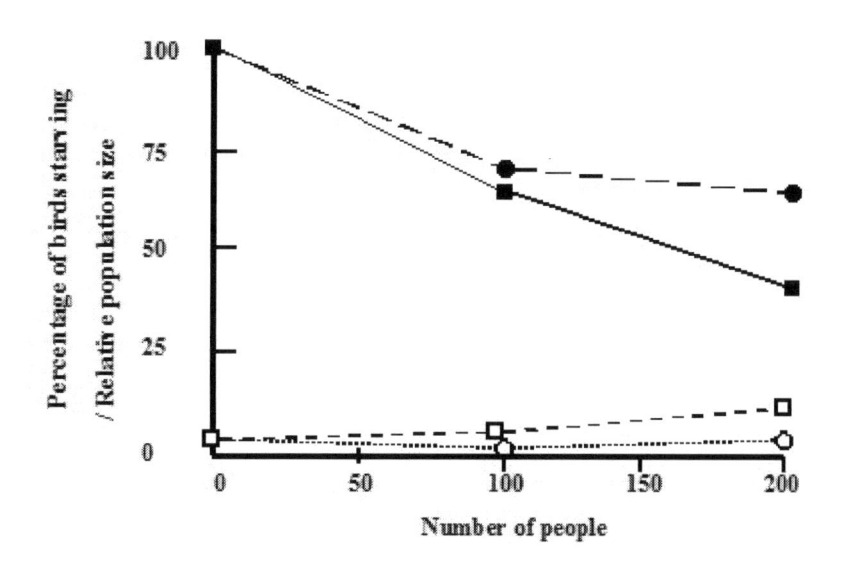

Figure 7.8 *The predicted effect of hand-picking (circles) and hand-raking (squares) on the mortality rate (open symbols) of oystercatchers over a single non-breeding season and the long-term equilibrium size of the population (solid symbols). The initial population size of the oystercatchers was 1550 birds. The population size of the birds is expressed as a percentage of the population there would have been without ant mussel-fishing taking place.*

Conclusions

The main fishing methods on the Exe at the time version 3 was being built and tested were hand-picking and hand-raking. The model predicted that the fishing methods used at that time and the amount of fishing that was done did not increase oystercatcher mortality or affect their body condition. Therefore, it would not have affected the size of their population either. At that time, the Exe mussel fishery was a low low-intensity operation and the mussel stocks were high relative to oystercatcher numbers. The simulations gave no reason to believe that more rigorous restrictions on the way in which the mussel fishery was operated at the time would have increased the numbers of oystercatcher on the mussel beds.

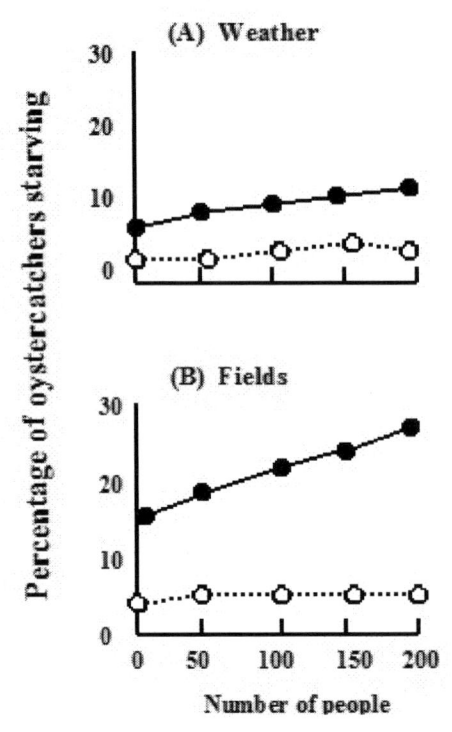

Figure 7.9 *The predicted effect of* **(A)** *the weather during the non-breeding season and of* **(B)** *the presence or absence of supplementary feeding in fields on the impact that shellfishing has on the mortality rate of oystercatchers.* **(A)** *Cold weather was simulated by reducing the temperature in mid-January from about 5^0 (open circles) to 0^0 (closed circles).* **(B)** *Fields present – open circles; fields removed – closed circles.*

But the simulations also showed that, had the fishing effort been substantially increased, and had more intensive techniques been employed, fishing for mussels could have affected oystercatcher survival and therefore numbers. The magnitude of the impact would have depended a great deal, however, on whether the methods employed to harvest the mussels decreased the area occupied by mussels and whether they also disturbed birds. Mussel-fishing techniques that reduced the surface area of the mussel beds (hand-raking and dredging) not only reduced the amount of food available to the birds but also forced them to feed at higher densities, thus increasing both exploitation and interference competition. In contrast, the other techniques did not reduce bed area but instead just reduced the density of the most profitable sizes of shellfish.

At the time, there had been no particular concern that mussel fishing might be affecting the oystercatchers, so the findings had no implications for the management of the Exe estuary fishery itself. The important thing about these early simulations was that they had shown how the consequences for bird survival of fishing for mussels at various intensities and using various methods could now be predicted, something that previously had just not been possible. Had it been available some decades earlier, it might have prevented the expenditure of much time and effort and oystercatcher lives on the cockle fishery of the Burry Inlet!

COCKLE FISHING IN THE BURRY INLET

A contract with the European Union allowed the Exe model to be applied to the cockle fishery of the Burry Inlet, the place that had played a major role in inspiring the development of the model in the first place. The Burry Inlet model was identical to that of the Exe but, of course, many of the parameters were changed following two years of additional fieldwork carried out in the Inlet. Apart from this, the only difference was that, at the time, interference seemed to be insignificant on the Burry inlet, perhaps because in the year the fieldwork was carried out, the prey were so abundant, so interference was assumed to be absent in this model. The model was seeded with 13 000 individuals to represent the then oystercatcher population.

On the Burry inlet, 50 shellfishing licences (for hand-raking) were issued annually, although not every fishermen fished every day. However, there was some casual and illegal fishing and, to allow for this and again to be cautious, 50 fishing units were used to represent the shellfishing regime at the time.

Hand-raking and suction-dredging cockles only select shellfish within a target size range and do not reduce the density of smaller ones or reduce bed area. Based on the evidence available at the time, hand-raking and suction-dredging cockles were assumed to have no adverse effects on the survival of shellfish outside the target size range.

The model predicted that the then current fishing methods and effort had no significant effect on the proportion of time that oystercatchers spent feeding at the end of non-breeding season and the use they made of fields over high water. Like the Exe model, the Burry model calculated intake rates on shellfish from an optimal foraging model. Accordingly, model birds took more of the small shellfish as the larger and more profitable ones were removed by intensive shellfishing.

A point came when many oystercatchers could not compensate by feeding for longer or by eating more of the smaller prey. At this point, the least successful birds in the model then drew on their energy reserves and so lost mass. The differences between the effect on the birds of the fishing methods were due to the different rates of depletion and disturbance caused by each fishing method. Suction dredges would have removed cockles at a much higher rate than hand-raking or hand-picking: 60 suction dredges could have killed all the Burry oystercatchers whereas 500 hand-rakers would have had no effect.

EXE AND BURRY INLET FISHERIES COMPARED

The main fishing methods on the Burry Inlet was hand-raking. As had been found on the Exe, the model predicted that the fishing methods and efforts then being employed did not increase oystercatcher mortality or affect their body condition. Both were low-intensity fisheries with large stocks of shellfish relative to oystercatcher numbers. The model gave no reason for believing that reducing the intensity of shellfishing on either of these fisheries would have increased oystercatcher numbers.

But the simulations also showed that increasing the fishing effort above the amount operating at the time and using more intensive techniques, such as suction-dredging, would have affected oystercatcher survival and numbers, although to different degrees, depending on the circumstances. The varying impacts of the different fishing methods reflected differences in the way in which they would have depleted shellfish stocks and whether they would also have disturbed birds.

The differences also arose from the degree of difficulty model birds had in meeting their energy demands in the absence of fishing. In the absence of fishing, or when fishing effort was very low, model birds in the Burry Inlet were able to meet their energy demands by feeding for only a fraction of the time for which the cockle beds were exposed. In contrast, many individuals in the Exe model needed to feed for nearly all of the available time. Small increases in fishing effort therefore caused some birds to die on the Exe, because these were only just surviving in the absence of fishing. By contrast, equivalent increases on the Burry Inlet did not increase mortality, because all birds had enough time available to compensate.

Mussel fishing on the Exe and cockle fishing in the Burry Inlet differed in the ways in which they affected shellfish stocks. On the Exe, mussel spat only settle where adults are already present, so the numbers of young mussels recruiting to the population are decreased when the density of adults is decreased by shellfishing. In cockles, on the other hand, spat recruitment is either unrelated to the density of the adults or actually increases as adult density decreases because the adults may eat the settling spat. This difference in the way in which the abundance of adults affects the amount of spat that is recruited means that shellfishing methods that strip the mussel bed clean reduce the area occupied by mussels in the long term. In cockles, however, shellfishing may even enhance subsequent spat settlement, if settlement is indeed inversely related to adult density - so long as the sediment is not rendered unsuitable by the method employed.

These simulations carried out for the Exe estuary mussel-feeding oystercatchers and the cockle-feeders of the Burry Inlet showed that the intensity of shellfishing at the time was insufficient to affect the birds' survival and body condition. However they also confirmed that shellfishing could do so if it was intense enough. They showed that the model could provide an answer to the questions: 'What would happen to the birds if we managed the shellfishery in a different way to the current way it is being managed?' The time had come to apply the model to some real management issues in other estuaries.

REFERENCES FOR CHAPTER 7

Goss-Custard, J.D. (1981). Role of winter food supplies in the population ecology of common British wading birds. *Verhandlung Ornithologische Gesellschaft Bayern*, **23**, 125-146.

Goss-Custard, J.D. & Verboven, N. (1993). Disturbance and feeding shorebirds on the Exe estuary. *Wader Study Group Bulletin*, **68**, 59-66.

Stillman, R.A. & Goss-Custard, J.D. (2002). Seasonal changes in the response of oystercatchers to human disturbance. *Journal of Avian Biology*, 33: 358-365.

Stillman, R. A., Goss-Custard, J. D., West, A. D., McGrorty, S., Caldow, R. W. G., Durell, S. E. A. le V. dit, Norris, K. J., Johnstone, I. G., Ens, B. J., van der Meer, J. & Triplet, P. (2001). Predicting oystercatcher mortality and population size under different regimes of shellfishery management. *Journal of Applied Ecology*, 38, 857-868.

Urfi, A.J., Goss-Custard, J.D. & Durell, S.E.A. le V. dit (1996). The ability of oystercatchers *Haematopus ostralegus* to compensate for lost feeding time: field studies on individually marked birds. *Journal of Applied Ecology*, **33**, 873-883.

West, A.D., Goss-Custard, J.D., Stillman, R.A., Caldow, R.W.G., Durell, S.E.A le V. dit & McGrorty, S. (2002). Predicting the impacts of disturbance on wintering waders using a behaviour-based individuals model. *Biological Conservation, 106, 319-328.*

CHAPTER 8:
Simplifying the Exe model and applying it to other shellfisheries

...in which the ways in which the model was further developed to enable it to be applied to oystercatchers and shellfish – cockles as well as mussels - much more quickly than had been possible on the Exe estuary are described.

COULD THE MODEL BE SIMPLIFIED?

Individual-based models (IBMs) are more complex than most of the traditional population models that over recent decades had been built for many species of animals. In individual-based models, the starvation rates, for example, are not explicitly included as part of the structure of the model as they are in traditional 'demographic' models. That is to say, there is no equation in an IBM that expresses the mortality rate as a function of, for example, the density of the animals or the ambient temperature. Instead, the starvation rate is a prediction of the model, after it has been built. The starvation rate 'emerges' from the decisions made by model individuals as to how they should best respond to changes in the virtual world of their model environment. The decisions themselves are derived from a number of behavioural processes that represent the animals' behavioural choices. As should now be clear from our experience on the Exe, these models also have to include many aspects of the natural history of the birds. Complexity therefore seems to be inevitable with IBMs.

But there is no point in the model being unnecessarily complex. Complexity can make it more difficult to understand how the model produces the output it does and increases the risk that errors will be missed. Finding the right balance between complexity and realism is a key element in all modeling and may be particularly challenging with individual-based population models. Therefore, components of the Exe oystercatcher-mussel were removed individually to find out if any of the many processes could be deleted without affecting the accuracy with the model predicted the birds' starvation rate and body condition.

The effect of removing components from the model

The tests were carried out with an oystercatcher population of 1550 birds, as had been used in the development of the model. The model prediction that was tested was the mortality rate. This decision was taken because it had already become clear by then that a change in the predicted starvation rate would be tracked closely by a change in the predicted body condition.

The sensitivity of the model predictions to the presence or absence of particular components was tested by removing groups of related parameters, assumptions or components from the model – the 'base' model (Fig. 8.1). The presence of mussel beds was the most important component of the model. Their total removal caused all birds to die. This means that none of the birds could survive by just feeding on the upshore and field areas. But even though these areas could not sustain birds on their own, they were still important as supplementary feeding areas. Removal of either of these supplementary sources of feeding caused mortality to increase greatly. This showed that some birds depended on these habitats to supplement their consumption of mussels over the low tide period and that they could not survive by eating mussels alone. It was therefore vital to include these two aspects of the birds' natural history in the model.

Component removed	Percentage mortality
Mussel beds	100%
Energy reserves	87%
Interference	
Seasonal decrease in mussel flesh	
Thermoregulation	
Assimilation cost	
Fields	
Day/night efficiency on mussels	
Dominance hierarchy	
Upshore areas	
Variation in foraging efficiency	
Day/night efficiency on upshore areas	
Change in mussel flesh down the shore	
Non-oystercatcher mortality of mussels	
Cost of storing energy	

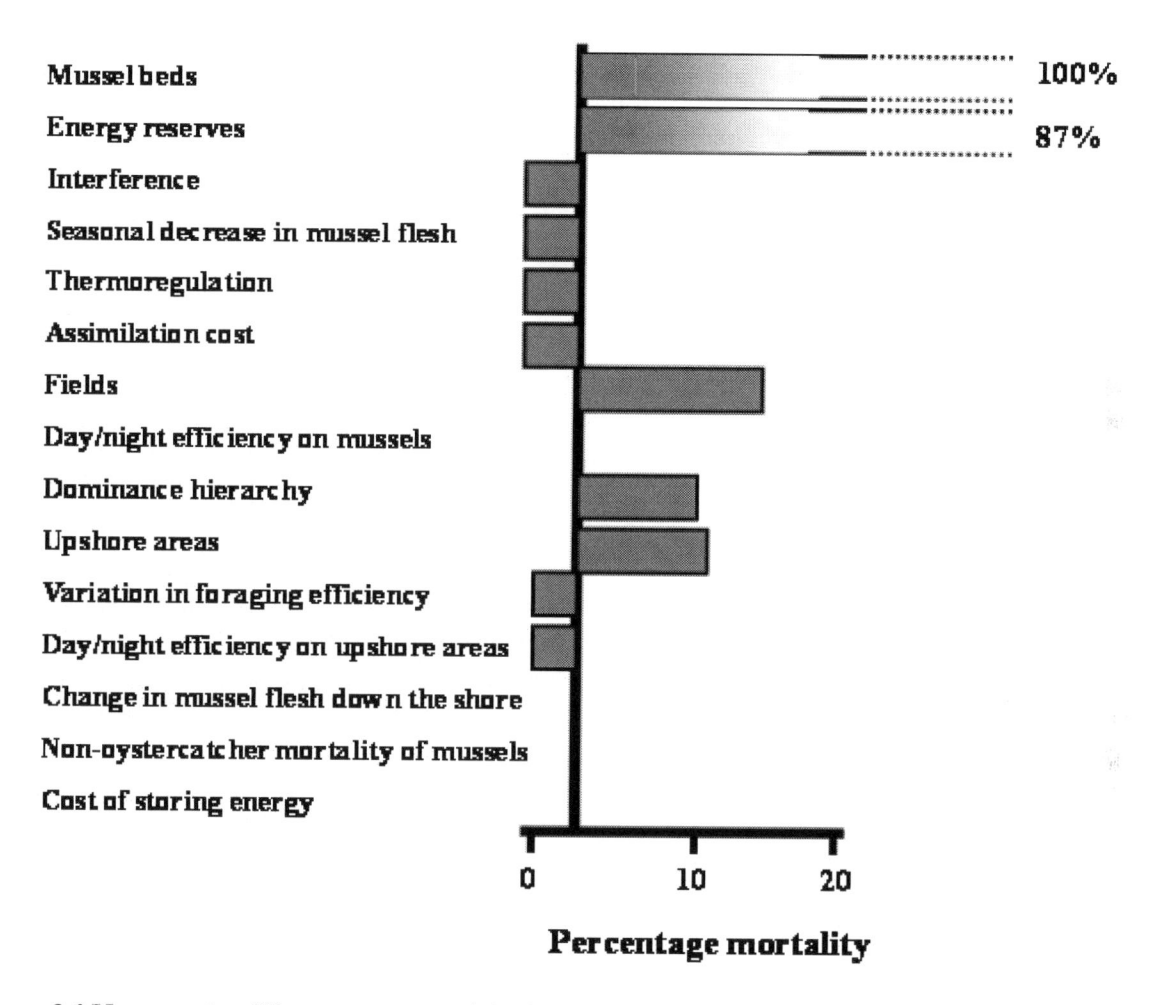

Figure 8.1 How removing different components of the 'base' model affects its predictions for the mortality rate over the non-breeding season. The bars show the predicted mortality rate when a given model component was entirely removed. The thick vertical line shows the predicted mortality rate with the full model with all the components included.

Other components dealing with aspects of the mussel food supply had a range of effects. Mortality was decreased greatly when the flesh content of the mussels remained at its high September value rather than declining steadily throughout the non-breeding season. Mortality was also decreased, although to a lesser extent, when the flesh content of mussels did not decline at the higher shore levels. In contrast, the removal of mussel mortality due to factors other than oystercatchers had little effect on the model's predictions because, on the Exe mussel beds, these losses were very small. As this might not be the case in all systems for which models might subsequently be required, it was considered vital to retain this component, despite its only trivial influence in Exe oystercatchers.

The oystercatchers' energy reserve was the second most important component. Without a requirement to store energy reserves, birds in the model only had to attempt to maintain their body mass at the starvation mass at the end of each 24-hour period of the non-breeding season. They therefore starved immediately if their energy requirements were not met during a single day for the simple reason that they had no reserves to draw upon! It turned out that most birds had at least one day during the non-breeding season when they had been unable to obtain their daily requirement for energy from foraging on that day alone. Accordingly, almost all of them died at some point when they were not allowed to store reserves to carry them over these 'bad' days. Two other energetic components, thermoregulation and assimilation costs, were also important because the presence of each of them significantly increased the predicted starvation rate. In contrast, the presence of energy storage costs did not influence predictions.

Interference was the third most important of the components that were tested. Without interference, no birds died at all, indicating that interference was one of the major factors killing birds in the model. In accordance with this, the presence of a dominance hierarchy was also very important. When all birds were of the same dominance, mortality increased because the average level of interference increased and affected all individuals in the model rather than just the sub-dominant individuals. With a dominance hierarchy present, only the subdominant birds suffered.

The removal of the other source of individual variation - feeding efficiency - meant that all birds were of average efficiency. With this component removed, the predicted starvation rate decreased because only the birds of below average efficiency died in the standard simulations with the base model. If all birds were set to be equally efficient, most of them were able to obtain their food requirements. Or to put it another way, the least efficient individuals in the base model were the ones most likely to starve at some point during the non-breeding season.

A huge number of parameter values were required for the foraging sub-model. Several parameters were estimated on each of several mussel beds for birds of each feeding method. In addition, the density of the different size classes of mussels was also estimated on each bed. A large part of fieldwork devoted to model parameterization had been concerned with this sub-model. As the parameters had been included in this sub-model because they were known to be important for predicting the birds' intake rates accurately, and as the predicted intake rate was known to be important to the starvation rates predicted by the oystercatcher-mussel model, there was little point in removing each of the parameters in the sub-model to find out what would happen to the predicted starvation rate.

So, by the end of this exercise, there appeared to be rather little that could be left out of the oystercatcher-mussel model without undermining its ability to produce reliable predictions for the starvation rate (and therefore body condition also) of mussel-eating oystercatchers on the Exe. There seemed to be little in the main model that could be jettisoned without undermining its predictive ability. This was to be expected, really, because the model had been built up over the calibration years, component by component, until it replicated the observed rates of starvation. This build-up process had come to a stop only when this had been achieved. In terms of predicting starvation rates, to remove a component would literally have been to take a step backwards.

Sensitivity analysis

These simulations showed that all the components that had been included were needed if the model was to make reliable predictions. But these were 'presence or absence' comparisons. The other question was how necessary it was to obtain very precise estimates of the value of every parameter in these components. It might be vital to include a component, but the model's predictions might not be very sensitive to the precise value of the parameter that is used to represent that component.

There were no fewer than 31 'main' parameters in this first oystercatcher-mussel individual-based model for the Exe estuary. The values of all these parameters had been obtained from fieldwork or from laboratory studies and, of course, these were only estimates of their true values: only seldom can one measure things like these without there being any possibility of error! From the point of view of predicting the starvation rate and body condition of Exe oystercatchers, though, the important question is whether the errors matter. Large errors in the measurement of some of the parameters may not really affect the predictions, whereas quite small errors in the measurement of others may greatly affect the predicted mortality rate and body condition of the birds. If you can identify the parameters that absolutely must be estimated accurately if the model is to give accurate predictions, you will know where to concentrate your research effort. Once the Exe estuary oystercatcher-mussel model had been built, these possibilities could be explored.

The sensitivity analysis asked the question: 'How much are the predictions for the rate of starvation and body condition affected by a given percentage change in the values of each of the parameters that are used in the model?' This analysis was carried out in the following way. Either single parameters or groups of related parameters were changed by increasing or decreasing their value in the model by 25%. Simulations were then run to calculate the resulting increase or decrease in the predicted mortality rate of the birds. For example, let's say that the value for the energy content of one gram of mussel that had been used in the model was, say, 20kJ. The model would be re-run using the values of 15kJ and then 25kJ instead. The predicted starvation rates resulting from these changes in this single parameter would then be compared with those obtained with the actual model – the base model.

When a group of parameters was being considered, the individual parameters were not necessarily all changed in the same direction; that is, they were not all increased by 25% or all decreased by 25%. Instead, they were changed in the direction that would have the same effect of either decreasing or increasing the survival chances of oystercatchers. For example, while the daily energy requirement would be *increased* by 25% - thus making life more difficult for the birds – the energy content of a mussel would be *decreased* by 25%, as this too would make it more difficult for the birds to balance their expenditure and consumption of energy. Both changes would therefore work in the same direction.

In all cases, changing the value ascribed to an individual parameter did indeed lead to predictions that were different from those of the base model itself. All parameters tested therefore had at least some effect on the predictions. The details of the effect of changing each parameter can be found in the paper published by Richard Stillman and others in 2000. Suffice to say here that changing by 25% the values of some of the parameters used in the base model had a particularly large effect on the predictions.

To summarise the results, the values of the parameters that were concerned with the energetics of the birds and of their prey were, not surprisingly, some of the most important in the model. These parameters changes were: increased assimilation efficiency, mussel energy density and ash-free dry mass and decreased energy expenditure and critical temperature, above or below which the birds have to burn extra energy to maintain their body temperature. All of these parameters, of course, concern the energy requirements of the birds and the rate at which they obtain energy from their prey. It was not at all surprising, of course, that these had a big influence on a predicted rate of starvation! What these sensitivity tests showed, however, is that even a rather modest error in the measurement of some parameters concerned with the energetics of the birds and prey could greatly affect the model's predictions for starvation rate. Clearly, in future applications of the model, every attempt should be made to obtain as precise an estimate as possible of the values of the parameters that relate to the energetics of the birds and their prey.

Changes in the values of many of the parameters that describe the behaviour of the birds also significantly affected the predicted starvation rate. However, changes in these behavioural parameters did not affect the outcome by as much as had the changes in the gross energetic parameters.

This remained the case even when behavioural parameters were grouped together so that their combined importance could be explored rather than individually (Figure 8.2). Nonetheless, interference clearly played an important role in the model. Increased seasonal interference, the value of the aggregation factor and the interference experienced by sub-dominant birds at the beginning of the winter were among the most important of the behavioural parameters. As obtaining the parameters required to represent these processes had taken so much effort over so many years, it was consoling to find out that all this effort had not been made without good reason!

The finding that the values used to represent interference were important meant that it would be important to measure accurately the parameters that represent interference when the model was to be applied to other species of birds and prey. The magnitude of the individual variation in the foraging efficiency of birds on mussel beds during both the day and night was also important, and more so than their efficiency on the supplementary prey. This suggested that measuring the magnitude of this variation should also be determined as accurately as possible in future modelling studies on new species.

The results of the sensitivity analysis led to two main conclusions. The first was that the prodigious effort that had been spent in measuring the individual variation in the foraging behaviour of the birds had actually been worth it! It would not have been good enough just to pluck imaginary values out of thin air and use them! The second conclusion was that applying the model to new bird and prey species would require us somehow to obtain precise estimates of many of the parameters that had taken so long to estimate on the Exe. A rather daunting prospect.

SPEEDING UP THE DEVELOPMENT OF FURTHER MODELS

The first reaction to the appearance of the oystercatcher-mussel model for the Exe estuary was that it would be very difficult to apply to other, less amenable shellfisheries. This was a justified concern because, even in an estuary and shellfish species that had been selected for their ease of study, the model had taken so long to develop and test – some 25 years or so! It had required a huge amount of work, with many research workers involved (and they are not cheap), and had benefited from some pretty remarkable good fortune. It would have been optimistic - at best - and ridiculous - in fact - to have expected that both these conditions to be met when a new oystercatcher-shellfishery had to be modeled. Apart from anything else, most feasibility studies and environmental impact assessments last only months or a very few years. In order to apply the Exe-estuary oystercatcher model to other shellfish species and to other estuaries in the time that was usually available, something had to be done.

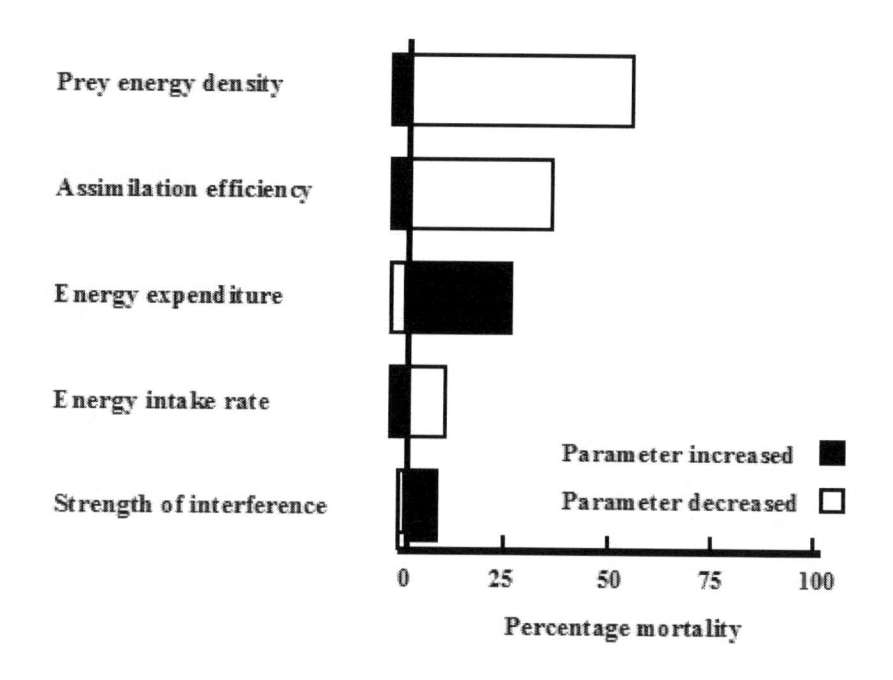

Figure 8.2 The sensitivity of the predicted overwinter mortality rate to changes in the values of groups of parameters. The bars show the predicted mortality rates when single parameters were increased (black bars) or decreased (open bars) by 25% of their standard value used in the 'base' model.

Functional response of oystercatchers eating mussels on the Exe estuary

The results described already in this chapter showed that little in the main model could be jettisoned without undermining its predictive ability. But there was one option for simplification that remained, however. This was to find a way to simplify the sub-model that predicted the intake rate of the average oystercatcher from the numerical density of each of the ten size-classes of mussels and their flesh content. This sub-model had taken a long-time to develop, not least because it contained so many parameters concerned with the 'micro' behaviour of a foraging oystercatcher. If a way could be found to predict much more simply the interference-free intake rate of the average bird at different times of the non-breeding season, it would be possible to apply in a lot less time the model to a different estuary and, perhaps, to oystercatchers eating cockles.

The solution that arose was to predict a bird's intake rate from a 'functional response' rather than by using a very detailed and parameter-rich foraging sub-model. The functional response is a curve that relates an individual animal's rate of feeding to the abundance of its food: a hypothetical example is shown in Figure 8.3. This shows how the numbers of prey captured and consumed by a single bird (the 'feeding rate') changes as the numerical density of the prey where it is feeding increases. When no prey are present, the bird's feeding rate is also (rather unsurprisingly!) zero. But as the density of the prey increases and the bird begins to find them increasingly often, its feeding rate increases. Where the food items are very scarce, so that their numerical density is very low, it takes a long time for the bird to find the next prey after it has swallowed the previous one. The 'searching time' between one prey capture and the next is therefore very long. But as the abundance of the food items increases, the 'searching time' between one prey and the next diminishes.

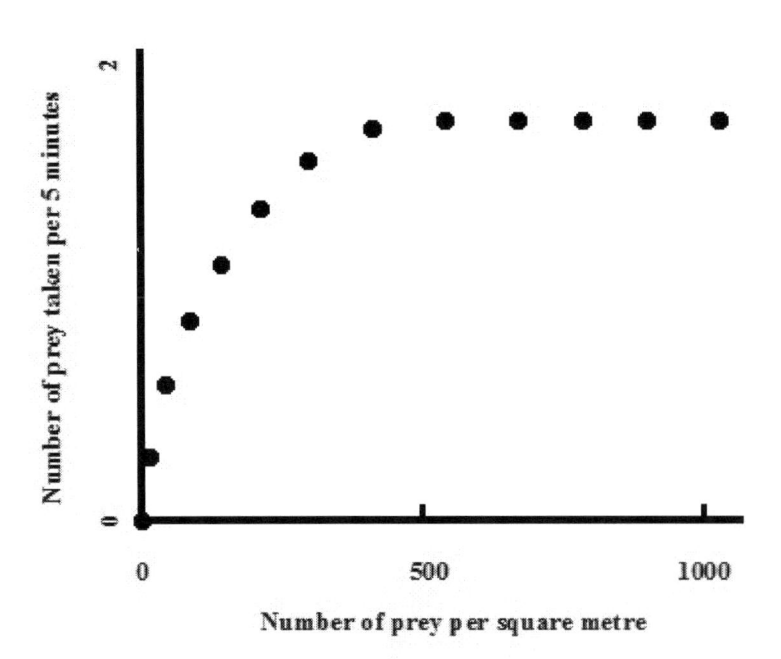

Figure 8.3 A hypothetical 'feeding rate' functional response. This shows how the numbers of prey items that a bird catches and swallows in one minute (its 'feeding rate') first increases and then levels off as the numerical density of the prey increases. Each dot represents the average interference-free feeding rate of an average bird in a single feeding location, such as a small area of mudflat or mussel bed.

Eventually, as the prey's numerical density continues to increase, a point is reached where the bird locates its next prey more-or-less immediately after it finishes dealing with the last one. From then on, the rate of feeding stays level, however much the food supply increases in abundance. The predator simply cannot consume any more prey per unit time when the searching time is virtually zero and the bird spends all the time in picking up, opening and swallowing a succession of prey items: imagine a stationary pigeon feeding on a pile of grains. The bird has then reached the plateau, or the 'asymptote', of the functional response.

Two more hypothetical functional response curves are shown in Figure 8.4. These are 'intake rate' functional responses in which it is not the *numbers* of prey consumed per unit time that is plotted against the density of the prey, but the *biomass* of the prey consumed per unit time - the 'intake rate'. Also, the abundance of the prey is not expressed as a numerical density but as the 'biomass density'. This is obtained by multiplying the numerical density of the prey by their average mass. As birds can't digest and assimilate minerals in their prey, and any water they might contain provides no energy, the mass of a prey item is usually measured in terms of their ash-free dry weight (AFDM), as described in *Box 8.1*. How the biomass density was measured is described in *Box 8.2*

In the lower functional response, the prey items where the birds are feeding are small. Therefore, its intake rate is very low, even when it has reached the asymptote. In the upper one, each prey item is large, and so the intake rate at the asymptote is much higher. It is the same for people: eating single peas, one by one, will give us a lower intake rate of energy than eating, for example, whole baby potatoes! As long as the time required to capture and swallow the large prey is not too great, the intake rate of the birds at a given numerical density of prey will usually be higher when the prey are large than when they are small.

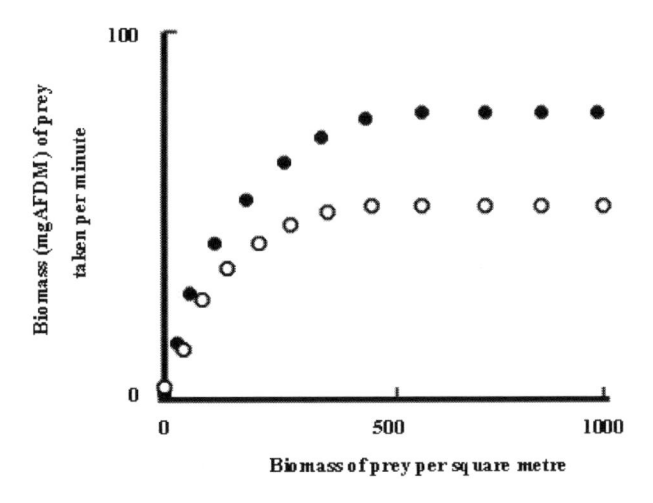

Figure 8.4 *A hypothetical 'intake rate' functional response. This shows how the biomass of prey items that a bird catches and swallows in one minute first increases and then levels off as the biomass density of the prey increases. Each circle represents the average interference-free intake rate of an average bird in a single feeding location, such as a small area of mudflat or mussel bed. The intake rate is measured as the mass of flesh of the prey consumed per minute – excluding indigestible inorganic material and water. Black circles refer to birds feeding in places where the prey are large and the open circles to where prey are small. The abundance of prey is not expressed as the biomass density of the prey where the bird is feeding measured in gAFDM per square metre. This is obtained by multiplying the numerical density of the prey by their average mass.*

The idea for replacing the foraging sub-model with something much simpler was based on the intake rate-prey biomass version of the functional response shown in Figure 8.4. If the intake rate of the average bird foraging in a place could be estimated from the average mass and the biomass density of the prey that are in its 'consumable size range' in the place where it is feeding, it would save huge amounts of time when setting up new models of oystercatcher-shellfish populations.

The data required to do this consisted of measurements of intake rate measured in places and at times when the biomass density of the mussels had, or could, also be estimated. Most of the data that had already been obtained were found to come from beds with middle to high numerical densities and sizes of mussels. The ranges of prey sizes and biomass densities over which the birds' intake rate had been measured were therefore too limited for them alone to be able to describe the whole functional response. To define the intake rate functional response over the entire span of biomass densities that occur in nature, and to avoid having the 'extrapolate beyond the empirical range of the data', new data were needed from places where mussels were unusually sparse or unusually dense or unusually large or unusually small. In other words, more winters had to be spent in the hides and on the sea wall (Box 8.3).

Plate 8.1 *Spot the mussels! A place where the density of mussels was extremely low. Compare this with the Plate 3.1 where the density of mussels was very high.*

An example of the resulting data is plotted in Figure 8.5. Each data point represents at least four days of fieldwork and often very much more in places where mussels and birds were scarce. The equations that describe these relationships were then calculated: the trend line for dorsal hammerers is shown in Figure 8.5. At any one biomass density of mussels, the intake rates in some sites were above trend while others were below the trend, of course. This variation around the trend was mainly due to the prey size differing between sites. Where the mussels in the size range consumed by oystercatchers were large and/or contained a high flesh-content (*i.e.* the sites were downshore or the data were obtained in autumn), intake rate was above the trend line. Accordingly, the mathematical equations describing the intake rate functional response included a measure of the mean AFDM of a mussel of standard length (47.5mm) where the birds were feeding. A point to notice is that the birds were able to maintain a high intake rate even when the biomass density was extremely low, for reasons that are still not understood.

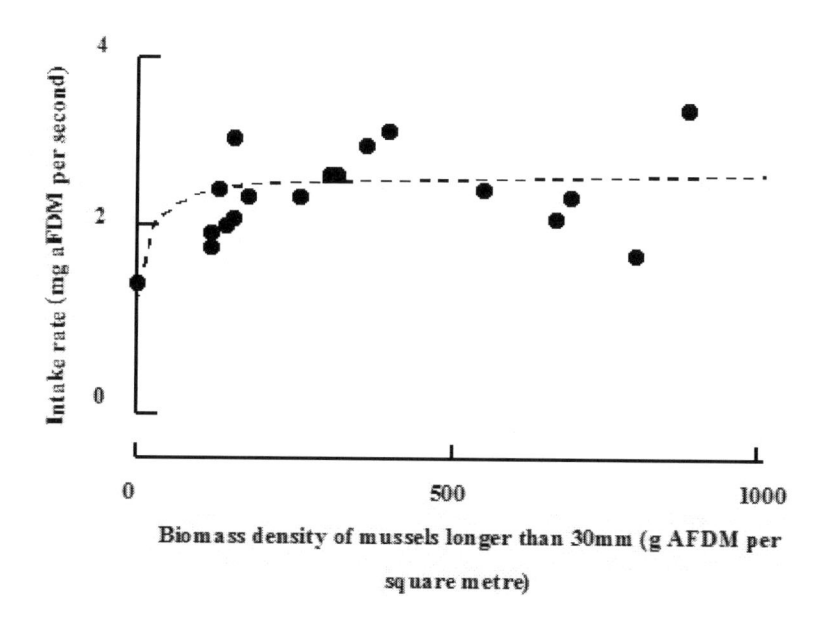

Figure 8.5 *The functional responses of oystercatchers eating mussels on the Exe in birds that opened mussels by hammering them open on the dorsal side. Similar graphs were obtained from birds that opened mussels by hammering on the ventral side or by stabbing.*

The equations fitted to each of these data were then used in the IBM to calculate the intake rate of the average bird feeding in a particular place at a particular time of the winter from (i) the biomass density of the mussels that was on the particular mussel bed at the time and (ii) the AFDM of a mussel 47.5mm long on the same mussel bed at the same time. This allowed the foraging sub-model (with its many equations and large numbers of parameters) that had been used up to this time to be replaced by just two equations – one for stabbing birds and one for both kinds of hammerers - with only four coefficients and parameters each!

Simulations were then run with the IBM over a range of September oystercatcher population sizes and, as usual, the starvation rate plotted against initial population size. The resulting density-dependent function was very similar to the one that had been obtained previously using the foraging sub-model. This suggested that the biomass functional response adequately captured the variation in intake rate within the range of conditions over which the data had been obtained. It confirmed that it might indeed be possible to simplify the IBM a great deal by replacing the foraging sub-model with a couple of simple equations. This was another important step towards reaching the goal of being able apply the model easily and quickly to shellfisheries and populations of oystercatchers other than those of the Exe estuary itself.

The functional response of oystercatchers eating mussels elsewhere or cockles

Fortunately, it also proved possible to go further and to extend the equation for the functional response so that it would apply not only to mussel-feeding oystercatchers in estuaries other than the Exe but also to birds eating cockles.

This is how this equation was developed. There was available a huge amount of published and unpublished information (which were generously provided by the researcher concerned) from all round the World on the intake rates of oystercatchers eating mussels or cockles. There were eight functional responses from mussel-eating and cockle-eating oystercatchers that confirmed that intake varied independently of prey density over a very wide range. The asymptote in most studies was reached at very low prey densities ($<150/m^2$), as had those of oystercatchers eating mussels on the Exe estuary. This was very useful confirmation that the overall shape of the functional response that had been found on the Exe applied elsewhere. It also meant that the many researchers who had measured intake rate in just one or two places, most of their data would have been collected at or near to the asymptote of the functional response. This is because you can be sure that most research workers do not like sitting by a mudflat devoid of birds because the prey there were too scarce or too skinny to attract oystercatchers! This, in turn, meant that it was possible to use these 'spot' estimates of intake rate to develop an equation that could predict the asymptote of the functional response quite easily because most of these data would have been obtained in places and at times when the birds were 'feeding at the asymptote' of the functional response.

There were 46 spot estimates of intake rate for oystercatchers eating cockles and 106 for oystercatchers eating mussels. Statistical analysis showed that neither the feeding method that the birds used to open the shellfish or whether they were detecting their prey by sight or by touch had a significant influence on the intake rate. Four factors had a highly significant effect, however. The first was the average mass of the prey being consumed: the larger the prey, the higher the intake rate. The second factor was whether the prey was a mussel or a cockle: for a prey of given mass, cockle-feeders had a rather higher intake rate than mussel-feeders, presumably because cockles take less time to open than mussels of the same flesh content. Two other factors also affected intake rate: whether the oystercatcher was breeding or whether it was free-living or held in captivity. The analysis therefore showed that the intake rate of shellfish-eating oystercatchers at the asymptote of the functional response was higher when the prey were large and was higher in breeding birds but was lower in mussel-eaters than in cockle-eaters and in captive oystercatchers. But as the model is concerned with free-living birds during the non-breeding season, only two of these four factors mattered: the average mass of the prey being consumed and whether the prey were cockles or mussels: luckily, oystercatchers don't often feed on both species simultaneously!

This analysis made it possible to work out the asymptote of the functional response from just two quantities: average prey mass and whether the prey were cockles or mussels. The model calculates the asymptote of the functional response of a bird of average foraging efficiency instantaneously from this equation using just the current mass of the prey in the patch in question, which is up-dated every day in the model simulations, for each species of shellfish. Rather than spending another several winters in the field measuring the asymptote of the functional response of oystercatchers eating cockles - as had been necessary for Exe estuary oystercatchers eating mussels - the asymptote could now be measured instantaneously within the model itself! Pity we didn't think of this sooner!

The gradient of the functional response – the narrow section where intake rate rises rapidly from zero to the asymptote - was measured as the prey numerical density at which intake rate had risen half way to the asymptote. The gradient was very steep in all the functional responses that had been measured and occurred at prey densities that were very low compared with the range of densities over which they regularly occur. The average of the available estimates of the gradient were therefore used in the oystercatcher-shellfish model. Any imprecision in the estimate of the gradient arising from this simplifying assumption was judged likely to have only a trivial influence on model predictions.

Interference in oystercatchers eating cockles

It wasn't only data on the intake rates and functional responses that were so generously provided by colleagues from all round the World. Although the Exe study itself had provided masses of data on interference in mussel-eating birds, none was available from oystercatchers eating cockles. Luckily, Patrick Triplet made available all his huge data set on cockle-feeding oystercatchers from the baie de Somme, in Picardie, north-east France (Box 8.4). These data played a vital role in allowing the oystercatcher-mussel model for the Exe to be extended to cockle-eating birds.

Prior to this time, several studies had been carried out by several research groups into the possibility that interference occurs in cockle-eating oystercatchers, but none had found any evidence that it did. The very large data set from the baie de Somme settled the issue quite decisively. The cockle stocks in the baie vary enormously in abundance from year to year. The average size of the cockles also vary between years. This means that the food supply is very rich in some years but very poor in others, when oystercatchers take a great many ragworms instead. The statistical analysis that was carried out on the data showed that interference between foraging oystercatchers – caused in cockle-feeders as in mussel-feeders by stealing - occurred only when the cockle stocks were low and only above a density of birds of 50-100/ha. When cockles were abundant, interference did not occur at all – even at the highest recorded densities of birds (Fig. 8.6). When cockles were large and abundant, it was no more advantageous for birds to steal mussels from other oystercatchers than it was to find them for themselves.

This result provided a convincing explanation as to why interference had been elusive in the previous studies. Either the density of the oystercatchers had been too low or the cockle stocks had been too rich for interference to occur. The slope of the interference functions varied according to the food supply but overlapped the range that had been recorded in mussel-eating oystercatchers of the Exe. This provided enough information for realistic values of both the threshold density at which interference begins to occur in cockle-eating birds and the subsequent slope to be included in the oystercatcher-shellfish model.

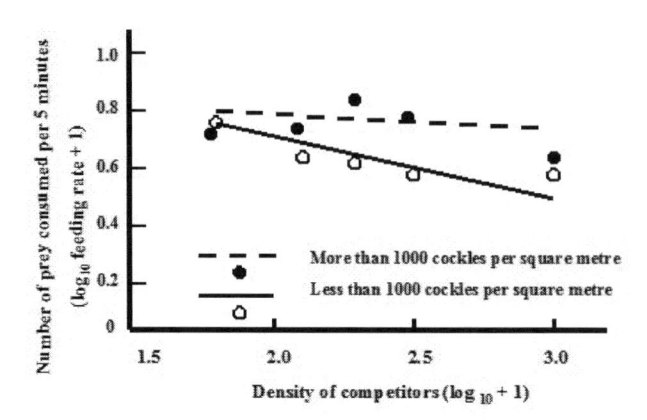

Figure 8.6 The effect of the abundance of cockles on the relationship between the feeding rate and density of oystercatchers in the baie de Somme. The dashed line is the statistically fitted line to the data (solid circles) obtained when cockles were abundant (above 1000 cockles/sq. m): the data are shown as grouped means of 1886 5-minute observation periods. The sold line was fitted to the 1278 5-minute observations that were obtained when cockles occurred at densities of less than 1000/sq.m.

Just one test of the oystercatcher-shellfish model

By this point, the oystercatcher-mussel model had been extended to the shellfish-oystercatcher model that could be applied to cockle fisheries as well as to mussel fisheries. It had also been simplified by replacing the very complicated foraging sub-model with one, very simple equation. It was time to test its predictions, an absolutely essential part of the process of developing a model.

A range of tests of the model's predictions will be presented in subsequent chapters, and just one rather encouraging one is presented here, by way of illustration. On the Burry Inlet, Wales, oystercatchers over the low tide feed either on cockle beds, on long-established beds of mature mussels or ephemeral patches of young mussels attached to cockles squeezed out of the sand by their own high density, the so-called 'mussel crumble'. The oystercatcher-shellfish predicted the observed distribution of oystercatchers across these three feeding areas quite well (Fig. 8.7).

It may not be immediately obvious, but this is a pretty impressive test of the model's predictions! This is why. In the absence of interference, all of the birds would have fed on mature mussel beds where the mussels were very large compared with cockles and so provided the highest interference-free intake rates. As the mature mussel beds occupied a rather small part of the whole Inlet, it seems that the model must have represented pretty accurately the interference that prevented all but a small proportion of them from feeding on the mussel beds. The results also suggest that the model must have predicted quite well the interference-free intake rates of the birds feeding on both cockles and mussels. And it also suggests that it must also have predicted the intensity of interference amongst cockle-feeding birds quite well too. In other words, this test suggested that the additional components that had been added to the oystercatcher-mussel model to upgrade it to an oystercatcher-shellfish model were working quite well. Since the predicted distribution depended on the intake rates predicted by the newly-installed equation and also the intensity of the interference occurring amongst cockle-feeders as well as mussel-feeders, there was plenty of scope for the model to make very poor predictions. The fact that it did not do so once again inspired confidence that it was adequately representing – and quantitatively - the main components of the interactions among the oystercatchers themselves and between them and the mussels and cockles.

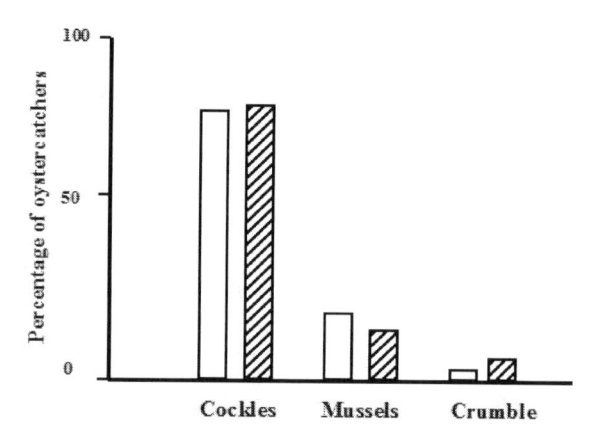

Figure 8.7 A combined test of (i) the simplified way of predicting the intake rate of oystercatchers when feeding on mussels or cockles and (ii) the way in which interference was calculated in the oystercatcher-shellfish model for both cockle-eating and mussel-eating birds. The test was made in the Burry Inlet where most birds fed on the very extensive cockle beds but some also fed on the much smaller established mussel beds and 'mussel-crumble', sheets of young mussels that had established themselves on cockles sticking out of the sand. The close correspondence between the model's predictions for the proportion of the birds that feed on each food source and the proportions that were actually observed in the field implies that the model calculated quite well the intake rates and intensity of interference of the oystercatchers.

The development and initial testing of this oystercatcher-shellfish model opened the way for investigations to be made of a number of conservation-shellfishery issues in other estuaries and coastal areas. The next chapter summarises the results of modelling carried out in shellfisheries other than the Exe using the simplified oystercatcher-shellfish model.

REFERENCES FOR CHAPTER 8

Goss-Custard, J.D., West, A.D., Stillman, R.A., Durell, S.E.A. le V. dit, Caldow, R.W.G., McGrorty, S. & Nagarajan, R. (2001). Density-dependent starvation in a vertebrate without significant depletion. *Journal of Animal Ecology*, **70,** 955-965.

Stillman, R.A., Goss-Custard, J.D., West, A.D., Durell, S.E.A. le V., Caldow, R.W.G., McGrorty, S. & Clarke, R.T. (2000). Predicting to novel environments: tests and sensitivity of a behaviour-based population model. *Journal of applied Ecology*, 37, 564-588.

Triplet, P., Stillman, R.A. & Goss-Custard, J.D. (1999). Prey abundance and the strength of interference in a foraging shorebird. *Journal of Animal Ecology*, 68, 254-265.

BOX 8.1 How the ash-free dry mass of a shellfish prey is measured

To measure this, the flesh is removed from individual shellfish and heated in a crucible at a temperature just sufficient to get rid of the water. The crucible and its contents are then weighed: say, x grams. Next, the flesh in the crucible is incinerated at a very high temperature so that all the organic matter is burned away and just the inorganic stuff remains; there may have been mud particles in the animals' guts, for example, or animal hard parts, such as mandibles or shell. The crucible and its now much-diminished contents is then weighed, say y grams. The amount x-y is the ash-free dry mass (AFDM) of the prey, and measures the biomass of the prey that is actually of value as food to the bird. As the amount of energy per gram ash-free dry mass (the 'energy density') is rather similar in different species of shellfish, the AFDM also closely reflects its energy content of a shellfish.

It is important here to remember that both the numerical density of the prey and their AFDM must only refer to the size range actually consumed by the birds. In hammering oystercatchers eating mussels on the Exe, for example, this would normally be mussels between 30 and 65mm long. Any mussel – of which there are very few on the Exe - that is much larger than this is not actually 'prey' to the birds as the bird is normally unable to break into the shell: to the bird, a huge mussel is about as useful as food as a tin of baked beans! At the other end of the size range, any mussel much smaller than 30mm is usually so unprofitable that it is not worth taking. So, for oystercatchers on the Exe, the biomass density of the food supply would normally refer to the biomass of mussels 30-65mm long.

Box 8.2 Measuring the biomass density of the prey.

The biomass density of the prey in an area is relatively easy to measure. All you have to do is to select out from the samples the prey items that fall into the size range taken by the birds and then take a random sub-sample to determine their average AFDM. As most prey items lie obviously either within the size range or out of it, only those near to the size-boundaries need actually to be measured, thus saving masses of time. In the mussels eaten by oystercatchers, the boundaries are 30mm and 65mm, although there were so few mussels longer than 65mm, it was seldom necessary to measure the very largest ones in the samples. In contrast, for the oystercatcher-mussel sub-model, each and every mussel in a sample had to be measured. This is a much longer procedure and being able to dispense with this approach would save much time.

Box 8.3 Finding places with very low densities of mussels.

It sounded easy to locate places where mussels are very scarce and small but it proved not to be so. The birds' intake rate is low where mussels are small and/or contain little flesh and the birds avoid such places. At low tide, when all the mussel beds were exposed, most birds fed in places where the food was good. But, once again, there was a bit of good fortune. There were a few small area of mussels close high up the shore and close to the seawall where the mussels were extremely scarce and rather small. On the receding tide, some birds fed in these places for a short while before more profitable feeding areas further down the shore had been exposed by the receding tide, to which they quickly moved, of course. There was therefore not much time on a single tidal cycle to collect data from the birds. Often, it was possible to record data for only 30 minutes before the birds had flown so that perhaps only three or four 5-minute long observations could be made. It was frustrating but, over some weeks in each of several winters, an adequate data set built up that proved to be very valuable.

The amazing thing was that the birds feeding there were able to find mussels they could open at almost the rate they achieved elsewhere, even though the mussels were very scarce and mussels in other places were extremely numerous – see Plate 8.1. We still have no idea how they did so.

Box 8.4 Patrick Triplet – un francais extraordinaire

One day in the early 1980s, out of the blue, a thick parcel arrived for me that contained a 250-plus page thesis on the foraging of oystercatchers on cockles and ragworms in the baie de Somme. This M.Sc. thesis was accompanied by a letter from Patrick asking that I be his supervisor for his Ph.D. project, likewise on the oystercatchers of the baie de Somme. After a word-by-word translation using a french dictionary (mainly in the pub after a day in the field), the request was gladly accepted. So began a highly stimulating and vital collaboration that had a large impact on the development of the shorebird IBM. It also led to an enduring and highly-valued friendship.

Patrick was (and still is) the nature manager for the coast of Picardy where there are plenty of conservation issues concerning shorebirds (along with many other organisms): shellfishing; hunting; disturbance from a whole range of recreational activities; erosion; encroachment of *Spartina* on to the higher mudflats used by shorebirds *etc*. Patrick carried out research himself and also managed teams working on shorebirds in the baie de Somme. Being an enlightened conservationist, he early recognised the force that well-conducted research could bring to his arguments for the conservation of the birds and the management of the places where they live. But being a realist, and recognising the rights of others to use the coast in ways that are environmentally friendly, and realising that it is easier to convince people of any need for self-constraint when the arguments are believed and therefore based on sound science, he also realised the potential benefits of the oystercatcher-shellfish model. He has over the years provided masses of highly valuable data and ideas, and has actively sought other opportunities for using the model in other parts of France. In return, the model has been used to advise him and his team on a number of coastal management issues in the baie de Somme.

He is incredibly hard-working and inspiringly devoted to the cause of the evidence-based management of the coastal zone for birds. His immense contribution to coastal management and conservation in Picardie was recently recognised by his being appointed Chevalier dans l'Ordre National du Mérite. Never was an honour so well deserved.

CHAPTER 9:
Applying the model to other shellfisheries

... in which the application of the oystercatcher-shellfish model to a range of management issues in shellfisheries elsewhere than the Exe is described and examples are given of the kind of management 'rules of thumb' that the model can be used to produce.

Apart from the Exe itself, the oystercatcher-shellfish model was quickly applied to the cockle and mussel fishery in the Burry Inlet, Wales, to the mussel fishery in the Menai Straights, Wales, to the cockle and mussel fishery in the Wash, England, and to the cockle fishery in the baie de Somme, France.

BURRY INLET COCKLE AND MUSSEL FISHERY

The management issue

The main fishery in the Burry Inlet, Wales is licensed hand-gathering of cockles which takes place throughout the year. There is also some occasional mussel fishing which is carried out both by hand and by dredging of mussels for re-laying in commercial fisheries elsewhere in the country. In the late 1990s, there was an extensive settlement of young mussels over areas of the cockle beds on Llanrhidian Sands and elsewhere in the Inlet. The cockle industry was concerned that this 'mussel crumble' would smother and kill the cockles lying in the sand beneath and thus remove some of the cockle stocks on which their industry depended. Accordingly, they requested permission to remove the crumble and to sell it for laying elsewhere to provide an additional source of income. But the conservation authorities were concerned that there might be circumstances in which the mussel crumble would be of great benefit to the oystercatchers by providing, for example, a supplementary food source in years when cockle stocks are low.

The effect of any change in the shellfishing regime would depend on how near the oystercatchers were to being 'food-stressed' at that time. That is to say, it depended on whether some birds were already having so much difficulty in meeting their energy requirements that they either starved or failed to store enough reserves to migrate to their breeding grounds. The observations that so many of them rested for long periods when the tide was out and the cockle beds were fully exposed and that very few of the oystercatchers fed in fields over high tide did suggest that most of them were unlikely to be finding it difficult to obtain their food requirements. Nonetheless, the IBM was contracted to explore how close to being food limited they were. This was done by exploring the consequences for the oystercatchers in the model of removing mussel crumble over a range of abundance of shellfish.

Setting up the model

This modeling work required the collection of some data additional to those provided by the annual surveys of the abundance of the birds and of the shellfish along with some local meteorological data. Apart from sampling the mussel beds - about which rather little was known - these extra data were mainly concerned with validating the model predictions. Accordingly, counts were made of oystercatchers to find out how many used each of the three main shellfish food supplies - cockle beds, mussel beds and mussel crumble - over low water and whether many of them used fields over high tide. In addition, data were collected on the amount of time the birds spent feeding over the exposure period and on their interference-free intake rates on both cockle and mussel beds. Were the model to predict these data reasonably well, it would imply that it had captured reasonably well the main elements of their foraging behaviour and distribution.

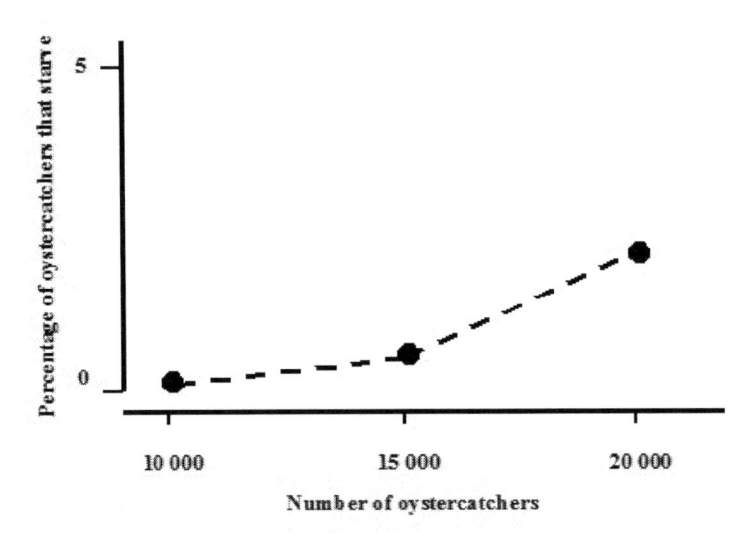

Figure 9.1 The mortality rate of oystercatchers in the Burry Inlet predicted by the model over the range of population size of 10 000 to 20 000 birds. In recent years, the population size had varied between 10 000 and 16 000 birds.

Testing the model

For unknown reasons, the model did not predict very well the numbers of oystercatchers feeding on particular cockle beds over the low tide period. But it accurately predicted the percentages of the whole population that were feeding on cockles, on mussels and on mussel crumble over the low tide period, as shown at the end of the last chapter (Fig. 8.8). The model also predicted that, in the winter of 2000–01, less than 3% of the birds would feed over high water in fields. This accords well with the observations that only very small numbers of oystercatchers were actually recorded feeding in the fields that year. Critically, the model also predicted the number of hours spent feeding by an average oystercatcher during a daytime tidal cycle with encouraging precision. Across all the four comparisons that could be made, the model over-predicted the time spent feeding by only 11% (40 min). That the predicted time was higher than had been observed meant that the model was making it more difficult for model birds to obtain their food requirements than it actually was for real birds in the Inlet. This was accepted as a suitably precautionary approach. The model's predictions therefore matched the observed behaviour of the birds quite well, indicating that the main processes and parameter values that determine the birds' foraging success had been satisfactorily represented.

Predictions of the model

Using the abundance of cockles present in 2000–01, the model predicted that very few birds (<1%) would starve during the non-breeding season at the then typical population size of 10 000 to 16 000 birds. The model did however predict that mortality rate would increase if the population size was to increase up to much higher levels than those that had typically been recorded in recent years (Fig. 9.1).

The cockle and mussel stocks are not constant from year to year, and the year 2000-01 may have been atypical. Therefore, further simulations were run with either more or less shellfish stocks than had been recorded in that year and over a wide range of possible oystercatcher population sizes. When mussel stocks alone were varied, there was relatively little change in mortality (Fig. 9.2). When cockle stocks were reduced, alone or in combination with mussel stocks, mortality increased gradually at first, then more steeply as stocks became very scarce (Fig. 9.2). At the lowest population size of 10 000 birds, mortality from starvation did not begin to occur until shellfish stocks were less than 50% of the values recorded in 2000–01. At higher initial population sizes, mortality began to occur at higher shellfish stock levels, and increased more steeply as stocks declined further.

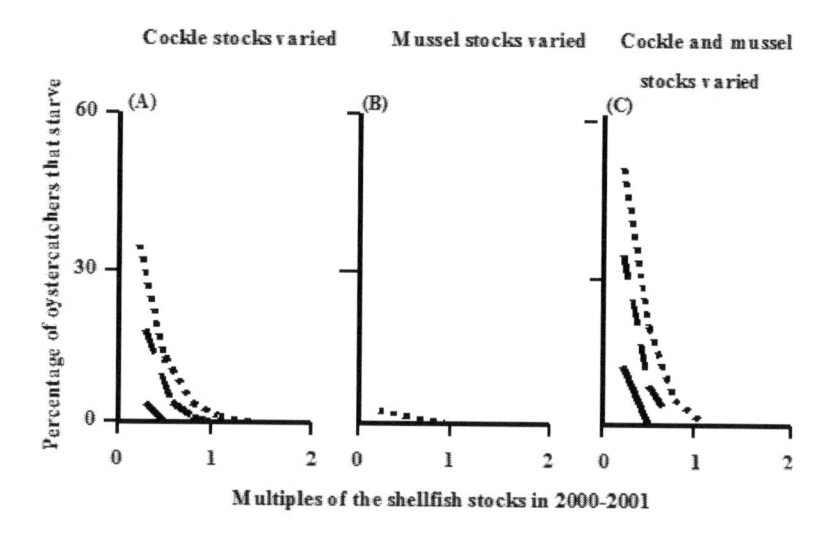

Figure 9.2 *The mortality rate of oystercatchers in the Burry Inlet as predicted by the model when the food supply was varied from half to twice that recorded at the start of the non-breeding season of 2000-01.* **(A)** *The cockle stocks only were varied;* **(B)** *only the mussel stocks were varied, and* **(C)** *both the cockle and mussel stocks were varied together. The results refer to three population sizes of oystercatchers: 10 000 birds, solid lines; 15 000 birds, dashed lines; 20 000 birds, dotted lines.*

At the population sizes and shellfish stocks occurring at the time, removing mussel crumble to uncover an equivalent area of cockles was predicted to increase mortality by less than 0.5% (Fig. 9.3). However, when the stocks of cockles and mussels in the Inlet were reduced below their actual levels, there were indeed circumstances in which removing mussel crumble would have made it more difficult for the birds to maintain their high survival rate. This increase was especially apparent when shellfish stocks were reduced below half of the 2000–01 levels.

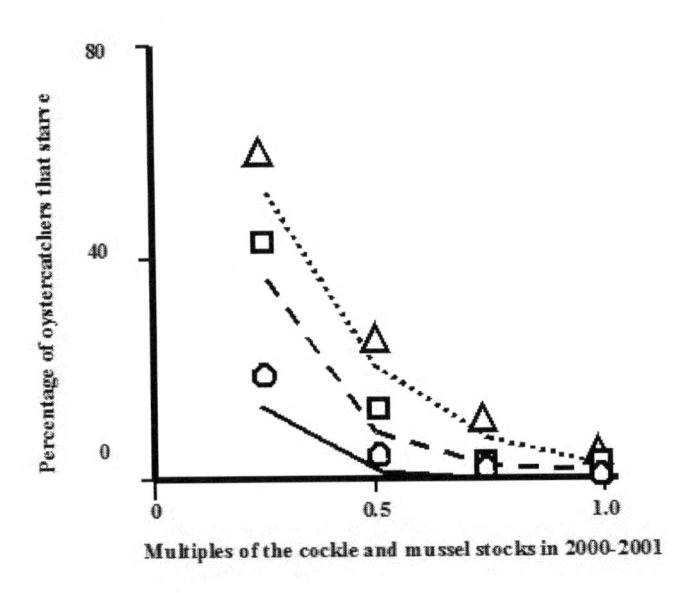

Figure 9.3 *The predicted effect on the mortality rate of oystercatchers over the non-breeding season of removing the 'mussel crumble' lying over some of the cockle beds in the Burry Inlet at four levels of cockle abundance: the same as the amount initially present in 2000-01 (1.0) and with three-quarters, half and one quarter present. The lines show the model predictions with the mussel crumble present. The symbols show the model predictions with the mussel crumble removed. The results refer to three population sizes of oystercatchers: 20 000 birds, triangles and dotted line; 15 000 birds, squares and dashed line, and 10 000 birds, circles and solid line.*

Management recommendations

The conclusion was that, regardless of the numbers of oystercatchers in the Inlet, removing mussel crumble would have little effect on the mortality rate, and therefore the number of birds supported by the Inlet, when the shellfish stocks were at or above their 2000–01 levels. Only if cockle and mussel bed areas were to be very substantially lower than they actually were – at an improbable 25% of 2000–01 levels - would the removal of crumble have become more important. In these circumstances, some 5-7% more oystercatchers were predicted to die if the crumble was removed, leaving only the underlying, and less profitable, cockles for the birds to exploit. Although the mussel crumble was predicted to increase the Inlet's capacity to support oystercatchers in years when shellfish stocks were extremely low, it was not doing so at the then current stocks and bird population sizes, nor at the stock levels that had been recorded over the previous ten years. Accordingly, the advice was that the removal of the mussel crumble would be very unlikely to have affected oystercatchers in the Inlet.

BANGOR MUSSEL FISHERY
The management issue

In many places, mussels are harvested by keeping young mussels – 'mussel seed' – in a suitable place and then waiting for a couple of years or so until they have grown large enough to harvest for human consumption. The seed mussel in such cultivated areas can be encouraged to settle there naturally by providing a suitable surface in an otherwise unsuitable location. But they can also be cultivated by collecting wild seed mussels 10-30mm long from elsewhere - usually from permanently submerged parts of the estuary or from the seabed - and re-laying them in a suitable plot. Such farming of mussels is widespread around the coasts of Europe and has been carried out by generations of fishermen for many years. (On the Exe estuary, for example, almost all of the mussel beds were created and farmed by fishing families and, without this, there would have been far fewer mussels – and therefore far fewer oystercatchers – than there have been.)

The amount of mussel seed available in the UK can vary greatly from one year to the next. Furthermore, an abundant settlement can de decimated or even wiped out by gales or by hordes of marine predators, such as starfish and crabs, coming onshore from the sea. Knowing this, mussel fishers often ask permission to dredge up the seed mussels before this happens. But often, they either fail to get the permission from the sometimes many authorities involved or the permission arrives too late and the seed mussels have already been wiped out. As a consequence, the mussel industry is economically vulnerable to an inconsistent supply of seed mussels. This uncertainty can lead to an over-exploitation of the natural resources in good years and to large year-to-year fluctuations in the harvestable stock, which is not very helpful from a commercial point of view.

One way of overcoming this unpredictability would be to store excess seed mussels in times of abundance in areas of the shore that are not normally used for cultivation. The traditional approach has been to lay seed mussels high up the shore where they are less likely to being eaten by crabs and starfish, these voracious predators of mussels being most abundant at the bottom of the shore. And because the young mussels are covered over high water for a relatively short time at the top of the shore, and so have little time for feeding, they do not grow very quickly. This means that they remain small – and thus ready to be 'grown on' – for longer. In subsequent years when the supply of seed mussels to the fishery is poor, they could then be transferred down-shore to where they would grow quickly and so be 'fattened' up ready for harvest. For this approach to be successful, the young mussels must not be removed by predators in such large numbers that few are left when they are needed.

What would be the best level of the shore to establish such a store, or 'bank', of seed mussel? As in most things ecological, a trade-off has to be made. On the one hand, the higher up the shore the mussels are banked, the slower their growth rate and the longer they can be stored before they reach marketable size and the fewer are eaten by marine predators that come in with the advancing tide. But the higher up the shore they are placed, the longer the seed mussels are exposed to predation by terrestrial predators, particularly oystercatchers. But on the other hand again, bird predation in up-shore areas may not be very heavy because the slower growth rate of the mussels there, and their lower flesh content, may make them insufficiently profitable to attract many oystercatchers. In fact, the most likely time they would be taken by oystercatchers would be when the birds are hard-pressed and thus forced to feed for as long as possible in up-shore areas, irrespective of the absolute profitability of doing so. When the surviving seed mussels are eventually moved down-shore to grow to a marketable size for the fishermen, they also grow into a profitable size for oystercatchers. They would therefore be subjected to much more predation by the birds which can sometimes remove 40% of the stock over a single non-breeding season.

Setting up the model

A contract was obtained to use the oystercatcher-shellfish model to find out the optimum way to bank mussel seed so that both the mussel fishery and the oystercatchers would benefit. The large mussel fishery at Bangor, north Wales was the site for this project where a large population of mussel-eating oystercatchers spend the non-breeding season. The main question was: 'Would it be financially viable to store seed mussels and, if so, at which level of the shore would it best be placed, given the likelihood that oystercatchers would exploit the bank? There were several other questions too: 'Was the mussel fishery having an impact on the survival of oystercatchers?'; 'Were oystercatchers – whose numbers had almost doubled in recent years – having a significant impact on the existing commercial mussel beds?', and, if so, 'Could the losses to oystercatchers be minimised by changing the way in which the fishery was managed?', and if so, 'What would be the consequences for oystercatchers were the management of the fishery to be changed'.

The principal food resources available to oystercatchers at Traeth Lafan consisted of five commercial mussel beds – or 'mussel lays' - that had been laid by the shellfishers themselves very low down the shore (to maximize growth rates) using mussel seed collected from coastal areas all around the UK. Seed mussels were laid straightaway on the place where they were to remain until harvesting. As the areas from where the seed mussels were obtained generally consisted of a single age-class, all the mussels within a particular lay were usually harvestable at the same time. Harvesting - by dredging, mainly from December to February - therefore cleared an entire area which then became available for re-seeding the following summer. Being so far down the shore, these commercial lays were only exposed fully on the biggest spring tides and did not expose at all on one third of all tides.

There were also three large natural mussel beds that were situated mid-shore and so higher up the shore than the commercial lays. Gathering mussels by hand still continued on the natural beds but this contributed very little to the harvest taken by the four shellfishing companies that were operating at that time.

When the mussel beds and mussel lays were covered by the tide, oystercatchers could feed on clams and polychaete worms on the higher mudflats up-shore and on earthworms in the surrounding fields. For the purposes of this project, an experimental lay of mussels was also laid out by the pier, and thus in a convenient location for observing the numbers and feeding behaviour of the birds that were feeding below and alongside. This also provided a useful opportunity to test some of the model's predictions.

As was also the case for the Wash, most of the data for the model were obtained from standard fisheries data that were collected by the commercial growers, from routine bird counts and from nearby weather stations Some additional fieldwork was also carried out on the birds and their food supply, particularly on the supplementary food supplies lying up-shore of the mussel beds.

Testing the model

The objectives of the first simulations were to test whether the model adequately replicated the behaviour of the birds, and particularly their distribution over the various sources of food and the proportion of the initial stock of mussels that they removed. These simulations were therefore run with the bird numbers, mussel densities, patch areas, tidal exposure patterns, and fishing harvests as measured in the winters of 1999–2000 and 2000–2001 when the study was carried out.

On the receding tide, an average of 36% of the birds were feeding on mussel beds. This increased to 91% over low tide when a larger area of mussels was exposed. Although the model overestimated the former and underestimated the latter, it did generate a marked increase in the number of birds feeding on mussels between these two stages of the tidal cycle (Fig. 9.4). No counts were available for the advancing tide with which to compare with model predictions for the numbers feeding on mussels then.

Fieldwork also showed that, on spring tides, the number of birds on the natural mussel beds in the middle of the shore changed through the tidal exposure period. Numbers were high as the tide first receded, when only the natural beds were exposed, then decreased sharply when many of the birds moved down-shore to the low-lying commercial lays as they became exposed over low water. Numbers increased again as the lays were being covered by the advancing tide. On neap tides, however, when few or none of the commercial lays were exposed at low tide, the numbers of birds on the natural bed remained about the same throughout the period they were exposed; *i.e.* on the receding tide, over low tide and as the tide advanced. As a result, across all tides, there was a strong negative relationship between the number of birds on the natural bed over low water and the "springiness" of the tide.

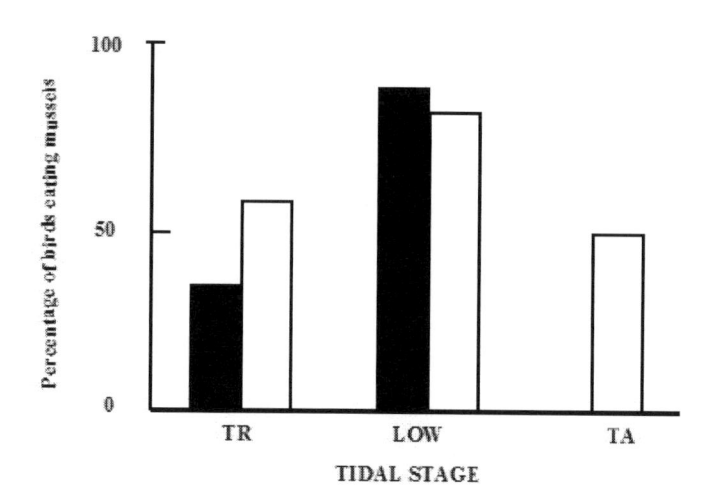

Figure 9.4 Comparison between the model-predicted (open) and the observed (black) percentage of oystercatchers feeding on the available mussel resources as the tide was receding (TR) and over low tide (LT) on the Bangor flats. No counts could be made as the tide advanced. The available mussel resources were only the natural mussel beds as the tide was receding but included both the natural beds and the commercial lays over low tide.

There was a close agreement between the model predictions and the actual counts on the rate at which the numbers of birds on the lays increased as the tides became more 'springy' (Fig. 9.5). It is worth noting that the maximum counts of about 1500 birds predicted by the model was by no means certain to arise. The similarity between the predicted and observed counts inspired some confidence that the model captured this important aspect of the birds' foraging distribution.

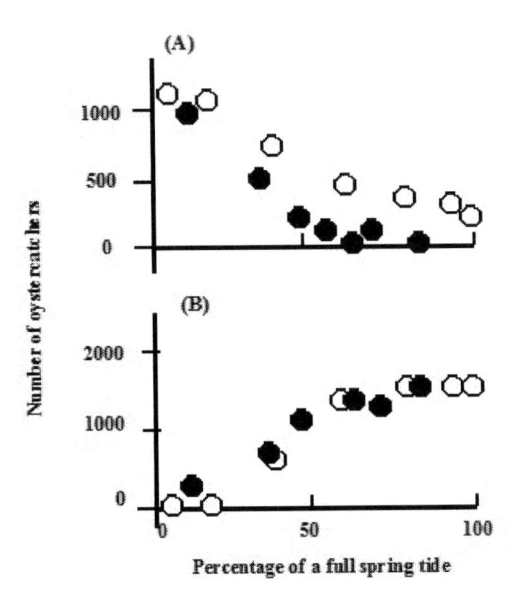

Figure 9.5 The observed (solid circles) and model-predicted (open circles) numbers of oystercatchers on the Bangor flats on (A) the natural mussel bed 1, and (B) three commercial lays over the low water period in relation to the height, or 'springiness', of the tide. A full neap tide is given the value of 0% and a full tide the value of 100%.

The experimental mussel lay also provided data with which the model predictions could be compared. In reality and in the model outputs, there was a significant increase from September to January in the number of oystercatchers using the experimental lay over low water, and statistically there was no significant difference between the observed data and model outputs.

As one of the main purposes of the model was to predict how many mussels the birds would consume under different management regimes, it was important that the model accurately predicted the numbers of mussels that the birds took over the non-breeding season. From fieldwork, it was estimated that oystercatchers consumed 397 677 mussels from the experimental lay over those months. As there had been 24 826 529 mussels within the size range taken by oystercatchers on the lay in September, the birds were estimated to have consumed 1.53% of the initial stock on this experimental lay. This was very close indeed to the prediction of 1.47% made by the model. Bearing in mind that, to get this close to the observed value, the model had to correctly predict the numbers of birds feeding over the winter on the lay and also their consumption rates during the night as well as during the day, the similarity between the observed and predicted impact of the birds on mussel numbers was very encouraging.

These comparisons between model outputs and field data indicated that model birds and real oystercatchers behaved similarly. In terms of the amount of time that they spent feeding, how feeding effort was distributed between stages of the tide, and how birds distributed themselves between natural beds and lays. Although the experimental lay was small and lacked the biggest mussels that would be most attractive to oystercatchers, the model accurately predicted the observed level and seasonal pattern of usage and predation pressure.

Predictions of the model: alternative ways of managing the commercial lays
Commercial lays and shore-level

The next simulations explored how the down-shore commercial lays might be managed so as to reduce the amount of mussels consumed by oystercatchers before they were harvested. One way to modify the management of these lays would be to change the density at which the seed was laid, and thus the area of ground they covered. Another would be to change their position on the shore, which determines for how long they are exposed over low tide and therefore accessible to oystercatchers.

In the baseline simulation, the exposure times of the commercial lays in the model were set as they really were. That is, they remained covered for over one-third of all the low-water periods that occurred during the non-breeding season. Placing the lays further down-shore (or up-shore) was simulated by altering their exposure time in such a way that they remained covered on half (or only one-fifth) of low the water periods instead.

On average, only about half of the area occupied by a lay actually had mussels on it. By reducing the extent of bare ground between mussel patches, the stock could be compressed into half the area it actually occupied. Accordingly, simulations were run in which the surface areas of the lays were halved and, therefore, the density of mussels doubled. For comparison, simulations were also run in which the areas were doubled and the mussel densities halved.

Would changing the location and size of the lays affect the impact that oystercatchers had on the commercial stocks in the lays? Changing the location of a lay on the shore would either increase or decrease the proportion of low water periods on which oystercatchers could feed there. As well as increasing the density of the mussels, reducing the area of a lay would increase the density of birds and so increase the chances that interference between birds would occur. This would reduce their consumption rate and might even reduce the numbers of birds on the lay if the less effective competitors moved to other feeding areas. Either way, the impact of oystercatchers on the mussel stocks would be expected to be reduced.

As expected, the losses of mussels of a marketable size to oystercatchers increased when the lays were moved up-shore and as the mussels were spread out so that their combined surface area was increased. The reverse occurred when the lays were moved down-shore and their surface area halved. Moving the lays down-shore reduced the amount of time when oystercatchers could feed there. Concentrating the mussels in a smaller areas increased interference among the birds and so reduced both their numbers and their rate of consumption.

Although these trends were not unexpected, the advantage of using the model was that it could quantify the numbers of mussels that would be removed by oystercatchers under alternative management strategies. The lowest loss of 12.5 million mussels occurred when the lays were moved down-shore and concentrated in a smaller area. The greatest loss of 24 million, almost twice as high, occurred when the lays were moved up-shore and spread over a larger area. The simulations suggested that the mussels lost to oystercatchers could be halved simply by laying the seed mussel in a different place and at a higher density than was the usual practice at the time.

What effect would these alternative management strategies have on the oystercatchers, however? The model predicted that 0.17% of mussel-feeding oystercatchers were starving under the then current management arrangements of the fishery. A total of 32 potential management options were considered by the study, although not all of them have been detailed here. Of these, 22 resulted in more birds surviving the non-breeding season, but the magnitude of the effect was small. In fact, most of the 32 options had rather little effect on the starvation rate of the birds. Only when all lays were moved further down-shore and their surface area halved was the starvation rate predicted to exceed 1% (1.5%, to be precise). Although this is a very small absolute rate of starvation, it means that, by moving the mussels down-shore and concentrating them in half the area, the starvation rate of oystercatchers would increase almost ten-fold, from 0.17% to 1.5%. The gain to the fishery arising from adopting this particular option would therefore be at the expense of the oystercatchers.

Removing entire mussel beds and lays

As the mid-shore natural beds were used a lot by oystercatchers, their presence may have had an influence on the birds' use of, and therefore impact upon, the commercial lays further down the shore. In order to explore the role of these natural beds, both to the birds themselves and to the losses experienced by the commercial mussel growers, simulations were conducted in which the three natural beds were simply removed from the model. For comparison, simulations were also carried out in which all of the commercial lays were removed instead. This latter represents the worst-case scenario that would arise if the commercial growers were to clear their lays of mussels when their leases expired or were to cease their business altogether for other reasons.

Removing the three natural mussel beds caused the impact of oystercatchers on the mussel stocks in the commercial lays to increase. If the birds could not feed on the natural beds, they had no choice but to go to the commercial lays, despite the increase in interference that would occur. Removing the natural mussel beds was predicted to almost double the impact of oystercatchers on the lays, increasing their take from 28 million to 48 million mussels.

What effect would the removal of the natural beds while leaving the mussel lays intact have on the birds? Because of the intensified competition and reduced amount of time available for the birds to feed at low water, the model predicted that the percentage of oystercatchers that would starve over the non-breeding season would increase from the baseline value of under 0.2% to 3.5% in 1999–2000 and to 19.7% in 2000– 2001, These were both massive increases in comparison with the actual rate. Removing the mussel lays while leaving the natural mussel beds intact was predicted to increase the mortality rate of the birds to 12.3% in 1999–2000 and to 11.4% in 2000–2001. Clearly, both the natural beds and the commercial lays played a very important role in keeping the starvation rate of oystercatchers at their normal very low levels. The simulations suggested that the complete removal of either of them would greatly increase the numbers of birds that would starve over the non-breeding season.

Seed banks and shore level

One key issue in determining whether banking excess seed mussels would be commercially viable was how many of them would be removed by oystercatchers. Accordingly, a 30-ha seed bank was added to the model, this being placed either mid-shore or down-shore, these being the only locations where there was sufficient free space.

The model predicted that the amount of seed mussels taken by oystercatchers from the bank would depend on its position on the shore. Losses of 1% were predicted if the seed bank was laid down-shore. Losses of 5-7% were predicted if the seed bank was laid mid-shore. (These figures correspond well to overwinter losses of 4% and 10% that were actually recorded on a trial seed bank of small mussels that had been established at Bangor in 2000). The addition of a seed bank – wherever it was located - was predicted to lead to only very minor reductions in the amount of mussels taken by oystercatchers from the commercial lays down-shore. The presence of a seed bank up-shore did not remove much oystercatcher pressure from the commercial lays down-shore.

The model therefore predicted that the losses of small seed mussels from a seed bank that would be inflicted by oystercatchers would be negligible, particularly if it was laid down-shore. However, such low shore areas were scarce at Bangor and were at a premium for growing older mussels to harvestable size. If the seed bank was laid further up-shore, losses were predicted to be between 5% and 7%, which is quite a lot. On the other hand, the tonnage removed by the birds would probably be offset by the more rapid growth of the remaining stock resulting from the reduced competition for food in the water column. Therefore, oystercatcher predation at this early stage in the life cycle might simply "thin out" the mussels and enable them to grow better: in fact, "thinning" is a technique that has been widely practiced in many mussel fisheries to increase production. By demonstrating that losses to oystercatchers from seed banks of a commercially viable scale would be negligible, the study suggested that "seed banking" was indeed a practical solution to the irregular and unreliable supply of wild seed mussels.

Management recommendations

Based on these model outputs (and on empirical work carried out in the same area simultaneously), the model led to the proposal of a novel way in which to manage the fishery.

The suggestion was this: Small seed mussels (15–20 mm) would be laid in mid-shore areas in mid-summer. Given that the larger mussels on lower intertidal areas were the preferred prey of oystercatchers, losses of these seed mussels to the birds would be very small. Similarly, losses to subtidal predators, notably crabs and to starfish, would be less than would occur if the seed were placed further down-shore, especially as mussels grown mid-shore would be likely to grow thick shells. Any losses to predators were believed likely to be compensated by a subsequently higher growth rate.

After one year, these seed-bank mussels would be re-laid further down-shore and spread over a larger area. Growing intermediate-sized mussels over a wide area would make them relatively attractive to oystercatchers. However, by both increasing the time for which the mussels were immersed over high tide and by reducing crowding, this would accelerate mussel growth, while reducing the time for which they would be accessible to oystercatchers. The thicker shells developed by mussels grown initially at mid-shore levels would be maintained following their transfer further down-shore. This would reduce the mussels' susceptibility to predation by both large crabs and by the majority (70%) of adult oystercatchers that hammer into mussels. The mussels would by then be too large to be eaten by small crabs.

In the spring and summer prior to harvest, mussels would be re-laid again but this time as far down-shore as possible. They would also be packed as tightly as possible without reducing by too much their rate of growth. Moving these large mussels so far down-shore would also minimize their accessibility to oystercatchers at a stage in their cultivation when they would be at their most attractive to the birds. By this time, the mussels would be too large for all but the largest of crabs. Although starfish would be able to exploit the mussels at such a low position on the shore, they would have a comparatively short period of time in which to do so.

What actually happened?

These were the suggestions but what happened when this revised management plan was adopted? Before the project had started, the practice had been to gather 25-30 mm long seed mussels and to leave them to grow to harvestable size for up to two years. This generally resulted in a typical harvest of 1 kg live mussel mass for every 1 kg of live mass laid as seed (a ratio of harvested to seeded mussels of 1:1).

The question was: 'How would this ratio be affected were the management suggestions if they were to be implemented?' Based on the recommendations, wild seed were gathered when they were 15–20 mm long and laid in early summer quite high on the shore. They were moved in their second summer to deeper water. A year later, in the summer prior to their harvest the following winter, the mussels were moved again to the very lowest areas for the last six months of their growth.

In line with the expectation that this approach would reduce losses to predators throughout their entire growing period, yields at harvest increased to 4 kg for every 1 kg of seed laid, *i.e.*, a ratio of harvested to seeded mussels of 4:1. At the prices then current, 10 tonnes of seed yielded an income of £22 000 ($37 400) compared to the previous amount of £5 500 ($9350): in contrast, the costs of moving 10 tonnes of mussels twice by dredger was just £40 ($68). A very substantial increase in yield to the fishery!

The natural beds were clearly of great importance to the sustainability of the oystercatcher population, but so was the continued success of the commercial mussel farmers. In the worst case scenario, in which all mussels on the commercial lays were removed and were not replaced by any natural re-colonization, in excess of 10% of the mussel-feeding oystercatchers were predicted to starve! This is yet another example of human activities not necessarily being detrimental to conservation. As the paper reporting this study concluded: *"With appropriate management, the interests of shellfish growers and competing shorebirds need not conflict."*

WASH SHELLFISHERY

The management issue

The oystercatcher-shellfish model for the Bangor mussel fishery had taken about three years to develop, and included a lot of new fieldwork that was carried out on the site itself. If the model was to be widely applied to some of the other shellfisheries in the UK and elsewhere, a way had to be found to produce accurate predictions using data that were already available or that could be collected within a very short time. The first opportunity to try this was provided by the massive shellfishery of the Wash embayment in eastern England.

The question was: 'Could the oystercatcher-shellfish be used to predict oystercatcher mortality rate using only the data that were already available from routine monitoring of the bird and shellfish populations and of the weather?' To answer this, the model was parameterized for oystercatchers feeding on cockles and mussels, both of which are abundant on the Wash. Ringing by the Wash Wader Ringing Group had shown that the mortality rate of oystercatchers over the non-breeding season on the Wash had varied enormously during the 1990s. Subsequent research had shown that this variation could be linked to changes in the cockle and mussel food supply: the stocks of both shellfish had also been monitored in order to manage the shellfishery. As the numbers of oystercatchers on the Wash had also been counted over the same years, there seemed to be enough data to apply the oystercatcher-shellfish model over a sample of years during which the birds' mortality rate had varied from virtually zero to almost 20%.

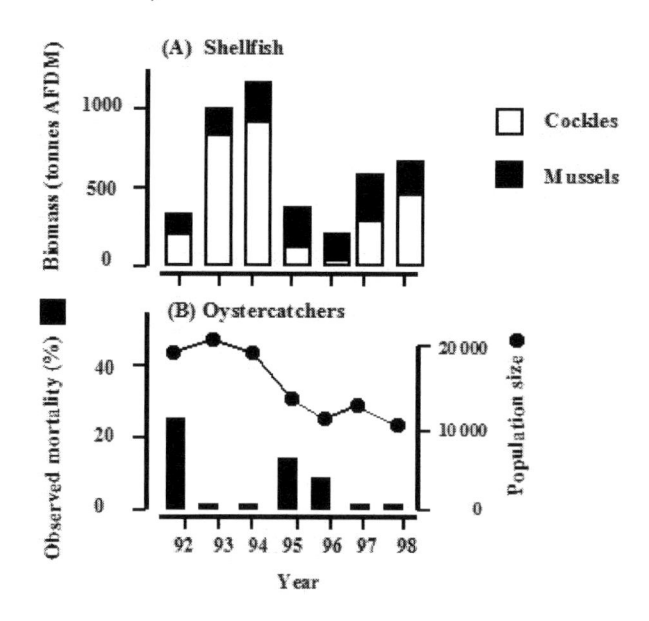

Figure 9.6 Annual variations in the shellfish stocks and oystercatcher survival and numbers on the Wash. (A) The annual variation in the biomass of shellfish over the seven years that were modelled, sub-divided into cockles and mussels on natural mussel beds and on lays. (B) The annual variation in the population size and mortality rate of oystercatchers over the same seven non-breeding seasons.

This is what happened over those years. During the 1990s, there had been an enormous variation in the mussel and cockle stocks (Fig. 9.6). The total biomass of the cockles present varied from 35 to 6269 tonnes AFDM and the area they occupied an area that varied from 4909 to 8388 ha. Mussel abundance varied from 123 to 482 tonnes AFDM and the area they occupied from 92 to 157 ha. Mussel beds were smaller than the cockle beds but had a much higher biomass density; 62–546 gAFDM/sq m compared with 1–16 g AFDM/sq m on cockle beds. The five mussel lays had an even higher biomass density (mean 466 gAFDM/sq m) than the natural mussel beds (mean 147 gAFDM/sq m). Although only a small proportion of the stocks were removed in most years, the size of the harvest varied considerably between years. Indeed, the wild mussel beds were often closed to fishing due to a large crash in their abundance having taken place in previous years. The shellfish stocks were lowest during 1992–93, 1995–96 and 1996–97, both in terms of the total stock available at the start of winter and the amount remaining after shellfishing, most of which took place before most oystercatchers had arrived on the Wash in autumn (Fig. 9.6(A)).

The mortality rates of oystercatchers between September and March also varied enormously between winters. They were very much higher during the winters 1992-93, 1995–96 and 1996–97, when shellfish stocks were low, than during the remaining years of shellfish abundance (Fig. 9.6(B)). Clearly, large numbers of oystercatchers starved to death in the winters when the shellfish stocks were very low whereas almost all of them survived in years of shellfish abundance.

Setting up the model

The model was parameterized for the period 1 September to 15 March for the seven non-breeding seasons of 1992–93 to 1998–99. A separate model was built for each year as the seven were known to differ in three important respects: the size of the oystercatcher population, the abundance of the cockle and mussels and the weather. They also probably differed in other important respects too but such differences had not been measured. Annual variations in the AFDM of the shellfish and in the intake rate attained by oystercatchers in the supplementary feeding areas upshore of the main shellfish beds were two, potentially very important gaps in the data available.

The target body masses of oystercatchers (the body mass that each individual attempts to maintain) were the average monthly masses of birds captured on the Wash. The percentages of hammering and stabbing oystercatchers was calculated from the shape of the bill tip of samples of birds caught by the Wash Wader Ringing Group between 1991 and 1999.

The abundance of shellfish within the oystercatcher size range in September each year, and the proportion of it removed by shellfishing, was derived from data that had been routinely collected by the Center for Environment, Fisheries and Aquaculture Science (CEFAS) and the Eastern Sea Fisheries Joint Committee (ESFJC). Ten cockle beds, six natural mussel beds and five mussel lays were identified and used in the model. Each of these 21 shellfish beds was represented in the model as a single patch. As no data were available from the Wash, published values of the flesh-content of mussels and cockles that had been obtained in other estuaries were used in the model. As most mussel and cockle fishing on the Wash is done from boats at high tide, it was assumed in the model that shellfishing did not disturb the birds.

The model could only include details of the mussel and cockle food supplies below the 4m contour as only these had been included in the regular surveys of the fishery. From previous studies on the Wash, it was known that very few oystercatchers fed above the 4m contour at low tide anyway, which suggested that the up-shore areas was less profitable for them than those down-shore. However, the model for the Exe had shown that feeding up-shore can be important to bird survival. Even if the intake rate there is relatively low, it can extend by a couple of hours the time the birds have for feeding over each tidal cycle. Up-shore areas were incorporated in the model as a single patch which exposed 1 hour before and covered 1 hour later than the shellfish beds below the 4m contour. There was no terrestrial feeding patch because oystercatchers seldom fed in the often dry and earthworm-poor arable fields around the Wash.

But relying only on existing information meant that the value of an important parameter was not known. This was the interference-free intake rates of birds feeding in up-shore areas. The Exe oystercatcher model had shown that the mortality rate of the birds was sensitive to the value given of this parameter. Although the intake rate in upshore areas was very low (0.67mgAFDM/sec) compared with typical intake rates on the mussel beds (2mgAFDM/sec) of the Exe, it had a large effect on how likely starving birds would be able successfully to compensate for an inadequate intake rate over the low water period.

There was no time or resources for additional fieldwork and so all that could be done at the time was to assume that the up-shore intake rate on the Wash in each of the seven years was the same as that recorded from extensive research on the upshore feeding areas of the Exe.

Testing the model

How well did the model predict these very different rates of mortality? During the four years when the actual overwinter mortality rate had been low (0·5–1·5%), the model correctly predicted a mortality rate of less than 2% in each year. In the three years when the actual mortality rate was high (10–26%), however, the model did not predict well the mortality rate that was measured in each year. However, it did accurately predict the average mortality rate over those three years, the predicted value being 17.1% and the observed value 16.8%. Close indeed!

But there may have been a large slice of luck in achieving such a encouraging comparison for the years when shellfish stocks were low. As Figure 9.7 shows, the predictions in the three winters when shellfish stocks were very low depended a lot on the value used for the interference-free intake rate on the upshore flats. The value used in the model was 0.67mgAFDM/sec, as had been measured on the Exe. Had a value of 1mgAFDM/sec been used instead, the mortality rate would have been almost zero! Had a value of 0.33mgAFDM/sec been used, the predicted mortality rate would have been twice as high, at about 35%! By contrast, in the years when shellfish were abundant, the value used for the intake rate of the oystercatchers on the upshore flats had very little effect. The very obvious reason for this is that, in years of shellfish abundance, the birds in the model – as in nature – did not have to feed on the upshore flats as they were able to acquire all the food they needed over low tide on the main shellfish feeding areas.

A very important lesson was taken from this result. Clearly, it is vital to represent the birds' intake rates on the upshore prey as accurately as possible, even though the birds may only feed on that food source only occasionally when they are hard-pressed. For most of the non-breeding season, only a few birds – if any - might use these supplementary food sources. It would be easy, therefore, to dismiss this feeding as unimportant and not worth spending too much time researching. But that could be a very bad mistake on those occasions that the birds really need to feed on that food source.

The average mortality rates predicted by the model were 17·1% and 0·1% in the years of low and high food abundance respectively which compares well with the observed values of 16·8% and 1·4%. By any standards, this is an encouraging comparison. But how much better it would have been had the upshore intake rate of 0.67mgAFDM/sec actually been measured on the Wash!

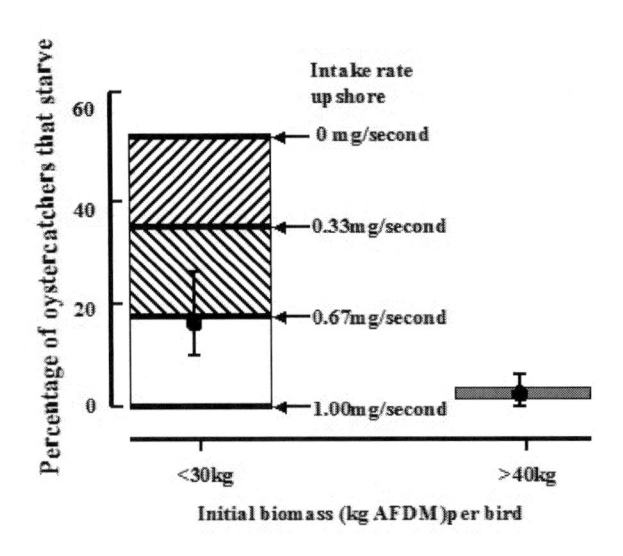

Figure 9.7 The relationship on the Wash between the shellfish stock and the average mortality rate of oystercatchers during the non-breeding season over the four years when shellfish were abundant (right) and the three years when they were scarce. The mean mortality rate of oystercatchers during each group of years is shown by the black circle, the vertical lines showing their 95% confidence limits. The amount of shellfish is measured as the kgAFDM per oystercatcher present on the Wash at the start of the non-breeding season. The model-predicted average values are shown as horizontal lines for four these conditions: the intake rate of oystercatchers feeding upshore of the mussel beds, above the 4m contour, was assumed in the model to be 1, 0.67, 0.33 or 0 mgAFDM/sec. In the years when the shellfish stocks below the 4m contour were high, the assumed intake rate above the 4m contour made little difference because the birds obtained all they needed from the shellfish beds and so did not need to use the upshore, supplementary source of food. But when shellfish were scarce, the value used to represent the upshore intake rate had a very large effect on the predicted mortality rate.

Implications for the management of other shellfisheries

The finding that the quality of the upshore feeding areas was so important to the survival of oystercatchers stimulated a potentially very useful idea. This was that the model could be used to advise conservation and shellfishery managers on the most efficient way of providing a new source of food to reduce an unacceptably high mortality rate in oystercatchers, should they occur. For example, one option might be to dredge mussels from deep waters (where they are permanently inaccessible to the birds) and to lay them in the intertidal area to provide extra feeding areas.

But how best to lay them and at what level of the shore should they be placed? In the case of the Wash, new beds could either be laid above (up-shore) or below (down-shore) of the 4m contour. Furthermore, a given amount of mussels could either be laid at high density, and so cover only a small area, or at low density, and thus cover a large area. Which of the four possible combinations of location and density would most help oystercatchers to survive the winter?

To illustrate how the model could be used to identify the most effective strategy, it was used to determine how the laying of an extra mussel bed in each of the four ways could have reduced the mortality rate of oystercatchers during 1992–93, the year with the highest observed rate of mortality of 26%. In these simulations, mussels laid above the 4-m contour were exposed for eight hours instead of six. These mussels were assumed to contain only 90% of the amount of flesh that mussels below the 4-m contour contained: as mentioned in an earlier chapter, the flesh content of mussels is low at the higher shore levels. Mussel density in the high-density simulations was set to the average density on mussel lays during 1992–93. Mussel density in the low-density simulations was set to the average density on natural mussel beds during 1992–93, which had much lower mussel densities than the mussel lays.

These simulations showed that both the location and the density of any new mussel lay would influence by how much oystercatcher mortality rates were decreased (Fig. 9.8). An addition of 600 tonnes AFDM laid at low density – and therefore over a large area - in an up-shore area was predicted to reduce the oystercatcher mortality rate from the actual rate of 26% to 1%, the approximate rate observed in the years of high shellfish abundance. By contrast, the same quantity added up-shore at a high density - and thus over a small area - only reduced mortality to about 5%. Adding the equivalent quantity of mussels to a down-shore bed only reduced mortality to, at best, 12%, depending on whether the mussels were laid at high or low densities. Even though the low-density, up-shore lay was assumed to contain mussels of lower quality than the low-density, down-shore lay, this 'handicap' was considerably outweighed by its location. Because it was exposed for longer, it enabled oystercatchers to feed on their most profitable food source – mussels – for eight hours during each tidal cycle rather than for just six, as is normally the case.

Interference between the birds was the reason why the size of the mussel lay had such an effect on predicted mortality rates. When the mussel density on the lays was high, the surface area of the lay was small and so the density of foraging oystercatchers was high. The greater interference competition between oystercatchers on the high mussel density lays meant that fewer birds could feed there successfully. Accordingly, small lays reduced oystercatcher mortality to a lesser extent than did the larger, low-density lays where there was enough room for the birds to spread out.

An important implication of the Wash model was that it showed that oystercatcher mortality rates on a shellfishery could be predicted using data routinely collected by shellfishery, shorebird and climate monitoring schemes. Apart from one thing – the intake rate of the birds in the upshore feeding areas - no new data were needed for oystercatchers on the Wash as their foraging behaviour and physiology were assumed to be the same as that in other areas. But the absence of this datum proved only to be critical in years when the shellfish stocks were so low that birds were in real danger of starving. When not able to include the upshore areas, one could view the model as being highly precautionary. That is to say, when shellfish were becoming too scarce for oystercatchers to survive easily on that source of food alone, the model would over-predict the mortality rate and thus provide an early warning that trouble was pending.

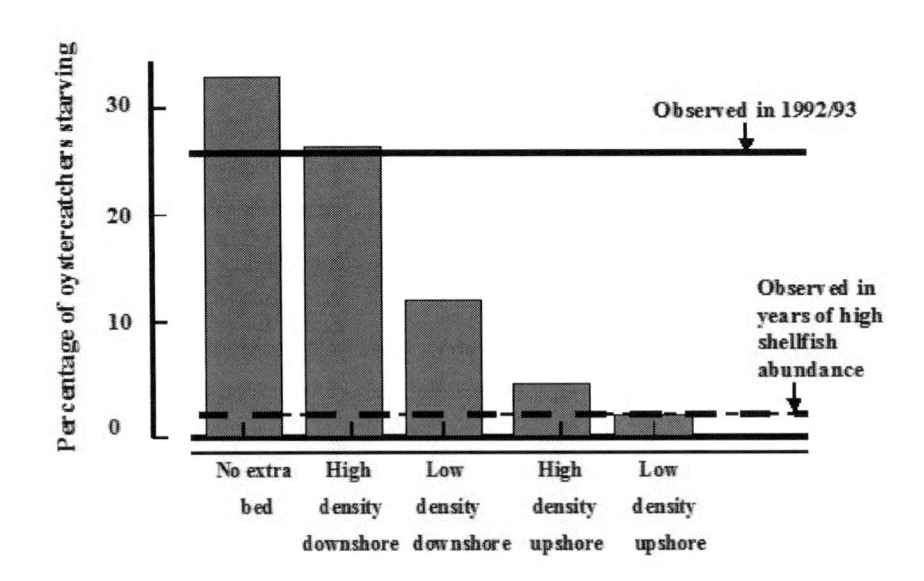

Figure 9.8 Four ways in which a given quantity of mussels could be laid upshore of the 4m contour line on the Wash to help oystercatchers survive the non-breeding season when the shellfish downshore of the 4m contour line were scarce. The abundance of cockles and mussels in 1992-93 were used in these simulations. The mortality rates predicted by the model are shown for each condition. Without any supplementary mussels being placed upshore, over 30% of the birds were predicted to starve, about 8% higher than the actual rate recorded in the field. The best way to mitigate for the scarcity of natural shellfish would be to spread the mussels over a large area as this would reduce the interference amongst foraging birds. As the right-hand column shows, this would reduce the mortality rate in a year of shellfish scarcity to the value typically recorded in years of shellfish abundance.

DISTURBANCE AND COCKLE-FISHING ON THE BAIE DE SOMME

The management issue

Much of the extensive area of mudflats and sandflats of the baie de Somme in north-west France is reserved for hunting shorebirds, and so many of the other activities that people like to carry out on intertidal flats take place in the areas outside – in the Reserve Naturelle. These activities are several, a minimal list including walking, bird-watching, horse-riding and kiting. There is also the licensed harvesting of cockles by professional shellfishers, along with some 'informal' cockle-picking by members of the public for their own consumption. On top of that, there are numerous birds of prey that regularly disturb shorebirds feeding or roosting on the flats. A request was made by the estuary management team that the model be used to devise ways of managing both shellfishing and disturbance of all kinds (apart from the uncontrollable raptors) so that the survival of oystercatchers would be affected as little as possible.

For the results to be useful to the estuary managers, it was necessary to devise very simple policy guidelines for deciding when the frequency with which birds are put to flight by disturbance reached the level at which the survival and condition of the birds begins to be reduced - the 'critical threshold for disturbance'. Thanks again to Patrick Triplet and his teams, the data required to establish the critical threshold were already available for three non-breeding seasons between which the feeding conditions varied greatly.

Setting up the model

When the oystercatchers arrive at the beginning of the non-breeding season, they eat cockles but turn to ragworms if the shellfish became depleted from both shellfishing and other natural causes, such as being washed out of the sand by gales and strong currents. The model was set-up for each of three winters that varied greatly in the abundance and quality of the initial cockle stocks, in the weather conditions and in the number of oystercatchers that arrived late in the winter from The Netherlands, from where they had been driven by severely cold weather. The results from only two of the winters are discussed here, this being sufficient to illustrate how the oystercatcher-shellfish model was used to establish the critical disturbance thresholds for the baie de Somme.

The food supply had been measured annually as part of a monitoring exercise of the fishery and many other parameters required by the model, such as the area and exposure times of the various patches of food, the energy content of the prey and their overwinter mortality due to storms, the numbers, age-distribution and feeding methods of the oystercatchers and the daily ambient temperature were already known. As in reality, there were included in the model three patches of cockles and an additional patch that contained only ragworms. No new fieldwork was required to parameterise the model and the only six months of fairly relaxed effort were required to set up the model and to run the simulations.

As the cockle harvest over the fishing season had been recorded annually, the losses of cockles to shellfishing – both licensed and 'informal' - were known for each year. The cockle stocks in the model were therefore reduced by the appropriate amount in early winter when most of the shellfishing took place.

It was rather a more complicated matter to incorporate realistically all the various forms of disturbance that occurred, including that arising from the shellfishers themselves. Shellfishing disturbance occurred only during the first 2 hours of low-water and then only in daylight on weekdays and only during the approximately six week fishing season in early winter. Other disturbers (human and raptor) occurred all through the tidal cycle throughout the winter, but only in daylight. As a result, there were often no birds left to be disturbed because they had already been driven away by an earlier disturber. Somehow, the model had to be set-up to take this important reality into account.

This is how disturbance was represented in the model. The tidal cycles was sub-divided into six, roughly 2-hour long stages. A disturber (or a group of disturbers of the same kind, such as shellfishers) arrived on the specified patch at the beginning of the specified tidal stage and stayed for a specified time. If any birds were present when the disturber(s) arrived, all the birds on that patch flew up and then alighted on the same or another patch, each bird choosing the patch that was now, for it, the most profitable. Each disturbed bird incurred a specified energy cost as they flew up but no time cost because field studies had shown that the flight-time was very short (*circa* 30 seconds). Birds roosted before resuming feeding, and the winter-average 'recovery' time of oystercatchers on the Exe was used. Birds remaining on the disturbed patch could not feed in a circular 'exclusion zone' around the disturber for as long as the disturber remained: 2 hours for shellfishers (*i.e.* the whole of one tidal stage), 20 minutes for other human disturbers and 2 minutes for raptors. Afterwards, birds re-occupied the exclusion zone at a rate that, again based on work on the Exe, increased through the winter

In the model, shellfishers did not overlap in space with other human disturbers or with each other; this was because, in practice, the whole patch fell inside their combined exclusion zone for the whole 2 hours. Constraints related to the structure of the model limited to one the number of disturbers - additional to shellfishers - per tidal stage on each day of the week yet, to achieve the observed (often very high) frequency of disturbance, there had to be up to three. To approximate this, the energy and time costs per disturber were increased according to the number of disturbances per tidal stage being represented. If one disturber cost 1 kJ and 30 minutes, two disturbers during a 1 hour tidal stage cost 2 kJ, because all birds fly up twice, even if the second disturbance occurs immediately after the first. However, the two recovery times (*i.e.* 30+30minutes) could not be summed because this would assume the second disturber always arrives just as birds resume feeding following the first disturbance. In fact, the second disturber could arrive at any time during the recovery period, or afterwards up until the end of the tidal stage yet the model required that the whole of the disturbance event had to take place within the specified tidal stage. It was therefore assumed that the combined recovery time from two disturbances would be 30+15minutes because there would be a 50:50 chance that the second disturbance occurred after the birds had resumed feeding. By the same logic, three disturbances in a tidal stage cost 3 kJ and 30+15+7.5 minutes.

In the simulations, all the birds in one of the three cockle patches or one ragworm patch flew up when disturbed whereas, in reality, only some of them may have done so. Because of this, these critical thresholds show how frequently a given group of birds can be repeatedly disturbed before their survival rate is reduced. Model simulations in which only a proportion of birds were disturbed produced, of course, lower mortality rates. The critical thresholds described here are therefore very precautionary because they assume that the same birds were repeatedly disturbed: in reality, many birds may have been much less disturbed than was assumed in the model.

Testing the model and its main predictions

It is convenient in this study to consider together both the predictions of the model and the limited number of tests that were possible with the data that were available.

1996-97: a difficult winter for the oystercatchers

In this year, the cockles were at typical autumn densities and of typical mean length and flesh-content. AFDM decreased by 31% over the winter, partly because shellfishing removed the larger ones but mainly because individual cockles lost mass. Most cockles disappeared over the winter (99.1%), primarily from causes other than shellfishing and oystercatcher predation which, between them, accounted for only about 15% of the loss. In the absence of their preferred shellfish prey, all cockle-eaters switched to ragworms during January, in the model as in reality. Mudflats froze for 2 – 3 days in late winter during a long cold spell during which 7000 Dutch adult cockle-eaters joined the 500 immature and 2700 adult cockle-eaters in the Reserve. The provenance from The Netherlands is extremely well-known from ringing studies. Based on the body mass of oystercatchers leaving The Netherlands during a severe spell of cold weather and on the likely energetic cost of flying to the Somme, Dutch birds were estimated to have on arrival in the baie de Somme a body mass of 402g. In the model, the Dutch birds left the Somme after the cold spell had ended in mid-February, just before the local adult birds also departed for their breeding grounds.

The difficult feeding conditions in 1996-97 due to the prolonged period of very severe weather in January and the almost complete disappearance of the cockles by the end of the non-breeding season made this year the most appropriate for doing extensive sensitivity tests, and these were duly carried out. But to avoid presenting a huge amount of detail, but to give a flavour of the findings, here is a brief summary. The mortality rate in oystercatchers that began the non-breeding season eating cockles was sensitive to: (i) their intake rate on the alternative prey, ragworms; (ii) the energy cost of disturbance; (iii) the duration of the post-disturbance recovery; (iv) whether birds were disturbed on consecutive or alternate days (when they had more time to recover); (vi) the efficiency of night-feeding on both cockles and ragworms; (vii) the body mass of arriving Dutch birds; (ix) the number of shellfishers; (x) the area of the main cockle beds; (xi) the length of time that a disturber remained on the flats; (xii) the severity of the winter weather; (xiii) whether the mean AFDM of cockles declined over the winter or remained at the October level, and (xiv) the duration of the exposure period. Quite a list!

On the other hand, the mortality rate was not very sensitive to (i) the width of the path disturbed by a raptor flying overhead; (ii) the radius of the circle disturbed by people; (iii) whether or not interference occurred amongst ragworm-eating birds (which was unknown at the time); (iv) whether all birds, or only the birds feeding at the time, suffered the time and energy costs of disturbance; and (v) the asymptote of the functional response of cockle-eating birds.

The scenarios that were simulated were chosen that were believed most likely to encompass the reality of the Somme cockle beds during that winter. These showed that, in all cases, mortality rate began to rise rapidly as the frequency of disturbance flights rose above a critical threshold of approximately 0.3/hour (Fig. 9.9(A)). This low value was mainly due to the severity of that winter and the associated influx of competing Dutch birds. With no influx and the daily temperature over the 21 days of the actual cold spell set at the average for a normal winter of 3.9°C (range 0.20 – 9.30), rather than the actual average of –3.7°C (range -9.1 – 0.4), the mortality rate only began to increase above about 0.8 disturbances/hour. This is one of the interesting things about modelling: you can ask yourself what might have happened had the conditions been different to what they actually were. A sort of thought experiment, but with numbers!

1995-96: a fairly typical and not especially difficult winter for oystercatchers

In this year, cockles were initially extremely abundant although they were rather small. Even so, mean flesh content decreased over the winter by 57.7%, not because individuals lost mass but because the rather scarce large ones just disappeared. By February 28th, 65% of cockles >15 mm had disappeared, primarily from causes other than shellfishing and oystercatcher predation. In the model as in reality, some oystercatchers switched to ragworms at the very end of the winter. But there was no prolonged severe spell. Mortality did not begin to increase until the frequency of disturbance had risen to 1–1.5 disturbances/hour (Fig. 9.9(B)). The critical disturbance threshold in this winter was therefore several times higher than in the winter when the feeding conditions for oystercatchers were very unfavourable.

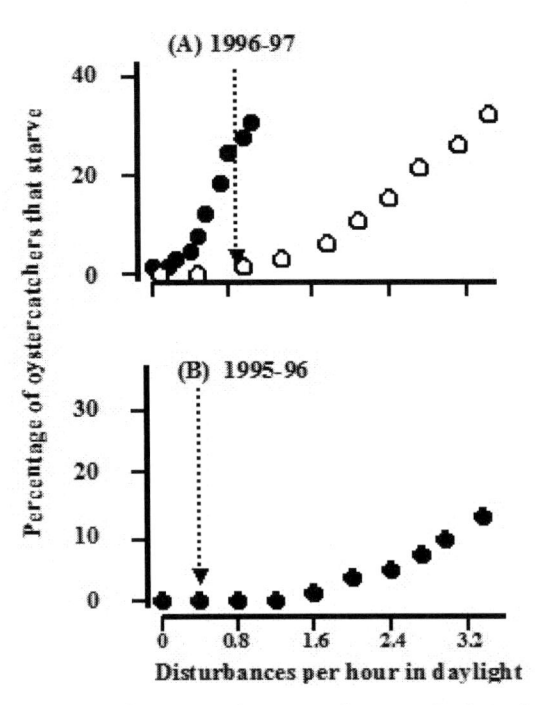

Figure 9.9 The model-predicted mortality rates of oystercatchers on the baie de Somme during the non-breeding season in relation to the frequency with which the birds are disturbed by people and raptors. (A) 1996-97 – This was a non-breeding season of particularly difficult feeding conditions for oystercatchers. The solid circles refer to the actual situation that year whereas the open circles show what would have happened had the cold spell and the arrival of the Dutch immigrants not occurred. (B) 1995-96 – This was a year of ordinary feeding conditions. The arrows show the typical frequencies with which birds were actually disturbed and put to flight in each of the two non-breeding seasons.

Implications for the management of the Reserve Naturelle

There was little evidence from this study that the removal of cockles by shellfishers in this highly regulated fishery had any impact on the oystercatchers. Cockles sometimes completely disappeared over the non-breeding season, but mainly for reasons unconnected with shellfishing. Furthermore, most of the disturbance from the cockle fishers occurred at the beginning of the winter before the hard weather arrived and the influx of Dutch birds took place. The main threat from disturbance arose later in the winter during periods of severe weather by which time almost all shellfishing had stopped. It was disturbance from other people and from raptors that sometimes posed a threat to the survival of oystercatchers.

The value of the critical threshold was particularly low (0.2–0.3 disturbances/hour) in 1996-97 when a prolonged period of severe weather occurred. This raised the birds' energy demands at a time when their intake rates were reduced for three reasons. Ice prevented them from feeding for a few days, the local birds had to compete for cockles with Dutch immigrants and the cockles disappeared so that the birds switched to the less profitable ragworms. Without severe winter weather and the associated influx of Dutch birds, further simulations showed that the critical threshold would have been a lot higher that winter (0.8–1.0 disturbances/hour). It would have been even higher had the birds not been forced to switch to less profitable ragworms at the end of the winter. By contrast, in 1995-96 when cockles remained abundant until the end of the winter, the threshold was comparatively high (1.0-1.5 disturbances/hour).

Oystercatchers wintering in the Reserve Naturelle were actually disturbed into flight between 0.513 and 1.73 times/daylight hour by people and raptors combined, depending on the winter. The highest disturbance frequency would only have increased mortality a little in the mild winter of 1995-96 during which cockles remained abundant throughout. Most birds could continue eating cockles throughout that winter and did not have to switch to the less profitable ragworms. But in another mild winter during which most cockles disappeared (1997-98), simulations not shown here suggested that mortality started to increase at 0.5–0.6 disturbances/daylight hr, and these frequencies of disturbance were common on the baie de Somme. In 1996-97, the critical disturbance threshold was only 0.2–0.3 disturbances/daylight-hour when, in addition to cockles becoming depleted, a prolonged period of cold weather occurred and many Dutch birds arrived. In other words, the threshold for disturbance varied between years depending on the food supply and the weather.

In the light of these findings, it was possible to provide a quite simple policy rule for the management of disturbance in the Reserve that took into account the negligible influence of the already well-controlled shellfishing. A frequency of flying up caused by people and/or raptors in autumn and early winter of <1.5/daylight hour could be allowed. However, if the cockles became considerably depleted by the end of December, especially if they were small, the frequency of disturbance – from both people and raptors - should be kept below 0.5/hour. This could mean that in winters with many raptors, people should not be allowed to disturb the birds at all. Similarly, no disturbance from people should be allowed during a prolonged cold spell with an influx of Dutch birds.

This example of the baie de Somme showed that individual-based model could be used to establish for the first time practicable anti-disturbance measures in a hand-fished shellfishery. The level of the critical thresholds would, of course, depend on estuary-specific features and so the ones established for the baie de Somme could not be regarded as being applicable everywhere. Because estimating the net impact of disturbance on the survival of oystercatchers had not previously been possible, most nature managers at that time usually made the precautionary assumption that, if the birds' behaviour was affected, there was a risk that their chances of survival might also be affected. However, as the baie de Somme model illustrated, this may often not have been the case and that the activities of people on the coast may often have been unnecessarily restricted.

A 'RULE OF THUMB' FOR MANAGING SHELLFISHERIES

The management issue

The study on the Wash stimulated an idea that should prove to be very useful to the managers of shellfisheries with the responsibility also to protect oystercatchers. Both the field data and the results from the model suggested a simple 'rule-of-thumb' for choosing the size of the annual shellfish harvest of shellfish. The observed mortality rates were low if more than 40kgAFDM of shellfish remained for each bird at the start of the non-breeding season (Fig. 9.10). But if less than 30kgAFDM per bird remained, the observed mortality rates were increased. It is important to notice that the quantity 40kgAFDM – the 'threshold' shellfish abundance required to maintain oystercatcher survival - is well above the amount of 9kgAFDM that is actually consumed by a single bird over the entire winter. In other words, the birds' 'ecological requirement' is very considerably higher than their 'physiological requirement'. It is necessary to apply an 'ecological multiplier' to the energy requirements of the birds to calculate how much food should be left over for them after shellfishing has finished.

This finding suggested how the Wash shellfishery might be managed very simply in an oystercatcher-friendly way. All that would be necessary would be to ensure that, after shellfishing had finished, at least 40kgAFDM remained for each bird that would return to the Wash in the following autumn. The quantity required is not hard to estimate with some confidence as oystercatcher numbers vary rather little between adjacent years in this (normally) long-lived species.

This possibility then prompted the idea that the model might be used for any shellfishery to calculate the amount of food that would have to remain after shellfishing to maintain the normally low mortality rate of oystercatchers during the non-breeding season. The Wash example had shown that this should be feasible in many shellfisheries because the data required – bird numbers, shellfish stocks and weather - are routinely collected. A policy guideline of not letting the shellfishing stocks after shellfishing fall below *c.*40kgAFDM bird per bird would maintain the mortality rate of the oystercatchers at the acceptably low rate of about 1% on the Wash, and so perhaps elsewhere. This could be a very useful 'rule of thumb' for managing many shellfisheries. This would be analogous to the simple 'rule of thumb' that had been devised for managing disturbance on the baie de Somme.

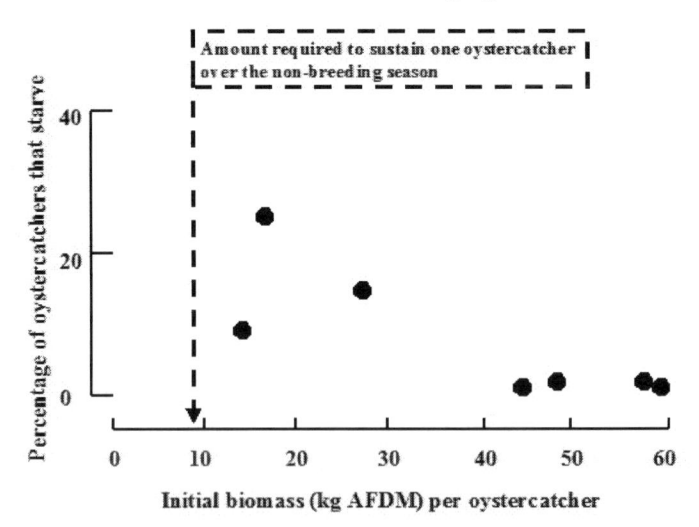

Figure 9.10 *The observed mortality of the oystercatchers on the Wash over the non-breeding season in relation to the quantity of shellfish at the beginning of the non-breeding season. The food abundance is measured as the biomass of shellfish per bird. The vertical arrow indicates the quantity of shellfish required to support one bird over the non-breeding season; i.e. the physiological food requirement of an individual bird.*

Ecological multipliers in other shellfisheries

The obvious question then was: 'Would the ecological food requirement of an oystercatcher at the start of the non-breeding season on the Wash, and therefore the ecological multiplier, also apply to other shellfisheries?

By this time, the results from five IBMs of oystercatchers eating shellfish were available to try and answer this question. These shellfisheries were the Wash, Exe estuary, Burry Inlet, Bangor flats and baie de Somme. Figure 9.11 shows the mortality rate of oystercatchers in relation to the abundance of shellfish present at the start of the non-breeding season, after shellfishing has ceased. Where shellfishing occurred during the non-breeding season itself, the harvest was deducted from the initial shellfish stock. The quantity kgAFDM/bird therefore represents the shellfish biomass that was available for the birds to use over the whole non-breeding season.

At high shellfish abundance (70-120kgAFDM/bird), the probability of starving over the winter is extremely low and independent of shellfish stock (Fig. 9.11). The probability increases sharply below this range but the increase begins at different shellfish abundances in the different estuaries. To compare the findings from the different estuaries, the dotted horizontal line in Figure 9.11 refers to a mortality rate of 0.5%. The mortality curve crosses this line over the range of 20 to 61kgAFDM/bird. This is equivalent to 2.5 to 7.7 times the gross food requirement (*i.e.* allowing for assimilation efficiency) of a single oystercatcher (Table 9.1). The starvation rate of 0.5% seems to be reached at a higher abundance of shellfish where mussels, rather than cockles, are the predominant shellfish. That is, a greater tonnage of mussels than of cockles is required to sustain a high survival rate in oystercatchers. Below these threshold values, the probability of starvation rises very rapidly to reach levels which, with no shellfish present, depend on (i) oystercatcher intake rates on alternative prey, (ii) the duration of the exposure period and (iii) whether birds can feed over high tide.

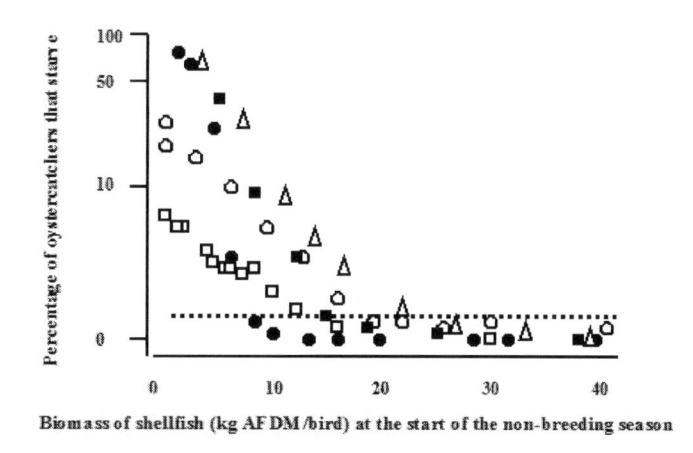

Figure 9.11 *The model-predicted probabilities of oystercatchers starving over the non-breeding season in relation to the shellfish stocks present at the start of the non-breeding season. The systems modelled are: Wash (solid circle); Burry Inlet (solid square); baie de Somme (open square); Exe estuary (open triangle) and Bangor flats (open circle). The horizontal line represents a mortality rate of 0.5%. Note that a logarithm scale is used on the vertical axis.*

Why are the ecological requirements so much higher than the physiological requirements? One reason might be wastage: oystercatchers leave scraps of flesh in the shells and, during daylight, also have shellfish stolen from then by other birds, such as herring gulls and carrion crows. These sources of 'wastage' require each bird to find up to an additional 20% flesh, depending on the estuary being considered. Furthermore, individual shellfish lose 33-50% of their flesh mass from autumn to spring. The decline in flesh mass is approximately linear, so the average over-winter reduction is 50% of the entire loss from autumn and spring. Calculations not shown in Table 9.1, however, showed that taking these factors into account only reduced the values of the ecological multipliers to 1.9-5.4. They are therefore still well above the value of 1 that would apply were the ecological and physiological requirements to be identical. Thus, flesh wastage and flesh loss only partly explain why the food supply in autumn must exceed by so much the amount which birds will actually consume if most of the birds are to survive until spring.

The main reason why the ecological requirements are so high is that interference between oystercatchers on the shellfish beds causes the threshold to be several times higher than the actual amount that each bird consumes. Generally speaking, large quantities of mussels occupy a larger surface area of the intertidal flats than do small amounts of mussels. The greater the surface area of mussels, the easier it is for sub-dominants to avoid interference from other oystercatchers. By reducing the area of the shellfish beds, and therefore reducing the biomass of shellfish available per oystercatcher, interference competition for food is intensified. As interference amongst mussel-eating birds is more intense than amongst cockle-eaters, the ratio has to be higher in estuaries in which mussels dominate the diet than in those where cockles dominate. It is mainly because of interference that leaving just the quantity of shellfish after harvesting that oystercatchers actually require may generally not safeguard their survival. In other words, providing enough food is actually not enough.

Implications for the management of shellfisheries

The results suggested a simple policy guideline for managing shellfisheries to sustain oystercatchers. The shellfish stocks remaining after the harvest from shellfishing has been deducted should not be allowed to fall in autumn below 2.5-8 times the biomass that the birds actually need to meet their food requirements. It is important, however, to stress that the shellfishing policy should maintain stocks above these critical threshold levels in the long-term, not just in the short-term within one year. This is a very important point, confusion over which led to some prolonged discussions on occasions with Dutch colleagues.

The confusion is easy to understand. Imagine a shellfishery in which modelling had shown that 29kgAFDM/bird of shellfish should be present at the beginning of the non-breeding season. By the end of the non-breeding season, then, 20kgAFDM/ bird would remain. Now imagine that the biology of the shellfish is such that it requires only 10kgAFDM/bird to recruit enough young shellfish over the following summer to replace the 9kg that has been taken by the oystercatchers over the preceding non-breeding season. Clearly, the 20kgAFDM/bird that remains is more than enough to replace the losses and probably sufficient to provide an excess for the shellfishery as well. But what if it takes 40kgAFDM/bird to recupe the losses? What remained at the end of one non-breeding season would be only half what is needed to maintain the shellfish population at a size sufficient to support the birds during the following non-breeding season. Although no example has yet been raised where this state of affairs exists, managers should be alert to the possibility that the threshold for the birds may be too low to maintain the long-term abundance of the shellfish for both birds and shellfishers.

		(i)	(ii)	(iii)	(iv)	(v)
				Ecological requirement	Physiological requirement	Ecological multiplier
	System	Predominant shellfish		Biomass density at which mortality reaches 0.5%	Biomass required by one bird over the non-breeding season	(iii)/(iv)
				(kgAFDM/bird)	(kgAFDM)	
	Exe (1976-82)	mussel		61	7.88	7.70
	Bangor (1999)	mussel		50	7.79	6.42
	Burry (2000)	cockle		44	7.88	5.58
	Wash (1994)	cockle		20	7.93	2.52
	Somme (1996)	cockle		33	6.56	5.03

Table 9.1 The ecological and physiological requirements of oystercatchers in five shellfisheries and the resulting ecological multiplier. The ecological requirement refers to the standing crop of shellfish present at the start of the non-breeding season, and does not take into account subsequent losses due to other mortality agents, flesh-loss etc.

THE NEXT STEP

By now, it seemed reasonable to use a prediction from the shorebird model as a pretty reliable guide as to how a shellfishery can be managed to ensure a high survival rate in oystercatchers and, as had been shown at Bangor, even increase it, while at the same time raising the yield of the fishery. But the shellfish-oystercatcher interaction is only one of the range of issues with which the managers of estuaries and other coastal regions where shorebirds abound must deal. It was time now to find ways of extending the oystercatcher-shellfish model so that it could be applied to many more shorebird species, shorebird prey and management issues.

REFERENCES FOR CHAPTER 9

Caldow, R.W.G., Beadman, A.D., McGrorty,S., Kaiser, M.J., Goss-Custard, J.D., Mould, K & Wilson, A. (2003). Effects of intertidal mussel cultivation on bird assemblages. *Marine Ecology Progress Series*, **259**, 173-183.

Caldow, R.W.G., McGrorty,S., Stillman, R.A., Goss-Custard, J.D., Durell, S.E.A. le V., West, A.D., Beadman, A.D., Kaiser, M.J, Mould, K & Wilson, A. (2004). A behaviour-based modelling approach to predicting how best to reduce shorebird-shellfish conflicts. *Ecological Applications*, **14**, 1411-1427.

Goss-Custard, J.D., Stillman, R.A., West, A.D., Caldow, R.W.G., Triplet, P., Durell, S.E.A. le V. dit & McGrorty, S. (2004). When enough is not enough: shorebirds and shellfish. *Proceedings Royal Society B*, **271**, 233-237.

Goss-Custard, J.D., Triplet, P., Sueur, F., & West, A.D. (2006). Critical thresholds of disturbance by people and raptors in foraging wading birds. *Biological Conservation,* **127**, 88-97.

Stillman, R.A., West, A.D., Goss-Custard, J.D., Durell, S.E.A. le V., Yates, M.G., Atkinson, P.W., Clark, N.A., Bell, M.C., Dare, P.J. & Mander, M. (2003). A behaviour-based model can predict shorebird mortality rate using routinely collected shellfishery data. *Journal of Applied Ecology*, **40**, 1090-1101.

West, A. D., Goss-Custard, J.D., McGrorty, S., Stillman, R. A., Durell, S. E. A. le V. dit, Stewart, B., Walker, P., Palmer, D. W. & Coates, P. J. (2003). The Burry shellfishery and oystercatchers: using a behaviour-based model to advise shellfishery management policy. *Marine Ecology Progress Series*, **248**, 279-292

CHAPTER 10:
Extending the model to species of shorebirds other than oystercatchers

....which describes how the need to find a much quicker way to produce models for shorebirds other than oystercatchers and prey species other than shellfish was realised and how this objective was successfully met so that, instead of taking 25 years, a model could be built in just a few months which enabled a variety of models to be produced for a wide range of shorebird species, both wading birds and wildfowl, and management issues at different spatial scales.

MODELLING NEW MANAGEMENT ISSUES

Over the years that the oystercatcher-shellfish model was being developed and tested, issues other than the impact of these birds on a shellfishery, and *vice versa*, were increasing in importance in the management of estuaries. Questions were being asked, for example, whether building a marina on the foreshore or a barrage across an estuary, or whether disturbance from a variety of recreation activities, would affect shorebirds and cause their numbers to be whittled away. At the same time, the regulations were being strengthened increasingly in favour of conservation interests. There was a growing need to be able to predict the effect on the survival and body condition of shorebirds of an increasing number of human activities that could be perceived as threats.

If the model was to be of use anywhere except for oystercatchers and shellfish, a way had to be found to parameterise and calibrate it for other bird species and prey species much more quickly, otherwise it would be of only academic interest - if that (Box 10.1)! This did eventually become feasible as a result of a combination of new ideas for measuring interference and research on the energetics of shorebirds conducted by scientists in many parts of the World. The next two sections briefly describe these two areas of research.

Energetics

A great deal of work had by this time been carried out on shorebirds in many parts of the World. This had resulted in there being a great deal of published information on the energetics of shorebirds and their prey that could be imported quite readily into a shorebird individual-based model for species other than oystercatchers and shellfish. Here is a list of the parameter values that could be gleaned straight from the literature as a result of all this work:

- The capacity of the gut to digest prey;
- The efficiency with which prey of different kinds could be assimilated by the gut;
- The energy content of different prey according to their size;

- The daily energy requirement of a bird according to its size and to the ambient temperature on the day in question;

- The energy required to fuel additional flights due to disturbance from people, along with the length of time before the bird resumed feeding;

- The efficiency with which ingested energy that was surplus to a bird's daily requirement could be converted to stored fat, and the efficiency with which it could be subsequently re-mobilised for use;

- The amount of fat required by birds of different species to be stored at different stages of the non-breeding season.

Many of these data could be included in the model as an equation that related something (such as the daily energy requirement of an individual bird) to the body mass of the bird. This was very convenient because it enabled the model instantly to work out a parameter for an individual from another quantity that was already in the model – the weight of the average bird of the species in question.

Functional response

Fortunately, it also proved possible to calculate the interference-free intake rate of any shorebird of any species using an equation that included the size of the bird as well as the average mass of the prey where it was feeding. Both these quantities were again instantly available within the model itself because it tracked, from day to day, not only the birds' individual masses but also the mass of the average prey in every patch.

The equation was developed in the same way as the one described in Chapter 8 for oystercatchers eating either cockles or mussels. The difference was that body size was also included in the equation. By this time (early 2000s), a huge amount of data – much of it unpublished - had been obtained from all round the World on the intake rates of many shorebird species eating a wide variety of kinds of prey. As with oystercatchers, these were often single, 'one off' or 'spot' estimates where someone had measured intake rate in one or two places, perhaps more. In addition, there were quite a few functional responses available. These were again mainly 'flat': that is, the intake was level over a very wide range of prey density. In fact, the asymptote in most studies was reached at very low densities of prey ($<150/m^2$), as in oystercatchers eating shellfish. Once again, it would be safe to assume that most of these data would have been obtained at some point along the asymptote of the functional response.

Thanks to the generosity of over 30 researchers from all round the World, 468 spot estimates of intake rates and were obtained from 26 shorebird species and were subjected to multivariate analysis. The resulting equation predicted all but 2 of the 28 estimates of the asymptote of the functional response with an average discrepancy of only 0.2% (Fig. 10.1). An equation of just four variables predicted the observed asymptote very successfully in 93% of cases. Indeed, if the birds were not breeding and were not oystercatchers eating mussels, equally reliable predictions were obtained using just two variables, bird size and the average biomass of the prey that were being consumed.

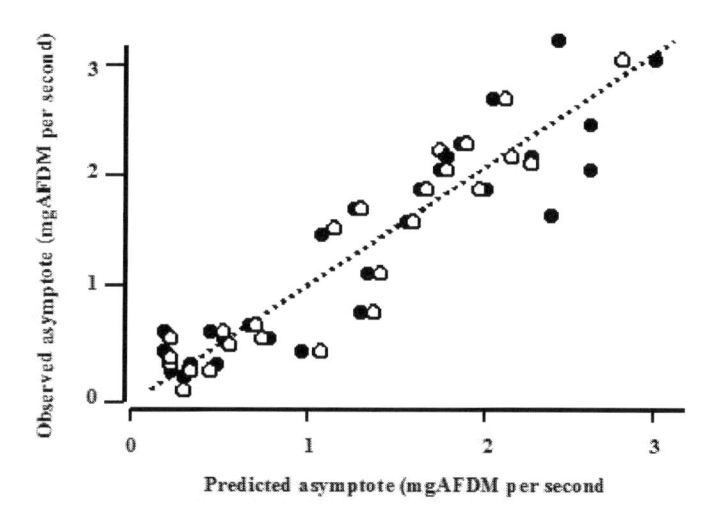

Figure 10.1 *A comparison between the predicted and observed asymptotes of the functional responses of shorebirds. The solid circles show the predictions obtained from an equation that predicted the asymptote from the mass of the bird, the mass of their prey and whether or not the bird was an oystercatcher or breeding. The open circles show the predictions obtained from an equation that predicted the asymptote only from the masses of the bird and its prey, and excludes oystercatchers that were eating mussels or breeding. The dotted line shows y=x, along which all the points would fall if the equation gave absolutely perfect predictions.*

The shorebird model now calculates the asymptote of the functional response of a bird of average foraging efficiency instantaneously from an equation that uses just bird size (a 'state' variable embedded in the model) and the current mass of the prey in the patch where the model bird in question is feeding, which is up-dated daily in model simulations. Rather than spend seven winters in the field measuring the asymptote of the functional response of oystercatchers eating mussels or earthworms, as had been necessary for Exe estuary oystercatchers, the asymptote could now be measured instantaneously within the model itself! Pity we didn't think of this sooner (Box 10.2)!

The gradient of the functional response was measured as the prey numerical density at which intake rate had risen half way to the asymptote. Because in all but two cases the gradient was very steep, the model for shorebirds uses an average value obtained across 21 field estimates. In shorebirds, intake rate seems generally to rise to half way to the asymptote at the very low prey densities of <150 prey/m^2. As with oystercatchers, any imprecision in the estimate of the gradient arising from this simplifying assumption was judged likely to have only a trivial influence on model predictions.

Interference

In shorebirds, interference occurs for two main reasons. Many mobile macro-invertebrate prey, such as some polychaete worms, escape a foraging shorebird by, for example, withdrawing rapidly into a burrow, beyond the reach of the bird's bill. As bird density increases, therefore, an increasing proportion of the prey become unavailable by being deep underground, beyond detection and capture by the bird above, whose intake rate therefore declreases. This is termed 'interference through prey depression'. In other cases, such as in oystercatchers eating large shellfish, interference arises through birds stealing from each other. This is called 'interference through kleptoparasitism'.

It had required years of intensive fieldwork to measure the interference functions in Exe estuary oystercatchers eating mussels. Given the probable crucial importance of interference in some shorebird systems, it was imperative to find a more rapid way to estimate the two parameters that describe the interference function in a given shorebird species consuming a given prey species. By way of a reminder, these parameters are: (i) the threshold bird density at which intake begins to decrease because of interference and (ii) the slope of the decrease thereafter.

In a series of innovative papers, Richard Stillman provided the breakthrough that allowed the strength of interference in different shorebird and prey species to be estimated quite easily. He identified three ways in which this could be done, depending on the biology of the prey and the kind of interference involved.

First of all, interference could be assumed not to occur in shorebirds consuming very small, surface-dwelling and immobile prey, such as the small snail *Hydrobia* spp. Such prey are picked up and swallowed so rapidly by shorebirds that other birds cannot steal them and so interference through stealing cannot occur. As they are not able rapidly to dive down a burrow, they are not able to avoid an approaching shorebird either. Interference through prey depression cannot occur either.

Second, interference through prey depression can be assumed to occur in shorebird species that consume mobile prey that are too small and too rapidly swallowed to be stolen by competitors but which do have anti-predator responses. For these cases, Richard Stillman constructed a behaviour-based model that predicted the interference function from details of the behaviour of both the bird and of their prey. Unfortunately, the threshold and slope of the interference function through prey depression had been measured in only one field study - redshank eating the crustacean *Corophium volutator*. Nonetheless, a comparison between the model predictions and this one set of field data indicated that this model did its job quite well if it was assumed – as field data strongly suggested was the case – that birds avoid areas that have recently been searched by other birds (Fig. 10.2).

Third, in shorebird species that take large prey that require a relatively long time (>5-10 seconds) to consume, interference often arises through prey stealing and through the need for subdominant individuals to avoid other birds that might steal their prey. By means of yet another behaviour-based model, Richard Stillman showed that the threshold and slope of interference functions caused by prey stealing are almost entirely determined by the distance from which one bird could attack its victim to steal its prey. This 'attack distance' itself depended on the time it took a victim to 'handle' its prey before swallowing it and this, in turn, depended on the size of the prey. There is more time for dominant individuals to attack a subdominant bird to steal its prey if the handling time is long rather than short, and so attacks can be made at greater distances. By using his behaviour-based model in which model birds attempted to steal prey from each other, Richard Stillman found that it was possible to predict the two parameters that measure the interference function from field data that were very easy to obtain, such as handling time. The predictions of this model were tested with generally encouraging results (Fig.10.3).

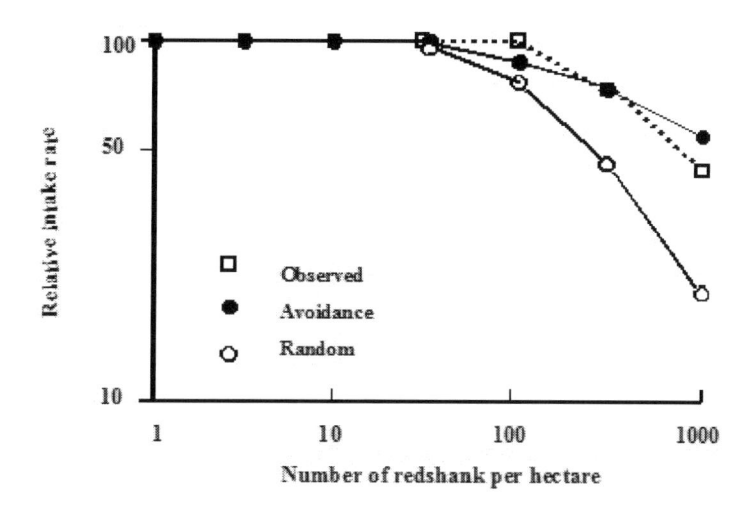

Figure 10.2 The interference function for redshank feeding on Corophium volutator, *a small burrowing crustacean. The open squares show the data obtained in the field on free-living redshank. The other two lines show the predictions of a model of interference from prey depression based on two different assumptions. The filled circles show the model's predictions when it was assumed that redshank avoided areas where other redshank had recently fed, a tendency which field data suggested is what happens in nature. The open circles show the predictions when it was assumed that redshank did not avoid previously searched areas and moved at random.*

The development of these two behaviour-based interference models was a major breakthrough. It meant that the parameters of the interference function could now be obtained instantaneously for a system from which no field estimates were available. With much relief, it was concluded that it would no longer necessary to carry out many years of time-consuming fieldwork to measure the parameters of the interference function in a new system, as had been required for Exe estuary oystercatchers. Along with finding a way instantaneously to predict the asymptote of the functional response, the discovery of how to predict the parameters that describe the interference function just as rapidly allowed the 'shorebird individual-based model' to be applied easily to a wide range of shorebird species anywhere in the World.

Local environment

To do this, data have first to be available on (i) the local climate; (ii) numbers of birds; (iii) the feeding patches along with the food supply they contained and their tidal exposure periods, (iv) the levels of disturbance (e.g. how frequently birds are disturbed and for how long), the shellfish harvest etc. All these have to be obtained locally although, often, most or all of the information is already available from previous surveys or from routine data collection programmes. Usually it is only the data on the food supply and its exposure through the tidal cycle that are not known. The methods required to measure the food supply in that way that the model requires have been described in publications and the work can usually be completed within 12 months. This is acceptable in most environmental impact projects.

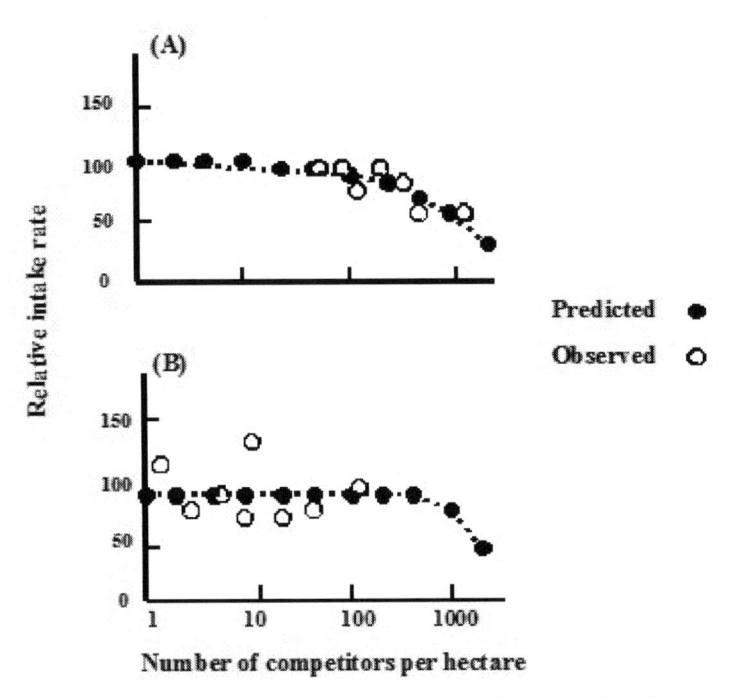

Figure 10.3 The interference functions of **(A)** oystercatchers feeding on cockles, and **(B)** bar-tailed godwits feeding on lugworms. The open circles show data recorded in the field in free-living birds. The solid circles show the outputs of a model that predicts the interference function due to prey stealing.

APPLICATION OF THE IBM TO THE MANAGEMENT OF MANY SPECIES OF SHOREBIRDS

The development of ways by which the parameters of the functional response and interference function could be rapidly obtained immediately opened the way for applying the model to solve many more coastal management problems. This was done on a number of occasions in the early 2000s, and continues today. Here are some of the early applications of the shorebird model.

Wading birds on the Seine estuary

The management issue

The estuary of the River Seine is one of the two largest estuaries in north-west France and supports nationally important numbers of shorebirds over the non-breeding season. The intertidal habitats used as feeding areas by these birds decreased in area throughout the 20th century, largely as a consequence of the development of the port at Le Havre and its associated industries. In the early 2000s, a new extension to the port - called Port 2000 - was proposed that would further decrease the amount of foraging habitat available to the shorebirds (Fig. 10.4). It was also feared that many of the activities associated with building and operating Port 2000 would cause increased disturbance of shorebirds feeding and roosting close to the port area. The Port Authorities were prepared to create areas designed to mitigate the effects of the development of Port 2000 on the shorebirds if it could be shown first that this was both necessary and likely to be effective. Accordingly, the shorebird IBM was contracted to test whether the loss of mudflat that would result from extending the port and the associated disturbance would reduce the survival of the shorebirds. If they would, then the model would be used to test whether the measures that were proposed to mitigate their impact would be effective and return the fitness of the birds to their pre-Port 2000 levels.

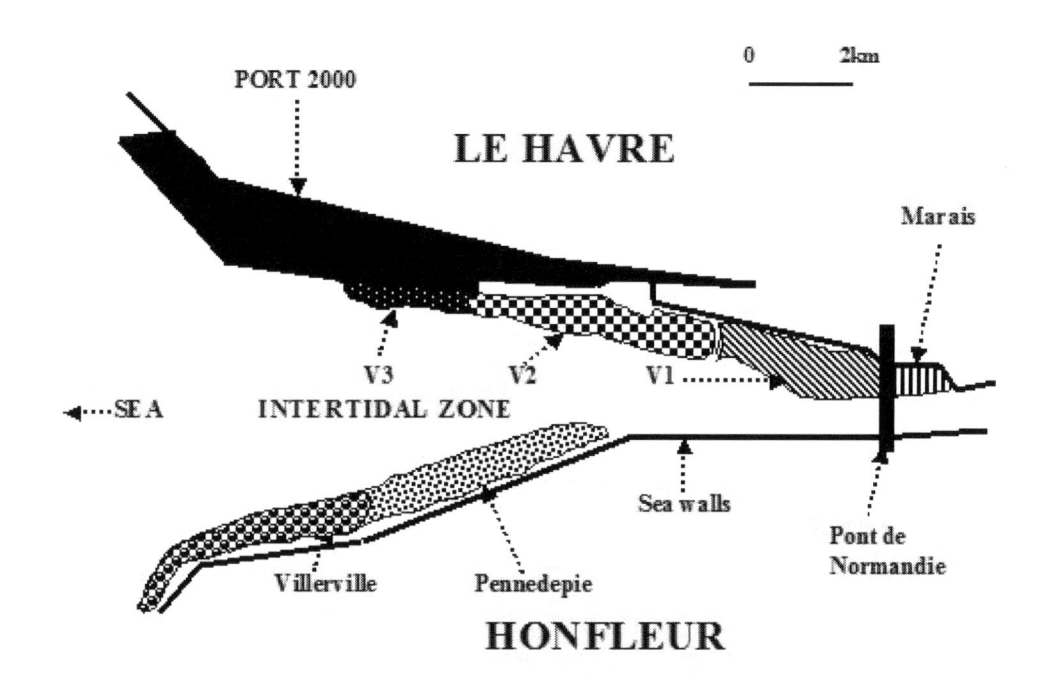

Figure 10.4 Estuary of the river Seine, showing the feeding patches used in the model and the Marais where the proposed mitigation was to be placed. V1 to V3 = the muddy patches Vasiè res 1 to 3.

Setting up the model

The data specific to the Seine that were needed to parameterise the model were collected on the shorebirds and their invertebrate prey over the winters of 2001/2002 and 2002/2003. Briefly, monthly counts were made of the more numerous shorebird species that were considered most likely to be affected by Port 2000, these being dunlin, curlew and oystercatcher. The counts made at high water determined the population size while those made at low tide provided information to test how well the model predicted where the birds fed. Observations on feeding birds provided information on the prey taken by each species and the number of disturbances to which they were subjected before the port had been extended. They also provided data to make another test of the model, namely the proportion of time birds spent feeding during the tidal cycle.

The benthic invertebrates that formed the food supply of these species were sampled in representative areas of the estuary in October, January and March in both 2001/2002 and 2002/2003, using standard techniques. The loss of prey due to factors other than consumption by the three shorebird species in the model was estimated by comparing invertebrate densities that the model predicted would still be present in March with those that actually remained in March surveys. The difference between the two values represented the loss of prey due to factors, such as predation by other bird species, crabs and so forth.

Each model run followed one winter, from 1 September to 15 March. The model was parameterised with the duration and timing of the neap-spring cycle and the day length cycle on the Seine during this period. On the basis of the results from the invertebrate surveys, and the distribution of the birds, the estuary was divided into five feeding patches. Three of the patches were on the north side of the estuary (Vasiè res 1, 2 and 3) and two were on the south side (Pennedepie and Villerville) (Fig. 10.4). As no data were available on the body masses of shorebirds on the Seine estuary, data from the Wash, east England were used to determine the mass of birds at the start of winter and their mean mass during winter.

On the Seine estuary, the main prey species were ragworms and clams *Macoma balthica*, which were taken by all three bird species, cockles taken by curlews and oystercatchers, the burrowing shrimp-like *Corophium volutator* taken by dunlins and mussels taken by oystercatchers.

There was already a certain amount of disturbance of shorebirds on the Seine estuary, mostly from walkers, but also from shellfishers and bait diggers. In the model, each disturbance event reduced the area available for feeding and stopped birds from feeding for 30 minutes, as had been measured in the field.

Simulations

The aim of the first model runs was to replicate the situation that existed before Port 2000 was built. As there were no data available on shorebird mortality rates on the Seine, the model was calibrated to give a 'best case scenario', where the mortality rate over the non-breeding season was close to 1%, and a 'worst case scenario', where it was close to 5%. In the event, however, there was very little difference in the results between these two scenarios, so only the results for the 1% mortality case are presented here. The model was calibrated by altering how efficient birds were at feeding on a particular prey until the predicted mortality rates matched the presumed values before Port 2000 had been built.

The first effect of Port 2000 on the shorebirds would be habitat loss, both through the direct removal of mudflat under the footprint of the Port itself and through a change in sediments outside the footprint. It was important to include the latter as some areas that had previously been mudflats were predicted to became mobile sands with very low prey densities of very small prey, and so virtually useless to the birds. The total mudflat area lost to shorebirds had been estimated at 105ha. Accordingly, simulations were run in which this amount of feeding ground was removed from the feeding patches on the north side of the estuary.

The second effect would be an increased frequency of disturbance. As no data were available on its likely strength and duration after Port 2000 had been built, it was assumed that disturbance would (a) exclude birds from feeding within a certain distance from the sea wall along Vasiè res 1 when the tide was out, and (b) disturb birds at the onshore roost over high tide. The distances from the sea wall at which birds would be driven from the mudflats over low water by human activities onshore had already been measured in the field. Two sets of disturbance simulations were run: (i) with disturbance occurring both day and night and (ii) with disturbance occurring in daytime only. Disturbance was assumed to be continuous throughout these periods. In order to simulate the effect of birds being disturbed when they were at the roost, simulations were run where it was assumed that birds incurred additional daily energy costs due because they spent more time in flight (which is energetically very expensive), this additional energy cost being calculated using a published equation.

As well as being useful for exploring the effect of the development of Port 2000 on shorebirds, the model was also used to predict the effectiveness of the proposed mitigating measures. One proposed mitigation was the introduction of a buffer zone next to the sea wall along the north side of the estuary to keep Port traffic away from feeding and roosting birds, thus reducing the impact of disturbance. A second proposed measure was to create of a new area of mudflat close to the Pont de Normandie - the Marais. It was assumed that this new area would have the same exposure time and the same invertebrate composition as the adjacent patch, Vasiè res 1 (Fig. 10.4). This meant that the mitigation patch exposed relatively early and covered relatively late in the tidal cycle and contained ragworms and *Corophium*. Simulations were also run which included both these mitigation measures in the model.

As plans for the new mudflat area had yet to be finalised, both the size and the invertebrate biomass of the new mudflat were varied in the model across the range that was believed likely to occur. Three different sizes of mitigation patch were tried: 50, 75 and 100 ha. Then, with a mitigation patch of 100 ha, prey densities of this patch were varied between 20% and 100% of the densities in Vasiè res 1. Levels of disturbance on this patch were assumed to be the same as for Vasiè res 1.

Testing the model

As has become by this time almost standard practice, the first test was to see how well the model predicted an important aspect of the birds' behaviour that can easily be measured - their distribution across the various foraging patches. In general, the Seine model predicted quite well the distribution of birds at low water in the middle of the non-breeding season (Fig. 10.5). The main discrepancies were that it underestimated the numbers of curlew and overestimated the numbers of oystercatchers feeding on the cockle beds at Pennedepie.

As no estimates of the mortality rates of shorebirds on the Seine estuary were available, the amount of time spent feeding was used to test the model's ability to predict the amount of feeding stress the birds had been under prior to Port 2000 being built. Data on bird feeding activity were available for only some of the feeding patches but these were believed to be representative of the whole estuary.

The proportion of time spent feeding by the birds as predicted by the model was very close to that observed on the mudflats Vasiè res 2, both at low water (Fig. 10.6(A)) and on the receding and advancing tides (Fig. 10.6(B)). The comparison between prediction and observation was also good for Pennedepie (Fig. 10.6(A)). The main discrepancy was in oystercatcher feeding activity at Villerville, where birds fed for longer in the model than was observed in the field. But overall, the agreement between prediction and observation was judged to be close enough to regard the model as good enough to explore the management issues that would arise from Port 2000.

Predicting the impact of Port 2000 on the birds

Model predictions for mortality and body condition were obtained for the end of January before the birds begin to leave the estuary. Body condition is expressed as the percentage of birds failing to achieve at least 75% of their target weight at departure.

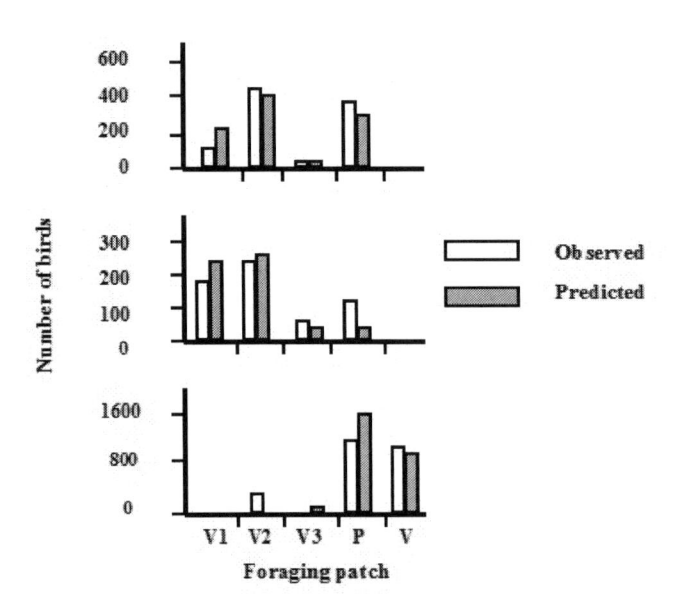

Figure 10.5 *Comparison between the distribution over the Seine estuary of the three species of shorebirds over the different feeding patches (open bars) and the predictions of the model (shaded bars).*

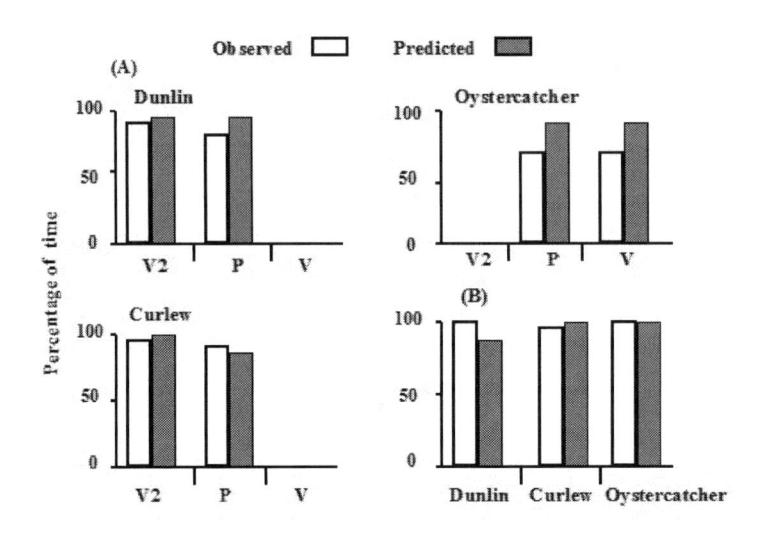

Figure 10.6 *Comparison between the amount of time spent feeding by the three species of shorebirds of the Seine estuary as measured in the field (open bars) and as predicted by the model (shaded bars) on (A) the different feeding patches over low water, and (B) when the tide was receding, low and advancing.*

Habitat loss was simulated by removing all of Vasiè res 3 from the model, and by reducing the area of Vasiè res 1 and 2 by 20%. With this amount of habitat removed from the estuary, the model predicted a significant increase in the mortality of both dunlin and oystercatchers and a significant decrease in their body condition (Fig. 10.7). In contrast, the mortality and body condition of curlew were not predicted to be affected by this habitat loss.

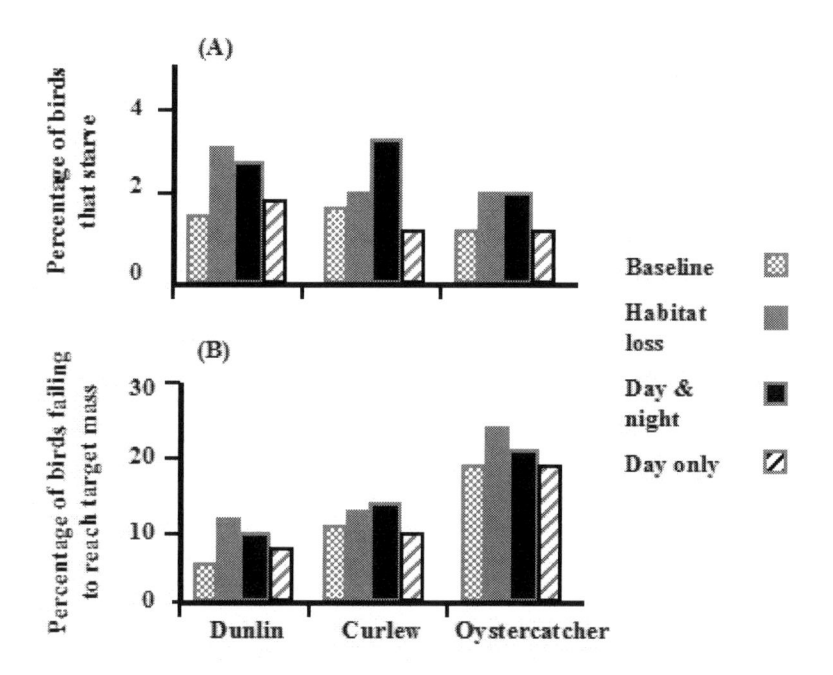

Figure 10.7 The predicted effect on (A) the mortality rate and (B) body condition on three shorebird species of the Seine estuary of habitat loss (grey columns), disturbance of feeding birds during the day and at night (black columns) and disturbance of feeding birds only during the day (striped columns) compared with the baseline rates without any of these activities taking place. Body condition is expressed as the proportion of birds failing to accumulate at least 75% of their target reserves.

Onshore disturbance was most likely to have excluded birds from the upshore part of Vasiè res 2 during the daytime. The model predicted no significant effect of this disturbance on the mortality rate in any of the three species. Only in dunlin was body condition significantly reduced by this disturbance. In fact, this was considered very likely to be a considerable over-prediction. This is because the model assumed that the upshore areas would have been disturbed throughout the exposure period on every day. Disturbance of birds on the feeding grounds by people onshore during the day could therefore be regarded as insignificant.

But if – improbably - the birds were also to be disturbed continuously at night, the model predicted that the impact would have been far greater. In fact, such intensive disturbance would have represented an additional loss of foraging habitat because disturbance would have denied the birds the use of these upshore areas at all times. If this disturbance had proved in practice to occur continuously day and night – again, very improbably - it could have easily been prevented by establishing a disturbance-free buffer zone along the top of the shore.

Frequent disturbance at the roost may have had an effect, however. This form of disturbance was simulated by increasing the birds' daily energy costs, a method which therefore assumed (again improbably) that the birds were disturbed at the roost on every day throughout the non-breeding season. When the birds' energy costs were increased by the equivalent of 10 min or more extra flying time a day, there was a significant effect on the mortality and body condition of all three shorebird species (Fig. 10.8). Such a high frequency of disturbance was considered by local experts to be most unlikely to occur in practice, however. But in the absence of any predictions as to how often the birds would be disturbed after Port 2000 had been extended, the precautionary approach was taken, and appropriate mitigation measures considered in the model.

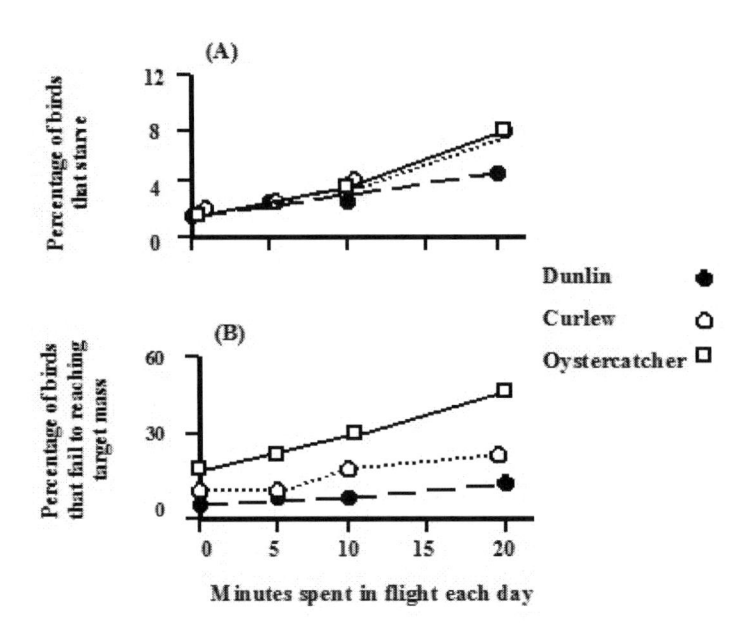

Figure 10.8 The effect of the extra energy cost of being disturbed at the high water roost on the Seine estuary on the (A) mortality rate and (B) body condition of three shorebird species. The amount of disturbance is measured as the amount of time the birds are in flight because of being disturbed.

Effectiveness of mitigation

Only the mortality rates and body condition of dunlin and oystercatchers were predicted to be affected by the loss of feeding habitat that would follow the construction of Port 2000. With this loss of habitat included in the model, a 50 ha mitigation area of the same quality as the adjacent mudflat proved to be sufficient to return the mortality rate and body condition of oystercatchers to their pre-Port 2000 levels. In dunlin, however, it was necessary to provide 100 ha to restore their mortality rate and body condition to previous levels. A 100 ha mitigation was also sufficient to mitigate the effect of disturbance at the roost in both dunlin and curlew, although not in oystercatchers. As it required a reduction of invertebrate abundance of almost a half before these areas of mitigation failed to restore the pre-Port 2000 feeding conditions, it was concluded that a replacement mudflat of 100ha was very likely to be effective, even if the assumed prey abundance proved to be rather over-optimistic.

Management implications

The loss of feeding habitat resulting from the development of Port 2000 was therefore predicted to have a significant impact on the mortality and body condition of two of the three main species of shorebirds that pass the non-breeding season on the Seine estuary. The 6000 dunlin that fed on the mudflats adjacent to Port 2000 throughout the tidal cycle were particularly likely to be affected. Although the main feeding areas for oystercatchers at low water were the cockle and mussel beds on the opposite side of the estuary to Port 2000, they too were predicted to be affected. This was because these birds did feed on the mudflats near to Port 2000 as the tide receded and advanced. Curlew may have been unaffected by Port 2000 because they occurred at such low densities that they could congregate in a smaller area without significantly intensifying interference between them.

A mitigation area of 100 ha was also sufficient to restore the mortality and body condition of dunlin and curlew to pre-Port 2000 levels when very high rates of disturbance at the roost were included, whereas in oystercatchers this was not so. In oystercatchers, the increased energy costs resulting from disturbance at the roost could not be met by feeding on worms alone. Accordingly, a mitigating area for oystercatchers would need to contain shellfish. As this was considered difficult to achieve, it was suggested that it might be more practicable to minimise disturbance of high water roosts and/or provide alternative roost sites.

The development of this model for the Seine represented an important stage in the development of the shorebird individual-based model. Sarah Durell had demonstrated that the model could deal with bird species other than oystercatchers, and with bird several species simultaneously. Her work also demonstrated that the IBM could provide predictions not only about the effect of a proposed development on the shorebirds of the Seine estuary but could also explore the efficacy of proposed mitigation measures. It was the first time that it had been possible to predict the efficacy of planned mitigation measures. The project also showed how an individual-based model could be used to predict the effects of both detrimental (habitat loss, disturbance) and beneficial (habitat creation, buffer zones) environmental changes on the mortality rate and body condition of shorebirds. Finally, it showed that the required parameters could be measured within a relatively short time span and that a 25-year research project was no longer necessary! This work represented another important step in the development of the model.

Redshank displaced from Cardiff Bay

The management issue

The river Taff in south Wales runs through Cardiff into the estuary of the Severn, a huge area of intertidal flats that supports many tens of thousands of shorebirds, mainly during the non-breeding season. In the early 1980s, a plan was proposed – and eventually implemented – to put an impermeable barrage across the mouth of Cardiff Bay in order to create a permanent stand of freshwater – a lake - over the intertidal flats of the Bay. The idea was to create the central feature of a new waterside development to replace what at the time was rather run-down part of Wales' capital city. What had previously been a large mudflat used for feeding by shorebirds at low tide would therefore become a fresh-water lake that would be quite unsuitable for these birds, and they would have to vacate the Bay (Fig. 10.9).

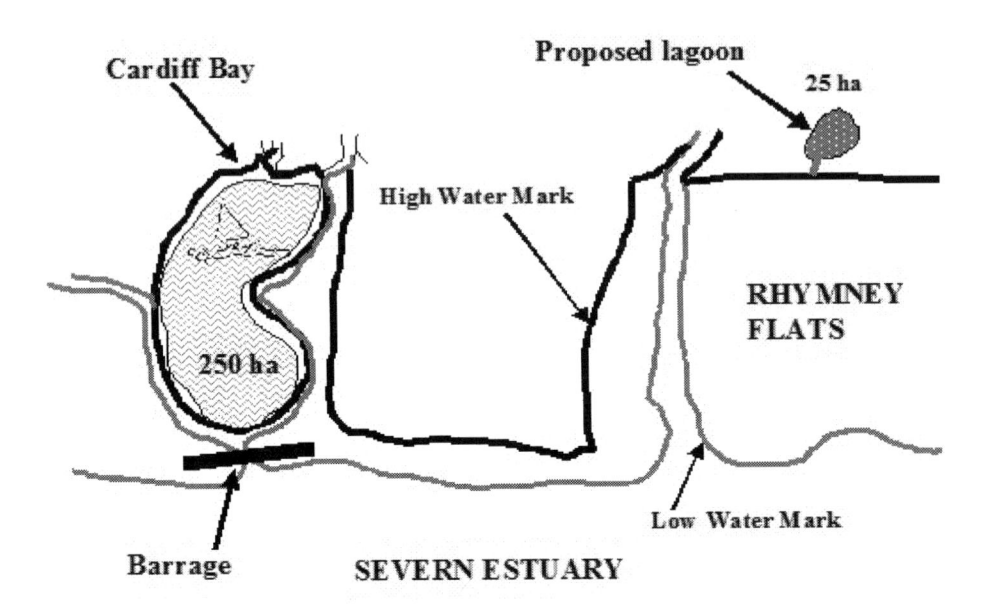

Figure 10.9 Shorebirds and the development at Cardiff Bay, illustrated with redshank. About 200 redshank fed in Cardiff Bay when the tide was out, along with large numbers of dunlin, curlew and shelduck. Shorebirds also occurred in large numbers outside the Bay, in the main estuary of the Severn estuary. The nearest mudflats outside the Bay were at Rhymney. When the barrage was built, the Bay became a freshwater lake, fed by the inflowing River Taff. The shorebirds could no longer feed there and moved out to the main Severn estuary, including the flats at Rhymney. As it was predicted that, in some species, the increased densities and of feeding birds at Rhymney would increase competition between them and raise their mortality rate above pre-barrage levels, a mitigation was proposed. This was to excavate a small lagoon in a field adjacent to the seawall at Rhymney to create a mudflat where the birds could feed when the mudflats in the main estuary of the Severn were covered at high water on Spring tides.

Amongst the many concerns that had to be addressed, of course, was the consequence for shorebirds of the removal of their foraging habitat in the Bay. Accordingly, the conservation lobby mounted a very effective campaign in an attempt to prevent the barrage from being built. An analysis conducted by the Exe estuary team as part of an extensive feasibility study into the consequences of building the barrage concluded that there was indeed a risk that the survival rates of the dunlin and redshank that fed in the Bay would be reduced, even though they would have moved onto the mudflats of the nearby Severn estuary. There were good reasons to believe that the intensified competition following their arrival on the feeding areas there would make it more difficult for more of the birds to obtain their daily energy requirements, especially in mid-winter. After peer-review, this advice was accepted. The team was then asked to devise a mitigating measure that would return their survival rates of the shorebirds to their pre-barrage levels.

The idea that came up was to punch a narrow hole in the seawall just upriver of the Bay to allow a new high-level mudflat to develop inside a bunded lagoon in an area that had previously been a grass field. Extensive feasibility studies were carried out, and it was eventually concluded that, though very costly, the lagoon might be effective, although the evidence was rather equivocal at that time. The Cardiff Bay Development Corporation subjected their plans to scrutiny by select committees in both the House of Lords and House of Commons and Parliament eventually passed the appropriate legislation that enabled the barrage to be built. (Box 10.3).

In the event, the barrage was constructed but the lagoon did not go ahead. For the Development Corporation, there would have been a permanent and heavy financial commitment to maintain the lagoon in a state suitable for shorebirds because it would have silted up and become overgrown quite rapidly with saltmarsh. For the conservationists, it was experimental and risky and so was not necessarily going to be successful, and their requirement was that any mitigation measure should be certain to succeed and actually be in place before the construction of the barrage had begun. Instead of building the lagoon, it was agreed that a new wetland area would be built that was not specifically designed to mitigate for the loss of Cardiff Bay but which would provide a great conservation facility, which it has proved to be.

The British Trust for Ornithology (BTO) was then contracted to monitor the survival rate of the redshank displaced by the barrage from the Bay. Redshank was chosen because it had been predicted in the feasability study to be the species most likely to be affected. The BTO study concluded that the mortality rate of these birds had indeed been increased by the loss of their foraging habitat in the Bay, even though they continued feeding outside on adjacent mudflats in the main Severn estuary. The risk of increased mortality that had been predicted by the feasibility study had proved to be correct, even though it had only been possible to deploy word arguments at the time the impact assessment had been made. At that time (1980s), the shorebird individual-based model was still being developed on the Exe estuary.

But by the early 2000s – a long time after the barrage had been built - the model had reached the stage when it could be used for species other than oystercatchers feeding on shellfish. The Cardiff Bay barrage provided an opportunity retrospectively to test the model's ability to predict the increased mortality rate in a situation in which – unusually - there was an actual estimate of the mortality rate. In addition, it also provided a retrospective opportunity to test whether the lagoon would have been an effective mitigation measure if it had it been built. This was thought likely to be a useful thing to know when other proposals for developments on estuaries were being considered in the future. Accordingly, a retired member of the Exe estuary team made it a priority to build a model of the redshank displaced from Cardiff Bay. The first objective was to test whether the model could accurately 'post-dict' the effect of the loss of Cardiff Bay on the mortality rate of redshank. The second objective was to examine whether the proposed mitigation lagoon would actually have been effective in restoring the survival rate of these birds to their pre-barrage levels.

Setting up the model

Local parameter values came from the following sources: (i) daily ambient temperature and daylength, were obtained from the local weather station; (ii) area and exposure time of each shore-level had been measured during the feasibility study; (iii) prey numerical density and size (body length) at each shore-level in mid-October had also been measured during the feasibility study; (iv) bird numbers and body weights had been determined during the BTO study, and (v) the diet of redshank, mainly ragworms during the day and *Hydrobia* at night was already known from studies that had been carried out previously by Pete Ferns and colleagues from Cardiff University.

The BTO monitoring study showed that the majority of displaced redshank moved to nearby mudflats at Rhymney to join other redshank that were already feeding there. The mortality rate between mid-October and mid-February of the *ca.* 200 redshank displaced from Cardiff Bay increased from 0.7% during the two winters before the barrage was built to 8.6% during the four winters afterwards. The mortality rate of the *ca.* 300 birds that had always fed at Rhymney remained the same throughout these six years at 4.9%. Thus, considering the combined post-barrage population of 500 birds that now fed on the Rhymney flats, the winter mortality increased by 3.2% from 3.2% pre-barrage to 6.4% post-barrage.

Simulations

As the model was required to post-dict the post-barrage mortality rate of redshank on just the Rhymney flats, a model was built for that area alone and not for Cardiff Bay itself. The Rhymney model parameterised with pre-barrage data considerably over-predicted the observed pre-barrage mortality rate of 4.9%. Accordingly, it was concluded that the model based on pre-barrage data had to be re-calibrated.

The most likely reason for the over-predicted mortality rate was that the predicted energy consumption of the average bird was too low. The most likely reason for this was that the values for intake rates used in the model for the daytime and/or night-time were too low. As the tests described earlier in this Chapter had shown that the predicted intake rates during the day were likely to be accurate, the model was re-calibrated by increasing the birds' intake rate at night alone.

This was done by increasing the night-time efficiency with which birds fed on *Hydrobia*, the one parameter that had not been estimated locally in the field. The first model had assumed that redshank only ate *Hydrobia* at night and did so at the same rate that they would feed on them during the day. Since this prey contains very little energy, the intake rate at night was therefore very low. However, as well as *Hydrobia*, redshank were known in that area to take some larger-sized prey at night, such as ragworms and winkles, and very few of these would be needed to considerably increase the intake rate from eating *Hydrobia* alone. As the size and, therefore, energy content of any of these large night-time prey were not known, the efficiency with which the birds were assumed to feed at night on *Hydrobia* was increased to mimic the extra intake rate they allowed the birds to achieve. Thus, a two-fold increase in the 'efficiency of feeding on *Hydrobia* at night' actually means that the birds, by taking a very small number larger-sized prey species, would have doubled the intake rate they would have achieved by eating *Hydrobia* alone.

Accordingly, the model was calibrated using pre-barrage data by increasing night-time foraging efficiency until the predicted mortality rate matched the actual pre-barrage mortality rate of the 300 Rhymney birds of 4.9% (Box 10.4). Having calibrated the model this way, bird numbers at Rhymney were increased from their pre-barrage total of 300 to their post-barrage total of 500. The only other parameter to be changed at Rhymney after barrage closure was the area of mudflats on which the birds could feed during the day. Disturbance from helicopters before the barrage was built had prevented redshank from feeding during the day on the mudflats adjacent to a nearby Heliport, although they did feed there at night. After the barrage had been built, redshank began feeding on the mudflat by the Heliport by day as well as by night. In the post-barrage model, daytime feeding was allowed to take place on the flats adjacent to the Heliport. Apart from this and bird numbers, all the other parameters in the post-barrage model remained as they had been in the pre-barrage model.

Predicting the effect of Cardiff Bay barrage

The model predicted a mean increase in the mortality rate in the 500 birds feeding at Rhymney after the barrage had been built of 3.7% which compared very favourably with the observed increase of 3.2%. The increased mortality implied that mortality was density-dependent. This was confirmed by simulation once bird numbers exceeded 100 (Fig. 10.10).

Effectiveness of mitigation

Although the proposed (but rejected) lagoon would have provided only less that 10% of the food resources and feeding area that had been lost in Cardiff Bay, it would have extended the time available for feeding on spring tides because the narrow breach would have delayed the inflow and outflow of water. In order to explore whether it would have been successful in returning redshank mortality rate to pre-barrage levels, 100 simulations were run. The surface area of the lagoon was set at either 15ha or 25ha and the tidal delays were set at either 0.75hr or 1.50hr, which represents the probable extreme values, as determined by hydraulic modelling. A 0.75hr delay means that, on the advancing tide, the lagoon would have remained exposed at the start of the high-tide period on spring tides for 45 min after all the mudflats in the main Severn estuary at Rhymney had been covered. On the receding tide, the lagoon would have uncovered 45 min after the Rhymney mudflats had been first exposed. The lagoon would have been exposed throughout the tidal cycle on high-tide neaps, as were all the upper shore-levels at Rhymney. The lagoon was seeded in the model with the same food supply as used for the high level mudflats at Rhymney because these two places would have been exposed for a similar amounts of time during a tidal cycle. All other parameters remained the same.

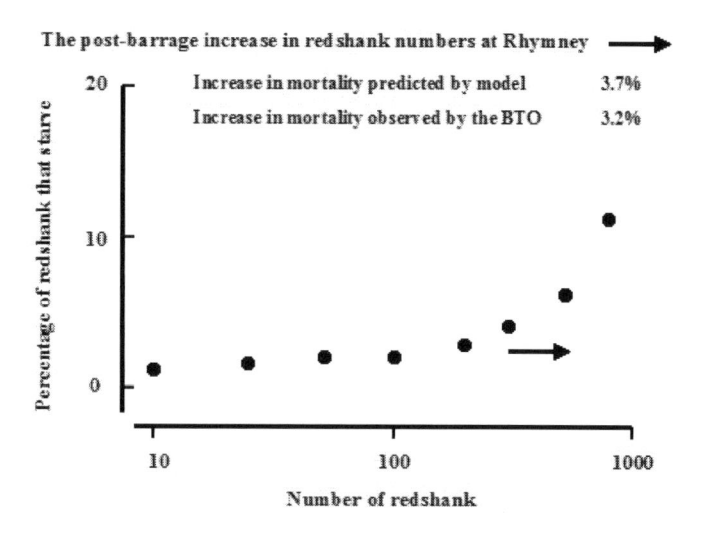

Figure 10.10 *The mortality rate of redshank feeding on the Rhymney mudflats as predicted by the model. A series of simulations were run with different population sizes of redshank, producing this density-dependent function. Note that the population size in on a logarithm scale.*

The results suggested that the lagoon would have returned mortality in the 500 Cardiff Bay and Rhymney birds combined from its post-barrage level of 6.8% to its pre-barrage level of 3.2%, and perhaps even lower (Fig.10.11). The difference in mortality rates between tidal delays of 0.75 and 1.50hr with the same mudflat area suggests that the tidal delay was in part the cause of the increased survival rate that was provided by the lagoon. This was confirmed by further simulations in which the lagoon was replaced by a mudflat of the same area but with the same tidal exposure pattern as the upshore areas at Rhymney; *i.e.* no tidal delay. Post-barrage mortalities were then only reduced by a very small amount (<1%), hardly different from the mortality rate with no lagoon at all (Fig. 10.11). This suggests the lagoon would have worked, not because of the additional feeding area it provided, but because of the delay it imposed on the tide. The lagoon provided mudflats that were available to the birds over high water on Spring tides when all the other intertidal areas were covered by water. According to these simulations, the lagoon would have been successful because if it extended the time available for redshank to feed on Spring tides.

Management implications

This study showed that, with surprising precision, the model could predict an increase in mortality rate that had been caused by a massive change in the feeding environment of the birds. Of course, this precision could have arisen just through good luck but was nonetheless seen as encouraging. The study also illustrated how the model could be parameterised in just a few weeks when no new fieldwork in the site itself was required.

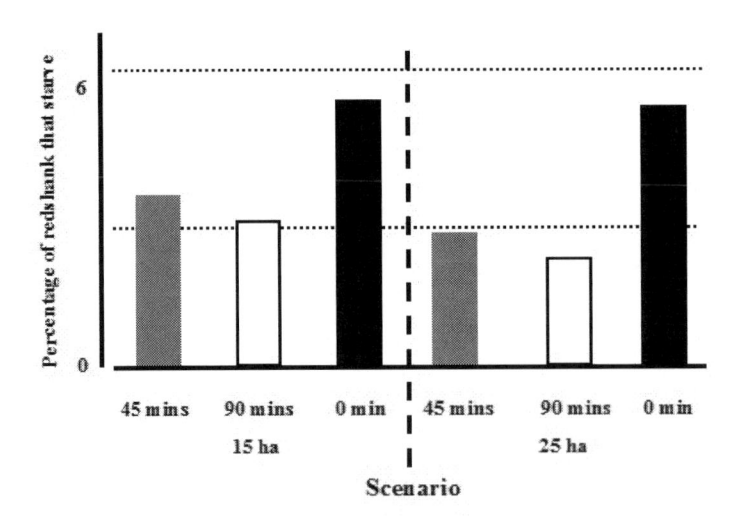

Figure 10.11 *The predicted mortality rate of redshank feeding at Rhymney if a tidal lagoon was provided adjacent to the mudflats at Rhymney. In one series of simulations, the surface area of the lagoon was 15ha (those to the left of the vertical dashed line), while in another series, the surface area was 25ha. In each series, simulations were run in which the tidal delay was either 45 minutes or 90 minutes long, or there was no delay at all (0 min.). The upper horizontal dotted line shows the predicted mortality rate with no lagoon provided. The lower horizontal dotted line shows the mortality rate that the mitigating lagoon was aimed at achieving; that is, the mortality rate before Cardiff Bay had been removed.*

As had the Seine model before it, the Rhymney model allowed the probable efficacy of a proposed mitigation measure to be tested. Importantly, the results suggested that it was not necessary to provide an equivalent area of mudflat to that lost in order to safeguard the survival chances of the displaced redshank: a 25ha lagoon represented only 10% of the area of Cardiff Bay that was lost. This contrasts to the mitigation proposed for the port extension at Le Havre where it was predicted that an area of equivalent size to that lost was needed to maintain the survival rate and body condition of dunlin.

This difference arose because the lagoon at Rhymney would have provided extra feeding time and not just replacement mudflat. The ability of shorebirds to obtain their requirements depends on a three-way trade-off between quantity (*i.e.* area), quality (*i.e.* prey abundance and profitability) and the time available for feeding. Prey abundance and quality in Cardiff Bay were similar to those found at Rhymney so it was the extended feeding time that the lagoon provided that would have returned the mortality rate of the redshank to its pre-barrage level. The contrast between Cardiff Bay and Le Havre illustrates the important point that the effectiveness of any proposed mitigation must be evaluated case by case; there was as yet no general rule that can be applied everywhere.

The redshank model for Rhymney could also contribute to evaluating the cost effectiveness of mitigation, an increasingly important part of the evaluation of alternative conservation options. The maximum numbers of waders and shelduck recorded in Cardiff Bay over the winter 1998-99 was 1,763, of which 786 were dunlin and 296 were redshank. At the time, it was being considered (1980s), the lagoon would have cost approximately £15million, or £8,500 for each bird whose habitat that winter was affected. This is a minimum estimate because this figure does not include the considerable (and indefinite) annual cost of maintaining the lagoon in a fit state for the birds.

As most of the redshank displaced from Cardiff Bay survived, the cost for each bird that would have been saved by mitigation (as distinct from per bird affected) would have been very much higher, of course. Of the peak of 296 redshank that used Cardiff Bay in the last pre-barrage winter, an estimated 6.8% died in each of the four post-barrage winters as a result of the habitat loss – 20 birds in the first winter but a total of 43 birds over the four winters combined plus, of course, an unknown number of other species, particularly dunlin. Because population processes are cumulative, the most appropriate measure of the cost-effectiveness of the lagoon would have been the cost of preventing the equilibrium population size of all the species concerned decreasing in the long-term, but predicting this at our present state of knowledge is problematical. So in view of this uncertainty about the long-term population consequences of building the barrage, it could only be concluded that the cost of preventing the population size decreasing by one bird was likely to have been very considerably more than the cost for each bird that was affected by being required to vacate the Bay, their former feeding ground.

Monitoring estuary quality for shorebirds
The management issue

Estuary managers are often required to monitor the quality of a site for shorebirds or to assess how a potential change to a site might influence its ability to support shorebirds. In European estuaries designated as 'Special Protection Areas' (SPAs), for example, countries are required to monitor site quality and to take the necessary steps to avoid any impending deterioration.

While the conservation importance of an estuary is appropriately measured in terms of the numbers of birds that use it, this is not a reliable way to monitor the quality of a site. This is because the number of birds using a site depends not only on the state of that site, but also on the condition at other sites where the birds might spend the non-breeding season. A decrease in bird numbers on one site might not be due to a deterioration in the quality of that site but be caused by an improvement in the quality of another which has drawn birds to it. Bird numbers on a non-breeding site may also depend on conditions in the areas where most of the birds breed.

So, rather than using bird numbers to evaluate the quality of a site, another method is required. Since the overall population size of any species is a function of the interaction between the mortality and reproductive rates, the best measure of habitat quality for an estuary used by shorebirds is one which, directly or indirectly, determines these demographic rates in the birds. In shorebirds during the non-breeding season, this means that habitat quality should be measured using factors that determine the mortality rate over the non-breeding season and the amount of fat stored by the birds prior to migration. If it can be shown that conditions at the site are sufficient to maintain the present-day rates of fat storage and survival at the current bird population size, then the quality of the estuary would be being maintained at a satisfactory level. If the population using the estuary decreases despite this, then the cause of that decrease needs to be sought elsewhere.

This is the kind of thing, of course, that the shorebird model can do quite readily. Two examples of its use in monitoring site quality are briefly described here: the Humber estuary and the Wash.

Setting up the models

There is no need here to repeat the details of how the data required to parameterise these two models were obtained, apart from saying that some new fieldwork was carried out to fill as many of the gaps in existing knowledge as possible. Both projects lasted about two to three years. Nine (Humber) and eight (Wash) species of shorebirds were included in the models, the largest species diversity that had at that time been attempted. In the Humber model, it was also necessary to include a terrestrial patch where curlews could feed, this being an important aspect of their natural history on that estuary.

Calibrating and testing the models

There were no data available to test the models' predictions for either the amount of time the birds spent feeding during the years of the study or their mortality rates. The models could only be evaluated by comparing the birds' real foraging behaviour with that predicted by the model. For the Humber, the behaviours for which this could be done were (i) the species of prey eaten by the various species of shorebirds, compared with the findings of a literature review of the diets of British shorebirds, and (ii) the distribution of the shorebirds over the estuary at low water, compared with the findings of low tide surveys conducted by the BTO between September 1998 and March 1999. Neither of these tests would tell us, however, whether the model predicted accurately the body condition and survival of the birds on the Humber estuary. Some data were available on the amount of time spent feeding by shorebirds on the Wash, but these referred to a period some twenty years earlier! It was therefore not possible to test and, if necessary, re-calibrate the models using values of mortality rate and of the time spent feeding that had been measured on the two sites during the study period itself.

Sometimes, time and resources don't allow models to be as thoroughly parameterized and tested as everyone would like, and these were two such occasions. The fact that the model had already performed well in other sites gave no grounds at all for having confidence in its predictions in these two sites. But the models had only been commissioned to show how *in principle* they could be used to assess site quality. As the following example illustrate, these two models did indeed illustrate how they could be used for this purpose, even if their actual detailed predictions at that time could not be relied on with confidence. For that reason, the models are best regarded as a theoretical exercise, rather than being used for making predictions.

Assessing site quality

On the Humber estuary, nine shorebird species were modelled; dunlin, ringed plover, knot, redshank, grey plover, black-tailed godwit, bar-tailed godwit, oystercatcher and curlew. With the exception of curlew, shorebird survival rates fell below 90% when the estuary-wide food biomass density at the start of the non-breeding season was less than about 4gAFDM per square metre (Fig. 10.12). Curlew survival rates fell when the initial food biomass density decreased below 8gAFDM per square metre. The initial prey biomass densities that had actually been recorded on the Humber were for all species, except curlew, well above the threshold prey density below which survival rates were predicted to decline. However, allowing curlew to feed in terrestrial habitats restored their survival rate to the high levels seen in the other species.

Eight shorebird species were modelled on the Wash; dunlin, knot, redshank, grey plover, black-tailed godwit, bar-tailed godwit, oystercatcher and curlew. The results were similar to those from the Humber except that birds began to starve when the estuary-wide food biomass density at the start of the non-breeding season was less than about 5gAFDM per square metre. The survival rate fell to below 90% when the prey biomass was reduced to 4gAFDM per square metre.

Management implications

These projects illustrated how the quality of a site for shorebirds could be measured in terms of the biomass density of the food supply from the survival rates predicted by the model. Other factors, such as disturbance, that might affect site quality could also be included, and indeed this was done with the Wash model. But as was stressed a little earlier, it would be unwise to regard these model outputs as an actual evaluation of the quality of the Humber estuary and Wash for shorebirds at that time. For this to be done, more parameters would need to be measured on site and, most importantly, the models' predictions for the time spent feeding and, if possible, the actual survival rate would need to be compared with measurements made at the time.

Nonetheless, the results were sufficient to illustrate how the shorebird model could be used to monitor the quality of an estuary as a non-breeding site for shorebirds. In order to do this, it would be necessary to measure the abundance and distribution of the invertebrate food supply at regular intervals – perhaps every five or six years. But this is a very time-consuming and expensive job, especially if the smaller-sized prey species are included (because they are so numerous and counting them in a sample takes a lot of time). But luckily, the simulations showed that site quality was unaffected by the biomass densities of two numerous small-sized prey – *Hydrobia* and *Corophium* – suggesting that limited resources would best be utilized by focusing on the larger-sized prey species, the annelid worms and bivalve molluscs whose abundance can be determined more readily. Quite rightly, though, the authors of the work cautioned that 'Further studies on other estuaries are required to determine whether these conclusions are more widely applicable.'

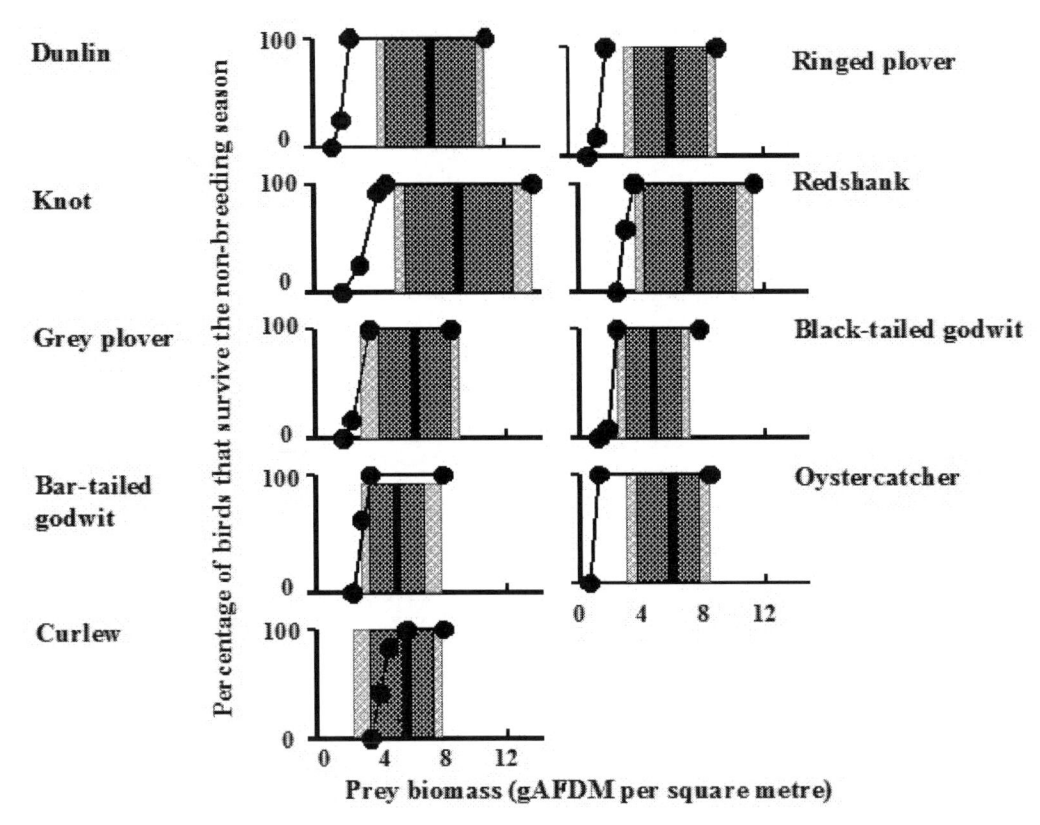

Figure 10.12. How the shorebird model can be used to determine the quality of the feeding grounds of an estuary, in this case, the Humber. The thick vertical line shows for each bird species the estimated biomass density of its food at the time the study was conducted. Because this is only an estimate based on a sampling scheme, the shaded areas on either side show the range within which the real food abundance is most likely to lie. The black dots show the model's predictions for the survival rate of each species of shorebird in relation to the biomass density of its food supply, taking into account the effect that competing bird species also have on their food supply. In all cases except curlew, the birds' survival rate was at, or very close to, 100% even when the food supply was less than the minimum it was likely to have been. Curlew is the exception, and it is believed that this species could only survive by feeding in terrestrial habitats over high tide.

Brent geese and barnacle geese across Europe

The final example to illustrate how the model was extended is that of brent geese and barnacle geese that breed in the Arctic and spend the non-breeding season in North-west Europe. This not only illustrates how the model could be adapted for herbivorous shorebirds but also how it could (i) include the energy and time costs of moving between geographically widely separated feeding areas and so can be applied to many non-breeding sites extending over a large geographical area; (ii) include the breeding grounds and the annual cycle as a whole, and (iii) model the size of a population and not just predict its density-dependent functions during one part of the year. These models are therefore both 'spatially explicit' and adopt a year-round approach.

Setting up and testing the models

The main point to appreciate about these models is that, within the non-breeding season, the populations could feed in a number of widely-separated sites, all of which had their own particular food supply; for example, the Wash and Humber estuary. Individual birds could move between sites if it was advantageous for them to do so and, while travelling, they would incur realistic costs in time and energy. In both models, there was also a single staging-site that the geese used in Spring when migrating from the non-breeding sites to their breeding areas where they built up their body reserves to fuel their onward journey.

The predictions of the model were extensively tested. Suffice to say here that there was a generally good agreement between the density-dependent functions that were measured in the field and those that were predicted by the model. Likewise, there was generally a good similarity between the models' predictions for the seasonal patterns in the distribution and movement of populations within and between sites and those that had been observed in nature. The models also predicted quite well the observed energy reserves of the two species of geese. The outputs of the models were also shown to be sensitive to many of its parameters, thus underlining again the need for the accurate estimation of many of their parameters if reliable and realistic predictions were to be obtained.

Movements between sites

A key innovation of the goose models was the opportunity for individual birds faced with deteriorating conditions in their current non-breeding site to move to another one where they might improve their chances of surviving the non-breeding season in good condition. The difference that the inclusion of this option might make to the size of the population was explored with the brent goose model.

The average population of the brent goose was reduced by over 40% when birds were not able to move from the non-breeding site where the deterioration had occurred. This arose because of changes to the shape of the density-dependent mortality function during the non-breeding season (Fig. 13(A)). First, the threshold density of geese at which birds first started to starve decreased markedly when starving birds were prevented from moving from the deteriorating site to another site. In fact, brent geese were predicted to starve at the population size that was current at the time this research was carried out. Secondly, at any given population size at any point across the whole range of population size explored, a higher proportion of the birds starved when they were prevented from moving to another site when they got into difficulties.

An unexpected consequence of the geese being allowed to move from one site to another during the non-breeding season was that, at the higher population sizes, the average production of juveniles per surviving female was predicted to be substantially lower when birds were allowed to move between non-breeding sites compared with when they were not allowed to do so (Fig. 13(B)). This probably arose because the greater mortality rate during the non-breeding season when geese were not able to vacate a deteriorating site may have reduced the subsequent competition between the surviving females on the staging area in spring.

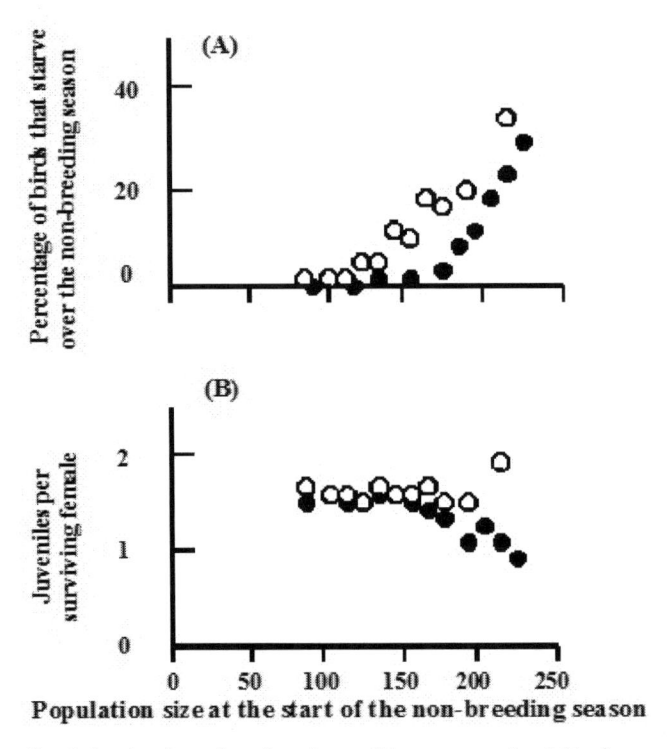

Figure 10.13 The model-predicted density-dependent functions of brent geese for (A) the rate of mortality during the non-breeding season and (B) the production of juveniles by each female when the birds are allowed to move between non-breeding season feeding sites (closed circles) and when they are not allowed to do so (open circles).

Management issues

Though the models had not been constructed to investigate a particular management issue, they were nonetheless capable of simulating the impact on these geese populations of an almost limitless number of possible changes in their foraging environment, both those caused naturally and those caused by man (Table 10.1). These changes could occur at either a local or a global scale. Just a few example outputs are shown here. Between them, they illustrate the need to adopt a spatially-explicit and year-round approach when the aim is to predict the impact of habitat changes on the size of migratory populations, such as brent and barnacle geese.

Removing habitat during the non-breeding season can be done either by removing a fixed area of habitat of identical size from every patch on every site or by removing entire sites. The difference that this might make to the predictions was explored with the brent goose model. When considering the removal of entire sites, up to five were removed sequentially in the simulations starting with either the one that was furthest from the staging site on which the population congregates in spring or with the one that was closest.

Habitat change	Causative agent
Global changes	
Removal of intertidal patches of *Zostera*	Recurrence of *Zostera* wasting disease
Reduced availability of intertidal habitat	Sea-level rise
Altered areas of managed grassland	Changes to Common Agricultural Policy
Altered timing of vegetation growth	Climate change
Loss of specific habitat (eg. currently managed grassland reverting to rough pasture when grazing livestock are removed)	Socio-economic factors
Local changes	
Removal of intertidal habitat	Reclamation, develpment, tidal barrages
Reduced area of managed grassland	Local development
Increased area of managed grassland	Creation of reserves
Increased nutritive quality of grassland	Fertilization of grasslan

Table 10.1 Some of the changes in habitat which could be investigated by the barnacle goose and brent goose models to predict their effect on the population size of the geese.

Removal of an area of feeding habitat equally from all non-breeding sites resulted in a virtually proportionate reduction in the size of the population in autumn when the birds returned from their breeding areas (Fig. 10.14(A)). That is, if 10% of each non-breeding site was removed, the average population size also decreased by about 10%. By contrast, the entire removal of those non-breeding sites that were furthest away from the staging site resulted in a sub-proportionate reduction in the population. That is to say, when 20% of the feeding habitats were removed, the population size decreased by a lot less than 20%. However, the removal of the sites that were closest to the spring staging site always led to a supra-proportional reduction in the size of the population. That is, if 10% of these habitats were removed, the population declined by a much greater amount than 10%. Presumably this occurred because the sequential removal of these sites gradually increased the distance the geese had to fly from their final non-breeding site to the spring staging site, thus putting them under increased pressure. The response of this population to habitat loss during the non-breeding season would clearly depend upon the precise spatial configuration of the habitat removal (Fig. 10.14(A)).

Feeding habitat can be removed not only from the non-breeding sites but also from the Spring staging site. The barnacle goose model was used to explore whether this affected the impact on population size (Fig. 10.14(B)). In both cases, the impact on population size was sub-proportionate. However, the impact of removing a given proportion of the staging site was less severe than it was when an equivalent area of the habitat used during the non-breeding season was removed.

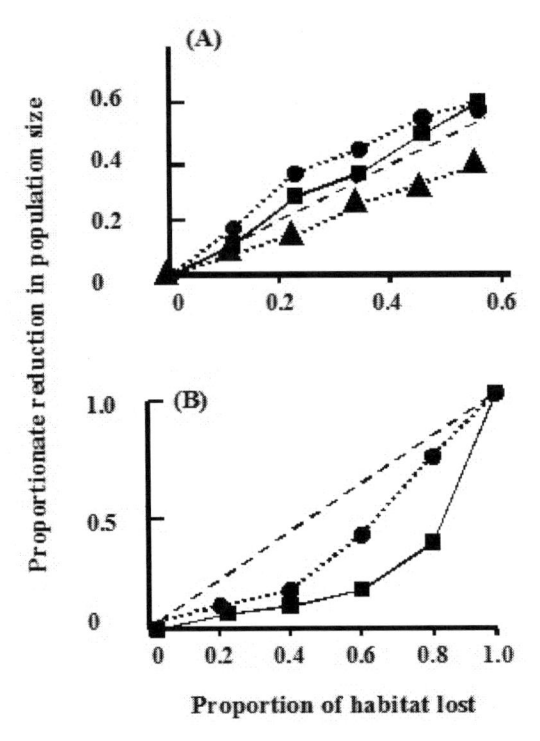

Figure 10.14 The predicted proportionate change in the equilibrium population size of brent geese and barnacle geese following the removal of feeding habitat in various ways: **(A)** Brent geese: 1. (square) removal of winter habitat from all sites equally. 2. (triangle) removal of consecutive sites that are most distant from the spring staging sites. 3. (circle) removal of consecutive sites that are closest to the spring staging sites. **(B)** Barnacle geese: 1. (circle) removal of habitat from wintering sites only. 2. (square) removal of habitat from the spring staging sites only.

Figure 10.15 shows the predicted immediate effect on the population size of barnacle geese of a hypothetical change in the socio-political or economic circumstances in Helgeland where the Spring staging areas are situated. These changes are assumed to result in the loss of one of the four different kinds of habitats that are used by these geese at this time of year. In all cases, changes to agricultural practices were predicted to lead to an immediate decline in the size of the population. This happened because individuals that had previously fed in the affected habitat found that the resource they had traditionally used was now missing, and it took time for replacement areas to be located. However, in all cases, this set-back proved to be temporary and was followed by a gradual recovery of the population. In some scenarios, indeed, the population returned to a size that was close to, or even above, its original size as the birds re-distributed themselves between the remaining habitats.

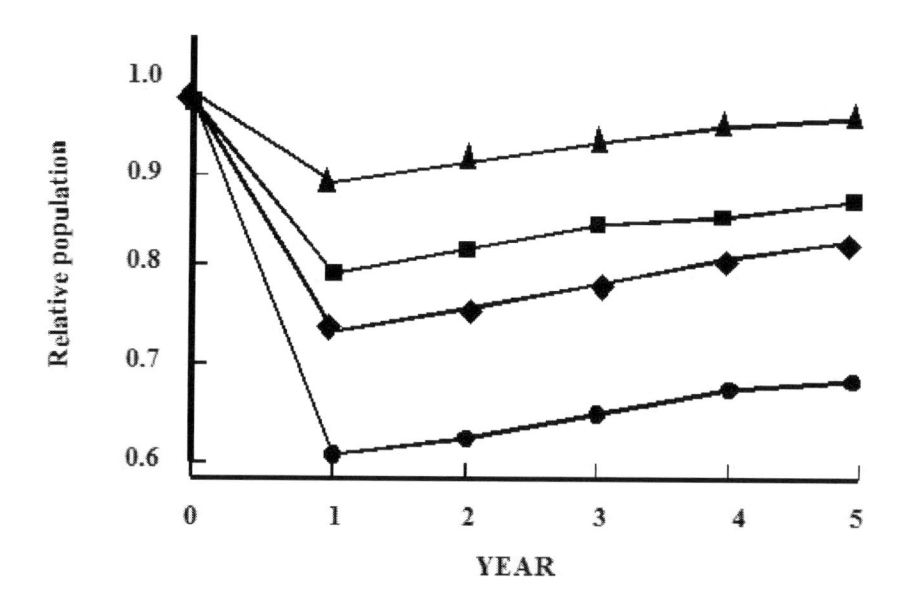

Figure 10.15 *The predicted population size of the Svarlbard barnacle goose population over a five year period following the removal of each of the four alternative habitats on the spring staging site: 1. (triangle) managed in the traditional way. 2. (square) unmanaged in the traditional way. 3. (triangle) agricultural land on islands. 4. (circle) agricultural land on the mainland. For details of precise way in which the land was managed in each scenario, and the way in which the geese exploited them, see the original paper.*

Importance of movement from site to site

Many valuable observations on the whole individual-based modelling approach as well as on the ecology and conservation of these geese populations arose from this study. Suffice to say here that these models contrasted most markedly with the previous shorebird models in being multi-site and year-round.

In the previous single-site versions of the shorebird model, birds that were *en route* to starving had no option but to try and reverse their predicament by adapting their behaviour on site. A starving bird might extend the time it spends feeding while the intertidal flats remain exposed or forage in terrestrial habitats over high water, for example. But real birds that are starving have another option, and that is to move to another site altogether. This is risky, of course, because the food supply in the new site may be no better than in the one they have left, or because the birds do not know the best way to exploit the new site or because of their possibly lowly competitive status as newly-arrived birds. Despite these risks, real birds often do move from a site where it has become difficult for them to feed fast enough to survive. The cold-weather movements of shorebirds in the non-breeding season provide many examples of this response to a temporary deterioration in the habitat, as noted earlier with Dutch oystercatchers moving to the baie de Somme.

The comparison of the output of the brent goose model when birds either were or were not allowed to move between feeding sites during the non-breeding season highlights the difference that this assumption can make to the predictions of the model. When birds were not allowed to leave a site when they were *en route* to starving, more birds starved than if they had been able to emigrate. This showed that single site models could considerably over-estimate the impact of an environmental deterioration on the size of the population as a whole. This confirmed the appropriateness of the precautionary assumption that had been made when using the single-site models: that is, there would be no impact on the population if the density-dependent mortality function in that site would not be affected.

But when an environmental change has been shown likely to reduce survival and body condition in the non-breeding season, the goose models underlined the importance not only of allowing between-site movement but also of modelling the population throughout the year. For example, the brent goose model predicted an increase in the non-breeding season mortality of brent geese when movements within that period of the year were prevented. But the model also predicted that this increase in the mortality rate during the non-breeding season would result in a slight weakening of the density-dependent reduction in breeding success for those females that had survived. In other words, preventing starving birds from moving to another site during the non-breeding season not only increased the numbers that died but also increased the productivity of those that survived. In terms of the long-term average size of the population, these were two outcomes that worked in opposite directions. One would tend to decrease the size of the total population, whereas the other would tend to increase it.

This raised the question of what would be the net effect on the population size of an increase in mortality during the non-breeding season but an increase also in the subsequent production of juveniles per female. The data available at the time suggested that the resulting increased reproductive success of the surviving females was not sufficient to exactly reverse the effect of the increased mortality rate over the non-breeding season. But had it been more marked, the increased reproductive output per female could have compensated for the increased mortality rate during the non-breeding season! If so, there would be no impact of habitat loss during the non-breeding season on the size of the goose population. An interesting but still hypothetical possibility!

Either way, this result emphasised the importance of taking a year-round approach to working out the effect of an environmental change on the long-term size of these migratory populations. It also again emphasized the vital need to test a model's accuracy in predicting the density dependence of key demographic parameters, such as the mortality rate over the non-breeding season.

REFERENCES FOR CHAPTER 10

Durell, S. E. A. le V. dit, Goss-Custard, J. D., Stillman, R. A., Triplet, P., Fagot, C. & Aulert, C. (2004). Les conséquences de la création de Port 2000 au Havre sur les Limicoles: première version d'un modèle prédictif. *Alauda*, **72**, 87-106.

Durell, S.E.A. le V., McGrorty, A.D., West, A.D., Clarke, R.T., Goss-Custard, J.D. & Stillman, R.A. (2004). A strategy for baseline monitoring of estuary Special Protection Areas. *Biological Conservation*, **121**, 289-301.

Durell, S. E. A. le V. dit, Stillman, R. A., Triplet, P., Aulert, C., Ono dit Biot, D, Bouchet, A., Duhamel, S., Mayot, S. & Goss-Custard, J. D. (2005). Modelling the efficacy of proposed mitigation areas for shorebirds on the Seine estuary, France. *Biological Conservation*, **123**, 67-77.

Goss-Custard, J.D. (1976). Variation in the dispersion of redshank, *Tringa totanus*, on their winter feeding grounds. *Ibis*, **118**, 257-263.

Goss-Custard, J.D. (1993). The effect of migration and scale on the study of bird populations: 1991 Witherby Lecture. *Bird Study*, 40, 81-96.

Goss-Custard, J.D., Burton, N.H.K., Clark, N.A., Ferns, P.N., McGrorty, S., Reading, C.J., Rehfisch, M.M., Stillman, R.A., Townend, I., West, A.D. & Worrall, D.H. (2006). Test of a behaviour-based individual-based model: response of shorebird mortality to habitat loss. *Ecological Applications*, **16**, 2205-2222.

Goss-Custard, J.D., West, A.D., Yates, M.G. and 31 other authors. (2006). Intake rates and the functional response in shorebirds (Charadriiformes) eating macro-invertebrates. *Biological Review*, **81**, 501–529.

Pettifor, R.A., Caldow, R.W.G., Rowcliffe, J.M., Goss-Custard, J.D., Black, J.M., Hodder, K.H., Houston, A.I., Lang, A. & Webb, J. (2000). Spatially explicit, individual-based behaviour models of the annual cycle of two migratory goose populations - model development, theoretical insights and applications. *Journal of applied Ecology*, **37 Supplement 1**, 103-135.

Stillman, R. A., Goss-Custard, J. D. & Alexander, M. J. (2000). Predator search pattern and the strength of interference through prey depression. *Behavioural Ecology*, **11**, 597-605.

Stillman, R.A., Goss-Custard, J.D. & Caldow, R.W.G. (1997). Modelling interference from basic foraging behaviour. *Journal Animal Ecology*, **66**, 692-703.

Stillman, R.A., Poole, A.E., Goss-Custard, J.D., Caldow, R.W.G., Yates, M.G. & Triplet, P. (2002). Predicting the strength of interference more quickly using behaviour-based models. *Journal of Animal Ecology*, **71**, 532-541.

Stillman, R.A., Goss-Custard, J.D., Clarke, R.T. & Durell, S.E.A. le V. dit. (1996). Shape of the interference function in a foraging vertebrate. *Journal of Animal Ecology*, **65,** 813-824.

Stillman, R.A., West, A.D., Goss-Custard, J.D., McGrorty, S., Frost, N.J., Morrisey, D.J., Kenny, A.J. & Drewitt, A.L. (2005). Predicting site quality for shorebird communities: a case study on the Humber estuary, UK. *Ecology Progress Series,* **305**, 203–217.

Triplet, P., Stillman, R.A. & Goss-Custard, J.D. (1999). Prey abundance and the strength of interference in a foraging shorebird. *Journal of Animal Ecology*, **68,** 254-265.

West, A.D., Goss-Custard, J.D., Durell, S.E.A. le V. & Stillman, R.A. (2005). Maintaining estuary quality for shorebirds: towards simple guidelines. *Biological Conservation*, **123**, 211-224.

West, A.D., Yates. M.G., McGrorty, S. & Stillman, R.A. (2007). Predicting site quality for shorebird communities: A case study on the Wash embayment, U.K. *Ecological Modelling*, **202**, 527-539.

Yates, M.G., Stillman, R.A. & Goss-Custard, J.D. (2000). Contrasting interference functions and foraging dispersion in two species of shorebirds Charadrii. *Journal of Animal Ecology*, **69**, 314 322.

Box 10.1 Simple and complex models

The shorebird models were sometimes dismissed as being just too complex. After so much effort, this could be a little irritating sometimes! It also seemed to be uncomprehending of our objectives. As should be clear by now, complexity was definitely not something that was sought for its own sake: to have done so would have been really silly. The model became gradually more complex because that was the only way in which its predictions could be made to match ever more closely what was happening in the real world. Experience showed that it was necessary to include many details of the natural history of both the birds and their prey. There would have been no point in having an elegant and simple analytical model if it under-predicted the birds' mortality rate and, worse still, was used to devise a policy that would lead to their extinction - as was pretty well the case with shellfish-easting birds in the Dutch Wadden Sea (as will be described in Chapter 11). This view of the IBM modelling was held by some, despite the fact that mature modelling disciplines, such as climate forecasting, hydrology and sedimentology, routinely use models a great deal more complex than the IBMs.

The shorebird models were, and still are, as simple as they could be made to be in order to do what ecological research ought to be able to do – but very frequently cannot. That is, to be able accurately to predict important aspects of the real ecological world, such as mortality rates and body condition, in novel environments beyond the current empirical range. This is the best test of your understanding of the system one is investigating, of course. To be able to make quantitative predictions successfully provides the best possible evidence that you might be on to something worthwhile, perhaps academically as well as practically.

Box 10.2 Another irritation but this time self-induced!

It was not just peers that could irritate (Box 10.1)! We could irritate ourselves just as well. In retrospect, some ideas, even simple ones, popped into the head after a ridiculously long time, and after much effort had been spent. But there we are; that's just the way it is sometimes!

Box 10.3 Select Committees in the Houses of Parliament

If you get a chance to be a witness at one of these Committees, grab it! It is fascinating! The buildings are wonderful, of course, and the paintings, statues, wood-lined rooms and corridors and well-carpeted floors create an impressive atmosphere. You also bump into many famous people of the day and, of course, are ever aware of the distinguished people who have worked in these buildings in the past. So much so that, when visiting the magnificent toilets, it is difficult not to think of all the famous bottoms that must have once sat there!

But it was the proceedings themselves that were most impressive. The questioning by the barristers was skilful and, it seemed, designed more to undermine the Committees confidence in an opposing witness than to convey the details of the scientific arguments. The questions from the Committee were often very acute, and implied that it really did matter to its members that the best possible decision was reached.

Impressive too was the intense considerations given to one issue in particular: the farm field where lagoon would have been built. The owner used this field to dispose of a great deal of very smelly pig slurry (*i.e.* pig poo). There was much debate as to where he might dispose of this stuff if the lagoon was built and removed his field. Even more impressive was the careful consideration given to one of the previous occupants of the farm. With determined seriousness, much time was spent debating whether the ghost of this person would be excessively disturbed by a change in land-use brought about by the construction of the lagoon. Apparently, the ghost did not like changes being made to the farm and threw things about the farmhouse to express its displeasure whenever it happened. I cannot remember how this matter was resolved, but it was impressive that a Committee of the House of Lords should devote so much careful attention to an issue that must have mattered only to a very few people!

Box 10.4 Calibrating the model

To some, adjusting a value of a parameter until the key output of the model – the mortality rate – is the same as has been observed in the real world smacks of fiddling. And so it would be if you just left it at that! You would definitely get the answer you wanted!

But this is not how proper calibration is carried out. The key element is that, once the re-calibration has been finished, you must to test how well the model predicts in different circumstances. In the case of the redshank model for the Rhymney flats, this test was provided by its successful forecast of the mortality rate after bird numbers had increased by 300 with the arrival of the birds displaced by Cardiff Bay. One must be careful that the parameter chosen for calibrating the model will not itself change when the model is applied to new circumstances, and this condition was certainly met with the Rhymney model.

Ideally, of course, calibration would not be needed. But if the alternative is to give up altogether rather than to re-calibrate, it really is a no-brainer so long as the re-calibrated model can be properly tested.

CHAPTER 11:
Some points to end with

..in which the notion of 'carrying capacity' is discussed and a new definition for shorebirds is developed and the importance of testing model predictions, of knowing the animals' natural history and of density-dependence are stressed

This where the story of the development and initial testing of the individual-based model of non-breeding shorebird populations comes to an end. Subsequently, the final version 3 of the model was replaced by its successor – MORPH – that was developed by Richard Stillman. MORPH is based on the same principles as the IBM shorebird models described in this book but is not shorebird-specific. It was developed in such a way that it could be used, and has been used, for a much wider range of animals than just shorebirds, including fish, diving ducks and flamingoes. It also included a wider range of behavioural decision rules, such as trading off the risk of being taken by a predator against the risk of starving. Papers that describe MORPH are listed at the end of this chapter along with a sample of publications describing how it is being used. There are also references to reviews of the IBM approach.

But before leaving the first shorebird model, there are a few points that arose over the three decades of its development and testing of its predictions which might be worth highlighting.

THE NOTION OF CARRYING CAPACITY

The term 'carrying capacity' is frequently used in discussions of how the value of a site for shorebirds during the non-breeding season might be affected by a change in the management of the resource it provides, usually the food supply. The common-sense idea underlying the notion is that there must be a limit to the number of birds that the food supply can support. Accordingly, the question is often posed: 'Will this proposal (eg. building a barrage or marina; allowing water sports *etc.*) reduce the carrying capacity of the estuary?' However, people use the term in very different ways so that there is uncertainty about how it should be defined and measured and therefore how one can answer the question. Nor is at all clear what deductions for informing management decisions can be made from its use.

Definitions of carrying capacity

In one definition that is widely used in theoretical models of animal populations of all kinds, carrying capacity is equated with the size of a population at equilibrium. As applied to migratory shorebirds, this definition can be dismissed easily. The equilibrium population size occurs when, on average, birth and death rates are equal. Were this definition to be applied to migratory birds, it would mean that the carrying capacity of the non-breeding grounds would be influenced by factors on the breeding grounds because equilibrium population size depends on processes that occur in both parts of the species range. Clearly, this completely misses the purpose of using the concept in relation to the ability of a non-breeding site to support the birds. What could a manager of an estuary in Devon do about the breeding conditions in the Arctic and feeding conditions in migratory stop-over points en route between his/her estuary and the Arctic?

Carrying capacity must therefore be defined in non-breeding shorebirds in a way that refers only to the non-breeding season itself. Two definitions have been used by scientists and conservation managers concerned with these birds. The first, and most widely used, is to define a site's capacity as the maximum number of bird-days that its food supply can support over part or all of the winter. This is the 'bird-days' definition. The second approach is to define carrying capacity as the maximum numbers of birds that are able to survive until the end of the non-breeding season in good condition. This is the 'number of survivors' definition.

Both definitions suffer from a fatal flaw. With carrying capacity defined in either way, birds emigrate or die well before carrying capacity has been reached by amounts that depend on various aspects of their natural history. This point is most easily illustrated using the 'bird-days' definition, the one that is most frequently used.

The issue is this: 'Would removing an amount mudflat by building a marina, for example, reduce the carrying capacity so much that the birds that currently use the site could no longer be supported there?' This is the 'Teesmouth question', as discussed in Chapter 1. As a reminder, imagine that each bird requires 10kgAFDM to survive the non-breeding season in good condition and that 100 birds usually spend the non-breeding season in the site. The population would consume 1000kg (10x100) before the birds departed for the breeding grounds. If the current food supply was 1100kg and building the marina would remove 300kg, leaving just 800kg, one would conclude that the carrying capacity would be reduced below the level required to support the present-day number of birds. If, on the other hand, the current food stock was 3000kg, we could conclude with this approach that, even after the marina had been built, easily enough food (3000 - 300 = 2700kg) would remain for the 100 birds. Therefore the carrying capacity – defined as bird-days - would be still sufficient to support the population of 100 shorebirds.

However, as described in Chapter 1, such a change in site management that apparently left sufficient food to support all the birds might nonetheless increase the mortality rate of the birds, and so reduce their numbers. This is because birds vary, and some will fail a long time before all the available resources of the site has been utilised. This point is illustrated again in Figure 11.1.

Regarding all individuals as being identical may be a conceptual convenience, but it has no basis in fact. The research carried out on shorebirds around the World since the 1970s had shown that it is overwhelmingly unlikely that individual non-breeding shorebirds do not vary in one or other component of competitive ability. Furthermore, to my knowledge, there is no case where a partial change in the feeding conditions has caused a 'step-function' response in the numbers or survival rate of the birds. That is, there is no example where the mortality rate, for example, has flipped suddenly from a very low to a high value (e.g. from 0% to 100%) so that birds became locally extinct. Even at Teesmouth, a partial reduction in the food supply led only to partial reductions in bird numbers and not to a total, 'step-function', collapse in the population. Some individuals left or died while others did not; i.e. they must have been differences between individuals in how they were affected by the loss of feeding habitat.

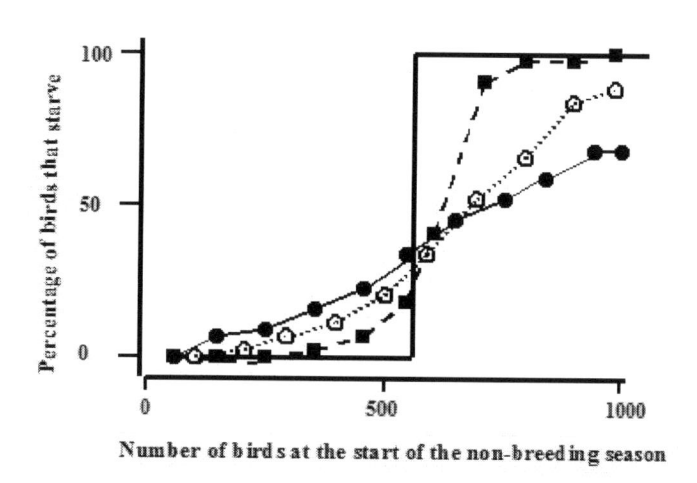

Figure 11.1 How the proportion of birds that starves before the end of the non-breeding season changes as the numbers arriving on the site at the beginning of the non-breeding season increases. The data refer to a hypothetical site where there is enough food to support 600 birds over the non-breeding season: that is, there are 600 rations, each of which would feed one individual for the entire non-breeding season. Defined in term of 'bird-days' or 'daily rations', the carrying capacity of the site is therefore 600 birds over the whole non-breeding season. The thick lines show how many are predicted to starve under this definition of carrying capacity in relation to how many birds occupy the site at the start of the non-breeding season. In the case of the thick solid line, all the birds are assumed to be identical and so there is no difference between them in their competitive abilities. If 599 birds arrive, they all survive. But if 601 arrive, they all starve because all the food runs out just before the end of the non-breeding season. This situation is a 'step function'. The other symbols and lines show what happens when individuals are assumed to vary in competitive ability. The magnitude of the variation amongst individuals is least in the solid squares and dashed line and most in the black dots and solid thin line. The variation is intermediate with the open circles and dotted line. To an increasing degree as the amount of individual variation increases, more and more birds starve well before the 'bird-days' carrying capacity of 600 birds has been reached. These results came from a series of simulations with a simplified version of the shorebird IBM, set up for a notional and typical shorebird species.

There are three fundamental problems with measuring carrying capacity as bird-days or daily rations. The first is that it assumes that the birds only starve when they have consumed all of the available food supply. But as was discussed in Chapter 1, shorebirds seldom eat out all their food supply, yet birds nonetheless starve. If the birds consume at present only 40% of their food supply and the change in management of the site removed another 10%, they would still only consume about 45% of the reduced food stocks, yet more of them would be expected to starve. In the sense of being able to maintain bird numbers, the capacity of the site to keep alive the same number of birds would have been reduced even though its capacity defined in terms of bird-days, or daily rations, was still nowhere near to being exceeded.

A real-world example that illustrates the dangers of using the bird-days/daily rations definition of carrying capacity approach comes from oystercatchers on the Wash. During the 1990s, high winter mortality rates (and low body condition) were recorded in three winters of low shellfish abundance. Chapter 9 describes how, even in years when the carrying capacity defined in terms of the consumable food present was nowhere near fully utilised, many birds starved. Even excluding the stocks of supplementary prey, such as ragworms and clams, the birds did not eat all the food supply available to them, yet up to 20% of adults starved (Fig. 11.2). Had the bird-days carrying capacity of the Wash each winter been used to decide how many shellfish should be harvested, very many oystercatchers would have starved or lost condition every year, and not just during the years of extreme shortage. The resulting high mortality rates repeated annually would have slashed the population by an even greater amount than actually occurred. It is therefore not safe to argue that, because spare bird-days or daily rations carrying capacity would remain after a change in coastal management regime had been implemented, the birds would be unaffected. In fact, the change in regime might substantially reduce their numbers. A real case where this disastrous approach was used to decide the policy for harvesting shellfish is described in Box 11.1.

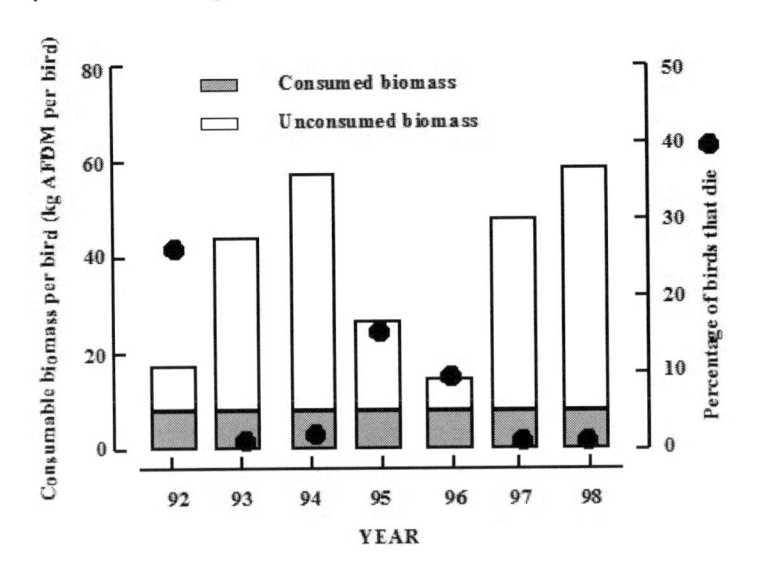

Figure 11.2 How much of their shellfish food stocks were eaten by oystercatchers on the Wash in relation to the mortality rate of the birds over the non-breeding season. Irrespective of the amount of food present per oystercatcher at the start of the non-breeding season, and irrespective of the mortality rate of the birds, there is always a great deal of food left uneaten by the end of the non-breeding season, even in years of very low initial stocks when very large numbers of oystercatchers starved to death – eg. 1992.

The second objection is that the bird-days carrying capacity approach cannot predict the effect of a change in coastal management on the demographic rates that determine population size. This difficulty is not immediately apparent and is often over-looked because of the superficial similarity between the two concepts: "bird-days" and "population size". But predicting the bird-days carrying capacity of a site is not the same as predicting the effect on population size. Bird-days carrying capacity is simply the maximum numbers of birds that the food supply, in principle, could support.

It is not equivalent to a demographic rate – the reproductive rate and the mortality rate - which are the parameters that actually determine population size in the long-term. In fact, it is just another way of measuring the food supply. Instead of using the total biomass of food present, or the total amount of energy or nutrient, the unit of measurement of the food supply is the number of daily rations that are present at the beginning of the non-breeding season.

As discussed above, the bird-days carrying capacity approach assumes that all individuals are identical, which is never the case. As Figure 11.1 illustrates, this assumption would mean that either all birds survive or all the birds starve or emigrate. In fact, as empirical studies on oystercatchers (Fig. 11.3) and modelling studies on, for example, brent geese (Fig.11.4) demonstrate, the proportion of birds starving increases gradually as the density of birds increases rather than as an all-or-nothing step function. This is because the worst competitors start dying quite early as numbers rise because they cannot collect their daily energy requirements in the time available even though plenty of food – in principle – remains. Food acquisition is not simply a question of picking up a packaged daily ration of food, as if in a supermarket. It is a rate process in which the rate of intake of food-stuffs must at least match the rate at which they are used up by the birds if starvation is to be avoided. Factors that affect the rate of feeding, such as the presence of competitors and individual differences in foraging efficiency, and factors that affect the amount of time the birds have available for feeding – such as the tidal conditions - therefore have an important influence on the birds' chances of surviving the non-breeding season in good condition.

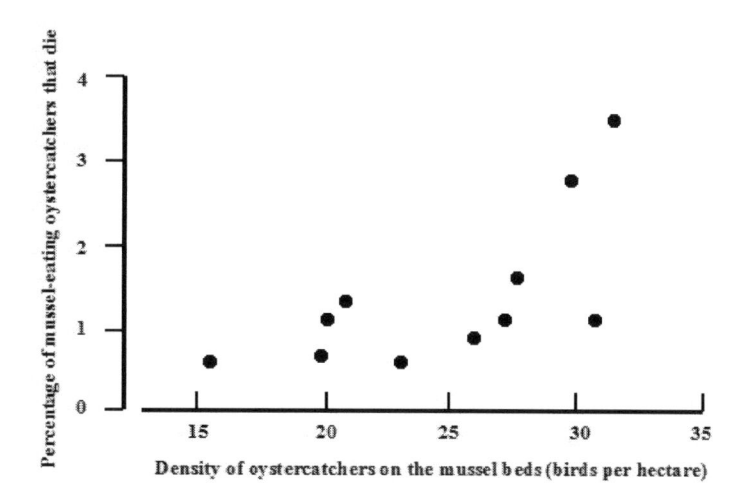

Figure 11.3 The density-dependent mortality of mussel-eating adult oystercatchers on the Exe estuary. Much of the variation in the mortality rate recorded in individual years could be explained by whether the winter weather was severe or clement.

This point can also be illustrated by the results of the IBM of the Wash shellfishery. As described in Chapter 9, the model was used to predict by how much winter survival rate would be improved in years of general shellfish shortage if artificial mussel beds were laid somewhere in the intertidal zone. The reduction in mortality varied enormously according to the level of the shore at which the mussels were placed and the area over which they were spread (Fig. 9.8). Putting a tonne of mussels at high shore-levels reduced the mortality rate by a great deal more than did putting the same amount of mussels lower down the shore. This is because placing mussels upshore extended the amount of time for which birds could feed on this highly profitable and preferred food over each tidal cycle. Spreading a tonne of mussels at a particular shore-level over a large area rather than a small one was also more effective at reducing the mortality rate. This happened because spreading the mussels out reduced the amount of interference because the sub-dominants could more easily avoid being attacked by dominants in the greater amount of foraging space that was available. These model results show that, because consumption is a time-constrained rate process, a tonne of mussels can have very different value in terms of bird survival, and therefore bird numbers, depending on its location and how it is provided. In contrast, the bird-days carrying capacity approach attributes the same value to a tonne of food, wherever and however it is provided.

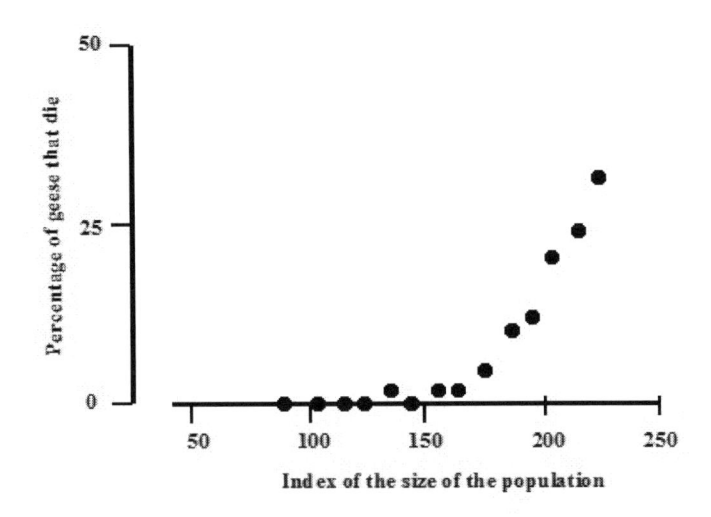

Figure 11.4 *The mortality rate of brent geese predicted by the multi-site model when the birds are allowed to move to another site when they are beginning to lose body condition.*

A similar result emerged from the model of the putative lagoon proposed for the Rhymney flats to mitigate for the loss of Cardiff Bay (Chapter 10). A given amount of food in the lagoon increased the survival rate of redshank substantially whereas the same amount placed on the main mudflats of the estuary made no difference (Fig. 10.11). This contrast again arose because the lagoon provided extra foraging time for the birds rather than extra food. The lagoon's narrow entrance held back the advancing tide for 40 minutes after the mudflats outside in the main estuary had been completely covered.

Ignoring the fact that feeding is a rate process, and therefore is constrained by the time available, was a very bizarre consequence of thinking in terms of bird-days and daily rations. It was also potentially very dangerous to the cause of conservation, as the experience in the Wadden Sea showed (Box 11.1). As a consequence of just leaving enough food after the shellfish harvest to provide for the physiological requirements of all the birds that ate shellfish, a great many of them starved and their populations declined until the policy was abandoned. Indeed, the Wadden Sea population seemed to be heading for extinction had the previous shellfishing policy persisted.

The third difficulty with the bird-days approach is how to decide what should be included in the calculation of the amount of food that is present. Consider a species, such as the oystercatcher, that uses supplementary sources of food, such as earthworms in fields, in addition to its normal intertidal prey species. They would first be expected to eat out their main bivalve and polychaete foods in the intertidal areas: *i.e.* to exploit all of the bird-days or daily ration carrying capacity of the intertidal zone. They would then switch to feeding on earthworms in coastal meadows, a switch that is probably very important for their survival and body condition. How would one then calculate the carrying capacity of the fields? As the earthworms in the first field to be utilised become depleted, the birds would move to the next and so on and so on and so on! Unlike an estuary, there is no obvious boundary to the area which could provide earthworms. At what point would one stop adding fields to the calculation of the total quantity of earthworms in the birds' food supply? In the case of brent geese arriving on the south-eastern coast of England at the start of the non-breeding season, they could in principle gradually graze their way along the food gradient until they reached Land's End at the extreme west end of southern England!

A better concept of carrying capacity?

Despite all these reservations about the definitions of carrying capacity that have been frequently used, the notion of carrying capacity may still retain some usefulness if a realistic and usable definition for it can be found. It really is useful when discussing a proposed change in the way in which an estuary is managed to ask whether it would affect its carrying capacity. The question: 'Will it reduce the capacity of the site' is a very simple question, the implications of which are easily understood by everyone – albeit invariably in a rather vague, and often different, way. But to answer the question with good science, a clear and relevant definition is required.

It is timely at this point to return to the logic set out in Chapter 1. This discusses how the idea of developing individual-based models began to take shape. In most cases where predictions are required, we need to be able to predict how a change in the quality, quantity and accessibility of the food supply (the "feeding conditions") will "affect" the birds; *i.e.* affect their chances of survival over the non-breeding season and their body condition as they set off on their Spring migration. As was described in Chapter 1, this usually means predicting the effect of a change in the management of the site on the intensity of competition amongst the birds. For example, a general reduction in the abundance of the food supply arising, for example, from a change in the nutrient status of an estuary, causes depletion competition to intensify because the food supply becomes depleted earlier in the non-breeding season as there is less food there at the start. Figure 11.5 shows that it also usually means that the surface area occupied by the best feeding areas will be reduced so that interference competition in these preferred feeding places will also intensify. A reduced area of food (e.g. arising either permanently from habitat loss or temporarily from disturbance, or from a general decline in the abundance of food) causes birds to feed at higher densities, so depletion and interference competition intensify, giving the same result. Reduced foraging time (e.g. by preventing birds feeding at the top of the shore as the tide ebbs and flows, draining coastal meadows or removing salt pans) reduces the chances that inferior competitors will be able to compensate for their competitive failure to obtain sufficient food supplies over the main low water feeding period.

Habitat loss reduces both the overall area available for feeding and the total amount and so permanently intensifies both depletion and interference competition. Disturbance has the same effect, but only temporarily.

Estuary managers should therefore not ask whether a proposed change would mean that the site in question would no longer contain enough food to sustain the numbers of birds that it presently supports. Rather, they should ask whether the proposed change is likely to decrease the percentage of the bird population that survive the non-breeding season in good enough condition to migrate successfully to the breeding areas at the end. For example, perhaps 5% of the birds currently starve over the non-breeding season. If the proposal was predicted to increase the mortality rate above this 'base' level to 6 or 7%. it would be correct to say that the carrying capacity was predicted to decrease.

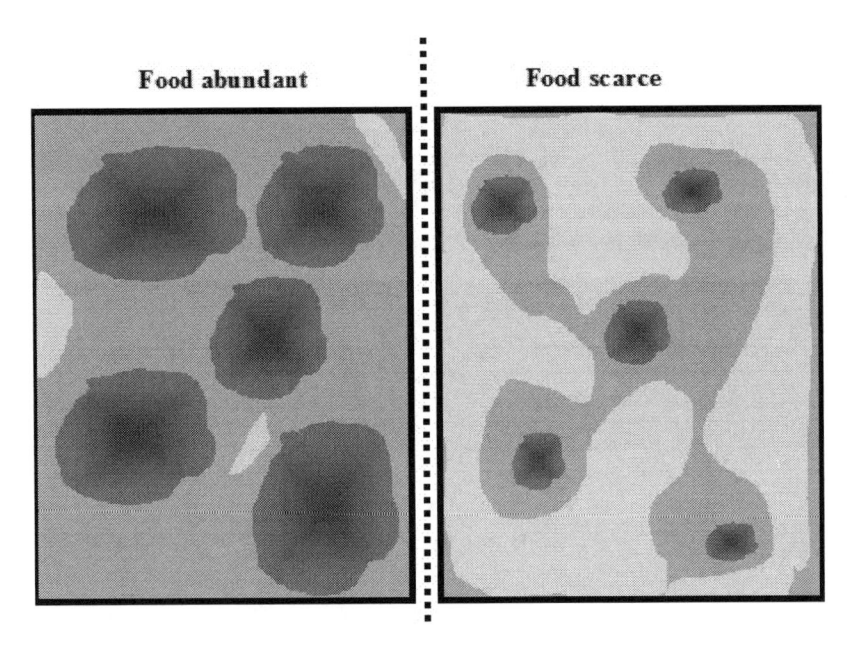

Figure 11.5 *How a general reduction in the food supply reduces the surface area covered by good quality feeding patches and thus intensifies interference competition. The dark blobs show the high-density or high-quality patches of food that provide the best feeding conditions for the birds, which therefore compete to feed there. When food is very abundant, large areas are covered by high quality patches whereas this is not the case when the food supply is generally reduced. There is no food at all in the palest areas.*

However, it is also important to take into account the fact that the numbers of shorebirds arriving in the non-breeding areas at the end of the breeding season will vary between years. If the mortality rate (and body condition) are density-dependent, it would be useless to use only one base value of the mortality rate (or average body condition) to define the carrying capacity of a site. Both the mortality rate and body condition would depend on the size of the population that arrives at the start of the non-breeding season. The base rate, as it were, would extend over a range of values, depending on the population size. And, of course, numbers would change for reasons quite unconnected with the management of the non-breeding site itself. The feeding conditions and risk of predation and disease on the breeding areas and in other non-breeding and stop-over sites within the birds' range would influence how many birds arrived on the 'subject' site at the start of the non-breeding season.

Any method for measuring carrying capacity must therefore incorporate the notion of density dependence. There seems to be only one solution and that is to define carrying capacity in a way that recognises that the mortality rate (and body condition) will vary in response to the fluctuating number of birds that occupy on the site at the start of the non-breeding season. Figure 11.6 illustrates a definition that would do this. The solid line shows the density-dependent function prior to the proposed change in the management of the site: this represents the current status quo. If a proposal is made that does not change this function, then it will not affect the survival of the birds or their body condition, however many birds happen to occupy the site at the beginning of the non-breeding season. Therefore, the proposal would not affect the size of their population and the conservation status of the site, its carrying capacity, would be maintained.

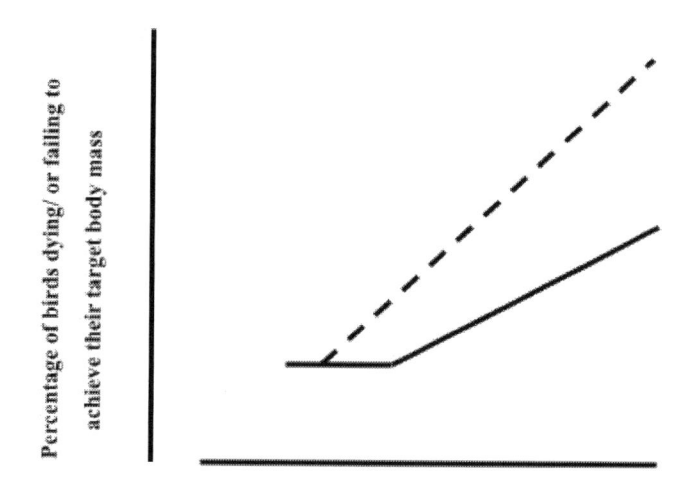

Figure 11.6 How the definition of 'carrying capacity' might be addressed. The black line shows the present-day, density-dependent mortality or body condition functions of the shorebirds occupying a site. A change in management has been proposed for the site; eg. building a car park over an area of mud. The dashed line shows the function that is predicted to apply after the mudflat has been removed. Because of this habitat loss and the resulting intensification of the competition amongst the birds, at any one initial population size, the mortality rate is higher or fewer birds achieve their target body mass by the time they migrate to the breeding areas. The conclusion is that the loss of habitat would reduce the capacity of the site to support birds in good condition over the non-breeding season. Note that, in the dashed line, the mortality becomes density-dependent at a lower population size and subsequently increases at a higher rate.

But if the proposed change in the management of the site would cause the density-dependent function to rise up the vertical axis, it would mean that, at a given population size at the start of the non-breeding season, an increased proportion of birds would starve or fail to reach their target body condition by the end (Fig. 11.6). Bird numbers would therefore decline, and the conservation status of the site would have been reduced. The carrying capacity of the site would have been reduced because its ability to support birds in good condition throughout the non-breeding season would have been reduced.

The main message, then, is that coastal managers should not ask whether a proposed change would mean that there would no longer contain enough food to sustain current bird numbers: remember the experience of the mollusc-eating birds in the Dutch Wadden Sea! Rather, they should ask whether the proposed change is likely to change the density-dependent mortality (or body condition) function. This is the key question. If someone asks: 'Will this proposal change the carrying capacity of the site?', everyone present should understand that this is a short-hand way of saying: 'Will this proposal change the density-dependent mortality function and/or the density-dependent body condition function of the shorebirds involved?' Answers can be sought in studies of present-day demographic processes and rates as a function of population size and of the food supply and by individual-based modelling, and probably other forms of modelling also.

An important caveat

In Figure 11.6, the mortality rate (or body-condition) is shown as being density-dependent across most of the range in the size of the population. This may occur regularly in non-breeding shorebirds, but not enough is known for it to be argued that density-dependence across the normal range of population size is the general case. It is entirely possible, in fact, that bird numbers are sometimes so low relative to the feeding conditions that the function is 'flat' across a wide range of population size and density; *i.e.* it is density-independent over a wide range of population size. This may increasingly be the case in many southern and western coasts of the UK if, in response to the warming climate, the numbers of wintering shorebirds continues to decline due to their movement to winter quarters nearer to their breeding areas, and so further to the north and east. The multi-site model of brent geese illustrates a case where there is a wide range of population sizes across which the mortality rate in the non-breeding season is independent of population density (Fig. 11.4).

When advising policy-makers, it is very important to know whether a population lies to the left or the right of the threshold population size or density at which mortality becomes density-dependent. We really need not be concerned about the effect of a proposed reduction in the feeding conditions if the population density currently lies well to the left of this inflexion point (Fig. 11.7). Even a series of habitat losses will have no effect on the birds until the inflexion point is reached. It is therefore no more appropriate to argue (as is sometimes done) that a series of piecemeal reductions "must have a cumulative effect the birds" than it is to say that summing any number of zeros still yields a total of zero! Only when the birds' density occurs near to or to the right of the inflexion point will a further deterioration in the feeding conditions reduce fitness and thus population size. In other words, the only consequence of a series of habitat removals in a density-independent region of the mortality function is to bring the site closer and closer to the threshold point at which the mortality will begin to increase following further habitat deterioration.

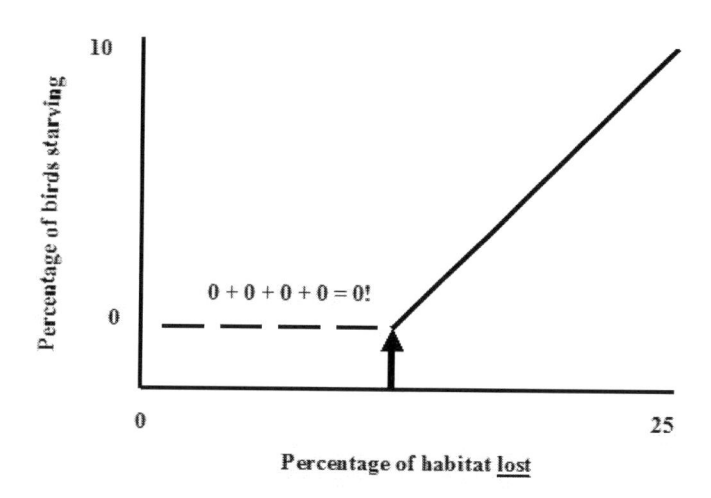

Figure 11.7 *A hypothetical example of how removing feeding areas will not reduce bird numbers by increasing their rate of mortality until a certain threshold value – shown by the thick arrow - has been reached. A series of small losses that have no impact on survival will, in combination, still produce a zero impact. What they will do, however, is bring the site closer and closer to the threshold, the point at which further reductions in the food supply will increase the mortality rate of the birds.*

SOME LESSONS FROM DEVELOPING THE SHOREBIRD IBM

The vital importance of testing model predictions

If I were a manager of the coast and a scientist said that a model could be used to predict whether a change in management policy would have an impact on the birds, my first response would be: 'OK: but first you need to convince me that I should have confidence in the predictions of your model. You must be able to assure me that I should believe what it says would happen if I changed our policy! And what's more, you have to be able to persuade me that it will also convince potential objectors from conservation organisation. Failure in this regard could involve me in an expensive and time-consuming enquiry'.

The very necessary task of raising confidence in model predictions is not made any easier by an apparently gut reaction of some people to be highly suspicious of models and unconvinced of their utility (Box 11.2). Again as in all science, the key to confidence is exhaustively to test the predictions against events in the real world – whether the predictions come from numerical models or from a theory or hypothesis expressed in words.

This is because the model represents the current understanding of what is important in the system that is being modelled – in our case, non-breeding shorebird populations. The shorebird model includes many components that have to varying degrees been tested, such as the equations that are used to predict the asymptote of the functional response and the parameters of the interference function. But even if every single such component has been thoroughly tested, it does not follow that, when they are put together into a model of a particular population in a particular estuary, the predictions of that model are themselves accurate. This is because the understanding, the conceptual model or the hypothesis upon which the whole thing is based, may itself be flawed. A wonderful model - much-loved by its creator – that may only contain thoroughly tested components may still fail miserably to make accurate predictions because, for example, some very important processes have not yet been discovered and so are not represented in the model.

In the case of the shorebird model, it is assumed – on the basis of quite good evidence - that the feeding conditions play a major role in determining the body condition and survival of the birds. But perhaps, in reality and still unknown to us, disease is actually more important. Imagine, for example, that most of the birds that die during a difficult period of the non-breeding season do not die because they starve but because, when they are in poor condition, they are finished off by a certain pathogen that is abundant in their non-breeding site. Without that pathogen being present, most birds would survive the difficult period and recover after it had passed. Now imagine two such sites that have identical feeding conditions but very different amounts of the pathogen. Removing 10% of the food supply in each site would be expected to make it more difficult for the birds to acquire their food requirements so that a few more would starve. In the pathogen-free site, the mortality rate would increase a little. But in the site with the pathogen, the mortality rate would rise by a great deal more when the pathogen wreaks havoc amongst the weakened birds. The model might predict the increased rate of starvation, and therefore overall mortality rate, in the first site very successfully, but it would greatly underestimate the increased mortality rate in the second because it does not include the lethal influence of the pathogen.

This example may – or may not – be far-fetched but it makes the point that a model is only as good as the appropriateness of the ecological understanding upon which it is based. The model is actually a quantified representation of our hypothesis as to how the mortality rate of the birds is determined. Since it is just an hypothesis, on scientific grounds alone its predictions should be thoroughly tested in the normal way of science. But as managers of the coast may base important management decisions on its output, there is an additional necessity to do so, and to do so thoroughly.

That accepted, it is then vital to test the predictions in the proper way. Much can be said about this, but there is one particularly important and astonishing failure that I have encountered in the shorebird community in the understanding of how to test model predictions (Box 11.3). It is illustrated in Figure 11.8. The plot at the top of the figure shows a case where there is a good correlation between the values that the model predicts and the values recorded in nature. The predicted and the observed values vary together very well indeed. A predicted high value is matched by an observed high value and *vice versa*. The correlation coefficient (R^2) that measures the closeness of the association between the predicted and observed values is very high, and almost at its maximum possible value of unity. The trouble is that the predicted values are several times higher than the observed ones! A model has only very limited utility if it can only predict where or when high values occur and where and when low values will occur if its predictions are massively too high.

The lower graph shows the ideal outcome. Here the predicted and observed values are, on average, identical: if the model predicts a value of 10%, the observed vale is also about 10%, and not 1%! Accordingly, when the predicted and observed values are plotted against each other, they fall along the line of perfect fit in which the slope is 1 and the intercept is 0. In other words, the data fall along the $y = x$ line of perfect fit across the whole range. This is the dream outcome of any such test!

Of course, the tests must not only be unbiased but also extensive, and meeting this condition has not been easy with the shorebird model. Figure 11.9 shows the results of the limited number of tests that have been made of its predictions for the mortality rate over the non-breeding season. They are encouraging, but there are good reasons for arguing that far more tests would be desirable.

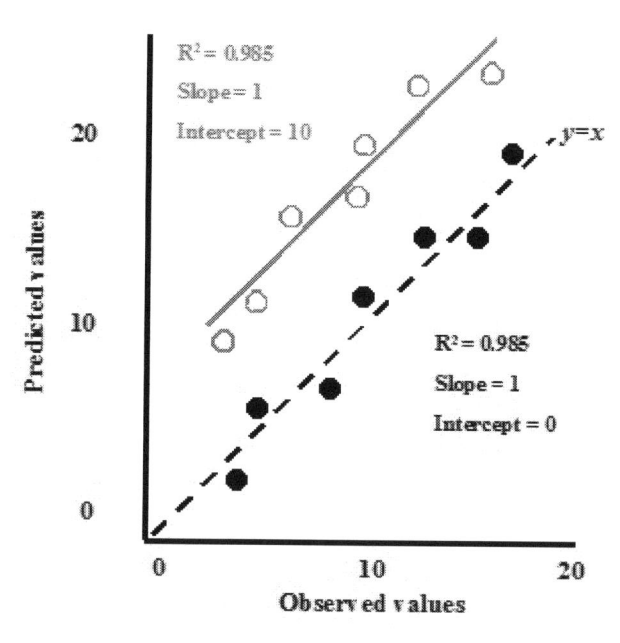

Figure 11.8 *Why a high correlation between real-world observed values and those predicted by a model does not necessarily mean that the model makes accurate predictions. The predicted and observed values need to fall along the line of perfect fit, where y = x.*

First of all, the two predictions for the oystercatchers on the Wash in years of shellfish abundance and shellfish scarcity depend for their accuracy on the estimated value of the intake rate of oystercatchers feeding upshore, and this was taken from the Exe and not measured on the Wash itself. Second, the prediction for oystercatchers in the Burry Inlet relies on the assumption that the mortality rate there was very low because so few birds fed in the fields over high water. Although this is very likely to be the case, there was no actual estimate of the real mortality rate in the Burry Inlet at that time. This means that there are only three really 'solid' tests of the model's predictions for the mortality rate in just two species: (i) the two for oystercatchers on the Exe at the low and the high population size, and its dependence on the density of the birds on the mussel beds, and (ii) the increase in the mortality rate of redshank at Rhymney after the birds displaced from Cardiff Bay arrived. Sadly, more tests cannot be made in the many other sites and on the many other species that have now been modelled. This is because the mortality of shorebirds over the non-breeding season have seldom been measured.

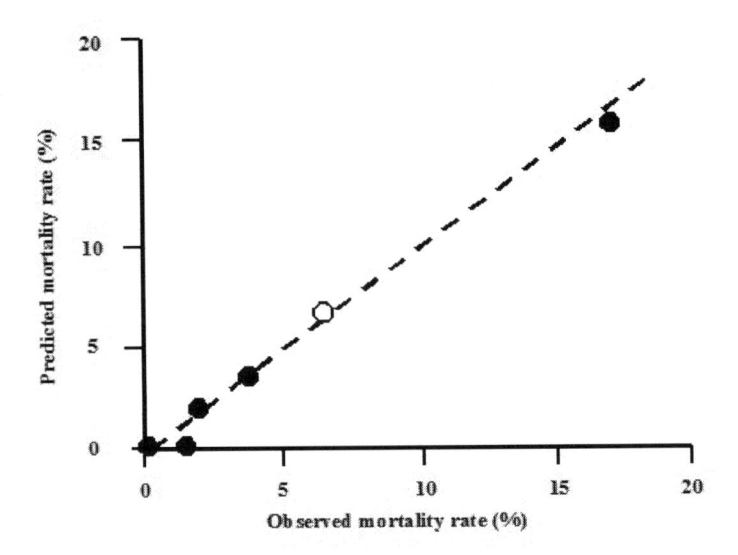

Figure 11.9 Comparison between the predicted and observed percentage mortality rate of oystercatchers (solid circles) and redshank over the non-breeding season.

This is unfortunate, not only because of the need to test model predictions, but also because the observed values provide a means of calibrating the model, as the examples from the Exe and Rhymney illustrated. Ideally, the model should be calibrated for a period of years and then its predictions separately tested for another group of years: this is how it was done with the Exe mussel-feeding oystercatchers, for example. It was enormous boost to confidence when the model predicted that the mortality rate of mussel-feeders would be density-dependent across the range of densities that occurred over the 1970's to 1990's and did so at a time when this had not yet been established by observation in the field.

Such critical tests between predicted and observed mortality rates can seldom be carried out without a research project conducted on a scale that can only rarely be achieved. But fortunately, another measure for calibrating a model and testing its predictions is available. It is common sense - and something that has been well-established by field studies over several decades - that hungry shorebirds feed for much longer each day than do satiated ones. If at some stage during the non-breeding season most of the birds are feeding for every moment of the time for which food is accessible to them, we can be pretty sure that many of them are finding it difficult to meet their daily food requirements and that, probably, some of them are losing body condition and *en route* to starving. A comparison between the predicted and observed amount of time spent feeding by the average bird at the most critical periods – usually late in the non-breeding season - is therefore a good test of the model's ability to predict when the birds are 'hard-pressed' for food; that is, experiencing 'food stress'. Furthermore, the model can also be calibrated in the first place by adjusting the most appropriate parameter values until it predicts the amount of time spent feeding at another period of the non-breeding season, perhaps at the beginning when the birds are seldom hard-pressed.

Happily, it is not difficult to measure the amount of times spent feeding by the average shorebird in most sites. Such measurements have been made regularly for over 50 years now in places as variable in size as the diminutive Ythan estuary in Scotland and the huge embayment of the Wash. The occasions that this test has been applied to the predictions of the shorebird model up to the time of writing are shown in Figure 11.10. It is very encouraging that the predictions fall along and either side of the line of perfect fit; the 'y=x' line. It is especially encouraging too that that so many species in so many different places in Europe contribute to this result.

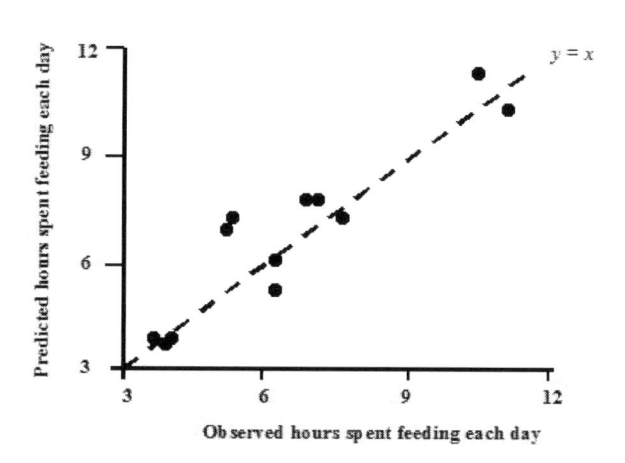

Figure 11.10 Comparisons between model predictions and the observed amount of time spent feeding by an average bird over a single daylight tidal cycle. The filled circles refer to oystercatchers on the Exe estuary, Burry Inlet and Bangor flats. The open circles refer to sanderling, curlew, dunlin and little stint on the Seine estuary and bahia de Cadiz.

There are other tests as well which add to the confidence with which the predictions can be viewed. The best ones are those that require many aspects of the model to represent the real world accurately in order to be able to 'get it right'. Here is an example, again from mussel-eating oystercatchers of the Exe. On the Exe estuary, surveys of the mussel stocks in autumn and in spring showed that, on average over 8 years, 12.1% of the mussels in the size range eaten by oystercatchers disappeared over the winter, and exclosure experiments confirmed that the great majority of the mussels that disappeared had been taken by oystercatchers. The model predicted that just under 12% would be taken by oystercatchers, which is pretty close to the amount that was actually taken by the birds (Fig. 6.13)!

There is plenty of opportunity for the model to have failed to predict the real outcome so well. Apart from the possibility that the daily energy requirements of oystercatchers may not have been represented well in the model, both the model birds and real birds ate many prey items other than mussels, such as clams and earthworms. That the model predicted with such accuracy the mortality inflicted on the mussels by oystercatchers suggests that it represented the important processes of mussel consumption with some precision.

These successful tests do not mean, however, that no further tests are required. Far from it! The ecology and feeding conditions of the birds vary enormously between sites and we cannot assume that a new model for a new site will be as successful as those shown in Figures 11.9 and 11.10. It is most important that every application of the shorebird model to a particular species or group of species in any site must include a test of how well the model's predictions for the amount of time spent feeding match the values that have been observed in the field in that site. The calibration of a model and its successful test using this method should, I hope, give managers of the coast the confidence they need to base their practical decisions upon it.

It can be important as well to test that the model accurately represents the precise way in which the birds use an estuary. Imagine a coastal manager who needs to know whether allowing people to kite surf in the vicinity of an important feeding area for shorebirds should be forbidden or, at least, controlled in some way. A model is therefore commissioned. The outputs show that there is no impact of the kite-surfing on shorebirds. This result might be very disappointing to those who don't like kite-surfing on aesthetic grounds or because they think that the shorebirds will regard the kites as potential – and enormous – threatening birds of prey: well, perhaps! But anyway, if the surfers are close enough, they certainly would disturb birds.

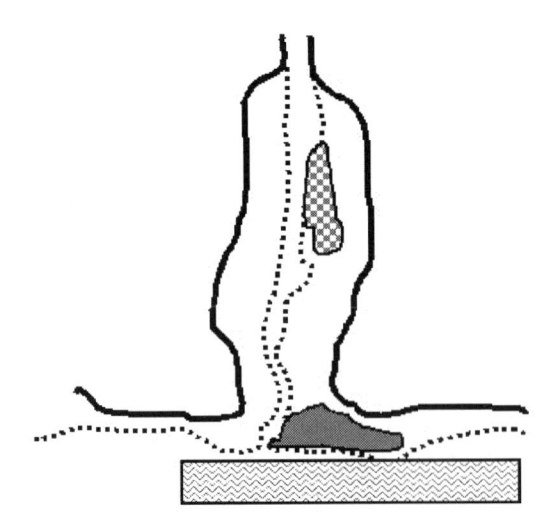

Figure 11.11 *Disturbance and where model birds feed. The rectangle shaded with wiggly lines shows the area where kite-surfing takes place in a hypothetical estuary. The area with solid grey shading is where the real shorebirds feed at low tide. The hatched area is where the first version of the model incorrectly predicts where the birds should feed. Clearly, model birds are at no risk of being disturbed by the surfers whereas, in the real world, they certainly are.*

But then somebody finds that the model did not place model birds in the part of the estuary where kite-surfing actually occurs *(Fig. 11.11)*. No wonder the model predicted no impact of kite-surfing! For some reason, the model had under-estimated the value to the birds of this part of the estuary, so none of the model birds fed there. The model must therefore be adjusted by increasing the relative attractiveness of the area adjacent to the kite-surfers until the numbers of model birds predicted to use that place is the same as the number that was observed: that is, a minor but vital re-calibration of the model is carried out. Now the model birds are subjected to disturbance from kite-surfers, as are real birds. Kite-surfing is now predicted by the model to have an impact on the birds' chances of surviving the non-breeding season in good condition. By the way, I might just as easily have used bird-watchers as kite-surfers in this wholly hypothetical example!

In other words, every possible test should be made, not only of the main predictions of the model – the birds' mortality rate and, if possible, body condition – but also for how well it represents the risks to which the birds are put by any proposal to change the management of the site.

For managers of the coast to believe what the model tells them and to risk being challenged in enquiries and courts at all levels of the 'system', they must have confidence in the predictions. In my opinion, no contract should be awarded for a model unless it contains critical $y=x$ tests of its predictions. In the absence of such tests, there is a risk that there will be a 'rubbish-in, rubbish-out' situation. This is bad for the objective manager of the coast, bad for the people subjected to the consequences of an ill-informed decision and bad for the reputation of the science on which the decisions are based. It is not good either for the cause of shorebird conservation.

Importance of the birds' natural history

In modelling, simplicity is widely regarded as 'good' because it makes it much easier to understand just how the model reaches its conclusions. A simple model has simple workings so that the provenance of its outputs can usually be easily understood and, if not, alternative explanations can be easily explored with further simulations. Often we are asked to model a particular system to provide advice that can be applied to the management of that site, and it would be very useful for all concerned if the resulting model was simple rather than complex. Accordingly, a number of attempts have been made by shorebird biologists to marry the 'virtues' of simplicity and of relevance in their models. It is hoped that not only will such models help resolve a particular management issue but they will also provide insights that would be expected to apply to many systems, and not just to the one being modelled.

But we must be very careful in our pursuit of simplicity not to leave out vital aspects of the natural history of the species in order to achieve it. This is another important reason why shorebird modellers should get out into the field themselves and see what actually happens: it can be very important to fully appreciate the natural history of the birds. The natural history of the birds is their survival strategy and, when predicting survival, it is self-evident that the birds' natural history should not be ignored if reliable predictions are to be obtained!

The development of the model for the Exe estuary mussel-feeding oystercatchers illustrated this point. It was only by adding yet more details of the birds' natural history in the third version of the model that the predictions for the mortality rate matched those that had been observed over the first five years of the study.

Details of the birds foraging environment can also be crucial. In the case of the Exe model, including the muddy feeding areas upshore of the mussel beds and in the nearby fields proved to be vital to the success of the model. So too was including the ebb and flow of the tide and its effect on the area of the mussel beds that was accessible to the birds at any one stage of the tidal cycle. This point is worth expanding as it will illustrate just how subtle can be some of the processes that affect the survival chances of oystercatchers.

In the absence of serious depletion, the density-dependent mortality function recorded in the mussel-eating oystercatchers of the Exe was suggested by modelling to be caused almost entirely by interference competition. We therefore expected that the individuals that would be most likely to use supplementary feeding areas over high water and also to starve would be the least dominant individuals whose intake rate would be most reduced by interference. However, as discussed in Chapter 6, fieldwork showed that, in fact, the individuals most likely to use the fields and to starve were the least efficient ones (Fig. 6.10). Surprisingly, there was little relationship between an individual's dominance and the frequency with which it used the fields and on its chances of starving.

At first sight, the suggestion that feeding efficiency is more important than interference in competition for food seems at variance with the conclusion that the density-dependent mortality is due to interference, not depletion. However, this is not so and the finding can be understood as follows. On the Exe estuary, the difference between the water level low tide and at high tide – the tidal range - varies from about two metres on Neap tides to well over four metres on Spring tides, this variation in tidal range being common in British estuaries. As mussel beds on the Exe mostly lie between mid-shore and extreme low water mark on Spring tides, the proportion of the mussel beds that is exposed and so accessible to oystercatchers varies through each tidal cycle and through the fortnightly Neap-Spring cycle too. The largest area of mussels is accessible to oystercatchers over low tide. Accordingly, over low water on most Spring and mid-tides, the birds can spread out so that their density is very low over most of the low tide period, as is shown by the profiles of the density of oystercatchers on a typical mussel bed in Figure 11.12.

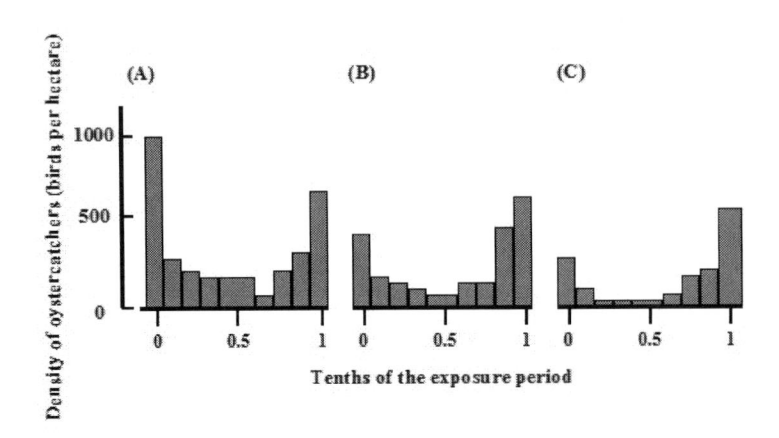

Figure 11.12 The average density of oystercatchers in 25x25m squares over one, typical mussel bed of the Exe estuary through the exposure period on (A) Neap, (B) mid- and (C) Spring tides. The length of the exposure period varies over the Neap-Spring fortnightly cycle, and also from day-to-day, according to the wind strength and direction and to the amount of fresh water coming down the river into the estuary. Accordingly, each exposure period was sub-divided into time periods of one-tenth of the exposure period. On mid- and Spring tides, the average density of birds was less than the 100-200 birds/ha, the threshold density at which interference begins to occur.

In fact, for much of the exposure period, the densities of oystercatchers on the mussel beds are well below the threshold density of 100-200 birds/ha at which interference begins to occur. Accordingly, for most of this period, interference will not affect the intake of many, if any, of the birds, even the least dominant. How well a bird forages at these low densities will depend, by definition, on its efficiency. It is likely that the most efficient birds will be able to obtain most of their food requirement over this part of the tidal cycle.

By contrast, it is likely to be mainly the least efficient individuals that will have to feed on the mussel beds as the tide recedes and advances at the beginning and end of the exposure period. These are, of course, the stages of the exposure period when bird densities are regularly high enough for interference to depress the intake rate of the sub-dominants. Although it is their sub-dominance that causes their intake rate to be depressed by interference at these stages of the exposure period, it is their low foraging efficiency that, in the first place, causes them to be subjected to it. Figure 11.13 illustrates this idea in schematic form.

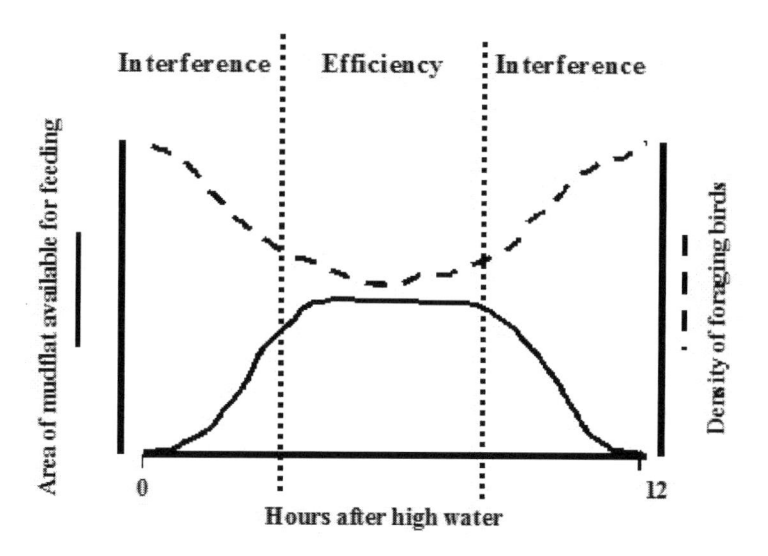

Figure 11.13 *A representation of how an individual's foraging efficiency and dominance influence its rate of food consumption at different stages of the tidal exposure period. Over low tide, when a large part of the mussel bed is exposed, the density of competitors is low enough for the bird's intake rate to be determined largely by its efficiency. At the beginning and end of the exposure period, however, its dominance is likely to be important since the density of competitors is high because much less of the mussel bed is exposed and so accessible to the birds.*

Hence, a bird's foraging efficiency is the pre-determinant of whether it will be at risk of interference, and it is their dominance that then determines how strong the effect of that interference will be on their rate of consumption at the more competitive stages of the tidal cycle. The situation in Neap tides is similar but, because so much of the mussel beds do not expose even at low tide, interference will affect the intake rate of subdominants for a greater proportion of the exposure period. Nonetheless, it is the most efficient individuals that will still be most likely to be able to avoid feeding at the beginning and end of the exposure period when competitor densities are particularly high. Although this explanation has yet to be tested in the field, it does explain satisfactorily why the foraging efficiency of an individual has so much influence on its use of supplementary upshore and terrestrial feeding sites and why the mortality rate – which only affects a small minority of the population – is nonetheless density-dependent.

The point of this story is that it illustrates how details of the natural history of the birds – that were entirely unforeseen - can be very important to both understanding of how starvation occurs but also to accurate prediction by the shorebird model. The model could have been greatly simplified by ignoring the variation in the exposure of the mussel beds and using the mean area exposed across all exposure periods and over the Neap-Spring cycle. But that would have left out an aspect of the oystercatcher's natural environment that proved to be rather critical to understanding how density-dependent mortality arises. And as was argued at the start of this book, density-dependence is the key to understanding how changes in the foraging environment of these birds will affect their chances of surviving the non-breeding season in good enough condition to return to the breeding areas in Spring. It is therefore very important that the density-dependent processes are represented in the model both accurately and realistically. And to achieve that, keeping a continuing close eye on the natural history of the animals and on their environment is vitally important.

REFERENCES FOR CHAPTER 11

Caldow, R.W.G., Goss-Custard, J.D., Stillman, R.A., Durell, S.E.A. le V. dit, Swinfen, R. & Bregnballe, T. (1999). Individual variation in the competitive ability of interference-prone foragers: the relative importance of foraging efficiency and susceptibility to interference. *Journal of Animal Ecology*, **68**, 869-878.

Durell, S.E.A. le V. dit, Goss-Custard, J.D., Clarke, R.T. & McGrorty, S. (2000). Density-dependent mortality in oystercatchers *Haematopus ostralegus*. *Ibis*, **142**, 132-138.

Durell, S.E.A. Le V. dit, Goss-Custard, J.D., Clarke, R.T. & McGrorty. S. (2003). Density-dependent mortality in wintering Eurasian Oystercatchers *Haematopus ostralegus*. *Ibis*, **145**, 496-498.

Durell, S.E.A. le V. dit. Goss-Custard, J.D., Stillman, R.A., & West, R.A. (2001). The effect of weather and density-dependence on oystercatcher *Haematopus ostralegus* winter mortality. *Ibis*, **143**, 498-499.

Goss-Custard, J.D. (1985). Foraging behaviour of wading birds and the carrying capacity of estuaries. *Behavioural Ecology: Ecological Consequences of Adaptive Behaviour*. (Ed. by R.M. Sibly & R.H. Smith), pp. 169-188. Oxford, Blackwells.

Goss-Custard, J.D. (1993). The effect of migration and scale on the study of bird populations: 1991 Witherby Lecture. *Bird Study*, 40, 81-96.

Goss-Custard, J.D. (2003). Fitness, demographic rates and managing the coast for shorebird populations. *Wader Study Group Bulletin*, **100**, 183-191.

Goss-Custard, J.D. & Durell, S.E.A. Le V. dit. (1988). The effect of dominance and feeding method on the intake rates of oystercatchers, *Haematopus ostralegus*, feeding on mussels, *Mytilus edulis*. *Journal of Animal Ecology*, **57**, 827-844.

Goss-Custard, J.D. & Durell, S.E.A. Le V. dit. (1990). Bird behaviour and environmental planning: approaches in the study of wader populations. *Ibis*, **132**, 273-289.

Goss-Custard, J.D., Ross, J., McGrorty, S., Durell, S.E.A. le V. dit, Caldow, R.W.G. & West, A.D. (1997). Locally stable numbers in the oystercatcher *Haematopus ostralegus* where carrying capacity has not been reached. *Ibis*, **140**, 104-112.

Goss-Custard, J.D. & Stillman, R.A. (2008). Individual-based models and the management of shorebird populations. *Natural Resource Modelling*, **21**, 3-71.

Goss-Custard, J.D., Stillman, R.A., Caldow, R.W.G., West, A.D. & Guillemain, M. (2003). Carrying capacity in overwintering birds: when are spatial models needed? *Journal of Applied Ecology*, **40**, 176-187.

Goss-Custard, J.D., Stillman, R.A., West, A.D., Caldow, R.W.G. & McGrorty, S.(2002). Carrying capacity in overwintering migratory birds. *Biological Conservation*, **105**, 27-41.

Goss-Custard, J.D., West, A.D., Stillman, R.A., Durell, S.E.A. le V. dit, Caldow, R.W.G., McGrorty, S. & Nagarajan, R. (2001). Density-dependent starvation in a vertebrate without significant depletion. *Journal of Animal Ecology*, **70**, 955-965

Stillman, R.A., West, A.D., Goss-Custard, J.D., Durell, S.E.A. le V., Yates, M.G., Atkinson, P.W., Clark, N.A., Bell, M.C., Dare, P.J. & Mander, M. (2003). A behaviour-based model can predict shorebird mortality rate using routinely collected shellfishery data. *Journal of Applied Ecology*, **40**, 1090-1101.

Sutherland, W.J. & Goss-Custard, J.D. (1992). Predicting the consequence of habitat loss on shorebird populations. *Acta XX Congressus Internationalis Ornithologici*, 2199-2207.

Papers that describe MORPH

Grimm, V., Berger, U., Bastiansen, F., Eliassen, S., Ginot, V., Giske, J., Goss-Custard, J. D., Grand T, Heinz, S., Huse, G., Huth, A., Jepsen, J. U., Jørgensen, C., Mooij, W. M., Müller, B., Pe'er, G., Piou, C., Railsback, S. F., Robbins, A. M., Robbins, M. M., Rossmanith, E., Rüger, N., Strand, E., Souissi, S., Stillman, R. A., Vabø, R., Visser, U., DeAngelis, D. L. (2006). A standard protocol for describing individual-based and agent-based models. *Ecological Modelling*, **198**, 115-126.

Goss-Custard, J. D. & Stillman, R. A. (2008). Individual-based models and the management of shorebird populations. Natural Resource Modeling, 21, 3-71.

Stillman, R.A. & Goss-Custard, J.D. (2012) Les modèles comportementaux appliqués aux oiseaux côtiers. In: Manuel d'étude et de gestion des oiseaux et de leurs habitats en zones côtières. (P. Triplet (ed.)). Syndicat Mixte Baie de Somme, Forum des Marais atlantiques, *Aesturia* **17**, 775 p.

Stillman, R. A. (2008) MORPH – An individual-based model to predict the effect of environmental change on foraging animal populations. *Ecological Modelling*, **216**, 265-276.

Stillman, R. A. & Goss-Custard, J. D. (2010). Individual-based ecology of coastal birds. *Biological Reviews*, **85**, 413-434.

West, A. D., Stillman, R. A., Drewitt, A., Frost, N. J., Mander, M., Miles, C., Langston, R., Sanderson, W. G. & Willis, J. (2011) WaderMORPH: A user-friendly model to advise shorebird policy and management. *Methods in Ecology and Evolution*, **2**, 95-98.

Papers that use MORPH

Durell, S. E. A. le V. dit, Stillman, R. A., Caldow, R. W. G., McGrorty, S., West, A. D. & Humphreys, J. (2006). Modelling the effect of environmental change on shorebirds: a case study on Poole Harbour, UK. *Biological Conservation*, **131**, 459-473.

Durell, S. E. A. le V. dit, Stillman, R. A., McGrorty, S., West, A. D., Goss-Custard, J. D. & Price, D. (2007) Predicting the effect of local and global environmental change on shorebirds: a case study on the Exe estuary, UK. *Wader Study Group Bulletin*, **112**, 24-36.

Durell, S. E. A. le V. dit, Stillman, R. A., Triplet, P., Desprez, M., Fagot, C., Loquet, N., Sueur, F. & Goss-Custard, J. D. (2008) Using an individual-based model to inform estuary management in the Baie de Somme, France. *Oryx*, **42**, 265-277.

Caldow, R. W. G, Stillman, R. A., Durell, S. E. A. le V. dit, West, A. D., McGrorty, S., Goss-Custard, J. D., Wood, P. J. & Humphreys, J. (2007). Benefits to shorebirds from invasion of a non-native shellfish. *Proceedings of the Royal Society, London, Series B*, **274**, 1449-1455.

Duriez, O., Bauer, S., Destin, A., Madsen, J., Nolet, B. A., Stillman, R. A., & Klaassen, M. (2009) What decision rules might pink-footed geese use to depart on migration? An individual-based model. *Behavioural Ecology*, **20**, 560-569.

Stillman, R. A., Moore, J. J., Woolmer, A. P., Murphy, M. D, Walker, P., Vanstaen, K. R., Palmer, D. & Sanderson, W. G. (2010) Assessing waterbird conservation objectives: an example for the Burry Inlet, UK. *Biological Conservation, 143*, 2617-2630.

Toral, G. M., Stillman, R. A., Santoro, S., Figuerola, J. (2012). The importance of rice fields for Glossy Ibis (*Plegadis falcinellus*): management recommendations derived from an individual-based model. *Biological Conservation*, **148**, 19-27.

Wood, K. A., Stillman, R. A., Daunt, F. & O'Hare, M. T. (2012) Individual-based modelling of mute swan foraging in a chalk river catchment. In: *River Conservation and Management* (P. J. Boon & P. J. Raven (eds.)). Wiley-Blackwell, pp. 339-343.

Box 11.1 A disaster averted in the Wadden Sea?

The huge shellfishery in the Dutch Wadden Sea was managed for a while using the 'bird-days' measure of carrying capacity. The policy was to allow the harvest to reduce the shellfish stocks to 70% of the amount of 'daily rations' that the huge population of mollusc-eating shorebirds required in order to sustain it through the subsequent non-breeding season. It was assumed that the remaining 30% of food requirements would be provided by other prey species, such as ragworms.

But year-by-year, the population of birds steadily declined, and many emaciated corpses of oystercatchers and eider ducks were found. Intensive studies were carried out to explore whether it was starvation rather than some other cause – such as poisoning – that was responsible. The evidence for and against the starvation hypothesis was debated vigorously and eventually came down heavily in favour of it. The harvesting policy, and the industrial scale methods that had been used to collect the shellfish, were changed.

Apparently, the findings of the shorebird-shellfish IBM that it might take up to **eight times** the amount of daily rations to maintain the previously high survival rate and body condition of the birds (Table 9.1) had some impact on decision-makers. Certainly, leaving after shellfishing only 70% of the birds' physiological requirements was nowhere near enough! The IBM had shown that it would require up to ten times this amount!

BOX 11.2 Responses to modelling shorebird populations

Models are required partly because most predictions should be expressed in numbers. It really matters whether the mortality rate is predicted to increase by 0.1% or 1% or 10%, for example. Such quantitative predictions can only be obtained through numerical means, hence the need for a model.

Models also make the reasoning that underlie the predictions very clear and explicit. The processes involved in making the predictions are clearly set out, and the currently best estimates of the coefficients and constants used in the equations are there for all to see. They make the whole process of prediction about as accessible and accountable as it can be!

Unfortunately, for those of us trying to provide the means to make quantitative predictions, this does not seem to be the view of everyone in the world of ecology, conservation and shorebirds! Some conservationists have treated the shorebird model with open hostility as if fearful that it might undermine their ability to argue against a particular proposal for a change in estuary management. Knowledge will always be a threat to someone!

A bizarre case arose when a person at a meeting argued that the predictions of the particular shorebird model under discussion might provide a 'useful guide' to what might happen but that he/she felt it important to use his/her 'judgement' to interpret the outputs. I took this to mean he/she wished to retain the right to ignore the model's predictions even if the science was agreed by everyone to be sound. When asked why he/she had this view, he/she argued that a model is just a 'black box' whose outputs depended on the unknown processes going on inside. I pointed out that every single assumption, process and parameter value in the model was fully available for public inspection, as in other models. In fact, I said, the only black box in this instance was his/her brain because nobody present had a clue as to the experiences, influences and processes that would determine his/her judgement – and so his/her re-interpretation - of the model outputs!

I suspect that this view arose partly out of a reluctance to do the hard work of thoroughly understanding the way the model is constructed, on its processes and so forth. This book has been written partly in the hope that it will enable more people to understand its simple workings more easily and to have more confidence in its predictions, where they have been properly tested.

ACKNOWLEDGEMENTS
and some photographs

I am very grateful to Pete Ferns and Patrick Triplet for reading the book in draft and making many very useful suggestions as to how it could be improved.

As should be obvious from this book, I am also indebted to a great many people who either worked with me on this very long-term project or contributed ideas, data and time to help us get there in the end. They really are too numerous to mention individually and, as they will know who they are and that I am very grateful to them, there really is no need to do so. Many thanks also to Bruno Ens, Richard Caldow, Richard Stillman, Ralph Clarke and Sarah Durell for providing photographs.

Grateful thanks also to Jason Ingham of Lympstone village who helped me on many occasions with the exhausting job of building tower hides and for designing and constructing the very nifty 'in boat' hide that proved invaluable when the research switched from mussel beds to mudflats.

I am also indebted to a succession of bosses at all the various levels in CEH and in NERC who kept their faith in us and our program and supported the project over such a very long period.

We did not take a lot of photographs during this project, but the few that we took and have not lost are shown in the following pages. They include most of my former and very highly appreciated colleagues in CEH – I could not have had better people to work with - and some of the generous people from other organisations who helped the project in very important ways. There are also photographs of some of the methods we used in the field and some pictures of the estuary itself, along with the odd bird or two.

And finally, I would like to thank Tim O'Grady for formatting this book and for putting it on-line with Kindle Direct Publishing and laying out this version for paperback and print on demand. His technical skill and courteous and rapid help were very much appreciated. He made a task that would have been very difficult for me very easy and enjoyable. You can find him at: PublishOnKindle.co.uk

There is now the Exe Estuary Trail for cyclists and walkers that runs alongside both sides of the estuary which, along with the excellent bird hide near the main shorebird roost on Dawlish Warren, and the bird watching boat trips from Exmouth, enables the visitor to see the estuary and its shorebirds very easily. It is a beautiful place in which to see beautiful animals, and I recommend it to you without reservation. And there are excellent pubs along both sides of the estuary as well.

John Goss-Custard
26th March 2014

Your author sitting comfortably on a Boates Box on the Bull Hill mussel bed of the Exe estuary. He is recording the number of mussels consumed by an oystercatcher during a ten-minute period. The plate of mussels is not his lunch but shows how many mussels a single oystercatcher eats in a single 24-hour period.

A young Bill Sutherland, also taking it easy while recording oystercatcher behaviour in North Wales during his Ph.D. research on oystercatchers foraging on cockles. With Professor Bill Hale of John Moores University, Liverpool, your author had the great pleasure of supervising Bill's project.

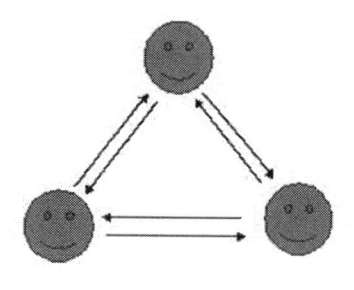

This was not a lineage but a reciprocity of inputs, as represented in this flow chart.

Richard Stillman who played a central role in developing the IBM and also created the vitally important models of interference. Here he is holding an Exe brent goose for colour-ringing so that individual birds could be identified at a distance and their behaviour recorded to provide data for the model of the brent geese of North-west Europe. Richard did a Ph.D. project at the University of East Anglia, Norwich, where Bill Sutherland was his supervisor.

Richard Caldow, another key player in the development of the shorebird IBM. He not only contributed a great deal to the oystercatcher-mussel model – as seen here - but also developed the multi-site model for brent geese for the whole of North-west Europe, an immense task and a critical step in the development of the IBM. Using the IBM, he also designed a way of re-stocking of the Menai Straights mussel fishery to the benefit of both the fishery and the oystercatchers. A genuine win-win outcome.

Sarah Durell who was another vitally important contributor to the development of the oystercatcher-mussel shorebird model. She was particularly responsible for the work on density-dependent mortality of oystercatchers and on body condition, feeding methods, sex ratios and modelling bird populations. She is holding oystercatcher 'right leg, orange above, thin, thick, blank (green sandwich)'.

Mick Yates, whose knowledge of the shorebirds and invertebrates of the Wash were critical for developing and testing the Wash model and whose fieldwork on redshank and godwits enabled the behaviour-based model of interference by depression to be tested.

More vital contributers to the development and testing of the Exe estuary oystercatcher-mussel IBM. Colleagues from Furzebrook Research Station join members of the Devon and Cornwall Wader Ringing Group (DCWRG) at a cannon-net catch of oystercatchers on Dawlish Warren, probably on a freezing cold dawn.

The magnificent mussel men: Selwyn McGrorty (near) and Andy West in the boat. Unfortunately, there is no photo of the third key member of this team, Chris Reading. Under Selwyn's leadership, not only did his team produce one of the best population studies ever done on an intertidal invertebrate, but without their efforts the whole IBM enterprise would have been dead in the water. Andy also helped develop the software for the IBM in its several manifestations and used the model to answer a wide range of both theoretical and applied issues of many kinds.

Humphrey Sitters, a key member of the DCWRG, holding an adult oystercatcher on a cannon-netting expedition on Dawlish Warren. He was also a pioneer in investigating the foraging behaviour of shorebirds at night, which he did on oystercatchers foraging on the mussel bed just to the south of Lympstone. Sadly there are no photographs of Roger and Barbara Swinfen, other vital members of the DCWRG.

On a ferry en route to the island of Texel to discuss our oystercatcher-shellfish model with Dutch ecologists (Box A.1). From left to right: Ralph Clarke, our colleague in CEH who played an absolutely vital role by writing the excellent software for versions 1 and 2 of the IBM. He was also our hard-working and very much appreciated statistical advisor throughout the entire development, testing and application of the IBM; Richard Stillman and Andy West; Ken Norris and Ian Johnstone, of the University of Reading and the RSPB respectively, who worked with us on the model of the Burry Inlet shellfishery; the author and Richard Caldow.

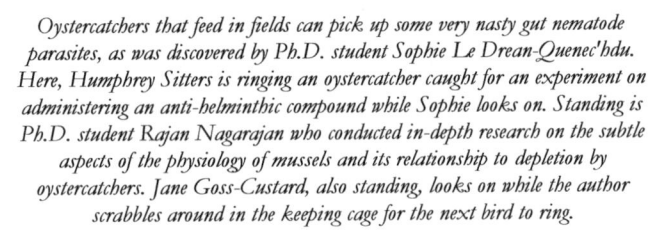

Oystercatchers that feed in fields can pick up some very nasty gut nematode parasites, as was discovered by Ph.D. student Sophie Le Drean-Quenec'hdu. Here, Humphrey Sitters is ringing an oystercatcher caught for an experiment on administering an anti-helminthic compound while Sophie looks on. Standing is Ph.D. student Rajan Nagarajan who conducted in-depth research on the subtle aspects of the physiology of mussels and its relationship to depletion by oystercatchers. Jane Goss-Custard, also standing, looks on while the author scrabbles around in the keeping cage for the next bird to ring.

Patrick Triplet who provided invaluable data from the baie de Somme that enabled the IBM to be used for cockle-eating oystercatchers as well as mussel-eaters. He also worked with the Exe team on a number of occasions in applying the model to a range of management issues on the baie de Somme and in the estuary of the river Seine. In this photograph, he is in west Africa.

There were many Ph.D. students and research workers who worked on the Exe on various aspects of the biology of oystercatchers, as the references at the end of each chapter will testify. Unfortunately, there are very few photographs of them. But here, Thomas Bregnballe from Denmark gets ready for a day in one of a hide.

Bart Ebbinge kindly came over from The Netherlands to share his enormous knowledge of brent geese. Here he weighs a goose in a bag using a spring balance suspended from the tripod that was normally used for telescopes while Richard Stillman watches.

Bruno Ens brought the tower hide to the Exe early in the project and from it carried pioneering research on interference in mussel-eating oystercatchers on the mussel beds at Cockwood. Subsequently, Bruno and the Exe team collaborated on a wide range of research projects. On the left, Bruno when a student, is holding an armful of oystercatchers in the Netherlands. On the right, he is cycling under the railway bridge at Cockwood to begin yet another day's work in the tower hide.

Matthew Alexander videos foraging brent geese so that their foraging and social behaviour could be investigated in detail in the laboratory.

Selwyn McGrorty after he and the author had just constructed an exclosure on Bull Hill mussel bed off Exmouth. A tower hide is behind

The mussel beds at Cockwood, looking north towards Lympstone.

En route on the receding tide to the hide where he will spend the day, the author (near) drops Richard Caldow off at his hide, and makes a mental note to pick him up again on the way back when the tide is coming back in!

Sometimes hides were bashed about by a gale. A cormorant can just be seen sitting on the roof.

The boat floats downstream of the hide on the receding tide at dawn. Another hide can be seen beyond. Exmouth is in the far distance.

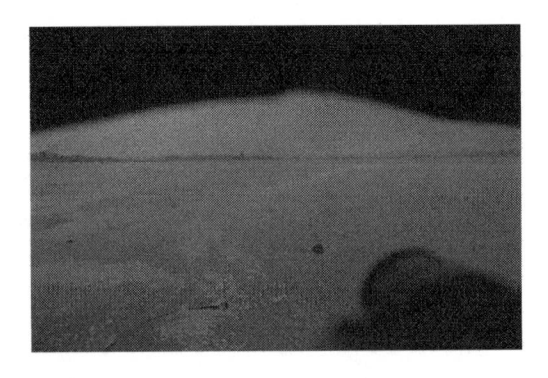

Waiting inside the hide for the tide to go down, telescope at the ready.

BOX A.1 Interference and that car key

The ferry journey back from The Netherlands was a legend in Dorset CEH. I drove the car to the Dutch ferry terminal and, being early, it was at the front of the boat and so would be the first off the ferry on reaching England. Then followed a journey devoted largely to an absorbing discussion of how interference might best be represented in the model. On arrival early in the morning in England, and still thinking about interference, I rushed off the ferry to catch a train back home, the rest of the party intending to travel home by our car. Slumping almost asleep on the still stationary and delayed train, my brain was (very luckily) just stirred by a muffled public announcement outside. It included a weird, double-barrelled word that I eventually realised, just might be mine, allowing for distortion and the difficulty most people new to the name have in mastering its pronunciation! 'Crumbs, that could be my name!' Off the train and returning to the ferry, I met extremely agitated, no, terrified, colleagues facing an army of incensed lorry drivers. I had forgotten to give the car key to someone else before rushing away! And the car was at the very front of the ferry and there were rows of impatient lorries parked behind! I arrived just in time to make it unnecessary for them to carry out their threat – to push the b.......... car over the side! What if the train had not been delayed?!! It just doesn't bear thinking about!

POSTSCRIPT

I have carried on working with the issues described in this book since my retirement in 2002, and with colleagues from Bournemouth University, I have continued to contribute to scientific papers. Many of the references and some of the work itself can be found on my blog at: www.birdsandestuaries.blogspot.co.uk

Printed in Great Britain
by Amazon